Janáček

Music advisor to Northeastern University Press
GUNTHER SCHULLER

Janáček

Mirka Zemanová

Northeastern University Press

BOSTON

Copyright 2002 by Mirka Zemanová

Published in 2002 in England by John Murray (Publishers) Ltd., London.
Published in 2002 in the United States of America by
Northeastern University Press, by arrangement with
Mirka Zemanová and John Murray (Publishers) Ltd.

Library of Congress Cataloging-in-Publication Data
Zemanová, Mirka.
Janáček : a composer's life / Mirka Zemanová
p. cm.
Includes bibliographical references (p.) and index
ISBN 1-55553-549-6 (cloth : alk. paper)
1. Janáček, Leoš, 1854–1928. 2. Composers—Czech
Republic—Biography. I. Title.

ML410.J18 Z46 2002   2002022957

MANUFACTURED IN GREAT BRITAIN
06 05 04 03 02   5 4 3 2 1

For my mother

Contents

Illustrations

(between pages 176 and 177)

1. The church in Hukvaldy
2. The village school
3. The Augustinian 'Queen's' monastery in Brno
4. Antonín Dvořák around the time of Janáček's wedding in 1881
5. Janáček and his wife Zdenka shortly after their wedding
6. Janáček in 1904
7. Janáček's daughter Olga
8. Speech melodies of Olga's last words
9. Kamila Stösslová and her husband David in 1917
10. Janáček's cottage in Hukvaldy
11. Two of Eduard Milén's designs for *The Cunning Little Vixen*
12. A caricature by Oldřich Sekora of the performers in the Brno première of *The Makropulos Affair*
13. Part of the piano score sketch of *Jenůfa*
14. A drawing of Janáček by Eduard Milén
15. Max Brod in a 1909 drawing by Lucian Bernhard
16. The Janáčeks and the Stössels in 1925
17. Introduction to *From the House of the Dead*

The illustrations appear by kind permission of the following individuals and institutions: 1 and 2, Archive of the Janáček Festival, 'Hudební Lašsko'; 3, 5–9, 11, 13–14, 16–17, Music Division of the Moravian Regional Museum, Brno; 10, Miloslav Budík; 15, DACS. Plates 4 and 12 have been kindly placed at our disposal by private collectors.

Acknowledgements

Much of the work on this book was made possible by a scholarship from the Wingate Foundation and a grant from the Hinrichsen Foundation. My sincere thanks are due to the committees of both institutions.

Among those who provided various materials and advice during the research stage of the book, I am particularly grateful to the staff of the following institutions: in Brno, Moravian Museum (Music History Division); in Prague, Institute of Musicology, the Czech Academy of Sciences; National Museum, Theatre Division; State Library, Music Division; in Budapest, Bartók Archives, Hungarian Academy of Sciences and in London, Slavonic and East European Collections at the British Library. My sister Ludmila was invaluable in helping me to obtain other necessary material.

Quotations from *Janáček's Uncollected Essays on Music*, edited and translated by Mirka Zemanová, appear by kind permission of Marion Boyars Publishers, London. Janáček's mother's letters, Janáček's letter to his uncle, and his correspondence, including that with Kamila Stösslová, first appeared in Czech in the editions cited in the notes. Janáček's letters to Zdenka, which were written in German, were first published as a collection by Jakob Kraus (see notes). All translations throughout the book are mine, unless otherwise specified.

Above all, I am greatly indebted to my agent, Mandy Little of Watson, Little Ltd, and to Grant McIntyre, the Editorial Director at John Murray, for their encouragement, enthusiasm and patience.

Guide to Pronunciation

Czech is a Slavonic language and is today largely spoken by some ten million inhabitants of the Czech Republic, which is made up of Bohemia and Moravia. In English two adjectives are used to refer to the inhabitants of Bohemia: 'Bohemian', derived from what the Romans thought the Celts originally settled in the area called themselves, and 'Czech', derived from the name used by the Czechs themselves. In the present volume 'Bohemia' is used purely as a geographical term, and the adjective 'Czech' is used as an ethnic and linguistic term. 'Moravia' and 'Moravian' are used in a geographical and ethnic sense. The term 'Moravian' is never used as a linguistic term: there is no 'Moravian' language (and, for that matter, no 'Bohemian' one) – Czech is spoken in both regions. However, like other Czech speakers from Moravia, Janáček does sometimes modify the grammatical structure and word order.

Czech vowels are open and pure, very much like Italian vowels. They are known as either 'short' (a, e, i, o, u, y) or 'long' (á, é, í, ó, ou [a diphthong, pronounced as 'ow'], ů, ú, ý). The diacritical signs indicate the length. The short vowels are pronounced approximately as follows:

a   as 'u' in 'hut'
e   as in 'net'
i   as in 'it'
o   as in 'otter'
u   as in 'put'
y   is similar to the Czech 'i'

Most consonants in Czech are pronounced approximately as in English, except for the following:

c   is similar to 'ts' in 'cats'
g   is always hard, as in Gibson

ch   as in 'loch'
j   is pronounced as 'y' in 'yes'
r   is always rolled

A 'háček' [hook] is another diacritical sign which, if placed over a consonant, modifies the sound:

č   is pronounced as 'ch' in 'church'
š   as 's' in 'sure'
ž   can be likened to 's' in 'treasure'
ř   a rolled 'r' and 'zh' pronounced simultaneously
     (the most difficult Czech consonant)

Some consonants are further softened if followed by 'ě', as in the name Věra (pronounced 'Viera'). Whenever 'd', 'n' and 't' are followed by 'i', they are also softened. These consonants are also softened whenever either a 'háček' or '" is indicated (as in 'd", 'n", and 't"). The consonants 'b', 'd', 'g', 'v', 'z', or 'ž' at the end of a word are pronounced as 'p', 't', 'k', 'f', 's', and 'sh' respectively; 'h' at the end of a word is pronounced as 'ch' (as in 'loch'). The 'voiced' consonants therefore become 'voiceless'. The consonants 'l' and 'r' are known as 'syllable-forming' (in words such as 'Vltava' [the Czech river Vltava] or 'prsten' [ring]).

The stress in Czech is invariably on the first syllable of a word, while the length of the syllable is indicated by the diacritical signs mentioned above. The stress and the length do not always coincide – viz. the names of two of the most famous Czech composers, Dvořák and Janáček (notoriously difficult to pronounce for non-Czech speakers). However, whenever a word is preceded by a preposition, the preposition draws the stress onto itself (as in 'na zemi' [on earth], or 'za stromem' [behind a tree]). The preposition and the following noun are joined and pronounced as one word.

Words are also subjected to changes as a result of declension: thus Janáček, but 'Janáčkovi' [to Janáček]. Czech is an inflected language, and such changes enable it to modify the content of a word, bringing it at the same time into different relations to other words in the same sentence. In English this is done by prepositions and pronouns, and the word usually does not change, except for an indication of the plural (whenever applicable).

'If speech melody is the flower of the water-lily, it nevertheless buds and blossoms and drinks from the roots, which wander in the waters of the mind.'

From Janáček's *feuilleton* 'Moravany! Morawaan!',
Lidové noviny, 6 April 1918

Introduction

THIS BOOK HAS three aims. First, it will tell general readers largely
familiar with Janáček's music something of his life and his background; second, it will lead operatic and concert audiences who have
heard perhaps one or two of his operas or orchestral and chamber
works on to others that he composed. Third, it will bring scholars
and serious students of Janáček significant new scholarship hitherto
unavailable in English.

Although no biography of Janáček has been published for over
twenty years, a number of additions have been made to the literature
on him since the revised edition of Jaroslav Vogel's classic life and
works appeared in 1981. Some of Janáček's writings have been translated into English; his important correspondence with his sometimes
reluctant muse Kamila Stösslová has been published both in Czech
and in English; and various aspects of his life and background have
been researched in depth. Taking advantage of these books and individual studies, I have been able to correct some of the previously
published information and throw greater light on some parts of
Janáček's life story.

Scholars may also be interested in the descriptions of local contexts
throughout the biography. As a Czech now also writing in English, I
hope that I have been able to portray these contexts successfully and
conjure up locales and situations vividly enough for the book to serve
also as a picture of Janáček and his world.

This book is not a standard 'life and works', and I have not
attempted to offer major new insights into Janáček's compositions;
in-depth criticism was not part of my brief. Although I have discussed Janáček's music in the context of his life and of contemporary
political and social events, and I have included excerpts from many
contemporary reviews, I have not analysed his works exhaustively.
Comprehensive documentary accounts of Janáček's operas, their
genesis and stage history, are now available in English, as are some

analyses. On the other hand, I have described in greater detail Janáček's orchestral, choral and chamber music, especially works which are less well known outside his native country. Musical examples and further commentary will eventually be available on my website (details will be announced in the musical press).

Above all, this is a book about Janáček as a man – a lonely chorister far away from home, an impecunious student, a passionate patriot in his native region of Moravia (which, for much of his life, was part of the Austro-Hungarian Empire), an aspiring reformer of musical life in his adoptive home town, and an erudite writer with an acerbic wit. I hope that the reader will be able to picture this handsome, imposing but also somewhat gauche, figure: dressed as Faust at a fancy dress ball to which he accompanies his teenage bride; grieving at the deathbed of his daughter Olga, or borne on the musicians' shoulders after the triumphant première of *Jenůfa*, his third opera and the first masterpiece. Here he is listening avidly to singers and musicians during his folk-song collecting expeditions, there, working through night after night to develop his style; solitary and misunderstood, he hammers on the piano a vigorous peasant dance or touches the keys with exquisite tenderness in the musical memory of a blown-away leaf – or perhaps a lost love letter: I hope these sketches of Janáček at work will also whet the reader's appetite for more of his music.

Old age did not change Janáček, At the age of 63, still an impressive man, he fell in love with a woman thirty-eight years his junior. From the time he lay in wait to see her coming out on to the balcony at the fashionable spa where they met, to his death eleven years later, Kamila Stösslová – with her cloud of raven hair, her tremendous vitality and charm – kept him spellbound.

The true nature of their relationship cannot now be fathomed, and no amount of sleuthing will help to discover whether it was consummated or not. In the end, it does not matter; the world of fantasy was very important to Janáček and, despite her often distant attitude and complete lack of any understanding of music, Kamila never failed to feed his imagination.

Although success on an international scale – which Janáček enjoyed with touching naivety – did not come to him until his sixties, he was rarely short of helpers and advocates. Early in his career several of his colleagues helped him selflessly; later on, the Czech singer Marie Calma-Veselá and her husband fought ceaselessly to get *Jenůfa* staged at the National Theatre in Prague. The Czech lawyer and publicist Jan Löwenbach brought Janáček to the notice of the

German-Jewish writer, translator and Kafka's biographer Max Brod; without Brod, Janáček would probably not have broken through in the German-speaking world. Yet Janáček did not always treat these admirers and advocates with the gratitude they deserved. And, as his wife remarked in her memoirs, he had many good acquaintances and colleagues, but never a close male friend. Janáček's fierce independence and pride – which belied his shyness – may have contributed to his difficulty in finding genuine friendship.

Janáček was a complex personality, and it is not easy to comprehend his motives and contradictions. Some were probably due to emotional deprivation at an early age. There was a deep bond between him and his mother, but they were separated for several years during his early teens and his schooldays had never been happy. These factors may have contributed to his well-known fear of being abandoned, his lack of emotional delicacy, and the bouts of deep loneliness throughout his life. In his correspondence, and the contemporary accounts from which I have quoted, the reader will also be able to detect his astonishing energy, industry, programme of self-education, his ambition and social aspirations, his generosity and kindness. The reader will also encounter his fiery temper, together with his tendency to put women on a pedestal during the initial stages of a relationship, only to drop them later in favour of a new prospect. And while he glorified women on the stage, he was capable of emotional cruelty to them in life.

Zdenka, Janáček's wife of forty-seven years, is usually portrayed either as a long-suffering spouse who gave up everything for the sake of his art (which is also, as shown in her memoirs, how she saw herself), or as the wrong kind of woman to be the wife of a genius. Neither view can be right. Although much in Zdenka's memoirs rings true, they were ghosted, and the skilful Czech journalist who collaborated with Zdenka may have taken her side: according to other contemporary accounts Zdenka was not always appreciative of Janáček's music. And dismissing her as unworthy of Janáček is patronizing. They were, quite simply, mismatched: each had emotional expectations that the other, for a variety of reasons, was unable to fulfil. But why did Zdenka, despite Janáček's infidelities and maltreatment, cling to him and to her role as dutiful wife? One of the reasons was surely the fact that she had no one else to care for and, had they divorced, nowhere to go. Their children died young, and her parents and her brother lived abroad. As she had no money of her own and no profession, she would not have been able to support herself. In many ways, she was just as trapped as Janáček thought himself to be.

Although Janáček lived most of his adult life in a provincial town, he was not completely isolated there. He was able to follow the developments and trends in contemporary music by studying scores, and could also see operas and attend concerts in Prague, Leipzig and Vienna, and later in life elsewhere in Europe. Among composers he met were Dvořák, Tchaikovsky and Richard Strauss; he also heard Grieg, Anton Rubinstein and Stravinsky play their music. Janáček also met Bartók – twice in 1925 (when at his invitation, Bartók played his own music in Brno), and once in 1927. On this occasion, after Bartók's concert in Prague, their conversation was described as 'a firework display'.[1]

Since the second half of the twentieth century Janáček's operas have become part of the core of the operatic repertoire in Europe as well as the United States. Why do these operas seem to speak so directly to contemporary audiences? Their themes are universal, and audiences anywhere can readily recognize the aspects of human existence which Janáček explores. These encompass such themes as unrequited love and the association of love with harsh fate, false pride, guilt, compassion and redemption, mortality and renewal. Moreover, although Janáček's music is based on the speech patterns and rhythms of the Czech language and the folk idiom of his native region, the unique blend and the moods and mental states it describes are equally comprehensible to non-Czech speakers – whether the operas are given in the original Czech or in translation – precisely because the moods are portrayed with such accuracy. As Janáček himself wrote after the rehearsal of *Jenůfa* at the Vienna Court Opera (where this opera was sung in German), a part of him was 'present in each of those foreign words . . . I comprehend their expression, they comfort me with their warmth, and I come to understand even their tinge of sorrow.'[2]

Yet during Janáček's lifetime his specific method of composition was much criticized, and he was often dismissed as merely a regional composer. He always protested vigorously against this. The rich material of his native Moravia, which surrounded him for the first eleven years of his life and to which he returned as a young man, was very important: it was a pure, complete experience. But Janáček knew that to write as a 'Moravian composer' would inevitably lead to being labelled as an exotic, and prevent him from reaching wider audiences. He strove to assimilate his material, and his mature style is not 'folksy' in any way. In addition, his almost filmic technique of complementing the wide sweep by zooming in on small details (notably in *The Cunning Little Vixen* and *From the House of the Dead*) was ahead of his time, and his ability to abbreviate enabled him to say a great deal in a short space of time, whether in his operatic, choral, orchestral or piano music.

Some of the characteristics and states of mind of Janáček's protagonists must have been born partly of his own neuroses, problems and mental processes. But while the men in his operas are almost invariably feeble, or trapped, and his female characters are almost invariably strong, one can see something of Janáček in each of his characters of either sex. The strong positive moral message in his operas often seems diametrically opposed to Janáček's own behaviour, but to make a direct comparison between Janáček's operas and his personal life would be simplistic and crude: real life and the nature of a composer's inspiration do not necessarily correlate. Although Janáček portrayed, for example, the sadistic and masochistic tendencies of some of his characters remarkably well, one does not have to regard the fantasies and passions of a composer's characters as those of the composer himself.

Nevertheless, in his life Janáček does sometimes give an impression of creating, consciously or subconsciously, certain situations and then exploiting them; in his correspondence with Kamila Stösslová, for example, he often dramatized even the most mundane details of their meetings, maintaining that any such experiences directly influenced his inspiration. Perhaps every experience in life, no matter how trivial, was grist to his mill.

Although Janáček sometimes wrote straight into the score, he often wrote at the piano. His relentless hammering of key phrases and even individual notes probably helped him to hone each motif into its definitive shape and test its sonority, and he may have also needed the repeated sound in order to immerse himself in a specific sound-world which gave rise to further ideas.[3] But it may also indicate that, at the most basic level, he believed the hypnotic role of music to be one of its fundamental functions. And he heard music everywhere – 'in a telephone receiver, in the dust of centuries-old registers, in the flag that flapped above the Castle in a mad whirl; yes, everywhere music sounded in a motif melancholy in its weeping, stabbing in its revenge. . . . Tame as a pet, predatory as a vulture, dry as a wilted leaf . . . it stuck to every kind of emotion.'[4]

I

Beginnings

(1854–1874)

'I HAVE ONE great joy,' wrote Janáček in 1916. 'Moravia by herself can give me all the inspiration I need. So rich are her sources.'[1]

What was it that provided such a wealth and variety of sources in Moravia, the small Central European province where Janáček was born, and where he lived all his life? One of the twin provinces that made up the former Crown Lands of Bohemia and today form the Czech Republic, Moravia differs profoundly from her larger sister, Bohemia. And her role in Czech history has often been overlooked.

'The Czechs were always the head, and we remained the tail of their kingdom,' declared Karel the Elder of Žerotín. A Moravian nobleman, a shrewd politician and an intellectual, he accurately described Moravia's status within the kingdom of Bohemia in 1620, after the fateful battle of the White Mountain which brought the country under Austrian rule.

The historical and cultural background of the two provinces is complex. Bohemia's name has always had a certain resonance: Anne of Bohemia married Richard II of England, son of the Black Prince; in the eighteenth century, Bohemian musicians were known and admired abroad, as were Bohemian craftsmen; and the names of the great nineteenth-century Bohemian composers Smetana and Dvořák need no introduction to music lovers.

But what of Moravia? When the kingdom of Bohemia was established in the tenth century, Moravia ceased to be the political centre of the surrounding lands. Yet in the years that followed, Czechs from Moravia created works which belong to and characterize the entire Czech nation.[2] And in the nineteenth century, Moravia – then still a part of the Austro-Hungarian Empire – was the birthplace of some of Europe's finest scientists, thinkers, artists and musicians: Sigmund Freud; the founder of genetics J.G. Mendel; the philosopher and first Czech president T.G. Masaryk; the Czech Art Nouveau painter

Alfons Mucha; the father of phenomenology Edmund Husserl; the architect Adolf Loos; the writer Robert Musil; and, among the most celebrated musicians, Leoš Janáček. Two other composers of genius, Mahler and Martinů, were born near the Czech-Moravian border. Great men and women are born without much reference to geography; what is significant is the environment in which they are nurtured. What were the traditions these luminaries encountered in their youth?

Today, Moravia covers an area about two-thirds the size of Switzerland, bordering Poland in the north, Slovakia in the east, Austria in the south and Bohemia in the west. Yet in the time of Charlemagne this future 'tail of the kingdom' governed a large territory, including much of Bohemia and Slovakia, with frontiers extending to Lake Balaton and the Hungarian Plain. This state, known as the Great Moravian Empire, was established in the ninth century. In AD 863, at the request of Duke Rastislav of Great Moravia, the Greek brothers Cyril (Constantine) and Methodius arrived to disseminate Christianity throughout the Empire. Cyril later developed the first Slavonic alphabet, *glagolice*, and translated the Bible and other religious writings into the earliest written Slavonic language, known as Old Slavonic.

The arrival of the Greek missionaries also counteracted the efforts of the German Empire to convert Rastislav's lands to Roman Catholicism: in Bohemia, Bavarian priests were active in the second quarter of the ninth century. And so, geographically and historically, Moravia became the crossroads where Eastern and Western cultures met. This was to be of great significance for her culture in general and, above all, for her folk music.

Eventually the old Slavonic (Byzantine) ritual was suppressed in favour of Catholic (Latin) worship. Disputes among Rastislav's sons followed, and by the beginning of the tenth century the Great Moravian Empire disintegrated. Slovakia was seized by the Magyars, and Bohemia became the dominant political centre of a new state which incorporated Moravia. Further turmoil within the Czech state meant that in 1182 Moravia was established as a margraviate, but the separation was short-lived: by the end of the century the territory was once again part of the Czech kingdom.

In the four centuries or so that preceded the Habsburg domination, both provinces made vigorous economic progress under enlightened monarchs from different dynasties.[3] In the fifteenth century religious strife gave birth to the Hussite movement, one of the strongest Reformation movements in Europe. In 1526, though, the Czech crown went to the Hapsburg dynasty; in 1620, Bohemia lost the battle of the White Mountain and ceased to exist as an independent kingdom. The Crown Lands remained under Austrian rule for almost three hundred years, with devastating effects on their economy, culture and language.

Before the religious wars of the fifteenth century exhausted the country, Moravia was not a backward province. There was a greater density of towns than in Bohemia; Moravia's silver mines, though less rich than the Bohemian ones, nonetheless greatly added to her wealth. The plains of central Moravia had always been the region's granary; there were vineyards in the south and deep forests in the mountainous north, where forestry, paper, coal and steel industries were to develop. Long-established merchants' routes ran from Moravia's southern border with Austria to the Polish frontier in the north and provided a link for trade between the Mediterranean and the Baltic. But politically Moravia never dominated the kingdom, although the Great Moravian Empire was clearly the nucleus of the future Czech state.

Nevertheless, during the Czech National Revival in the first half of the nineteenth century, the Moravian cities of Brno and Olomouc were its most important centres outside Bohemia. In the capital, Brno, various Moravian-born luminaries were active – the folk-song collector František Sušil, the composer Pavel Křížkovský and, in Brno's Old Town, the philosopher, poet, philosopher and journalist F.J. Klácel. And although the local clergy supported the conservative Moravian separatist party – with its old-fashioned ideology of tribal autonomy and 'purity of the Moravian nation' – once Czech grammar schools were established throughout Moravia after 1867, a new, progressive movement, Young Moravia, was formed.[4] Its aims were realistic; it was close to the radical *mladočech* ('Young Czech') faction of the National Party, and had ties with the Czech capital Prague.

Unlike Bohemia, Moravia retained for centuries a great variety of regional costumes, dialects and accents. The geographical and cultural multiplicity was also reflected in a variety of temperaments, and what the outstanding Moravian folklorist František Bartoš calls 'tribal spirit'; there are considerable differences between the individual regions. Although folk costumes are now only worn at festivals, many linguistic and tribal characteristics continue unchanged. The handsome, impulsive, fiery people of Moravian Slovakia, for example, known for their brave and jealous disposition, stand out all the more when compared to their slower, more prudent neighbours from the Haná region, whose placidity belies their humour. Those from the region of Valašsko and Dolňácko share some of the Moravian Slovaks' temperament, while those from Lašsko have some features in common with the neighbouring Poles. And, as Bartoš stresses, 'the entire tribal temperament resounded in song'.[5]

There are good historical reasons why folk-song in Moravia has come to reflect so accurately the province's spirit. Before the Czech National Revival, written Czech was barely kept alive, and spoken Czech survived largely only among the peasantry.[6] With no other means of expression, much of the nation's creativity was concentrated on music-making of all kinds: and in folk-song, language and music came together. In Moravia this resulted in poetic texts of great beauty, which reflect not only the many facets of tribal character, but also the diversity of landscape and climate. The deep 'black' forests, the green groves, the vineyards, orchards and gardens, the flowers and birds of Moravia all crop up in thousands of folk-songs.[7] Moravian folk music, with its rhythmical and melodic richness, depicts an exuberance of life and a depth of feeling that were to enchant Janáček, and which are mirrored in his own work in a variety of ways.

Janáček was born in the hamlet of Hukvaldy, in the region of Lašsko which lies on the banks of the river Ostravice in northern Moravia; Lašsko touches Czech Silesia and the industrial district of Ostrava in the north, and the picturesque Beskydy mountains in the south. 'A land of beauty, a quiet people, its dialect as soft as though you were cutting butter', Janáček wrote of it at the end of his life.[8]

The family surname, a derivative of Jan [John], was first documented near the Silesian town of Těšín in the second half of the seventeenth century; a branch of the family later moved to the small town of Frýdek, where Janáček's grandfather was born. He was the first family member to settle in Lašsko, in the small, entirely Czech-speaking village of Albrechtičky; his son Jiří, Janáček's father, arrived in Hukvaldy in 1848.[9]

Hukvaldy is one of the communities which make up the eastern-most part of the historical Czech territory in Moravia. For centuries, many different influences competed with each other in that area, and Silesian, German, Polish, Slovak and Hungarian cultures all left their mark; the name of the neighbouring region, Valašsko, derives from the district of Wallachia in Romania, from which successions of settlers had come.

A few houses, an inn, a church and a school form the hamlet below the ruins of Hukvaldy Castle, whose name commemorates Arnold de Huckeswage, its thirteenth-century warlord; among subsequent owners were two Hussite captains. After a series of sieges in the seventeenth century, the estate was the scene of a major peasant rebellion in 1695. In 1762 much of the castle and its archives were destroyed by fire; after another fire in 1820 the castle was left uninhabited. By 1848 the small, impoverished community at its foot had only some 570 inhabitants, whose principal occupations were weaving, sheep rearing and forestry. The school was a former manorial ice-store; its dilapidated building also housed the schoolmaster and his family. Janáček's father, who took up the post that year, was himself the son of a schoolmaster; as Janáček's first biographer Vladimir Helfert wrote, Grandfather Jiří was 'an extraordinarily striking figure', with 'many characteristics which later appear in his grandson Leoš':[10] a talent for music, enterprise, industry, and an explosive temperament. In the family lineage, as Helfert pointed out, he signified a turning point: 'after three generations of weavers there suddenly appears in him . . . the founder of [the family's] *kantor* and musical tradition'.[11]

At the beginning of the nineteenth century the tradition of the village schoolmaster-musician, the *kantor*, was still very strong in Bohemia and Moravia. The Latin equivalent, *cantor*, denotes the leader of the singing in church, but even in present-day colloquial Czech, *kantor* is still used to describe a teacher.

In the nineteenth century, though poorly paid, these schoolmasters enjoyed high social status, respect and indeed affection, especially in poor rural communities. Apart from the priest, the *kantor* was often the only educated man in the village. He would read and answer letters for the illiterate and mediate for them with the authorities; he would teach not only the usual syllabus but also music – singing, piano, organ and violin – and act as church organist and choirmaster. He would found reading clubs, disseminate new agricultural and gardening methods, and make musical instruments; sometimes he would even coach the children of the local nobility. The *kantors* also helped to keep Czech culture alive.

Grandfather Jiří was 'a passionate musician [and] an especially skilful organist': his son Vincenc wrote in the family memoirs that his improvised preludes easily grew into fugues which 'he executed in a masterly fashion'. A keen singer, he 'played and sang with such emotion that tears would run from his eyes'.[12] But he was also gregarious and an excellent raconteur, so he was popular, even though he was prone to terrible outbursts of rage and violence, particularly during his occasional bouts of drinking. At such times, wrote Vincenc, his placid and quiet wife – Janáček's grandmother Anna – was 'the golden pillar . . . against which the whole family would lean'.[13]

There were six children in Jiří's family, two daughters and four sons. Two of the boys, including Leoš's father Jiří, became teachers, the other two were chosen for the priesthood. Of the last two, Jan – who would become Leoš's favourite uncle – was also a good musician; Josef was an accomplished scholar, fluent in five languages, but bitter and somewhat eccentric. Vincenc eventually took over Jiří's post; the family memoirs and village chronicles that he produced towards the end of his life foreshadow the literary gift his nephew was later to show.[14]

Grandfather Jiří taught all his sons the piano, organ, and singing. His third son, also called Jiří, later attended the teacher's training course run by the Piarist order of clerics in the town of Příbor, and then, aged only 16, became an assistant teacher in a small Silesian village.[15] 'Here,' writes Vincenc, a 'little orphan [actually illegitimate] Pavel Křížkovský attached himself to the new teacher. The child's mother begged Jiří to teach the boy music and singing, as indeed he did, and he later found Pavel a choral scholarship at the Church of the Holy Ghost in Opava. Thus Jiří Janáček laid the foundations of Pavel's standing as a composer, a service Pavel later repaid to Jiří's son, Leoš.'[16] Pavel was to become Father Pavel Křížkovský, a renowned composer and Leoš Janáček's teacher.[17]

Jiří Janáček inherited from his father his 'outstanding teaching ability', and also his love of gardening; like all the Janáčeks, he was 'quick-tempered but also tenacious'.[18] In 1835 he was appointed *kantor* in Příbor, largely because of his music skills. Three years later he married there the 18-year-old Amalie Grulichová, a weaver's daughter, and for the next ten years they lived fairly comfortably, although Jiří was only an assistant teacher. But in 1848 nearby Hukvaldy was in need of a new schoolmaster, and so Jiří, Amalie and their five children moved into the dilapidated schoolhouse there.

'The Hukvaldy school: one large room, rough wooden benches', recalled Leoš Janáček later. 'One class on the left, for the little ones, one the right another for the older children. Two blackboards. Father and the assistant teaching simultaneously . . . . A huge stove in one corner, beside it a bed; there lodged the assistant.'[19] The school was damp, the roof badly in need of repair, the doors rotting away. The teacher's income − often paid in kind − was based on the number of fee-paying pupils. But the school was poorly attended. Meagre harvests and high taxes led to overwhelming poverty; hence the schoolmaster was just as poor as the villagers and sometimes poorer. Applications for a post elsewhere failed; by the time repairs were made to the school in 1858, time had taken its toll and severe rheumatism had weakened Jiří Janáček's heart.

In these often desperate conditions, nine more children were born to the Janáčeks. Only four of them, three boys and a girl, survived, though the three daughters and two sons born in Příbor all lived to adulthood.

Leoš (baptized Leo Eugen) was born on 3 July 1854, in a room where 'one window looked out on the church and the other on the brewery'.[20] He was the ninth child, the fifth born at Hukvaldy, and had his father's thick dark hair and his mother's small stature. His talent for music was clearly inherited from both parents, for Amalie was also very musical: she 'loved playing the guitar', had 'a beautiful voice', and often performed in the musicians' gallery of the local church.[21]

Life in a small mountain village like Hukvaldy in the 1850s still entailed a good deal of drudgery, and the yearly cycle of religious and other festivals had changed little since the Middle Ages. But when Leoš's father set up a reading and singing club, 'the humble Hukvaldy [soon] surpassed in singing and national consciousness the bigger villages and towns, then still dozing'.[22]

The children and adults alike delighted in the surrounding country-side. 'An old castle on top of the hill, below the neat parish. And the forest all around. Lime trees, some of which are five hundred years old,' Janáček was to write in 1918. 'Nowhere else have I found purer, healthier and stronger air and, during the summer days, brighter sunshine.'[23]

The child's world is inevitably a narrow one. 'The school's yard; some ducks in it. A cow in the byre . . . . In sister Vikýna's [Victoria's] cottage a loom,' reminisced Janáček in his autobiographical notes. 'Our apiary: I can only see the dark space of each beehive and the glistening honey.'[24] He never forgot the fire that broke out when he was four: 'It was at night, during the summer. They took us children in eiderdowns to the hillside by the deer park. My tears of terror and the blazing backcloth of the fire are, until today, all one in my mind.

And the echo of this is the key of C sharp minor in my *Overgrown Path*.'[25] There were also recollections of pilgrimages and winter trips to matins at daybreak. The first snow, the flickering lanterns, the deep forest with its wild berries – these early memories recall the innocence of a country childhood and give no inkling of the poverty the family had to endure.

Leoš, educated at the Hukvaldy school, was not among his father's best pupils. 'You child of the mountains, soft-hearted and playful! You feel with every little bird that chirps . . . you lose yourself in thought over a pebble at the bottom of the clear stream – why do your eyes flit over the page, as if you were dodging someone in the stubble field?', he wrote in 1909. 'These columns of words! Nineteen lines in one column. Substantives from *Aegyptus* to *Vergilius*, adjectives from *altus* to *septimus*! Where can these, with all the dust of the school, take hold?'[26]

Leoš excelled in music. 'Of course I did not come to music by chance,' he told an interviewer in 1928. 'Consider my whole background! When I was eight, people used to say: "That rascal will be better than his father." '[27] Music-making was one of the schoolmaster's duties, but also the family's chief entertainment; at six, under the strict eye of his father, he could already play some of Beethoven's piano sonatas.

But the real centre of musical life in Bohemia and Moravia, especially in small rural communities, was the church. From the moment when forcible re-Catholicization began in the seventeenth century, church and school were the pillars of an education system within which music was not only highly valued but formed an integral part of the curriculum.[28] Choral singing in particular was an important element of the Catholic ritual: the daily mass, the religious processions, the early morning Advent services and Christmas carols all constituted a cycle of musical events without which everyday life would have been unimaginable. Although later in life Janáček was to reject the faith, and would not 'step into a church even to shelter from the rain',[29] his early grounding in music was profoundly influenced by Catholicism.

The small gallery of the Hukvaldy church could only accommodate a few musicians. But the nearby village of Rychaltice was richer, and its church bigger. As its headmaster and choirmaster was friendly with Jiří Janáček (and, like him, a bee-keeping enthusiast), the Janáčeks often visited on Sundays to make music. The two villages would combine forces at festivals and important religious celebrations:

the Hukvaldy musicians helped out at Rychaltice, and in return borrowed the instruments their own small church lacked.

The pride of the Rychaltice church was its Baroque 'gilded organ, with plenty of registers on both sides of the manuals', recalled Janáček in his *feuilleton* 'Without drums'; by the window were 'two kettledrums as big as kneading tubs . . .'.* In 1861, the 7-year-old Leoš watched the Hukvaldy musicians practising for the Easter mass. 'There were violins, majestic trumpets and clarinets. But no – it can't be done without the drums, it isn't triumphant enough!' Even in a small Moravian village a high mass on Easter Sunday without timpani was inconceivable and so, unbeknown to his father, Leoš and a gang of local boys plotted to steal the drums from the Rychaltice church.[30] But the nocturnal raid was unsuccessful, and no drums were played at Hukvaldy that Easter: the expedition ended with Leoš getting a thorough beating with the drumsticks. Yet the instrument made an indelible impression on him: he could never resist giving the timpani a prominent part when the chance arose.[31]

When Leoš was 11 his childhood suddenly came to an end. His father, whose health was failing, wanted him to become a choral scholar at the Queen's Monastery in Brno, where he could study music. The Monastery ran a choir school, which had been founded in 1648; it had been endowed by Countess Sibylla Polyxena de Montani, née Thurn-Wallesassin, to enable a limited number of children from poor families to be instructed in the 'musical virtues' and the 'development of science'. Several outstanding men were associated with the Monastery: the composer Pavel Křížkovský, the philosopher, poet and journalist F.J. Klácel, the great folk-song collector František Sušil, and the founder of genetics J.G. Mendel; Revivalists such as the historian František Palacký and the writer and grammarian Josef Dobrovský (both of whom fought some of the first battles to revitalize the Czech language) had also had friendly contacts with the Monastery. The school's orientation was decidedly Slavonic: the prelate of Brno's Old Town, Viktor Napp – though not a Slav by birth – was in favour of the Slavonic cause and supported the Czechs from Moravia; and Sušil's Slavophile views on the characteristic features of Slavonic tunes and 'Slavism in music' were known from 1832.[32]

Leoš could of course have become a teacher and studied at nearby Příbor like his father. But the boy was talented, and the best musical

---

* *Feuilletons* were short essays printed in newspapers; Janáček wrote many in his lifetime – they suited his style – and they were later collected into a book.

education in Moravia was available only at choir schools; moreover, Křížkovský – the choirmaster at Queen's – was an old friend.[33] In the summer of 1865, Jiří took Leoš to sing and sight-read for Křížkovský, then ailing, at a spa near Opava.[34] In September, as a new *fundatista*, Leoš arrived in Brno.

'Mother and I spent the night, fearfully, in some dark closet of a room . . . I did not sleep a wink,' Janáček recalled later. 'At the crack of dawn, it was: out, quickly to be out. In the courtyard of the Queen's Monastery, Mother walks away with a heavy step. I am in tears. So is she. We are both alone now. I am among strangers – none is friendly; a strange school, a hard bed, and the bread harder still. No mollycoddling. My own world, exclusively mine, was beginning here.'[35]

The Moravian capital of Brno lies in the south of the province, in the valley between two rivers; on three sides it is surrounded by wooded hills. The historical centre – its characteristic outline with a fortress on top of the Špilberk Hill and the city at its foot – dates from the thirteenth century. During the Middle Ages the population of Brno was in fact German;[36] only the villages in the environs were Czech, and Brno's character did not change until the second half of the nineteenth century when these villages merged with the city.

Below the Špilberk Fortress once worked the bakers, locksmiths, tanners and other craftsmen after whom the streets are named; here merchants gathered at the Cabbage Market, a medieval square where a market still takes place daily. Brno resisted both the Hussites in the fifteenth century and the Swedish army during the Thirty Years War, although the surrounding areas were devastated. After 1620, following the enforced re-Catholicization, the city acquired its new, Baroque look; in the eighteenth century the Špilberk Fortress, with its dungeons built in a disused moat, became infamous as a Hapsburg gaol: many Hungarian Jacobins, Italian *carbonari* and Polish revolutionaries were imprisoned there.

In the early nineteenth century Brno changed its face once again. Although the city retained its ramparts until the 1850s, from 1839 it could be reached by railway from Vienna. Situated only some 100 km to the south of the Moravian capital, Vienna – its population in the 1860s still under 500,000 – had great influence on both of Brno's communities. The Brno Germans had close links with the city, and their pro-Austrian orientation also explains the strong nationalistic feelings in the Czech minority in Brno and throughout Czech-speaking Moravia, at a time when the Czech capital Prague had already passed this phase of nationalism.

Industrialization brought to Brno a large working-class population who lived to the south and the north of the centre, in overcrowded, dilapidated houses. But there was greenery around Špilberk and the Františkov Hill; further to the north, and west of the old quarter, were the city's parks, and beyond rose the green hills and woods of the Brno countryside. Yet the 11-year-old Janáček's world was largely confined to the enclosed grounds of the Monastery. 'To get to the Pisárky Park and to the Yellow Hill was virtually an expedition,' he wrote in 1927.[37]

Life at the choir school entailed a rigorous discipline. The day started at five o'clock with prayer and study until seven, when mass was sung. After breakfast, school continued until lunchtime, and the afternoon timetable included a walk and further study. Between six and seven there was an hour of singing practice, followed by supper and a short period of free time: 'Whenever I could, I sat at the organ, and Křížkovský once said: "Look at him – he already knows the motif from the mass we are going to perform." '[38]

There were many gifted boys at such schools, mostly from large, impoverished families. The choral scholars (ten in Janáček's time) were provided with rooms and board, and free medical care. The school fees (which were low), books, clothes and extras had to be paid for by the parents; the best pupils were exempt from fees. Further, paying choristers were admitted for the fee of 100 Austrian Gulden a year. Poverty was therefore a prerequisite for obtaining a place at the school, and the education acquired there gave its pupils a better chance in life. Yet they had to endure great loneliness.

> Bluebirds! This is what we, the boys from the Thurn–Wallesassin Foundation, were nicknamed . . . because of our light blue uniform trimmed in white. Lonely, and constantly watched over, we stood, in moments of melancholy, by the barred windows. From the prelate's garden, tiny bluish birds used to fly over to peck up what we had crumbled up for them . . . – they were also 'bluebirds', but these friends of ours were freer than us.[39]

Every day, each Bluebird practised singing, his particular instrument and the piano; in addition, there were quartet and ensemble playing classes. As each pupil spent part of the day at a grammar or secondary school, to study philosophy or classics, a strict routine had to be observed to cope with all the work, examinations and public performances.

On festive occasions the boys wore long red coats with blue collars trimmed in gold. '[At concerts,] their "harmony" welcomed ministers and other dignitaries. . . . They helped out at the theatre, and no church musicians' gallery could do without them,' wrote Janáček of their past history. 'Bluebirds played at grand balls and every day they entered the refectory "when the roast was served", to play at the table. Every day at the table and every Sunday an instrumental mass to praise God – and how much other music!'[40] At first a treble, Janáček became the best alto at Queen's, and sang a solo in a Beethoven mass. The boys sang mostly in church, but also appeared on stage; Janáček recalled participating in the children's chorus in Meyerbeer's *Le prophète*.[41] At the age of 11 he was already an excellent pianist, accompanying the soprano Eleonora of Ehrenberg (the first Mařenka in *The Bartered Bride*) at a concert. By then the German population of Brno and the city's Czech minority held separate concerts, though Czech operas were not given in Brno regularly until the 1880s.[42]

Music was not just a duty for the Bluebirds. 'No one who sang or played under Křížkovský would forget a single work rehearsed by him,' Janáček recollected many years later:

> We were a handful of assured singers. Voices grown pleasing through daily practice, and as steady as flutes; to conduct us was completely unnecessary. With our eyes we looked in front of us, but our ears were surely right at the back of our heads: we heard every little voice among the twittering violins behind us; we were pleased with Mr Štros when, at special religious festivals, he lamented on his oboe.[43]

Leoš also attended a German secondary school. Brno had no Czech school at the time; the first Czech primary school in inner Brno was not founded until 1881.[44] Once Austrian rule was established in the former Crown Lands of Bohemia, written Czech was only kept alive where possible.[45] But during the reign of the otherwise enlightened Emperor Josef II universal schooling in German was imposed, and in 1780 Czech was rendered all but extinct as a language of the educated classes: its teaching at grammar schools was abolished, not to be permitted again until 1816 (and then only as a non-compulsory subject).

Thus the nation was soon divided into the peasantry and urban lower class town-dwellers who spoke Czech and the aristocracy and the wealthy burghers who grew up speaking German. Any professional career required fluency in German, and so ambitious middle-class families also encouraged their children to speak German at home; by the middle of the nineteenth century, the Czech middle class had become virtually Germanized. In Brno itself there was, among the educated classes, only a very small Czech-speaking minority: Czech was considered the language of the underclass.

In the country the situation was quite different. As a village schoolmaster Janáček's father was one of the best-educated men in his community but although he had a good command of German, his background made him a Czech speaker. Thus at Hukvaldy Leoš spoke Czech with his parents, brothers and sisters, in the Lašsko dialect whose accent is notable for its clipped, staccato sound. But he wrote his early letters to his uncle Jan in German, as he was taught to do at school, and initially he also wrote in German to his brothers Bedřich and František, whose wives were both German.

Leoš never forgot the choir school discipline, which taught him how to plan and use his time. Křížkovský showed a paternal interest in him, at one time helping quietly to pay his school fees, and often using his influence on the boy's behalf. Once, when already at the grammar school, Leoš missed a maths exam because of illness, and was only allowed to resit it after much pleading by Křížkovský. The boy was often stubborn and fierce, though opportunities for pranks were few. Even a night raid for fruit in the Monastery garden was soon discovered: Křížkovský was waiting for the party of returning choristers in the doorway with a lighted candle. As the crestfallen boys reluctantly passed him, he beat 'a minor scale on us. For a few apples in our pockets – a minor scale in every octave,' recalled Janáček. 'I got a slap on the cheek in the highest octave.'[46]

A year after Leoš entered the school his father died, aged only 50.[47] By then Leoš's older siblings had either married or left home. Viktorie, sixteen years older than Leoš, is said to have gone with her husband to America in search of a better life, but this is not certain. The first-born son, Karel, ten years Leoš's senior, taught at various Moravian towns and later became a headmaster. Two other daughters, Eleonora ('Lori', 'Lorka') and Josefa ('Josefka'), respectively fourteen and twelve years older than Leoš, taught needlework; there was a strong affinity between Leoš and Josefka, who settled in Hukvaldy. Bedřich, eight years Leoš's senior, travelled a good deal; at one time he was a factory director in the Austrian region of Carinthia. Two brothers emigrated to Russia: František, two years Leoš's junior and his favourite brother, became an engineer in St

Petersburg; the youngest, Josef, was a teacher. All were said to be very proud of Leoš, and convinced of his talent.[48]

Janáček's mother was only 47 when she was suddenly widowed, with several children still in their early teens. The family lived in Hukvaldy in great poverty; for a while Amalie supplemented her meagre pension by resourcefully taking over her husband's duties as church organist. When the new teacher arrived a year later, she had to leave. Some of her older children took turns in providing accommodation for her, and later she found lodgings in the village where her daughter Eleonora taught. She only returned to Hukvaldy to stay with Josefka towards the end of her life, when she became seriously ill.[49]

Leoš continued to live in Brno; during his first four years at Queen's he was not allowed to spend a holiday with the family. Lonely and extremely poor, he was the only Bluebird who stayed on at the school during the short but cruel Prusso-Italian war with Austria in 1866, when the Prussian army swept through Brno. At the age of 70 he still remembered the sound of the band:

> Klášterní Square in Old Brno was filling up with the grey and red of the Prussian army during the summer holidays. The tin drums whirled and above them the high piccolos squealed. Predatory music. Even today it sits in my ears and buzzes. I, a lad of twelve, with my eyes popping out, followed the wild tumult of the Prussian army . . . .[50]

After his father's death Leoš was supported by his uncle Jan, a Roman Catholic priest.[51] The letters he wrote to him were full of sorrow and longing, and of humble requests for money: despite his scholarship, Leoš was not among the best pupils at Queen's and thus not exempt from school fees. There were laundry and cobbler's bills to be paid, as well as books; his allowance was not large enough to pay for a growing boy's clothing and in 1867 he spent money sent for school fees on new shoes.

At his German school, Leoš was registered as *böhmisch* (i.e. Czech), and so was a target for mockery and even beatings from his equally Czech but largely Germanized schoolfellows. At the Monastery, on the other hand, the Slavonic spirit was strong. Only two of the letters Leoš wrote to his uncle Jan are in German; the rest, written in Czech (albeit ungrammatical and clumsy), are already fiercely patriotic. 'Forgive me for not writing for so long,' he apologized in 1869:

I have written once or twice – and then burnt the letters, as I don't know whether you are a true Czech or a true German, or half and half. Oh, dear Uncle, you don't know how I love the Czechs, and you wouldn't believe how I hate the Germans . . . . On 5 June, twenty singers will travel from Brno to Velehrad, the whole Foundation including me. [. . .] You don't know how much I look forward to seeing that holy ground, where once stood the seat of Svatopluk and that of the Slavonic apostles Cyril and Methodius. I am not worthy to walk on it. May I express a wish, dearest Uncle? Would you please buy me a Slavonic outfit . . . . This is my most heartfelt entreaty, please answer it. At least promise that the outfit will be ready by the school holidays, then I swear most solemnly that I shall be the best at school.[52]

As a 14-year-old Leoš had 'shoulder-length locks, [and usually] a Sokol hat on his head'.[53] He wore high boots and wide trousers gathered at the bottom, with another pair inside to keep warm during the hard Moravian winters; with no overcoat, he put on two jackets, with two shirts and a waistcoat underneath.[54] When his voice broke he had to leave Queen's but continued his studies at the German grammar school, lodging with a young family for a very low rent. Křížkovský's door remained open to him, and Leoš visited the Monastery daily. An excellent pianist, he had there 'an equal partner, with whom he played Beethoven's symphonies' under Křížkovský's supervision.[55] As well as playing the organ he also continued his violin studies.

His first compositions, simple songs, date from this time. 'He wrote these songs down on special coloured paper: blue, pink and other colours. He always drew the staves himself,' recounted František Neumann, who recalled one song in particular: ' "If you don't want me, what of it, I don't care two straws. I shall climb a hill, and look around for another girl." A pretty song it was, and we both liked it terrifically!'[56]

During his time at Queen's, and later at the German grammar school, Leoš had no definite ideas about his future; at one time he wanted to become a forester. But in 1869, once he had completed his three years at the grammar school, he enrolled at the Brno Imperial and Royal Teachers' Training Institute, as his father had wished.[57] He was given an annual state scholarship of 100 Austrian Gulden – not a large sum but a fortune compared with his mother's miserly pension – and in 1872 he passed his examinations. Apart from singing and organ playing he distinguished himself in history and geography, though his practical teaching was only 'fair to middling'. He was greatly impressed by the psychology lectures given by Dr Parthe and the Institute's director Emilian Schulz, Janáček's future father-in-law, and became particularly interested in the works of the German physiologist and philosopher Wilhelm Wundt, which he later studied in detail.[58]

In the autumn of 1872, at only 18 and while he was still training as a teacher, Janáček was appointed Křížkovský's deputy choirmaster at Queen's, though without salary. His principal duty was to rehearse the choristers for an hour each afternoon, for the Sunday mass. New applicants also sang for him; the future famous Art Nouveau painter Alfons Mucha, who eventually became a chorister at another foundation in Brno, often helped out, singing under Janáček's baton.[59]

Janáček had fortunately completed his studies at Queen's before the Caecilian Reform movement changed the character of teaching and music-making there. This movement was established in the late 1860s but harked back to sixteenth-century polyphony, considered 'pure'; thus Lassus and Palestrina replaced Bach and Haydn, the Monastery's large orchestra was disbanded, the boys' instrumental tuition ceased, and their vocal concerts were restricted to church precincts.

Janáček's teacher Křížkovský, although at first opposed to the movement, was later entrusted to carry out these reforms in the city of Olomouc in central Moravia, and was often away from Brno. As his deputy, Janáček therefore had a first-class opportunity to conduct a large, mixed repertoire – including Lassus and Palestrina, preferred by the Caecilian Reform, but also Haydn and Brixi, in addition to new church music by German and Czech composers. The works were painstakingly rehearsed and the Monastery's church of St Martin's soon became one of the focal points of musical life in Brno. Křížkovský returned only rarely, 'to make sure everything was as it should be "under my management" ', as Janáček remarked later.[60]

In 1873 Janáček was appointed choirmaster of the Brno working men's choral society, Svatopluk. Founded five years earlier, this patriotic society was little more than a singing club; its members – mainly weavers – met originally in the city's taverns and did not aspire to more than light entertainment. Yet under Janáček's dedicated leadership the society's repertoire widened considerably and its concerts at the newly built Beseda House began to attract attention. Janáček, who refused to be paid for this work, never forgot the men's enthusiasm:

Outside it is raining, snowing, freezing. But the worker, as soon as he steps out of the factory where he has toiled the whole day in the deadly dust, still remembers that one more duty awaits him: his singing rehearsal. Perhaps he is hungry and thirsty; his wife and children wait for him at home. What keeps him from going home, why does he hurry to the rehearsal room? I cannot answer this question – but I admit that nowhere have I found such devotion, diligence, love and assiduousness among singers.[61]

Janáček's fierce independence was not always an advantage to him: his participation in the city's concert life coincided with a compulsory two-year period of teaching, also unpaid. Fortunately, his very low rent was paid by Křížkovský, and the Monastery kitchen provided lunches and suppers. In return Janáček helped out as organist, and played the violin at some masses. And Křížkovský, who hoped that Janáček would eventually become choirmaster at Queen's, would occasionally slip him some cash; at that time deputizing was the only possibility, as Janáček was still far too young for the post.

But his work at the Monastery and with the Svatopluk did not go unnoticed. Janáček's 'considerable musical erudition, outstanding . . . talent in the field of composition, his fervent love of the arts and iron discipline', wrote the correspondent of the Prague music magazine *Dalibor* in August 1873, were 'the guarantee that one day he would surely occupy a worthy place among our outstanding musicians'. At a concert the society gave in April that year, the 19-year-old Janáček attracted attention 'both for a precise, finely honed performance of the choir, and for one of his compositions, in purely national spirit (a very prettily arranged Serbian [folk] song)'. Janáček's other chorus, *War Song*, performed in July, 'was no less liked', the critic noted:

> though perhaps its musical form and the text did not entirely tally. But let this not frighten Mr Janáček! We wish him, with all our heart, the best opportunity to extend his musical education and cultivate his gift for composition; for then he will certainly justify the wonderful hopes which we rightly place in him.[62]

In July 1874, having assiduously attended lectures at the Moravian Academy, Janáček did extremely well in Czech and Czech literature; he was to pass his final examination at the Teachers' Training Institute in November. His teacher's diploma would qualify him to teach

Czech, history and geography at schools where the pupils were taught in their native language, and he would at last be able to earn his living.

But by then Janáček – aged 20 – knew that he did not want to become a teacher: his real vocation was for music. Křížkovský predicted a great future for him and so, also encouraged by Emilian Schulz,[63] Janáček had decided to continue his music studies at the Organ School in Prague. At the end of the summer he set off for the Czech capital.

2

Prague and Abroad

(1874–1880)

IN THE 1870s Prague's oldest parishes – the Old Town, the Little
Quarter and the New Town – were still surrounded by the city's
fortifications. The villages of Karlin, Smíchov, Žižkov and others
were only beginning to grow into future suburbs. 'I entered through
[the Horse Gate] one Sunday, on a sunny afternoon,' wrote Janáček in
1925, recalling a walk more than fifty years earlier. 'I walked up a
dusty road; small trees planted alongside were already withering in
autumn fatigue; acres of fields to the left and to the right. Here and
there the first few of the tall houses stuck out. Královské Vinohrady
[Royal Vineyards]: it had not yet dreamt of the town it was to
become.'[1]

Today, Vinohrady is part of Prague's inner city. Štěpánská Street in
central Prague, where Janáček found his lodgings in the autumn of
1874, is barely twenty minutes' walk away. Prague had begun to
acquire the look of a modern metropolis from about the middle of
the nineteenth century, but its historical centre had hardly changed
since Mozart's *Don Giovanni* was first performed at Prague's Estates
Theatre in 1781.

During the 1850s, under the rule of the infamous Austrian minister of the interior, Count Alexander Bach, there was no Czech
political life in Bohemia and Moravia, and no political journalism.
Literature languished, and performances of Czech opera in Prague
were few, although Czech plays, at least, were staged regularly. In
1867, the new Austro-Hungarian Empire was established. But the
redistribution of political power brought political equality only to
the Hungarians – not the Czechs, who had already failed to achieve
any of their objectives in the Revolution of 1848.

Protests and demonstrations erupted in Prague. The Slavonic spirit
grew strong and frustration manifested itself in new ventures such as
independent Czech newspapers and patriotic choral societies. Czech
balls, which took place during each carnival from 1840 onwards,

were now attended by thousands; there Czech, considered the language of servants, could be spoken freely and without embarrassment. After 1862 the 'foreign tailcoat' was almost entirely supplanted by the patriotic black *čamara*,[2] and in 1868 ladies wore dresses in the national colours of white, red and blue. Not even the city police commissar dared to appear in a uniform. And on 16 May of that year the foundation stone of the Prague National Theatre was laid, during a three-day festival which was not just a national and political demonstration but 'a semi-religious rite'.[3] Yet by 1872 there were quarrels between the *staročech* ('Old Czech') and *mladočech* ('Young Czech') factions of the National Party, and their subsequent long-drawn-out debates were to influence attitudes towards individual Czech composers.

The National Theatre, where both drama and opera were eventually performed, was funded almost entirely by public subscription and justifiably aroused national pride: although it was not completed until 1881, this was to be the Czech theatre for the Czechs, in an independent Czech state. And in 1874 a competition was announced for the design of a new concert and exhibition hall further down the Vltava, on the site of a former prison: in 1884 the well-appointed neo-Renaissance Rudolfinum Hall was opened, its building funded largely by the Czech Savings Bank.[4]

Before the completion of the National Theatre there was another theatre in Prague for the Czechs alone, provided in 1862 by the state and commonly known as the Provisional Theatre. It was a small neo-Renaissance building which seated only 900, and occupied what was to be the rear of the National Theatre. The company – which gave performances two or three times a week – was the first permanent and exclusively Czech ensemble; it was led by Smetana, who composed for it and became its chief conductor. There were also several concert-giving societies in Prague (chamber and symphonic concerts were attended by both Czechs and Germans), and a number of Czech choral societies.

The Organ School, established in 1830 in the Old Town, was by the 1880s one of the two most important music schools in Bohemia. Its purpose was to train organists; modulation, counterpoint, fugue, liturgical chant and orchestration were also taught. It formed part of the Institute for the Cultivation of Church Music, and maintained arch-conservative values: contemporary music was not in favour, and attitudes only improved under the directorship of the enlightened František Skuherský,[5] a composer of church music but also of operas.

The core of the three-year course of studies that Janáček undertook at the Organ School was the second year, which focused on
composition; he also studied theory of music and aesthetics. He was
granted only a year's leave from the Teachers' Training Institute in
Brno: as an accomplished musician he had remission from the first
year, but was obliged to cram the remaining two years into one.

His application was absolutely exemplary; he showered his teachers with homework, and the manuscripts of his compositions were
extremely neat, unlike the hasty, frantic script he was to develop later
in life. He read widely on aesthetics, and even attempted, with his
former schoolfellow František Bílý, to translate into Czech the
General Aesthetics of Forms by the German theoretician Robert
Zimmermann.[6] He also took a keen interest in contemporary
harmony, taught by Skuherský, and in the study of church modes.
Much Moravian folk-song is 'modal', and this study was to be of
great importance for Janáček's later work.[7] Not content with all that,
he also studied French and mastered the Russian alphabet.

Janáček graduated as the best student, though his extra-mural
activities – including reviewing for the music magazine *Cecilie* – were
not always appreciated. Some six months after entering the Organ
School he published an extremely critical review of a Gregorian mass
conducted by Skuherský. Four days after its publication Janáček
was asked to leave the school. 'A memorable day,' he noted in his
textbook. 'They have wronged me for telling the truth.' He was only
re-admitted, after a prolonged Easter holiday, through the interven-
tion of the magazine's editor, Father Lehner, and of a former scholar,
the tenor Jan Ludevít Lukes. In fact, Skuherský was well aware that
his pupil, if tactless, was very gifted. Three years later he gave him a
handsome letter of reference, praising him for his 'extensive knowledge of musical literature, a subtle ear as well as a thorough command
of musical theory and aesthetics which give him the right to activities
as conductor and critic'.[8]

Money was scarce. František Neumann, his former fellow scholar,
sent half the fees he earned from taking over Janáček's private pupils
in Brno, but it was far from sufficient. Cold and hunger did not deter
Janáček from working all the harder but they did alter his looks: a
photograph taken at the time shows a bespectacled, clean-shaven,
emaciated and somewhat tight-lipped youth, who bears little
resemblance to the future dashing young composer. The hardship
is obvious, but so is the seriousness of purpose and exceptional
will-power.

Janáček had not even enough money to hire a piano. He practised Bach's preludes on a 'keyboard' drawn on his table with chalk. 'It was maddening,' he recalled. 'I was longing for the living sounds! [. . .] One day, out of the blue, a piano appeared in my little room in Štěpánská Street.' When Father Lehner, Janáček's frequent host, was told of the instrument's miraculous arrival, 'a sly smile appeared on his kind face. At the end of the year the piano vanished from my room in the same mysterious way.'[9]

Poverty also prevented Janáček from taking advantage of Prague's musical life. He paid regular visits to Sv Vojtěch [St Adalbert's] Church where he made the acquaintance of its young organist Antonín Dvořák, whose champion and lifelong friend he was soon to become. Yet even though the foundations of the Czech national operatic style were being laid at the Prague Provisional Theatre, there was no sign at this time that so much of Janáček's own work would take the form of opera: he saw no opera at all in Prague, not even Smetana's *The Bartered Bride*. Just as Janáček's early grounding in music was profoundly influenced by Catholic ritual, so the works he wrote in Prague during 1874 and 1875 conformed to the ethics and aesthetics of the Caecilian ecclesiastic movement: the *Graduale (Speciosus forma)*, *Introitus (in festo Ss Nominis Jesu)*, *Benedictus*, *Exaudi Deus* (his first published work, 1877) and *Communio* are all for mixed choir and, apart from the *Graduale*, are based on or closely follow original Gregorian chants. His two *Intradas* were written for four violins, and the *Sounds in Memory of Arnošt Förchtgott-Tovačovský* for three violins, viola, cello and double bass. The three works for the organ, Prelude, *Varyto* and Chorale Fantasia, and the funeral song *Take Your Rest*, also date from that time.

He could rarely afford the treat of going to a concert. 'How I managed – on a fixed income of 5 Gulden a month – to get to a concert in honour of Bedřich Smetana, I have no idea,' wrote Janáček in 1925. Smetana had become deaf in 1874 and had to leave his post at the Provisional Theatre; two of his tone poems, *Vltava* and *Vyšehrad*, were played at this concert for his benefit.[10] 'The performance had just come to an end and the deafening storm of applause came together in one cry: "Smetana"! [. . .] They led the ailing composer up the staircase. Only his face imprinted itself on my soul.'[11]

Janáček completed his studies at the Organ School in July 1875 with a performance of his Chorale Fantasia for organ and Bach's Toccata in C. He was given top marks in all subjects except for playing from a figured bass. He had now reached the highest standard of education possible within his country and, according to his diploma, was 'excellently qualified' to fill the office of an organist; in October he returned to Prague to take the state music examination in singing, organ and piano, and passed that also with honours. But in the meantime he was back in Brno, and fully involved in the city's concert life.

In those days Brno had no Czech opera house. The Königlich-Stadtisches Nationaltheater (popularly known as the Redoutensalle) had served the city's German speakers since 1786; the new, well-equipped German Stadttheater was to open in 1882, and the Czech Provisional Theatre, staging both opera and drama, in 1884. But throughout the 1870s there was plenty of lively activity among the musical clubs and societies of the Czech minority. The Reading Circle, founded in 1861, was one of the most important centres of Czech cultural life in Brno; Janáček had become a member before his studies in Prague. There were also societies devoted to physical education, and to religion. A women's educational society, Vesna, which started in 1870 as a singing club for girls, went on to establish patriotic schools and clubs where thousands of Czech women were trained in home economics; most of these societies also offered their members musical evenings, as well as dances and theatre performances.

Although music was usually on the statutes of many such societies, their ideas of programming were often not very advanced. Czech cultural life in Brno was still far from sophisticated, and Janáček burned with the desire to deliver it from its provincial amateurishness.

At the beginning of 1876 he was elected choirmaster to the leading Czech choral and concert-giving society in Brno, the Beseda; founded in 1860, it owned its own premises from 1873. The newly built Beseda House included a concert hall and immediately became the main centre of local Czech cultural and social life. The Beseda was an all-male choir and its artistic standards were low at the time (although Czech operas by Smetana and Blodek were occasionally performed), but its funds were sound. The society was now looking for a capable conductor and Janáček, aware of its potential, seized the opportunity. At first he also continued to conduct the Svatopluk Choral Society but soon resigned to devote himself to the Beseda.

There was much to do. The Beseda's members – like those in many Czech middle-class societies at the time – had little musical training, and music-making was often merely part of a social event. From the start, Janáček refused to take part in any entertainments. 'I will remain true to my decision,' he was to stress again in 1880. 'I shall not conduct performances of songs alongside beer drinking. Only if this "entertainment" is turned into performances without the obligatory beer, performances that are at least musical, even if not exactly of a classical content, would it conform to my views as to the dignity of a musician.'[12] Within two months he transformed the Beseda into a proper mixed choral society, supplementing the choir on occasions with the Monastery choristers and pupils from the Teachers' Training Institute. And instead of giving medleys of popular items as was customary before his arrival, Janáček introduced large works previously only undertaken by Brno's much wealthier German Musikverein.

In his efforts to elevate the Beseda's standards he had had, since early 1876, tremendous support from Amalie Wickenhauser-Neruda, an accomplished pianist. Tall, thin and dark-haired, Amalie was the 42-year-old wife of the conductor of the city's German Theatre, and she had been born in Brno into a musically gifted Czech family. With her brothers and sisters – all prodigies – she travelled throughout Europe, both as a soloist and as a member of the celebrated Neruda Quartet; her younger sister Wilma became the world-famous violinist Norman-Neruda, and later Lady Hallé.[13]

When, in August 1876, Janáček became a provisional teacher of music at the Teachers' Training Institute, he had already resumed conducting the choir at the Monastery, where he also took part in a concert, playing on the magnificent new Steinmayer organ. At the end of that year he decided to give two chamber concerts a year at the Brno Reading Circle, with Amalie. An experienced performer and a highly regarded piano teacher, she was most likely Janáček's mentor and adviser on programming, both at the Reading Circle and at the Beseda. Several chamber works by Beethoven, Mendelssohn and Schumann – in some of which Janáček participated – had been in her family's repertoire; Brahms, in whose works she excelled, was her favourite composer, and another sister, the violinist Marie Arlberg, joined her in Grieg's Violin Sonata.[14] Amalie also stimulated Janáček's passionate interest in the Russian composer and virtuoso Anton Rubinstein; she had known and loved his music for years, and had performed it in Brno. Now she introduced Rubinstein's works at the Reading Circle, and performed his Third Piano Concerto at the Beseda, where Janáček joined her in the Fantasia for two pianos.[15] He also performed Mendelssohn's Piano Concerto in G minor (this was Mrs Wickenhauser's tour de force, and no doubt she coached him)

and Saint-Saëns' Piano Concerto No. 2 in G minor, both under the
baton of her husband Ernst.[16] Thus Romanticism reigned during the
entire first period of Janáček's work with the Beseda (1876–9).

The Beseda's performance of Mendelssohn's *Psalm 95*, within a
year of Janáček's appointment, was also Amalie's idea; Mozart's
Requiem, at Easter 1878, was a joint project, with each covering part
of the expenses.[17] A year later the society achieved a high point with
Beethoven's *Missa Solemnis*. The choir numbered a hundred singers
and the leading Prague soloists included the soprano Eleonora of
Ehrenberg (whom Janáček had accompanied at a concert as a boy
of 11). The orchestra, 'such as was never heard in Brno before',
comprised thirty violins, thirteen violas, seven cellos and seven
double basses.[18] Janáček's programmes also included works by his
former teachers at the Monastery and the Prague Organ School.

Amalie was the best ally Janáček could have found in Brno; as contemporary reviews make clear, he made 'enormous progress' in his
piano studies under her tuition,[19] and even considered becoming a
professional pianist. She, meanwhile, was apparently 'attracted by the
ambitious, self-assured youth with organizational ability'[20] and by his
drive. The two are said to have had an affair in 1876.[21] Whatever the
relationship, it suddenly ended in 1879 and the circumstances surrounding the rift were 'very strange and unfortunately unclear'.[22]
Janáček later made unflattering remarks about her, and cast aspersions
on her pianistic and teaching abilities. Much fêted at the Beseda until
then, Amalie badly missed working with the Society and soon ceased
performing at Czech musical institutions in Brno – as did her famous
sister Wilma and her brother František. This was a serious loss to
Czech musical life in the city.[23]

Janáček also promoted Czech composers in Brno, and he cham-
pioned Dvořák's music with almost boundless admiration. In 1877 he
conducted Dvořák's *Serenade* for strings, op. 22; the *Moravian Duets*
and some choral works followed, with Dvořák himself – thirteen
years Janáček's senior – at the piano. Four of the newly orchestrated
first series of *Slavonic Dances* were heard in 1878. Dvořák was made an
honorary member of the Beseda, and throughout the next decade
the society hardly gave a concert without one of his works on the
programme.[24]

During his time at the Svatopluk Janáček continued to write
choral works, mostly settings of folk music. But with an orchestra at
his disposal at the Beseda he now also tried his hand at instrumental
compositions. No copy has survived of his orchestral melodrama

Smrt ['Death'], to a text by Lermontov, his first work in a series of compositions inspired by Russian literature. In Janáček's first extant instrumental composition, the six-movement Suite for string orchestra (1877), various writers have seen the influences of Liszt, Bruckner, Wagner, Smetana, Suk and even Beethoven.[25] The overall style of this traditional, mellow-toned but technically not very accomplished piece is certainly rather archaic, far from Janáček's later personal idiom – originally, its third movement was even entitled 'Saraband'. The slow, lyrical second and fifth movements are more discernibly Czech, but in the uncharacteristically slow finale we can hear an echo of Tchaikovsky's *Serenade* for strings, op. 48, a work Janáček loved. Although he was later very critical of the Suite, it is often performed today as an interesting example of his early work.

In the seven-movement *Idyll* (1878), Janáček's technique is equally far from faultless, and the work still shows dependence on other composers, especially Dvořák (the fifth movement includes a *dumka*). But the writing is clearer here, as is Janáček's sense of mood, orchestral colour and key structure, as well as his use of certain irregular rhythms typical of his later style. Both works were performed by the Beseda under Janáček's baton, with Dvořák – in Vogel's words, the spiritual 'godfather' of the *Idyll* – attending the première.[26]

Janáček's reforming zeal at the Beseda was not universally appreciated, and there were constant demands for a return to the previous mix of social events and light music. Only Janáček's decision to go to Leipzig to continue his studies prevented this conflict from coming to a head: although in 1878 he finally passed the long-delayed examination in violin playing and was fully qualified as a music teacher, he now knew his true calling.

To become a composer meant further study. First he wrote to Anton Rubinstein with whom he would have liked to study piano as well as composition, but after a year the registered letter 'came back into my hands unopened'.[27] Since German was the only foreign language Janáček spoke fluently, he decided to go to Leipzig, famous both for its Conservatoire (which, unlike that of Prague, included composition in its syllabus) and the traditional excellence of its musical life.

Leipzig is set in the open, flat landscape of Saxony, roughly halfway between Prague and Berlin, and was then principally a mercantile and university town. In the 1870s it still enjoyed a reputation as a major intellectual, publishing and musical centre. German and foreign students flocked to the university where Goethe, Fichte and Schumann had been educated.

The Conservatoire, founded in 1843 by Mendelssohn, equally attracted students from all parts of the world. Leipzig had a long-standing musical tradition: J.S. Bach's B minor Mass and *St Matthew Passion* were written for the celebrated Thomaskirche, where he had served as Kantor; Schumann had been active in the town as a composer, performer and critic; and Mendelssohn had for twelve years been conductor of the celebrated concerts at Leipzig's Altes Gewandhaus concert hall, famous for its acoustics. And between 1876 and 1882 the city became the base of the Wagner operatic company which, under Angelo Neumann, gave the first *Ring* performances in London, Amsterdam, Brussels and Venice. World-famous instrument makers such as the piano firm of Blüthner were established in Leipzig, and by the end of the century there were some sixty music publishing firms in the city.

Janáček arrived in October 1879, and enrolled in a number of Conservatoire classes. He threw himself into his studies with tremendous vigour, this time attempting to cram three years' curriculum into one. Every single day he practised the piano for four to five hours, wrote a fugue for his counterpoint class, studied scores and read widely, attempting at the same time to work on his French grammar. He disliked the crowded, smoke-filled cafés and taverns – favourite student haunts – in the heart of the city, preferring long, solitary walks down Leipzig's streets and promenades.

Before long, suffering from overwork, he had to drop some subjects. The poorly equipped practice room at the Conservatoire deterred him from continuing his organ studies; he also lost his interest in choral singing, although his own voice was pronounced capable of development.[28]

Most of his professors at the Conservatoire were too old, overworked or simply second-rate; some could not keep class discipline. Janáček's piano teacher, the 71-year-old Ernst Wenzel, who had once been Schumann's collaborator, used to reminisce during Janáček's lessons, or simply doze off. He also told Janáček that his technique was insufficiently developed to cope with the repertoire he had played in Brno. Oskar Paul, whose lectures in history and theory Janáček attended both at the Conservatoire and the university, failed to notice two mistakes Janáček had left in a fugue, and lacked even a basic understanding of pre-Classical vocal scores.

Janáček soon became disillusioned. And although he had been able to take paid leave from the Institute, as his colleagues generously covered his classes without demanding extra payment, once again he had little money to spare. Life in Leipzig was expensive and Janáček had to economize. Many of his fellow students were younger than him, and with neither the time nor the funds for socializing he made no real friends. His only relaxation was to write daily to Zdenka Schulz, daughter of his principal at the Teachers' Training Institute, with whom he had fallen in love earlier that year.

There had been no serious love affairs in Janáček's life before Zdenka. In 1874, shortly before his studies in Prague, he had become infatuated with one of his pupils, the 16-year-old Ludmila Rudišová, daughter of a Brno factory owner. A year later, there had been an unrequited holiday romance at his uncle's in Znorovy, but he never told Běta Gazarková, 'a girl like a flower', of his love. 'The end of the holidays came, and with it the end of a fairy tale.'[29] A few initials and brief descriptions were all Janáček later revealed of his other infatuations and flirtations, and he never mentioned his rumoured affair with Amalie. But the 14-year-old Zdenka 'bewitched' him.

Pretty, round-faced, with an aquiline nose and fair plaited hair, Zdenka was a gifted pianist. She had been a pupil of Janáček's since the age of 12, and was in great awe of him:

> There was something sombre to me even in his appearance. He was slim then and rather small in stature, his pale face strongly contrasting with a coarse curly beard, thick black curly locks and very expressive brown eyes. Even then I loved his small, full, white hands which took on a life of their own whenever they touched the keyboard.[30]

Born on 30 July 1865, Zdenka was the only child of a mixed marriage; her father, although Czech by birth, belonged to the Germanized middle class in Brno, and her mother was German but with some Polish ancestry. 'Beautiful, slender, elegant, with austere moral principles,' wrote Zdenka of her mother, 'she lived solely for her household which she managed simply and economically.'[31] And since Emilian Schulz yielded to his wife in everything, Mrs Schulz also brought up Zdenka to speak German; the family only spoke Czech to the maid. The Schulzes' comfortable middle-class background allowed Zdenka to be educated at home and sheltered from every possible hardship. She was loved and cherished by her parents, but 'yearned for the company of children', and grew up very much alone.[32]

For about a year Janáček gave Zdenka three piano lessons a week and was 'never as harsh . . . as had frequently been said of him', she commented in her memoirs.[33] 'Then I suddenly matured, so that at the age of 13 I already had the appearance of a young lady.'[34] She soon realized, from watching her teacher's reflection in the mirror on the sly, that his interest in her was not purely academic; early in 1879 he offered her free Sunday morning lessons in duet playing. He could be charming when he wanted to, and he soon became friendly with Zdenka's family too; both her grandmother – who adored music – and her mother 'loved him as their own'.[35]

Janáček brought to Zdenka's placid life 'so much new, exciting [and] artistic that he became an axis around which all my thoughts revolved'. One day 'he suddenly went down on his knees . . . and, his whole body shaking with ardour', declared his love, proposing marriage.[36] Stunned, Zdenka simply nodded and Janáček began kissing her passionately. 'I was terrified,' she recalled. 'I was a girl and attracted to my teacher as if under a spell, but in my heart and spirit I was still a child . . . .'[37]

Neither of them took account of this; soon, when he found that she had been crying because she missed him, Janáček asked Zdenka's parents for her hand. But Mrs Schulz did not want her daughter to leave home yet: Zdenka was too young, and should continue her schooling. 'But we shall not be leaving you,' objected Janáček passionately, 'and you will, apart from having a daughter, also have in me a son.'[38] Nonetheless, no official engagement was announced: Zdenka's father may have hoped that when Janáček left for Leipzig the relationship would die away naturally.

Janáček's letters to Zdenka from Leipzig, and later from Vienna, show otherwise: the 169 letters written between October 1879 and June 1880 are one of the most touching collections of love letters ever written by a young musician. They also make very clear how lonely Janáček had felt since his childhood. Isolated and impecunious, he had never before met anyone to whom he could offer such love and devotion. 'My soul is nothing but a shrine and you are the saint on the altar,' he wrote to Zdenka in January 1880.[39] Battling with unfamiliar surroundings and a strict schedule, afraid of falling ill, anxious for the respect of his teachers and fellow students, Janáček wrote to Zdenka about everything. Living abroad depressed him: he felt uprooted and abandoned; his lodgings at No. 1 Plauenstrasse were light but draughty and over-furnished; he often suffered from colds; he disliked German food – particularly the bread – and restaurants were expensive. He made his own coffee, 'hot as fire . . . black as the night . . . and as sweet as love.'[40]

Janáček's life in Leipzig was to some extent an internal journey, filled with anxieties and hopes. He reports conversations with his teachers, but few with fellow students. Although he writes to Zdenka in German, his style is poor and he complains of difficulties with the Leipzig accent: 'I understand just about every tenth word and have to say everything to people twice.'[41] Although he reads German newspapers he never mentions politics or politicians; he goes to many concerts but mentions no impassioned discussions on culture. 'With no one else', he writes to Zdenka in October 1879, 'can I talk as freely as with you, dearest Zdenči.'[42] The letters are full of private love talk, though during their courtship he and Zdenka never became lovers; a mere month after his departure from Brno, Janáček makes wedding plans and presses his 14½-year-old object of devotion to shorten the waiting time to a year. And although Zdenka's letters have not been preserved, she, too, was bewitched, as she made known later in life.[43]

Their attraction apart, Zdenka also represented for the young Janáček the world to which he aspired. Hers was a family of good social standing in Brno, and Zdenka, even as a very young girl, showed a poise and composure that the fierce and occasionally gauche Janáček lacked. He still wanted to become a composer, but now – in order to support a family – he also needed the further qualifications to obtain a suitable position in Brno. His mind was overflowing with plans. His future father-in-law gave him useful advice and soon also financed Janáček's private lessons with his composition teacher, Leo Grill. Zdenka and her mother sent him food parcels: ham, Czech bread, fruit, nuts and pastry. Nor did Zdenka forget pen nibs, Czech music magazines, a hat and gloves. A fur coat was dispatched before Christmas to help Leoš face Saxony's bracing cold and snow. Special gifts were exchanged: a cabbage-rose was enclosed so that Leoš could pluck its petals one by one, counting the days until he saw Zdenka again at Christmas. Zdenka's photograph adorned the desk where he wrote to her by candle-light: 'Isn't that right, my own Zdenči, that true love is only such love that ennobles one?'[44]

The letters also paint a vivid picture of Leipzig's musical life. Janáček had free tickets to concerts and orchestral rehearsals at the Old Gewandhaus, where he sat in the gallery right above the orchestra, enraptured: the acoustics of the hall allowed great clarity of sound and dynamic strength. He also went to the chamber concerts of the

Euterpe society, and listened to motets at the Thomaskirche. He did not study instrumentation at the Conservatoire but read the German translation of Berlioz's *Traité d'orchestration* in his spare time, and paid close attention at rehearsals particularly to the wind instruments and their special effects.[45]

He reported to Zdenka on many concerts. Carl Reinecke, the chief conductor of the Gewandhaus Orchestra and Janáček's professor at the Conservatoire, gave a performance of Brahms's Symphony in C minor. Janáček also heard Lilli Lehmann, then active in Berlin;[46] he enjoyed Schumann's Fourth Symphony, and the Leipzig-educated Grieg playing his Piano Concerto.[47] Clara Schumann performed Beethoven's Piano Concerto in G 'with lightness and correctness of touch, neither sharp nor too emphatic'.[48] A concert including works by Schumann, Mendelssohn and Gade took place under the direction of Arthur Nikisch, 'a good enough theatre Kapellmeister'.[49] But as in Prague, Janáček never went to the opera, nor did he hear any works by Berlioz, Liszt or the Leipzig-born Wagner.

He did have an opportunity to admire his idol, the Russian pianist and composer Anton Rubinstein. 'I haven't so far heard a greater artist,' he wrote to Zdenka. 'The fire, the way he can talk to one's soul, this is what I can find nowhere else but in his compositions. He is so natural, never looks for effects . . . [and] unfettered by any musical doctrine, he reaches right to my heart. And what a distance there still is between him and me!'[50]

But by the end of the 1870s musical life in Leipzig began to stagnate. Although Brahms was welcomed there, and his symphonies played at the Gewandhaus, the orchestra's tradition of presenting a wide spectrum of new music dwindled. 'Leipzig is past its true prime,' remarked Janáček after only two months. 'The authorities cannot stand anything new – only Mozart, Bach and Beethoven are always played.'[51]

His mind was often in a state of flux: 'I still don't know which way my creative spirit will turn,' he wrote in November 1879.[52] His frequent changes of views and plans were not lost on Zdenka and her parents; he still contemplated becoming a concert pianist, but when he proposed studying with Saint-Saëns in Paris, Zdenka and her family expressed alarm. Janáček quickly abandoned the idea; he certainly did not want to become 'a travelling virtuoso', though a suspicion inevitably formed in his mind that the family wanted to put obstacles in his path.

Of Janáček's teachers only the 33-year-old Leo Grill eventually came up to his expectations. But he was a stern disciplinarian, and Janáček, who wanted 'no chains' in music,[53] at first resisted the 'iron armourplate of rules'.[54] Later he began to doubt his talent, a problem that was to dog him for many years. He strove hard to master the techniques required of him, and his reports were good. Nevertheless, early in 1880 he decided to leave Leipzig.

After spending three weeks in Brno with Zdenka and her family over Christmas, Janáček felt he could no longer bear being apart from her. He returned to Leipzig determined to transfer his studies as soon as possible to Vienna, which was only a few hours by train from Brno. He dreamt of Zdenka constantly, planning their future household and impatiently asking when the engagement was to be announced. By the end of January 1880 his anxiety had risen to fever pitch. 'Today', he wrote to Zdenka on the 30th from Leipzig,

> my state of mind was dreadful; I had no idea that it could be like that with me. [. . .] Was it home-sickness? Dissatisfaction with my teachers? Yes, doubts have been thrown on my high and cherished hopes, and I therefore sank into a very depressed mood. And the more I became absorbed in such thoughts, the worse I felt, until my state of mind was unbearable. Against this I put the picture of you and the thoughts of [our] future . . . . I called out your name, and I prayed for the first time so that I could keep you in my spirit during these excited states of mind, as only in you can I draw the strength to master all this emotional turmoil . . . . There was a moment when I completely lost my self-control, because I was afraid . . . . I came to a deeply felt conclusion then: I hold you so dear that I cannot live without you. And I was also convinced that I could no longer stay here in Leipzig.[55]

Of the numerous compositions that Janáček wrote in Leipzig only three have survived. The fourth of the four *Romances* (1879), a short, lyrical piece, was published only after his death, along with the *Tema con variazioni* for piano in B flat, subtitled 'Zdenka's Variations' (1880). Janáček thought of the theme for the variations early one morning in January, while still in bed: 'I jumped up, my watch fell on the floor but did not stop. I almost completely split the trousers I was putting on; I quickly got another pair and wrote down the theme. It is pretty and it will be easy to vary it.'[56] The sprightly, spiky rhythms in the third variation are reminiscent of Schumann, while the insistence on the interval of the fourth in the passage-work of the seventh variation recalls Smetana. But a more independent voice emerges in the concluding section of the main theme: the repeated, dance-like rhythmic figure circles around the same note, and this is further emphasized in the harmony. Another piece for violin and piano from the same period, the *Dumka* in C minor, was not performed until 1885; an earlier *Dumka* for piano (1879) has not survived.

Janáček left Leipzig at the end of February 1880 after giving a successful performance of several of his recently composed exercise fugues for the piano. Taking stock of his position, he felt certain that his time in Leipzig had not been wasted. Yet he left the city with few regrets. After spending Easter in Brno he arrived on 1 April 1880 in Vienna.

In the last third of the century the capital of the Austro-Hungarian monarchy was flourishing. The Hofoper, the Musikverein-Gebäude and later the Burgtheater were the most famous and grandiose public buildings in Europe. Vienna's wealth was not due to any economic miracle: vast sums of money flowed in from the Empire's many provinces, among which the neighbouring Bohemia and Moravia also provided most of Vienna's servants. Politically, the city saw a safe guarantor of her status in the Kaiser, Franz Josef I, a dependable bureaucrat. But Vienna's true king was Johann Strauss, whose specially composed waltzes would open the famous Viennese balls; and the city would throw itself into merry-making – and malicious gossip – with even greater enthusiasm than Paris.

Vienna was also very expensive: Janáček's lodgings cost 12 Gulden a month and, compared with his Leipzig rooms, were 'a terrible hole'.[57] He was not interested in Vienna's 'agitated, noisy life', nor in sightseeing. But he felt less alone, and was calmer: here he could visit Zdenka's uncle, and talk about Zdenka with her grandmother, who often visited. He wore a bracelet Zdenka had given him as a keepsake and revisited her within a fortnight.

At the renowned Vienna Conservatoire composition was taught by one of the city's most famous composers, Anton Bruckner. Janáček was taught by the 64-year-old Franz Krenn, and studied the piano with Josef Dachs, both of whom taught Mahler. But his 'Leipzig touch' was considered too soft[58] and soon he abandoned the piano to concentrate entirely on composition. He resisted the influence of the prevailing 'Wagnerian bombast' favoured by his fellow students.[59] Yet although Krenn 'mocked' established rules, by now Janáček had come to prefer the exacting discipline of his Leipzig teacher Leo Grill. Having to work mostly on his own, he was irritated by the incessant practice at the music school close to his lodgings and the itinerant musicians playing in the courtyard. But he worked hard on a violin sonata (now lost), a song-cycle (*Frühlingslieder*, to words by Vincenz Zusner, a popular but mediocre poet) and a quartet (also lost). Encouraged by Krenn, he wanted to enter his works for the public competition at the Conservatoire. He was anxious to gain further qualifications, and also to establish a reputation, particularly in Brno.

He went to fewer concerts than in Leipzig. He heard music by Wagner and Beethoven in the opulent Musikvereinsaal, famous for its acoustics. By today's standards it is quite small. Yet Janáček wrote to Zdenka that the hall, 'wonderful beyond imagination', seemed too big: 'The tone of all the instruments appears thin, puny.'[60]

As Zdenka's father continued to help out financially, Janáček was able to afford tickets to the Hofoper, like the Musikvereinsaal about ten years old. But he was clearly not impressed with either the music or the performance of Weber's *Der Freischütz*. 'Surely it is already much overplayed,' he wrote to Zdenka. Another opera he saw, Cherubini's *Les deux journées*, did not interest him at all, 'except for one spot'.[61]

By now he had again become very tired and depressed; his violin sonata did not even pass the qualifying examination for entry into the Conservatoire competition, having been pronounced 'too academic' by the jury. Janáček wrote a letter to the director, demanding another hearing. Only the slow movement entitled *Adagio* was played, indifferently, by a violinist who had also entered a work of his own in the competition. Janáček was convinced that the selection of the *Adagio* put him at a disadvantage, and threatened to expose the affair in a music magazine. Krenn also pleaded on Janáček's behalf but to no avail. It was a matter of principle, Janáček was told in the end. He was certainly not without talent but would need to forget all he had learnt in Prague and in Leipzig: Vienna was far more advanced.[62] He decided to wait for the results of the song competition, but again he was unsuccessful.

Thus, after a mere two months in Vienna, Janáček once again decided to move on. Not having completed the course he could not receive a formal diploma, but was given a private report by Krenn. He thought of finishing his studies with Dvořák in Prague but soon abandoned that plan. His self-confidence was crushed. Eight months previously his study trip had been announced in the *Tagesbote aus Böhmen*, the German daily published in Bohemia and widely read in Brno, and Janáček had boasted to Zdenka of the effect this would make on the 'nobodies' of Brno.[63] Now, feeling an utter failure, he did not want to return before the end of term. Early in June, shortly after finishing the third movement of the string quartet, he left Vienna to stay for a few days with his uncle Jan in the country before returning to Brno.

Janáček's letters to Zdenka reflect his gradual loss of confidence; the process of evaluating his talent and creativity was accompanied by great anxiety. And the crucial complication of not having found even a path to a specific style clearly impeded his development as a composer. No matter how hard he strove to master the traditional Classical musical forms, this vehicle was not for him. Janáček was born earlier in the century than the late Romantic composers such as Mahler, Wolf, Strauss and Reger. Yet although much of his musical language is rooted in the nineteenth century, the formal structure of his music differs fundamentally from theirs, and from those of his Bohemian contemporaries such as Fibich. Despite his initial training in counterpoint and sonata form Janáček did not care for either, although both were among the main features of the musical tradition throughout the Austro-Hungarian Empire, as well as Germany. And the different melodic structure of his music is already evident in his early works, even before his involvement with Moravian folk music. To force this elemental voice into foreign moulds could only make it sound stilted. Janáček's frequent bridling against the shackles of musical form was an instinctive defence of his own style even before it was fully formed.

In the summer of 1880, aged 26, Janáček returned to Brno to settle there for good. His engagement to Zdenka was announced, and a year later they married. During the next few years he composed little; instead he set out to establish in Brno a new and badly needed school of music where native students from Moravia could receive the best possible education. It was only in the mid-1880s that the full impact of Moravian folk-song made itself felt;[64] Janáček's first attempts at recording speech melodies (on which his distinctive idiom is based) also date from this period. But the development of his individual style was to take a long time, and was accompanied by immense self-doubt.

3

Back in Brno

(1881–1888)

FOUNDING AN ORGAN school was a long-standing dream, dating
from the time of Janáček's studies in Prague. 'The project of the
Organ School in Brno is an idea to which I have been truly devoted
since my first years of independent thought,' he wrote to Zdenka in
November 1879 from Leipzig, '. . . and I see in its realization one of
my most important tasks.'[1]

The first step was to found the Society for the Promotion of
Church Music in Moravia, which would eventually run the school.[2]
In the meantime, he threw himself wholeheartedly into teaching
music at the Teachers' Training Institute, the directorship of the choir
at Queen's, and the Beseda.

His engagement to Zdenka was announced on 1 July 1880, and
complete happiness seemed for a while within reach. Not quite 15 at
the time, Zdenka was growing prettier by the day. Slim, with a beautiful figure, long, golden hair and fair complexion, she was now a
little taller than Janáček. 'I don't want you to grow any more,' he had
written to her from Vienna in April.[3]

On his return to Brno, Janáček took lodgings[4] not far from the
Institute, where the Schulzes had a flat. His mother lived close by, in
a flat rented for her the previous year;[5] as she made her living by
letting part of the flat, often to female students from the Institute,
social decorum, quite apart from the Institute's rules, made it impossible for Janáček to live there.

Soon, Zdenka and Janáček became involved in the lively social
life of the Czech minority in Brno, attending concerts, theatre
performances, dances and meetings. In October 1880 they saw
a Czech production of Gounod's *Faust*, with the outstanding
young Czech bass Vilém Heš in the title-role;[6] Janáček reviewed the
performance.[7] Zdenka, enchanted by the opera, wanted to become
Marguerite at least for a day; at the next masked ball of the Reading
Circle – her first – she appeared in a blue dress with a small ruff collar

and full slashed sleeves, a tiny bag on her belt. French marguerites were braided into her long heavy plaits.[8]

Janáček went as Faust, Zdenka on his arm. His 'black velvet jacket became him extremely well, [contrasting] with his pale face, black beard, black locks and dark eyes'; he wore a plumed beret, and a sword at his side. To complete the picture, his friend and colleague Berthold Žalud dressed as Mephistopheles. The striking trio created a sensation in the ballroom; no one could take their eyes off them.[9]

Soon after their engagement Janáček insisted that he and Zdenka speak only Czech. Although schooled in German, and used to speaking German at home, Zdenka had no objection to communicating with her future husband and his colleagues in their mother tongue. But to Zdenka's grandmother and mother, both German by birth, Czech was a language fit only for servants;[10] although fond of Janáček, the grandmother insisted that the wedding ceremony be conducted in German. Janáček took this attitude as an affront. Soon it became obvious that the differences between his and Zdenka's backgrounds were likely to cause further tension; the roots of the problem were too deep-seated ever to be completely eradicated. Papa Schulz, who also knew Janáček's temper, worried that Zdenka might be too young and too delicate for him. Relations between Janáček and the Schulzes became strained, and Zdenka now often cried. Yet she always answered her family's predictions of inevitable unhappiness with Janáček by saying: 'I would rather be unhappy with him than happy with someone else.'[11]

Eventually a four-roomed flat was found for the couple in the street where Janáček's mother lived, and the Schulzes bought not only the furniture but also an excellent Ehrbar grand piano which Janáček chose. The wedding took place at Brno's Old Town church on 13 July 1881, two weeks before Zdenka's sixteenth birthday; Janáček was 27.[12] The bride wore pale pink satin, a small headdress of myrtle and orange flowers, and a long white veil. Yet she felt as if she were 'dressed for her own funeral', and the Schulzes were horrified when Janáček appeared at the church wearing the patriotic black *čamara* tunic, the Moravian pattern on his shirt embroidered by Zdenka herself; on his insistence the wedding ceremony was conducted in Czech.[13] It was a beautiful summer day, and the bridegroom beamed with happiness; members of the German theatre orchestra turned up to play at the reception, held at the Beseda House.

The marriage seems to have been a failure almost from the beginning. It has been suggested that Zdenka was frigid, and a prude.

But she was only 16, sexually inexperienced, and brought up in a repressive society, whereas Janáček was a highly-sexed and passionate young man. Throughout his studies in Leipzig and Vienna he had been convinced that Zdenka was the great love of his life; dreaming about their life together, he had painted for her a picture of their future happiness. Now his child-bride clearly failed to live up to his expectations.

During their honeymoon the couple made a series of excursions. They spent two weeks in Bohemia with Zdenka's Czech grandfather, a retired doctor;[14] during a week in Prague they visited the Provisional Theatre several times and managed to see the newly-finished National Theatre building (soon to be destroyed by fire).[15] Driving over the Charles Bridge one day, they spotted Dvořák in the crowd. Overjoyed, Janáček quickly stepped out of the carriage and brought Dvořák over to introduce his wife. '[But] what a child you have chosen!' exclaimed Dvořák, unable to conceal his surprise. He met the Janáčeks several times during their stay, and even joined them for an outing to the Karlštejn Castle.[16]

These were relatively happy days for Zdenka, but she could not share her impressions with her parents. 'My husband did not wish me to write to them,' she recalled.[17] And he was dismissive of Zdenka's uncle Gustav whom they visited on their return journey to Brno. 'He was a German and mama's brother, and that was unforgivable.'[18]

Back in Brno, Zdenka soon felt awkward with Janáček; he was no longer 'the attentive lover from the time of our engagement'.[19] After a week in their new flat the couple visited Janáček's favourite uncle Jan in Znorovy; Janáček then showed Zdenka his native Hukvaldy, which she loved. They also planned to meet Janáček's old benefactor Křížkovský in Olomouc, Zdenka's birthplace. Yet by now both were disillusioned. 'How strange and cold was the honeymoon forty-five years ago!' wrote Janáček in 1928. 'Not a single warm memory remains . . . .'[20] And Zdenka was horrified to learn, on their way to Olomouc, that they were short of money: for the first time in her sheltered life – honeymoon or not – she had to go hungry for a day, until Křížkovský generously helped them out.[21]

At that time Janáček was teaching piano, organ, violin and singing at the Teachers' Training Institute. This brought him a modicum of security,[22] and he applied himself wholeheartedly to choral singing. Teaching the violin, however, was 'torture', he recalled later,[23] although 'very good-natured', he was 'quick-tempered . . . nervous and beside himself when angry', recollected a former pupil.[24] 'As a

musical poet he belonged elsewhere,' wrote another, the writer Alois
Mrštík.[25] In 1881 Janáček was finally appointed director of the new
Organ School; here, from 1882, he taught only students who wished
to take up music professionally. At last he could express his own views
on teaching.

Janáček taught theory of music, rhythm and musical forms at the
school, and there were also classes in organ playing, singing, history
of music and liturgy; his father-in-law taught psychology, an inno-
vation at the time,[26] and also helped by offering the school the
Institute's premises on a temporary basis.[27]

Although the law required classes at the Organ School to be
conducted in both Czech and German, the school contributed enormously to musical education in Moravia by concentrating on students
of Czech origin. At the beginning there were only nine of them, but
during almost four decades of Janáček's directorship no fewer than
1,300 were taught there, many of whom became outstanding musicians. By the 1890s, when the school had three grades, harmony was
the most important subject, with six lessons a week given by Janáček
himself. Another six were devoted to organ playing; figured bass and
score-reading were taught twice a week. Janáček also added two hours
of piano playing and of choral singing a week, as well as counterpoint.
The history of music, both Czech and foreign, was also taught.

Thus the Organ School eventually provided virtually the same
education as a conservatoire, with the added possibility of a state
diploma.[28] Although the school was founded originally to train future
organists, choirmasters, music teachers and conductors, Janáček also
aimed from the outset at providing suitable training for future composers. The school became the focus of new thought in musical
theory; in 1905 Janáček described it as 'a school of composition, that
is to say the highest discipline within the subject of music teaching'.[29]
A strict teacher, Janáček nevertheless allowed each student to develop
at his own pace. Many students regarded his often irascible behaviour
as simply part of his nature. The composer Jan Kunc, who was among
Janáček's students at both institutions, remembered

> lessons full of poetry and love . . . particularly the lessons devoted to
> musical forms when Janáček impressed upon us his artistic beliefs.
> Whenever he taught . . . he had the subject matter perfectly organized
> and logically arranged, and he expressed himself as concisely and fit-
> tingly as possible. 'Accuracy in speech reflects accuracy in thought'
> was his slogan.[30]

There were also extra-curricular sonata evenings (offering in-depth analysis of the pieces played), lectures and concerts. Bearing in mind the high standards reached at the Prague Conservatoire, Janáček continually added new subjects, such as violin, woodwind and brass playing.

Yet serious disputes took place between Janáček and his father-in-law Emilian Schulz soon after the opening of the Organ School. In December 1881 Janáček asked the Ministry of Education in Vienna for permission to accept the directorship of the school, giving assurance that the post would not interfere with his duties at the Teachers' Training Institute. But just a week later he suddenly applied to the Brno Regional School Council for a transfer to another branch of the Institute, outside Brno. The application, it transpired, was submitted in the aftermath of an internal dispute; it concerned payment of an artist engaged by Janáček, which Schulz refused to settle. This was only the beginning of a breakdown in communications with the entire Schulz family.

Earlier in the autumn of 1881 Janáček's mother went to live with her daughter Eleonora, a needlework mistress at a small village school in Moravia;[31] 'and you won't have to worry,' she wrote to Janáček in December, 'that you will ever see me in Brno again, for I have, with a bleeding heart, left the city for good'.[32] Although Janáček and his brothers continued to support her, it is clear that she had been hoping to live with the young couple. Whatever her plans, her stay with Eleonora was short-lived; the following spring they unexpectedly fell out and she found her own lodgings in the village.[33]

Meanwhile, the crisis that had been developing since the beginning of Janáček's marriage came to a head. More than anything, the constant shortage of money prayed on Zdenka's mind. Janáček had 'a decent income' (and also pocketed Zdenka's monthly allowance from her parents).[34] But, supporting his mother, one of his brothers, and paying off various debts, he was 'unable to budget sensibly', and would not let Zdenka manage their finances.[35]

His 'hostile attitude' to her parents also greatly pained Zdenka: they were not allowed to visit, and she could only visit them on the sly.[36] Janáček's mother, too, stood between them: 'Leoš always spoke about her as if she did not like me and was not happy with me.' In the end, Zdenka was 'afraid of her'.[37]

By now she was also afraid of Janáček. 'Apart from the wild explosions of my husband's passion,' she confessed later, 'there was none of the tenderness and warmth which I was used to at home.'[38] When she became pregnant, Janáček 'showed no pleasure'; angry scenes intensified and Zdenka 'longed to return home'.[39]

In August 1882, not yet 17 and heavily pregnant, Zdenka had to oversee the move to a new flat Janáček had found for them.[40] Her labour pains began next morning; during her confinement she stayed with her parents but Janáček would not even accompany her there. In great pain, Zdenka constantly called for him but when he was sent for, he did not respond. Their daughter Olga was born later that afternoon. Janáček, enjoying a cigar after a banquet at the Monastery, only agreed to see Zdenka and the child following a rebuke by one of the priests.[41]

Olga was ailing but Janáček, afraid of the expense, refused to call the doctor. 'He never cradled her in his arms, never played with her,' Zdenka recalled sadly. Their quarrels continued; during one Janáček knocked against Zdenka roughly.[42] Soon he threatened to bring his mother back to Brno: 'She will give you short shrift.'[43] Fearful, Zdenka could only think of returning to her parents, taking Olga with her.[44]

Since their estrangement was now complete, Zdenka's father applied on her behalf for a formal separation, with divorce to follow. Janáček – after first sending a mediator round – agreed.[45] He did not disclose to his mother the reason for the break-up of his marriage, nor invite her to live with him. But she was not fooled; sending Christmas presents for little Olga at the beginning of December 1882, she wrote several letters. 'Why are you not frank with me, and why do you not tell me the reason why I may not visit the director's family?' she asked when she was finally told about the separation. 'I have done them no wrong. Perhaps the reason is that you are still supporting me? [. . .] Oh, how the other brides [Zdenka's sisters-in-law] would thank me if I sent them a present, and what do I have from yours? Only ingratitude, I think. I beg you not to conceal from me the reason for all this.'[46]

Meanwhile, at the Schulzes, Zdenka and Olga quickly recovered; her family accepted the situation though Zdenka's father worried about the divorce proceedings more than he revealed. In February 1883, Emilian Schulz also asked the Brno Regional School Council to commence disciplinary proceedings against his son-in-law and to help repair their working relationship as the situation at the Institute had now become impossible. His accusations included taking time off without permission, unwillingness to work extra hours on behalf of an indisposed colleague, rudeness towards the director and other members of staff, shirking various duties and 'nationalist fanaticism giving an impression of madness'.[47] But even before Janáček wrote a lengthy letter of defence, further developments brought about a complete rupture.

The divorce court allowed Zdenka to recover everything which had come with her dowry – furniture, linen, china, even the piano. On 2 March 1883, accompanied by her father, she went to the flat to organize the removal. An ugly scene took place: Janáček snapped at Schulz that he was not wanted there. 'And then my papa, always so kind, boiled over,' recollected Zdenka. 'You ungrateful young scoundrel,' he exclaimed, rushing towards Janáček who, barely managing to beat a retreat, called for the police. Zdenka and the school caretaker managed to restrain Schulz; Janáček – although impulsive himself – never forgave his father-in-law for this outburst.[48]

In the formal protocol completed later that year Janáček refuted most of Schulz's accusations in connection with the Institute: the director's own conduct was far from blameless. Several witnesses affirmed that Janáček was a conscientious teacher; the quarrel was entirely a family matter. No further disciplinary steps were taken, and Janáček was allowed to remain at the Institute. A kind of 'armed truce' ensued.

After his return from Vienna in 1880, in addition to his other work Janáček took up his old post as choirmaster of the Beseda choral society; on the occasion of the Emperor Franz Josef's visit to Brno he conducted it in the provocatively entitled *Fatherland* by Förchtgott-Tovačovský, and Javůrek's *Moravia*.[49] At the end of the year, he included in one concert – with the Beseda board's approval – his *Autumn Song*, written for the society's twenty-first anniversary; the following January he put on the programme his Violin Sonata and the Minuet for clarinet and piano. When some of his conservative detractors accused him unfairly of promoting his own compositions, Janáček resigned. But there was no one to replace him, and a year later a newly-formed board invited him back; Janáček continued to concentrate on the society's concert repertoire, while his colleague Berthold Žalud remained responsible for light entertainment.[50]

As before, the main composer on the repertoire was Dvořák. Janáček conducted two of Dvořák's large-scale cantatas (*Stabat Mater* and *The Spectre's Bride*) and two symphonies (D major and D minor), as well as some of his other choral works.[51] Steeped in Dvořák's music, he promoted it enthusiastically, both at the Beseda and at the Institute.[52] Here was a true Slavonic composer: his subject matter, his melodic invention, his Slavonic sympathies and lively interest in folksong (including that of Moravia), all pointed firmly in the only direction Janáček felt possible.[53] And Dvořák was now also successful abroad. Small wonder that Janáček's admiration for his old friend bordered on adoration: Dvořák embodied all his hopes for Czech music, which Janáček so wished to be known outside the confines of Bohemia and Moravia.

Soon Janáček began to review and analyse Dvořák's works, praising his dramatic instinct and musicianship. Dvořák, who visited Brno six times, clearly enjoyed listening to his pieces there, and often participated. 'He improvised the piano accompaniment to choral pieces,' Janáček recollected in a commemorative article, 'and sat down with the violas in Rhapsodies and *The Spectre's Bride*'.[54] Their friendship, formed in the mid-1870s in Prague, became even firmer; they corresponded from 1880, and in 1883 went on a walking trip together in southern Bohemia, visiting places of historical interest to Czechs.[55] And although their conversation, as Janáček remarked, 'could have been tied into a very small bundle', the bond was deep. 'Do you know what it is like when someone takes your words out of your mouth before you speak them? This is how I always felt in Dvořák's company. [. . .] He has taken his melodies from my heart. Nothing on earth can sever such a bond.'[56]

Apart from Dvořák, Janáček conducted at the Beseda two movements (*Vltava* and *Vyšehrad*) from Smetana's symphonic cycle *Má vlast* as well as some of his choral works. Smetana's orientation was more specifically Czech than Dvořák's; thus the cycle symbolized national consciousness for Czechs both in Bohemia and Moravia. Other composers on the programme included Brahms, Schumann, Liszt, Křížkovský and Bendl.

Another Slavonic composer whom Janáček admired all his life was Chopin.[57] In Leipzig, he had studied Chopin's nocturnes; back in Brno he began to analyse his works systematically, absorbing their harmonic structure, their form and various stylistic details. And once again he 'was practising furiously and knew no restraint'.[58] Before their separation, Zdenka often had to make way for him; soon, she realized that her own playing was deteriorating and, feeling disappointed, she 'no longer enjoyed the piano'.[59] And Janáček was too busy to continue teaching her: mornings and afternoons he taught at the Institute, at lunchtimes he rehearsed at the Monastery, after 4 p.m. he taught at the Organ School, and many evenings were spent at the Beseda.

The Beseda had no orchestra of its own; whenever Janáček planned to give a large cantata or symphonic work, he had to summon help from the local German theatre. To engage musicians from the local military band posed a problem as such bands had no string players. In 1882 Janáček at last successfully established a school of singing and violin playing at the Beseda.[60] Future musicians for the orchestra and choir were thus secured, but it was still extremely difficult to form and maintain a professional symphonic orchestra in Brno. Chamber music fared no better, and Janáček's suggestions for programming were often unsuccessful. Although he understood the necessity of popular concerts and light entertainment, he was irritated and offended by the board's amateurishness and unnecessary caution. For over two years, he felt, he had been attempting to build a musical tradition on shifting sands.

The initial enthusiasm of the Beseda's members did not last. Eventually, attendances slackened; there were complaints about deficits in the concert budget, and further demands were made on Janáček to supervise light entertainment.[61] Once again he refused; besides, the work exhausted him, and in June 1888 he resigned his unremunerated post for the second time.

This was doubly regrettable as Janáček was clearly a gifted conductor, with excellent relative pitch, energy, initiative and formidable willpower. Even as a young choirmaster at Queen's, he commanded the singers from the organ 'merely by moving his head', yet exercised absolute power over them.[62] He was always 'perfectly prepared', and 'would not tolerate mediocrity,' wrote the Beseda's chronicler; with his outstanding musicianship, he could tackle any score.[63] Under Janáček's baton, the society's orchestra 'sang, rejoiced, grieved and lamented,' recalled his former pupil František Mareš, who also witnessed other performances: 'I saw in the faces of the singers and players in front of you how the spark of your energy leapt across . . .'.[64] And 'pale, somehow austerely lost in thought',[65] Janáček 'could really build up the piece in the grandeur of its form, the plasticity of its dynamics and its perfect rhythm', wrote his former colleague, the conductor Pavel Dědeček.[66] Although later in life Janáček had to give up conducting for health reasons, he was 'a conductor in his own right, not just a composer who could also conduct'.[67]

After his divorce, Janáček lived on his own in an almost empty flat; although he passed Zdenka and his daughter virtually every day on his way to the Institute, he ignored them. He paid towards Olga's upkeep but Emilian Schulz would accept nothing on Zdenka's behalf.[68] In the harmony of the Schulzes' home, she and Olga flourished; like Zdenka's 2-year-old brother Leo, Olga called her grandfather 'tata [papa]'. And Zdenka grew even prettier, earning herself the sobriquet 'the Rose of Old Brno'.

A few months after their divorce, out of the blue, Janáček began to greet Zdenka most courteously once again, and asked for permission to see his daughter.[69] Yet when the young family met, 'he did not know what to say to her', recalled Zdenka.[70] She soon realized that the visit was a pretext: Janáček – 'once again . . . the beguiling Leoš from the time before our wedding' – began to court her anew, also accompanying her regularly to the door of the German Theatre.[71] When he asked her to return to him, Zdenka – though only too aware that she still loved him – hesitated. But divorce was, at that time, still a social disgrace; she was also afraid that Janáček could eventually take his daughter away from her.[72] Soon, he also charmed Zdenka's mother who 'forgave him everything'; once again the Schulzes accepted the situation and invited him to spend Easter 1884 with them.[73] The divorce was annulled shortly thereafter; after taking a bronchial cure together in Austria that summer,[74] the couple moved back together.

In November Janáček's mother died of cancer; she had moved back to Hukvaldy to stay with her daughter Josefka when she became seriously ill. But she lived to hear of the reconciliation. 'I write to you, I am sure, for the last time in my life,' she had written in October 1884.

> I shall say goodbye and wish you happiness and health in this world; do not forget your loving mother. I kiss Zdenka and Olguška with all my heart, and am so very sorry that I shall never see any of you again.[75]

Although he paid for the funeral, Janáček was unwell and did not attend.[76] For a while he sank back into a depressive mood, and once again stopped visiting the Schulzes. But although the initial happiness after the couple's reconciliation did not last long, there was at least peace at home. The Janáčeks' financial situation had improved[77] and, as before their wedding, they led a busy social life.

In December 1884 the first Czech theatre opened in Brno. This was an important event, though at first its standards were not very high. The National Theatre had no permanent company; the orchestra consisted of no more than twelve players until Karel Kovařovic, its first permanent conductor, managed to increase their number to eighteen the following season, and to direct it from a rostrum rather than from the harmonium on which the parts of the missing instruments were usually played.

Under the circumstances Janáček was hardly inspired to compose for the theatre, but he nonetheless wanted to encourage and promote it. Even before its opening, he launched a new musical periodical, *Hudební listy* [Musical Letters]. The journal, published from November 1884 under the auspices of the Beseda Society, appeared several times a month, and commented on performances throughout the season.

Unlike the prose of Schumann, Weber, Berlioz and Wagner, Janáček's writings are still little known outside his native country. Yet they deserve a wider readership: he was a perceptive reviewer, and vigorously attacked the weaknesses and follies of musical life in his adopted home town. Five operas by Czech composers (including Smetana's *The Bartered Bride* and *The Kiss*, and Blodek's *In the Well*), were given at the Brno Provisional Theatre in its first year, as well as operas by Gounod (*Faust*), Weber (*Der Freischütz*), Verdi (*La traviata* and *Il trovatore*), Flotow and Adam. Janáček wrote not only about the performances, analysing intonation, ensemble and orchestral playing in detail, but also commented on the structure and psychology of the works themselves. In an effort to raise the theatre's standards, he also devoted a good deal of space to repertoire planning, recommending that of three operas a week, two be by Czech composers. His pet hate was operetta; Strauss's *Die Fledermaus* earned itself the shortest review ever: 'The production was satisfactory.'[78]

The second season included a new Czech opera (Šebor's folk-based *The Frustrated Wedding*), Škroup's well-produced *The Tinker* (the first Czech opera, written in 1826), and good performances of *Faust* and *The Bartered Bride*. But *Norma*, not surprisingly for a theatre with an inadequate orchestra and chorus, and inexperienced soloists, was 'a scandal'. 'Complete stagnation at our opera house!' thundered Janáček halfway through the 1885/6 season. 'No point therefore in talking about such a desert.'[79] Instead, he outlined with great clarity a plan for maintaining and training a small but excellent orchestra of thirty-three and a chorus of twenty-four singers, with salaries 'governed by the results attained'.[80] Competing with the new German Stadttheater in Brno required great determination. This modern, well-equipped and well-lit building, opened in 1882, could rely for its repertoire and visiting artists on the Viennese and German opera houses.[81] 'I am convinced', wrote Janáček, 'that an opera house with a perfect orchestra and chorus, with perhaps less skilled and refined solo singers, would be a greater success than if the reverse structure obtained.' Such an 'academy of artists' would also need to cultivate its aesthetic judgement; Janáček therefore recommended setting up a well-organized archive, although that would be expensive.[82]

The article is the first to indicate Janáček's deep interest in speech on stage, and in the study of characters. 'Self-aware, correct and beautifully spoken Czech' needed to be heard, and he advised actors to study not only the many Moravian dialects but also regional characteristics: 'In our villages we find healthy, unspoilt characters, pithy, richly effective, full of the strength found in the truth and humour of their life.'[83] Sharp observations on the staging of Smetana's *The Bartered Bride* mingle with memories that speak straight from the heart:

> Do you know the bustle during a village festival? It is in the after-noon, after the 'litany'. Up there, on the hill, from the church with its slender spire surrounded by gingerbread stalls . . . festively-dressed crowds stream in all directions. Soon, all indulge in merriment. Old folk and children, in picturesque groups, are in front of those white-washed, gaily decorated cottages. The young are dancing.[84]

Authentic staging of Czech plays and operas was therefore of para-mount importance, for 'in Vienna and Berlin, it is as clear as daylight, they will not stage them well for us'.[85] Moreover, Janáček earnestly advised the existing Czech music institutions to unite to create an 'academy of music'. 'Let us be ourselves in music, too,' he declared, clearly referring as much to national independence in the arts as to his own aims.[86]

Janáček's reviews also reveal what music made a strong impression on him at the time. '*Carmen* with Miss Wollnerová!' he wrote in 1887, enthralled. Yet even then, he thought the details 'more inter-esting than the whole'; by 1891, his interest in Bizet had waned – he felt that he had been overwhelmed by 'the sheer *novelty* of the material'.[87]

Scrutinizing Smetana's style in *The Two Widows* and *Dalibor*, Janáček did not fail to notice a 'similarity with Wagner's operas'; nev-ertheless, the overall effect was 'powerful, complete – resembling a kind of trance'.[88] And in his review of *Dalibor* he commented that Milada, the opera's heroine, sang 'tunes formed specifically according to the flow and rhythm of speech'. Janáček believed that the melodic rise and fall and the rhythmic fluctuations of everyday speech reveal our emotions and states of mind. These years mark the beginning of Janáček's speech melody studies; his earliest surviving notations date from 1885. By the end of February 1888, when the *Dalibor* review was published, he was preoccupied both with speech melody and prosody.[89]

His frankness did not always pay off. His review of Kovařovic's first comic opera, *The Bridegrooms* (given in Brno in January 1887 when the composer was only 25), was so sarcastic that Kovařovic was not likely to forget it.[90] Relations between the two men cooled; after Kovařovic's appointment in 1900 as chief conductor and musical director at the Prague National Theatre, this became a considerable problem.[91]

Janáček had been contributing to various dailies and periodicals since his student days in Prague, but four years of working regularly as a music critic of *Musical Letters* had sharpened his perception.[92] His reflections show a subtle and sophisticated mind; although some ideas are thrown off rapidly and there are clichés, his comments are always thought-provoking. What emerges is unmistakable energy and originality, and a considerable literary gift.

In the mid-1880s Janáček returned to composition, writing several choral works (*The Wild Duck* and *Four Male-voice Choruses*). Two further settings of folk poetry (*On the Bushy Fir Tree* and *On the Ferry*), thought to be from the same period, were discovered in 1956.[93]

The Wild Duck, a mixed-voice chorus based on a Moravian folk-song, was written for a school songbook published in 1885; the *Four Male-voice Choruses* (*The Warning*, *O Love*, *Alas the War* and *Your Beautiful Eyes*) were probably written early that year. The first three are settings of folk poetry; the words of the fourth chorus are by Jaroslav Tichý, a Brno professor who wrote romantic poetry and opera librettos.[94] In *The Warning*, a setting of an east Moravian folk-song, Janáček's interpretation of the text transforms a simple poem into a miniature drama. The words of *Alas the War* were notated by the great Moravian folk-song collector František Sušil, and again Janáček probed beneath the text; *O Love* is a version of a folk-song he had heard some years previously while on holiday in Znorovy, his uncle Jan's parish.

Dvořák, to whom the cycle is dedicated, was at first taken aback. 'I found many a passage startling,' he wrote to Janáček, 'particularly as far as the modulations are concerned: I was dismayed.' But after he had played them several times on the piano, Dvořák's ear became accustomed to them 'and I said to myself, well yes, this can be done, though we could find plenty to quarrel about. But no matter,' he added. 'They are original, they radiate . . . a truly Slavonic spirit . . . and they contain passages that will have a magical effect.'[95]

Dvořák was not the only musician to be surprised by these works. As Helfert reports, Czech musicians in the circle of the Prague publisher František Urbánek 'simply could not believe that Janáček could have written these choruses', and refused their settings as 'an inappropriate solution'.[96] Given the Czech choral repertoire at that time, Janáček's 'new, fierce and passionate tone' was misunderstood, and the choruses – whose first performances took place in Brno in 1886 and 1889 – vanished without making an impact.[97]

Yet *The Warning* and *Alas the War* signal a definite turning in Janáček's style. The dramatic and the lyrical are powerfully combined, and his former emphasis on the structure gives way to a 'concentrated intensity and thus also to a condensed musical expression'.[98]

After a strenuous academic year, Janáček usually went for a spa cure during the summer, alone; his finances prohibited him from taking Zdenka. And she felt that he 'wanted to be alone'; when she visited him during his first stay in the Moravian spa of Luhačovice in 1886, she left inconsolable: Janáček was 'very unkind', even to little Olga, neglecting them for new flirtations.[99] Later that year Zdenka found a love letter in his jacket pocket, from one of the spa visitors. Janáček snatched it and burned it on the spot, but she had seen enough to be extremely angry; she only calmed down when he begged her forgiveness.[100]

In the 1880s Janáček turned for the first time to opera. During his years as choirmaster and conductor of the Beseda orchestra he had mastered choral and orchestral techniques; now the impetus provided by the first Czech opera house in Brno opened up new horizons for his natural dramatic instinct. Only a month after the building's inauguration in 1885, he sketched in his diary a synopsis for a romantic opera based on Chateaubriand's *Le dernier des abencérages*.[101] But conditions at the theatre were unsuitable, the story's events too remote, and he soon abandoned the idea.

In 1887 he came across *Šárka*, a 'music drama' written in 1879 by the renowned Czech poet Julius Zeyer, and based on the myth of the Czech warrior women and their eventual defeat.[102] Published in three instalments in the review *Česká Thalie* [Czech Thalia], it was brought to Janáček's notice by the music critic Karel Sázavský, and Janáček soon set to work on his opera of the same name.[103]

Zeyer's text was brimming with Romantic, indeed Wagnerian symbolism; the hero, Ctirad, reminded Helfert of Siegfried, and Šárka of Isolde.[104] As a staunch anti-Wagnerian, Janáček had to cut and de-romanticize wherever possible. Yet *Šárka's* style does grow from Wagnerian music drama, even though '*musically* it succumbs to it relatively little'.[105]

Janáček wrote two overtures for the opera, one for each version.[106] From a formal point of view, the first – of which only the piano score survives – was not ideal. The second is formally concise, and successfully introduces the atmosphere of the opera.

A brief motif in Act 1 – a quintuplet composed of descending thirds and fourths – introduces the warrior Ctirad. Suitably varied, this motif then surfaces in all the situations which signal his impending downfall, including his descent into the tomb of the dead prophetess Libuše in order to obtain the magic mace and shield hidden there. A variant of this motif, in an augmented form and combined with the 'tomb' motif, even accompanies Šárka's announcement of her intention to enter the tomb; thwarted by Ctirad, she vows revenge, and once again the basic tragic motif appears, suitably augmented.

Act 2 consists of an opening chorus, three big arias, and a dramatic conclusion. The fine women's chorus, 'Now the stars have waned', again combines the basic tragic and 'tomb' motifs. A variant of the basic motif appears in a later chorus, and a new motif only emerges in Šárka's aria 'Oh, you deceiving illusion'.[107] Šárka's ruse (her entrapment of Ctirad) and love for him are portrayed by two long, linked arias. This scene originally consisted of Šárka's passionate confession and a love duet; in the third version (1918), Janáček cut the duet, replacing it by a short aria for Ctirad, with substantially simplified harmony. However, the motif of the original duet appears in the overture and Act 1.[108] The ending of Act 2 – also radically cut in the 1918 version – is once more governed by the basic tragic motif.

Stylistically, the outline of Act 2 was determined by the lyric nature of the text. Yet from the motivic development point of view, Janáček managed to tie the individual sections into a cohesive whole; and linking set numbers in an unbroken flow, he demonstrates the growing individuality of his dramatic style.[109]

Act 3 describes the funeral of Ctirad (murdered by Šárka), her arrival at Vyšehrad Castle, and her suicide. Janáček viewed this act as 'a scenic oratorio', with several key solo parts.[110] Once again Šárka's main aria derives from the basic tragic motif (also used in the women's chorus that follows); the final mixed chorus is derived from the motif of Šárka's ruse, but its original passionate character is transformed into 'a broad cantata gesture'.[111]

Thus, stylistically, *Šárka* is not homogeneous. Although Zeyer's text led Janáček into the world of Wagnerian music drama, in Acts 2 and 3 he distances himself from it, deploying instead the Classical variation principle.[112]

Helfert was also the first to note the various influences manifest in *Šárka*: Act 2 is close to Smetana while in Act 3 the style is on one hand closer to cantata and oratorio, and on the other to Gluck's operas. This is not surprising – at that time, Janáček was intending to stage Gluck's *Orfeo*, and studied the score in great detail. Thus, rather than a mixture of styles, *Šárka* is 'a sequence of styles, determined by Wagner, Smetana [and] Gluck'.[113]

In *Šárka*, notes Helfert, Janáček entered the sphere of myth for the first and last time in his operatic canon. The subject was simply too remote for him. Although his youth – spent in a tiny, remote village at the foot of an old castle, and later at the gloomy Queen's Monastery – was conducive to evoking Romantic notions and moods, he was not a Romantic by nature. His primary source of inspiration was village life as he had experienced it.[114]

Janáček was therefore not interested in Zeyer's mysticism or indeed his decadence; rather, he saw in the text 'a drama of fierce human passion, betrayal and reconciliation'.[115] As in his choruses, he chose to portray in music 'the emotional and dramatic substance dormant beneath the surface of the word'.[116] He avoided Romantic and mythical stylization: even in the hero's evocation of the dead prophetess Libuše, for example, Janáček seems to have expressed his own grief over his mother's recent death.[117]

Hence the entirely tragic hue of *Šárka* never changes, not even in the love scenes, and the tragic tone also underlies Janáček's lyrical passages. Even in his first opera, his eroticism is 'always mingled with some tragic conflict'.[118] Moreover, Janáček saw Zeyer's bleak depiction of Šárka's death as the catharsis of the piece, and this type of ending – tragedy as a catharsis – is typical of most of his subsequent operas.[119]

Although Janáček shunned the Romanticism of Zeyer's mythical story, he must have been enchanted by its locale. The courtyard with its old linden trees and the untouched valley described in the text must have reminded him of the Hukvaldy game reserve and forests.[120] Helfert thought Janáček's evocation of this natural wilderness reminiscent of Debussy; the music describing the world of Přemysl (the consort of the prophetess Libuše) reminded him strongly of the general mood of *Pelléas*.[121]

Janáček continued to develop his individual style in *Šárka*, but his Classically orientated musical grounding still shows: his ability to create a great variety of motifs from a given theme is the hallmark of the Classical compositional method.[122]

Unlike Wagner with his leitmotif, Janáček does not automatically repeat his basic motif whenever the situation demands it: Janáček's motif 'lives an intense dramatic and emotional life' of its own, its shape and content always dictated by changes in the psychological situation.[123]

A degree of Smetana's influence cannot be denied in *Šárka*; the protagonist also appears in the famous Czech legend about the prophetess Libuše, the subject of Smetana's eponymous opera. Janáček's psychological dependence on Smetana, as Helfert points out, particularly shows in the festive scenes.[124]

Yet by far the strongest influence in *Šárka* is Dvořák, even though one can clearly see that Janáček had already embarked on his own individual journey: his expression 'grows organically from Dvořák', gradually freeing itself.[125] At times it is difficult to say 'where Dvořák ends and Janáček begins',[126] but far from copying Dvořák, Janáček was simply thinking along similar lines. The deep musical bond between them explains the fact that in Act 3 of *Šárka* one occasionally hears in the harmony what appears to be an echo of Dvořák's *Rusalka*, yet to be composed.[127] In his instrumentation of the first two acts, Janáček was also leaning on Dvořák, although he had not reached Dvořák's depth and sonic clarity.[128]

Despite all these influences, Janáček – plainly conscious of his growing individuality – reaches in *Šárka* greater clarity and transparency. The type of melodic line deployed – largely new in Czech music at the time – was to be used again in Janáček's future music, and there are signs of his future vocal style.[129]

The harmony is rich and varied and Janáček's modulations are fluent and mobile. A Wagnerian type of harmony occasionally colours the melodic line;[130] a chord of the ninth is frequently used to evoke a particular mood, and once again Helfert found this reminiscent of late Dvořák as well as of Debussy.[131] Janáček's liking for three-bar periods, typical of his later works, is also apparent; this type of periodization was equally new at the time, and clearly influenced by folk music.[132]

Thus, though stylistically not truly independent, *Šárka* shows that Janáček was already capable of original expression. In the history of Czech opera, Janáček's *Šárka* represents – after Dvořák's *Dimitrij* and Fibich's *The Bride of Messina* – a novel response to the tradition of Czech tragic opera.[133] It was the conclusion of Janáček's first creative period, at the age of 33, as well as a portent of his next stage of development. In *Šárka*, Helfert concluded astutely, 'Janáček arms himself for his future rebellion'.[134]

Longing to hear his mentor's opinion, Janáček sent Dvořák the piano score of *Šárka* in the late summer of 1887.[135] In October Dvořák finally invited Janáček to Prague, to talk about 'this very serious' matter.[136] His opinion, as Janáček later noted down, was 'sufficiently favourable', though as always he wanted 'more melody'.[137]

Only after obtaining Dvořák's opinion did Janáček ask Zeyer's permission to use his drama. The distinguished poet refused, peeved at having his text radically altered by an unknown young composer; his letters of 10 and 17 November 1887 do not display a particularly accommodating attitude. 'Your music, I presume, will not be wasted,' he added tetchily. 'You can use it for something else.'[138]

In a note on Zeyer's first letter, Janáček later commented: 'It was a misunderstanding. I was not sure whether I would succeed in my first opera, and hence worked quietly – and for myself.'[139] Disappointed but undeterred, he carried on revising and scored the first two acts before giving up; as a result of the poet's refusal, Janáček was not to see his first work staged until 1925, when he was 72.[140]

Unhappy with much of his work, Janáček 'tore up many compositions at that time', recollected Zdenka.[141] Compensation came in another form: on 16 May 1888, the couple's long-awaited son Vladimír was born, and welcomed 'like a prince'. Janáček 'took pride in him, cradled him in his arms, played with him – how completely different he was with Olga, and only because she was not a boy,' Zdenka observed sorrowfully.[142] Shortly before the boy's birth, Olga fell seriously ill. Having nursed her devotedly for two months, Zdenka became very weak, as did little Vladimír. In the doctor's opinion only a wet nurse could save his life. Yet Janáček refused: 'I am not a baron to pay for a wet nurse.'[143] In despair, Zdenka turned to her parents. Once again they helped, by paying the nurse's wages.[144] The boy quickly improved, and 'peace, indeed, happiness returned to us,' recalled Zdenka.[145]

By 1888 the hopes that Janáček had cherished in Vienna eight years previously were still unfulfilled. But he had returned to composition, and Dvořák's opinion, so vital to him, was encouraging. Soon he would embark on a folk-song collecting expedition which would provide a much-needed impetus for his style; he would at last shake off 'the shackles of tradition'.[146]

4

Return to Sources

(1888–1896)

JANÁČEK'S NATIVE VILLAGE, Hukvaldy, lies within a diamond bounded by Mount Lysá in the east, the town of Příbor in the west, Mount Radhošť in the south and the town of Frýdek-Místek in the north; the views from both mountains are magnificent. Further west of Příbor lies the lowland through which the river Odra runs north towards the city of Ostrava and the Polish border.

Janáček revisited this wooded, hilly countryside below Lysá in 1885, and the trip made a powerful impact on him: 'Below Hukvaldy Castle,' he recalled many years later,

> in a valley so narrow that you could throw a stone over to the other side, stood the small Harabiš Inn. The windows look like glowing fires, inserted into the darkness. Inside the inn you could almost cut the air, thick with smoke and smells. Žofka Harabišova flies from arm to arm. What a dancer! [. . .] The room is crowded with boys and girls, old women hold children in their arms. [. . .] Body to body; the passion of dancing . . . . Flashing movements, the faces sticky with sweat; screams, whooping, the fury of fiddlers' music: it was like a picture glued on to a limpid grey background.[1]

Janáček's first attempts at collecting folk-songs probably date from this time; in 1886 he published a significant review of the first volume of Ludvík Kuba's collection, *The Slavonic World in its Songs*.[2] In 1888 he returned to the region at the invitation of the foremost Moravian folklorist of the time, František Bartoš, then principal of the Czech Gymnasium in Brno. Bartoš began by studying Moravian dialects and folk customs; in the 1880s he began to include folk-songs, in order to supplement an enormous collection by František Sušil, the publication of which was completed in 1860.[3] As Bartoš was more interested in the words than the music, he had to seek help to notate the tunes for his 1882 collection, *New Moravian Folk-songs with Tunes Included*;

when he published his second collection, he had been working since 1886 with Janáček. This led to a serious ethnographic collaboration, which continued for several summers; Janáček also became the joint editor of all the collection's later editions.[4]

Throughout Europe folk-songs have always been shaped by the activities they traditionally accompanied, as well as by the landscape – its terrain, its isolation and so on. Moravian folk-songs, particularly those in the areas bordering Slovakia and Poland, also display some distinctly archaic musical features. Unlike their Bohemian counterparts, which are largely folk versions of seventeenth- and eighteenth-century art music, Moravian folk-songs are much freer and more irregular in their metrical and rhythmic structure, and more varied in their choice of melodic intervals; they also make liberal use of minor and modal scales.[5] The character of these modes gives the music its distinctive sound, much more exotic to Western ears than a melody in a major scale; whenever Moravian folk-songs do not employ modes, they frequently modulate to quite remote keys.

The peasant musicians that Janáček heard did not know the names of these modes, but they had their own ways of referring to them. The folk-song collector Vladimír Úlehla, for example, recalled musicians talking of 'playing in the thin key', and he observed that they tuned their bagpipes automatically in the most frequently used modes.[6] Úlehla even identified what he calls the 'Moravian' scale; Janáček himself considered the 'Moravian modulation', as he called it, a characteristic of this region's folk-songs in general.[7] And the melodic shape of the song is dictated by the words; this close association of words and music was of particular interest to Janáček.

During the summer of 1888 Bartoš and Janáček visited several villages in the Lašsko and Valašsko districts; Janáček notated not only tunes but also their instrumental accompaniment and made notes on the choreography of the dances.[8] He preferred not to organize special performances but notated the songs on the spot, sometimes inviting the singers and players to further sessions. Some villagers were shy at first but by November 1891, when a grant enabled Janáček to make an expedition to the countryside around Hukvaldy and to the northeast, many of those who had sung, played or danced for him before promised to attend more sessions, and bring old dances and tunes.

'Collecting folk-dances is immensely important, since here we are at the source of harmonized folk music. We Czechs do not yet know it – it was thought that we have none at all. Collecting . . . folk-dances in Moravia without delay must therefore be our sacred duty,' wrote Janáček in his application to the Czech Academy in Prague for a stipend of 200 Austrian Gulden:

> Why, the cymbalom players I have met in the Valašsko region are old men . . . . And they already have such difficulty remembering the old tunes! There is therefore a most justified concern that with the death of these unique connoisseurs many an important testimony to our culture would be lost for good.[9]

By this time Janáček had already composed his first ballet, *Rákos Rákóczy*, which came into being in a rather complicated way. The folk-dances that Janáček had seen became the inspiration for several orchestral dances, initially called *Dances from Valašsko* (later *Dances from Lašsko*). This set of six dances as it is known today was not conceived as a cycle – the dances were composed separately, and several were performed early in 1889 in the city of Olomouc and later on in Brno. 'In Janáček's *Dances from Valašsko* everything is still in a ferment, everything roars, forcefully elbowing its way into the score,' wrote the critic of *Moravian Letters* that December.[10]

The Brno concert was attended by the Moravian-born Augustin Berger, a young ballet master at the National Theatre in Prague;[11] he had been sent to Brno by the theatre's director F.A. Šubert, to whom Janáček had offered the piece. The National Theatre was about to stage a three-act ballet by Karel Kovařovic, *The Tale of Happiness*, and Berger specifically asked for some Moravian dances. Kovařovic's ten arrangements did not appeal to him; Šubert did not like them either and proposed to Janáček that some of his dances should be included in Kovařovic's ballet. This was hardly what Janáček had in mind. Turning the offer down, he suggested writing a ballet of his own, *Dances from Valašsko – an Idyll*, which was to include all the dances.

In a sketch he submitted to Berger, following Václav Kosmák's scenario, Janáček outlined a story set in Hukvaldy at the time of the Empress Maria Theresa. Twin brothers Vojtěch and Václav, both about to marry, are threatened with conscription, but they are given a chance to compete against each other: the one who outdances the other gets a reprieve. Neither wins; fortunately, Janek, the clumsiest boy in the village, offers to be conscripted in their stead, as this bolsters his ego. All ends well, with everyone celebrating.

The subject 'appealed greatly' to Berger; dancing itself was an essential part of the story and peasant musicians, including a cymbalom player, were to be used to add local colour. Yet in September

1889 the National Theatre's management returned the score to Janáček: for 'artistic reasons' it was deemed unsuitable.[12]

Teaching, writing, collecting and arranging folk-songs and folk-dances kept Janáček busy in the late 1880s, and he was also much involved in the social life of the Czech minority in Brno. His family life was happy at that time. Unlike his daughter Olga, his son Vladimír – who inherited his father's dark eyes and eyebrows but his mother's fair hair and complexion – showed clear signs of musical talent from a very early age, beginning to sing as soon as he started to talk. By the age of 2 Vladimír also liked to copy Janáček's mannerisms; he often watched his father composing at the piano but, as soon as Janáček got up, 'Vladíček [a Czech pet name for Vladimír] took his place, thumped at the piano and made doodles in the music. Vladíček was allowed everything,' recalled Janáček's maidservant Marie Stejskalová. 'Master would only put his arms around him and, full of joy, would exclaim: "You little rascal, you'll be a musician!" '[13]

In October 1890 first Olga and then Vladimír caught scarlet fever. Meningitis followed and the boy – always physically frail – died on 9 November. Little Olga wept so bitterly at her brother's tiny coffin that his face was drenched with her tears. Zdenka grieved for a long time, but Janáček never referred to the boy again, refusing to join Zdenka when she visited his grave. The wound went too deep.

In 1891, perhaps as a farewell to the son he loved so much, Janáček wrote a brief Adagio in D minor for orchestra. The thematic material of this short piece is related to the first version of his opera *Šárka*; like several of Janáček's works it was later discovered by his pupil, the conductor Břetislav Bakala, in the painted chest from Moravian Slovakia, in which Janáček stored his manuscripts.[14]

By 1890 Zdenka – still only 25 – and Janáček had not lived as husband and wife for some time; during the summer holidays of 1888 Janáček had found another object of devotion, the married daughter of the Hukvaldy brewer. After Vladimír's death Zdenka – though still desperately jealous – wanted another child. Janáček's cold refusal, as she confessed in her memoirs, killed all her desire for him.[15]

In 1891 an opportunity finally arose for Janáček's ballet to be performed at the Prague National Theatre. To celebrate the provinces' advances in industry over the past century, a Provincial Jubilee Exhibition was organized in Prague that summer; boycotted by the city's German population, the exhibition soon became a demonstration of Czech national unity. For political reasons, the organizers wanted as much local colour as possible: arts and crafts were exhibited, and a model of a 'Czech cottage' was displayed. Prague was packed with visitors from all over the country; between mid-May and the end of August the National Theatre played non-stop, with a Czech repertoire – including operas by Smetana and Dvořák, as well as works by Fibich and Bendl – amounting to half of all performances.

Once the theatre's management realized how popular the Czech repertoire was, it moved fast. The Czech writer Jan Herben[16] was commissioned to put a story to Janáček's dances which, although he never heard a note of the music, he completed in two days. Without having seen Herben's libretto, Janáček also added a few dances from other districts in Moravia. The première of *Rákos Rákóczy* (originally subtitled 'Scenes from Moravian Slovakia') took place on 24 July 1891; it was not so much a ballet as a sequence of folk-dances and songs for solo voices and chorus.

The dances and songs were combined without much attention to their origins – those from Lašsko appear alongside those from other districts, and none is from Moravian Slovakia, the district mentioned in the original subtitle. The work is not accurate from a folklorist's point of view, nor is Janáček's orchestration always satisfactory. Yet, judging by the critical response in the Czech press in Moravia, *Rákos Rákóczy* was a spectacular success: in *Moravian Letters*, it was hailed as the first attempt at 'a Slavonic national ballet'.[17] Only the reviewer from the magazine *Prague* thought that the actors showed little understanding of the nature of this folk drama. The peasants in *Rákos Rákóczy* 'shouted themselves hoarse in the introductory scenes,' he wrote, 'gesturing needlessly and explaining every little phrase with such an emphasis and so slowly as if trying to make a point to a deaf mute'. Thus the one-act ballet dragged on 'boringly'.[18]

In 1891 Janáček also began composing his second opera, *The Beginning of a Romance*, based on a story by Gabriela Preissová (1862–1946). He had been searching for a new libretto for some time, despite the disappointment caused in 1887 by Julius Zeyer's refusal to let his text be used so that Janáček's first opera, *Šárka*, could be performed.[19]

Preissová – popular with both critics and readers – was an obvious choice: she was born in Bohemia and lived most of her life in Prague but her writing was greatly influenced by the time she spent in Moravia. As a young girl, she fell in love with the beauty of the folk-songs, costumes and colourful dialect of Moravian Slovakia. At the age of 18 she married Jan Preiss, a wealthy official in the town of

Hodonín, and often travelled with him through the surrounding Czech-speaking villages, talking to the villagers, observing their customs and collecting their beautiful embroidery. Although Preiss spoke only German, he was sympathetic to Czech culture and supported his wife's pursuits wholeheartedly. In 1886, introducing the first of three volumes of short stories based on her impressions, Preissová declared enthusiastically: 'I am Czech, and [also] completely Moravian Slovak.'[20]

In 1888, when Janáček first asked Preissová for a libretto, she refused: she had always resisted commissions, convinced that they would involve her in a mechanical routine which she disliked.[21] Some two years later Janáček repeated his request, probably on the advice of František Bartoš.[22] This time Preissová enclosed an outline of *The Beginning of a Romance*, ready to be put into verse; Janáček might have discussed the libretto with her in January 1891, when she lectured in Brno on her two enormously successful plays, *The Farmer's Woman* (1889) and *Her Foster-daughter* (1890). Astonishingly, at the time of their premières neither Janáček nor Bartoš thought them suitable for operatic treatment (although Bartoš noticed that Preissová's short stories included much dialogue).

Preissová stressed that she had only sketched the libretto for *The Beginning of a Romance* out of respect for Bartoš, suggesting that the opera would have to be 'an operatic idyll, never a comedy – there is too little action in the piece . . .'.[23] When Smetana's librettist, Eliška Krásnohorská, declined the task of versifying the text, Janáček approached the poet Jaroslav Tichý, who provided the libretto within about a month.[24]

Janáček's correspondence with Preissová shows how fast he worked: beginning on 15 May 1891, he completed the piano sketch on 2 July, and a few days later played some excerpts to her. At the end of the month she reported to a friend that Janáček wrote 'in too massive – too classical a manner; it could be lighter'. Still, she had 'high hopes' of him.[25]

Janáček finished the full score around the middle of December 1891, offering to bring the work in person to the Prague National Theatre's director F.A. Šubert. He was – as he wrote – not submitting the opera 'officially', but was merely interested in Šubert's opinion; should this be favourable, he would offer the work to Brno. This was not strictly true, since Janáček delivered the score to the Brno opera as soon as he had completed it;[26] he also asked Preissová to put in a good word for him in Prague. Throughout the early part of 1892

Janáček continued his negotiations with Šubert, resubmitting the work and reporting further revisions. Encouraging Janáček to be patient, Preissová echoed his feelings: 'A piece by a Czech composer can always wait, but when Mascagni writes something they telegraph at once to get it . . .'.[27] In May – on the advice of the conductors Adolf Čech and Mořic Anger – the score was refused as unsuitable.[28]

Although the opera was accepted in Brno at the beginning of 1892, problems followed; initially, the soprano Marie Wollnerová returned the part of the female protagonist, Poluška. Writing with exaggerated, ironical courtesy, she claimed that she could not do the role justice; she had obviously been offended by Janáček's earlier criticism of her as Santuzza in Mascagni's *Cavalleria rusticana*.[29]

Then the production itself was postponed. In September the director Václav Hübner finally explained what was happening. He had always held Janáček in high esteem, he wrote, and the postponement was not his fault but the conductor's: František Jílek simply refused to study the work. Apparently, 'this was [his] revenge for your not wanting to write favourably enough about him and the opera ensemble'.[30] Not for the first time, Janáček's pugnacious criticism had backfired.

By the 1890s Janáček was well established as a music journalist and critic in Brno. He wrote for several journals: from 1887 for *Hlídka*, and from 1890 for *Moravian Letters* (following the closure of his own *Hudební listy* in 1888); he also contributed to various Prague music magazines, such as *Cecilie*, *Dalibor*, *Hudební revue* and *Listy Hudební matice*.[31]

In 1893 a new liberal daily, *Lidové noviny*, was established in Brno. This was a considerable achievement for Moravia's aspiring Czech community: it was a broad-based intellectual newspaper and it attracted some of the most distinguished local contributors. It backed the *mladočech* ('Young Czech') political faction and quickly became very popular. As it had a particular interest in promoting culture and the arts in the city, it represented a new and extremely useful outlet for Janáček.

He wrote his first *feuilleton*, 'Music of truth', for the paper's first issue, and continued to contribute to it until his death; the *feuilleton* form suited Janáček's own loose, idiosyncratic style well.[32] He had a wide range of interests and also published reviews and travel pieces as well as commentaries on his own compositions and their origins. Many of his *feuilletons* were devoted to his speech-melody studies, and in 1894 he also wrote a series of theoretical articles called 'The new trend in musical theory'.

Janáček was one of the foremost Moravian folklorists and his contributions on this subject too were welcomed by *Lidové noviny*; as a new wave of interest in folk culture swept through Bohemia and Moravia in the 1880s, Czechs from all levels of society enjoyed reading about their distinctive heritage. Janáček's first piece also reflected his artistic programme. 'Names, empty names of songs and dances!' he wrote with an almost audible sigh, describing his recent field trip.

> How would the contents of this *feuilleton* stand out if all the songs could sound and the dances could be spun out! How much love, longing, happiness and joy there is in these songs – how much truth, everywhere and always the truth. In music too there is *truth*. 'He does not always play truthfully,' Trn told me about his *kontráš*. What a comprehensive statement this is, musically speaking! He does not play the way the spirit of the songs commands, he does not think harmonically in the way the style of our music, our song commands . . . . *And how many Czech composers there are who still do not write the 'truth'!*[33]

The same year, Janáček's *Dances from Valašsko* – based on the fruits of his expeditions – became known under another title, *Dances from Lašsko* (first used for the orchestral dances that probably derived from his *National Dances in Moravia*, 1888–9). This latter collection included twenty-one dances arranged for piano or voice and piano, as well as piano arrangements for four hands; number 6 ('The Ancient') was written for the dulcimer.[34] Initially, *Dances from Lašsko* contained five dances, not identical with those in the work in its present form; earlier in 1890, Janáček succeeded in having the score of the first two dances ('The Ancient' and 'The Cudgel Dance') published in Prague. The material was recycled several times – Janáček also included some of the dances in *Rákos Rákóczy* and in *The Beginning of a Romance*, as well as in the orchestral Suite, op. 3 (both written in 1891). That year, another orchestral arrangement of four dances was given at a concert of the Vesna Society in Brno.

The whole project was to undergo further modifications: in 1904, a new piano version was made for both the 'Saw Dance' and 'Čeladenský', but as late as 1906 Janáček still referred to all the dances under the old title, *Dances from Valašsko*. The material was reorganized only in 1924, when Janáček also made some changes in the orchestration; the score of the cycle as we know it today was not published until 1928.[35]

By 1893, Janáček – still relatively unknown outside Brno – was also looking for another operatic subject, and expressed interest in Preissová's play *Her Foster-daughter*.[36] This was the drama of Jenůfa and her devoted foster-mother, the village sacristan – a story of wild jealousy and false pride, in which wisdom and forgiveness are learnt only through great suffering.

At first, Preissová was not in favour of the idea. 'I think that the material of P.[astorkyňa, i.e. *Her Foster-daughter*] is decidedly unsuitable for setting to music,' she wrote to Janáček. 'Perhaps we shall find something more suitable in time.'[37]

Meanwhile, the Brno première of *The Beginning of a Romance* was announced for 10 February 1894. Šubert was invited from Prague but he was unable to attend any of the performances. Instead, Mořic Anger – whom Janáček knew well – was sent to Brno at his request, and Šubert was sent the final version of the full score.

Notwithstanding their goodwill, the directors of the National Theatre did not change their opinion of the piece. The opera presents a romantic view of village life – a jolly story seen through urban eyes. The plot is naive and the peasants talk in a versified literary Czech while dialect is used in the songs. The effect is, predictably, stultifying.

The response of the leading dailies in Brno was polarized. *Lidové noviny* acknowledged the work's popular reception but was critical of the libretto and the lack of dramatic action; the orchestra (under Janáček's baton) was too loud, and the opera was thought to be the work of a novice.[38] *Moravská orlice*, on the other hand, welcomed it warmly as the product of an artist 'whose slogan about the "music of the truth" . . . sounds so engaging in this time of new ferment in our young art';[39] the newspaper's reviewer, Karel Sázavský, found the opera to be 'in the spirit of national and Moravian music', the first work 'written in a completely modern manner'.[40] Yet only four performances were given, and the work was not revived during Janáček's lifetime.[41]

Today, most scholars agree that in *The Beginning of a Romance* Janáček fought a losing battle. He was aware that the libretto – a kind of folk singspiel – was poorly constructed; at first he resisted the librettist's idea of including folk-songs but in the end only about a third of the score was freshly written. From Janáček's sketches and revisions it is clear that he was dissatisfied with the work; he burnt part of it and thirty years later dismissed it: '*The Beginning of a Romance* was an empty farce.'[42] Nevertheless, there are interesting features in this opera. Although the orchestration bears some relation to

Dvořák's music, Janáček's individual voice can also be heard. The melodic structure, rooted in Moravian folklore, also demonstrates the development of his style, with typically brief, terse, ostinato motifs and quick changes of mood.[43] *The Beginning of a Romance* therefore served as a testing ground for *Jenůfa*, and its few performances at least enabled Janáček to learn from his mistakes.[44] Later he obtained a reproduction of the painting of the same name by Jaroslav Věšín (which may have inspired Preissová's story); he kept it in his study, eventually taking it to Hukvaldy.

Earlier in 1892 Janáček had thrown himself with great enthusiasm into preparations for a Czecho-Slavonic Ethnographic Exhibition, planned in Prague for 1895. A committee for Moravia was set up, with František Bartoš presiding; on 20 October a concert of music from Moravian Slovakia was given in Brno. Although the peasant musicians and dancers from the village of Velká whom Janáček brought down felt inhibited in the hall, he was undeterred: in February 1894 he accepted an invitation from the Central Committee in Prague to take charge of the Moravian section. He planned to bring to Prague the best village musicians and dancers he could find from every part of Moravia and Czech Silesia. Lucie Bakešová, the dance coach of the Vesna Society, was engaged to plan the dances;[45] Janáček took charge of the rest. Organizing, travelling up and down the country and persuading the musicians to practise and rehearse took a great deal of his time.

The early 1890s were stormy years for the Czechs: in the 1891 elections the political ferment in Bohemia led to the victory of the 'Young Czech' wing over the 'Old Czech' one; the students, disenchanted with both factions, formed a new progressive movement, '*Omladina*'. In 1893, when the Austrian authorities refused the Prague council's request to replace the city's bilingual German-Czech street names with Czech ones, an impassioned popular protest followed. That summer, the police and the army were summoned to suppress demonstrations, and bloody clashes followed. A state of emergency was imposed and all public assemblies banned; in February 1894, in an attempt to intimidate the Czech population, sixty-eight followers of the '*Omladina*' were tried and jailed.

The Ethnographic Exhibition therefore became one of the few channels available to the Czechs to express patriotic sentiments and aims. The diverse, colourful and highly individual folklore of Moravia was bound to make an impression in Prague, and Janáček knew the opportunity was unique.

'Our life in Moravia, from now on until the Exhibition,' he declared in an article published in June 1894, 'is itself to be a trial exhibition.'[46]

In July, a 'trial' event did take place in the village of Velká, a bastion of folk art where folk-songs were still part of everyday life. Among the spectators there were many Czech artists and writers: for Czechs from Bohemia, Moravian Slovakia was then still virtually a foreign country, exotic in the richness and variety of its customs and traditions. For three days and three nights everyone drank wine, played, sang and danced, intoxicated by the music; a legendary contest between two folk fiddlers who were there was remembered for decades.

By then Janáček had already begun working on his third opera, *Her Foster-daughter*. The dates he jotted down in his copy of Preiss-ová's play, which served him as a libretto, indicate his reading of the text and sketching of the music, but he also revised extensively – ten months elapsed between the first date, '18 March 1894' (end of Act 1), and the second, '17 January 1895' (end of Act 2).[47] After the last date, '11 February 1895' (end of Act 3), he began detailed work in full-score but in 1897 he stopped working on the opera, concentrating instead on another large-scale work, the cantata *Amarus*.[48] He returned to *Jenůfa* (as *Her Foster-daughter* eventually became known in English-speaking countries) at the end of 1901, and it was during its completion that he matured as a composer. In the meantime composing was, as he often said, largely a matter of stealing time.[49]

5

Crystallization of Style

(1895–1903)

IN JULY 1895 the Ethnographic Exhibition in Prague opened its gates to thousands of visitors from the provinces and abroad; the 'Moravian Days' section of the Exhibition went on for ten days and Janáček brought out for the occasion a special publication entitled *Traditional Festivities and Customs of Moravia*. On the opening day Janáček himself – clad in black *čamara* tunic – led a colourful procession of Moravian dancers and singers to the exhibition site.[1] His daughter Olga, aged thirteen, was among the excited spectators; Janáček 'held his head as proudly as a king'.[2]

'Moravian Days' created a sensation. Czech artists and musicians met at the 'Hudeček' inn, one of the exhibits in the section. Moravian wine and the famous plum brandy, *slivovice*, flowed; the village band, led by the Velká *primáš*, Pavel Trn, was a triumph. Among the many visitors, the Czech writer Alois Jirásek danced with the actress Hana Kvapilová.[3] Wedding ceremonies were held at the inn, with the Prague mayor himself acting as a witness; and the voice of the folk singer Kateřina Hudečková enchanted everyone. Yet outside the confines of the twin Czech-speaking provinces of the empire, this full-blooded Moravian exoticism was only slowly making itself known, and it did not make a wide impact at the time. In the 1890s Europe fell in love with Japan: Japanese style penetrated all the arts, and Slavonic exoticism did not makes its full impact until after 1913, by which time Stravinsky's *The Rite of Spring* had caused a scandal in Paris.

In the few years preceding the new century Janáček composed little. In 1895 he made an outline of an organ sonata but got no further. His brief but striking hymn *Lord, Have Mercy*, written for four solo voices, two mixed choruses, brass octet, harp and organ, was premièred in 1896.[4] The following year he wrote the short *Festive Chorus* for male voices. His lyric cantata *Amarus*, the turning point in his compositional style, began to take shape around that

71

time, but before the new idiom became rooted Janáček once again turned to literary and educational activities.

His series of perceptive opera reviews for *Moravian Letters* continued in 1896 with a searching analysis of Tchaikovsky's *The Queen of Spades*, given in Brno in January of that year; for Janáček, Tchaikovsky was 'the genius of originality, character and truth in music'.[5] He had known Tchaikovsky's music since 1882, when he had conducted his *Serenade* for strings, op. 48 (a work he loved and admired), but his interest in Russian music dates from earlier still, 1878, when he had planned to study with Anton Rubinstein in St Petersburg. It was only a matter of time before he embraced other aspects of Russian culture: Russia was, as Janáček put it, 'the mother of all the Slavs'. In 1896, some six months after the Brno première of *The Queen of Spades*, an opportunity to see the country presented itself: the All Russia Industrial and Art Exhibition in Nizhny Novgorod. Janáček travelled via Poland first to St Petersburg, where his brother František had settled some years before, and then to Moscow and beyond. He took with him a copy of *Russian in Nine Lessons* (he spoke the language at that time, but badly), and he made enthusiastic entries in it right from the beginning of his two-week trip. 'At last the feeling of a Slavonic state,' he wrote at midnight on 18 July, after crossing the Austrian-Russian border. 'Throughout Galicia I was depressed. Now I am jubilant . . . I shake off slavery. Russia, here I come!' Ironically, Janáček had overlooked an important historical fact: he was not on Russian but still on Polish soil. Poland, also a Slavonic country, had ceased to exist as an independent state at the end of the eighteenth century when it was divided among Austria, Russia and Prussia, and would not be reunited until 1918.[6]

After a week in St Petersburg which he loved, Janáček went to Moscow and Nizhny Novgorod. He found the exhibition disappointing, but was fascinated by the famous old town on the river Volga. Returning via Moscow, he was enchanted by the Kremlin and the city's panorama. Russia's history, her language (related to Czech), her folklore and her literature were powerful stimuli for many Czech intellectuals at that time and Janáček was no exception. Above all, Russia seemed free from foreign oppression, and Janáček's short stay made a lasting impact on him.

He met no composers during his visit, heard no opera and went to only one concert, dedicated to Anton Rubinstein's memory.[7] At St Petersburg's 'zoological gardens' he witnessed a grand spectacle with music but, to his disappointment, there were no Russian composers on the programme. Fortunately, he had a chance to hear a Russian church choir at a *panychida* (a mass for the dead), and he much admired the characteristic features of Russian orthodox music.[8]

On his return to Brno Janáček wrote three articles for *Lidové noviny*, extolling Russia's independence and individual national spirit.[9] Soon afterwards he founded the city's Russian Circle, and began to read Russian in the original; Russian literature became a powerful source of inspiration for him.

In the spring of 1897 Janáček completed his lyric cantata *Amarus*, a setting of a poem by Jaroslav Vrchlický (1853–1912). Vrchlický was an accomplished poet, dramatist and translator, and above all an outstanding lyricist. His *Amarus* (the name translates as 'bitter') is the story of a young monk 'dying of thirst for love and life': an illegitimate child, he enters a monastery to escape prejudice, and prays to be allowed to die. An angel foretells that he will do so the night he forgets to refill the altar lamp. Years later, about to refill the lamp as usual, Amarus spots a pair of lovers in the church. Mesmerized, he follows them and watches them embracing in the churchyard under a lilac tree. Next morning the perpetual light is out – and Amarus is dead, prostrate on his mother's grave.

The theme was bound to attract Janáček. 'The long, cold, quiet corridors', he wrote in 1928, 'nearby hangs the silver eternal light and Amarus's quiet steps are pressing deep into the silent gloom. Add my youth, and how could the work not come about?'[10]

In an account which he wrote of his work on the piece, 'How ideas came about', Janáček gives a fascinating description of his compositional process. He had worked out the shape of the cantata in his mind when he suddenly awoke at night:

> I look down into my soul. Innumerable notes are ringing in my ears, in every octave; they have voices like small, faint telegraph bells. I would tune them all to an *a′′′′* – only the *a* stands out clearly – and on the left, out of this whole cobweb of sounds, I would also place the buzzing *a* which, with firm strokes, interrupts the deep and regular breathing of my daughter at the back. This is the sound of silence. [. . .] [Hearing] the tune and the stream of chords sounds so extraordinary, so pure, . . . and *somewhere other than* this buzzing . . . . I am listening to the music of the soul – I see it quite clearly noted down.[11]

The musical examples in the article do not tally with the work in its final version, but it is clear that the initial inspiration contained the pitch, harmony and rhythm. Janáček also instinctively thought in terms of specific voices, specific instruments and their combinations: he mentions the 'fuller tone' of the soprano; 'the colours of the melancholy oboe . . . darkened by the tone of the strings *con sordini*', and 'the sound of the muted harp'.[12]

He set the poem in five movements. At first the role of the narrator is divided between the baritone solo and the mixed chorus but in the third movement it is transferred to the tenor solo (which, in the second movement, represents Amarus). The baritone takes over again in the fourth movement and, as in most earlier movements, the chorus completes the story. The final 'Marcia funebre' is a rather odd march – in a major key, with jubilant brass chords entering after a brief ostinato in the bells and horns. The chorus returns briefly after the central lyrical 'trio' but more jubilant chords follow, though the work finally ends in A minor (the key of the opening movement).

Amarus displays many traits of Janáček's mature style: intervals such as a second and a fourth are emphasized in the melodic line, there are short, nervous, repetitive figures, motifs are progressively compressed into ever shorter units, and there are occasional brief, beautifully shaped instrumental solos. Throughout the piece the tenor solo has the typically high tessitura that Janáček was to favour in many subsequent works. The dramatic mood and the lyricism are well sustained over the five movements of the piece: *Amarus* represents the peak of Janáček's choral writing up to that time. 'I am convinced that you have succeeded in it entirely,' wrote Vrchlický to Janáček in June 1897.[13] Yet, sadly, the work was badly performed at its première in 1900 and was not heard again for fifteen years.

In 1897 and 1898 Janáček published a series of four articles on Dvořák's symphonic poems, *The Water Goblin*, *The Noon Witch*, *The Golden Spinning-Wheel* and *The Wood Dove*, based on Czech mythology as retold by the poet K.J. Erben.[14] Although these articles are not exhaustive analyses, Janáček's shrewd observations throw much light on Dvořák's type of melodic invention, his intervallic structure, instrumentation and sense of drama. The secret of 'effectiveness' in Dvořák's music was based on 'his maturity in all aspects of formal aesthetics, completeness of melodic, harmonic and rhythmic expression'.[15] Janáček also comments on the 'Czechness' in Dvořák's music: his tunes 'grow freely out of the same soil as folk-songs'. Czech composers, Janáček adds, 'ought to be, in the style of Czech music, phoneticians as well as symphonists.'[16]

This leads him on to 'speech melody': in *The Golden Spinning-Wheel*, Janáček also draws his readers' attention to a melodic line which corresponds to the poem's verse: 'Buy it, my lady! It is not dear.' In the original Czech, this motif, in the flute part, resembles unmistakably an established speech pattern.[17]

This was not an accidental find: by then Janáček had been absorbed in the study of the melodic curves of a person's speech, the speech melodies, for some time. No composer of opera, he asserted in many subsequent articles on the subject, should overlook the subject. 'When, during a conversation, we quote the words of someone else, we are halfway to a theatrical performance,' he wrote in 1924. 'We even quote the speed of speech, a thin little voice or a coarse one; a sing-song tone, a nasal intonation . . . an angry expression, a reproachful look, or a look of unctuous tenderness. And we quote even the tonal register of the speech and its melodic rise and fall.'[18]

Janáček's speech melody theory must not be confused with musical declamation, nor was he concerned with a precise imitation of speech and its intonation in vocal music. 'Speech melody is a true, momentary musical description of man; it is a photograph of a moment,' he explained. 'Speech melodies are the expression of the whole state of the organism and all the phases of the mental activity which follow from it.'[19]

He constantly stressed the extent to which everyday speech is affected by changes of mood and situation. Although the contour of speech melody is shaped by the characteristics of speech peculiar to each person, Janáček based his study solely on research and observation of states of mind. 'Whenever someone spoke to me', he told an interviewer in 1928,

I may not have grasped the words, but did I grasp the rise and fall of the notes! At once I knew what the person was like: I knew how he or she felt, whether he or she was lying, or upset. [. . .] Sounds, the intonation of human speech, indeed of every living being, have always had for me the deepest truth.[20]

Nevertheless, one must bear in mind that Janáček's conclusions were sometimes subjective: even a composer of his considerable intuition, and remarkable power to observe acutely the human psyche,[21] cannot accurately notate every nuance of human behaviour.

The first evidence of Janáček's systematic notation of speech melodies dates from 1897. More and more enthralled, he continued in his research, noting down precisely the time, circumstances, appearance of the person concerned, his or her reaction to outside impulses and so on. Children, lovers, soldiers, musicians, old peasant women, gypsies, beggars and many other characters – later even animals and birds – are all portrayed in these hurriedly sketched fragments of speech and other sounds. Later he began to use an instrument known as Hipp's Chronoscope, to help him measure time intervals of very short duration. He jotted down thousands of speech melodies, frequently on whatever was to hand, but mostly in tiny notebooks which he always carried with him. The speech melodies were usually notated in the key of C major, but occasionally they were in other keys where this better determined the speech melody in question.[22]

The speech melodies were not to be sung. Writing about an afternoon spent notating children's speech melodies, Janáček insists: '. . . please, only read, do not sing the notated stories. Read them with such a flow as shown by the black dots of the notes. The children's speech will ring in your ears. You will recognize the children at once and take a liking to them.'[23]

As time went on, Janáček attempted to classify his collection, though never into rigid categories; instead, he talked of 'attitudes'. He based his classification on the theory of emotional contrasts as outlined by the German philosopher W.M. Wundt, whose *Principles of Physiological Psychology* he read with enormous interest;[24] it is clear that Janáček wanted to turn his study of speech melodies into a scholarly discipline.

Although Janáček was convinced that the structure and expressiveness of speech melodies made them easily comprehensible to anyone, the speech melodies were never intended to be used as possible thematic material: they signified an entirely new approach to the voice line and vocal stylization, serving also as a pattern for setting the narrative.

Thus the characteristic sound of Janáček's new musical language began to take shape. In *Jenůfa*, his third opera and his first operatic masterpiece, speech melodies and folk music influences merged into a style which has no analogy in Western European music. Janáček began Act 1 early in 1895; it was finished and copied in 1897, the year he also completed *Amarus*. A long hiatus followed before he returned to Act 2 in December 1901.[25]

★

By the turn of the century the Janáček household had an established routine. In 1897 they no longer lived in the flat in Měšťanská Street; a few years earlier Janáček had found a new, four-roomed flat at No. 2 Klášterní (now Mendlovo) Square, on the top floor of a large, two-storey tenement house.[26] Unusually, all the tenants were Czech families; a Czech primary school occupied the ground floor and part of the first floor.

The house was extremely well placed: the Monastery where Janáček held the post of choirmaster was directly opposite and the Teachers' Training Institute, where he still taught, was only a few steps away. Brno's Old Gymnasium, where he taught singing, had a few classrooms at the Institute and this again saved him a journey. Only the Organ School was a fair walk away up the hill.

Although the flat lacked modern amenities such as electric or gas light, it was light and spacious. Zdenka filled it with flowers, and both she and Janáček frequently bought beautiful antique folk embroideries, about which he was very knowledgeable.

His sanctuary was the study. At first he used to compose at the piano in the dining room but, since he often worked through the night, the piano was moved to his study at the back, where he also slept. Zdenka now shared the main bedroom with the teenage Olga.

The large windows of the flat overlooked the Špilberk Hill and the castle with its ramparts; from the nearby Church of the Assumption one could hear the sounds of the bells and the organ, and sometimes even singing. This did not distract Janáček, but he greatly disliked the loud street music which could often be heard coming from the square, frequently used by visiting circuses and merry-go-rounds. On such occasions he would storm out of the house, returning late in the evening when everything was quiet again.

Janáček was 40 now, and 'such a very handsome man', recalled his maidservant, Marie Stejskalová, in her memoirs:

He was rather small of stature but robust and held himself erect, head high. He was quite swarthy, with thick black curly hair, a black curly beard and brown eyes full of sparkle and, whenever he was angry, burning like fire. But when he smiled, it was as if warm sun fell on one's face. [. . .] He had beautiful, small hands, white, chubby but strong and firm. Whenever he disliked anything or was angry, he used to shake his head so quickly that it looked as if it was trembling of its own accord. Only his teeth were not nice; they were small [and] blackish, and he frequently had toothache.[27]

The family led a busy life: Janáček had many visitors, and there were always projects to work on. The day usually began with breakfast at six o'clock after which Janáček would return to his study, as classes at the Institute did not begin until ten; Olga went to the school on the ground floor. The family met again at lunchtime; Janáček enjoyed good food and his frequent bouts of moodiness were often dissipated by his favourite dishes.[28] After a short nap he returned to the Institute. Classes there finished at five, when he went straight to the Organ School, returning for supper with the family at half-past eight, unless he and Zdenka went out.

As Olga grew, Janáček came to love her, and his relationship with Zdenka – always volatile – recovered. The atmosphere in the Janáček household was harmonious. 'When Oluška was a little girl and healthy, she was playful, cracked jokes as children do, and had many witty ideas,' remembered Stejskalová, who spent forty-four years with the family. Janáček was 'cheerful at the time, quite different from later on. Even madame often burst out laughing, and I was a notorious giggler, so those evenings were full of fun.'[29] After supper, Janáček – an excellent raconteur – sometimes talked about his childhood, about friends such as Dvořák, and frequently discussed books he was reading. But soon he would return to his study, often working into the small hours.

The Janáčeks were well respected among the city's Czech-speaking minority, and had many social commitments: they went to the theatre and concerts, and attended lectures and club meetings. Whenever Zdenka and Janáček went out together, 'it was a joy to look at the two of them', remembered Stejskalová. 'A little taller than he, slim and blond, she had beautiful blue eyes, serious and sincere, a finely shaped nose, and white skin as soft as silk. She had a sprightly gait and was known as an excellent dancer.'[30]

The Janáčeks supported the Czech cause at every opportunity, which was costly; money was also needed to buy Janáček essential books, magazines and scores. And plenty was given away, for neither Zdenka nor Janáček could bear to see poverty and suffering. As a result the Janáčeks rarely entertained and could not afford to travel. But, like many married women of her class, Zdenka had a *'jour fixe'* once a week, an open day when friends would visit for coffee and pastry without an invitation.

Their summer holidays were spent at Janáček's birthplace, Hukvaldy, where Janáček also liked to spend time at Christmas: he loved seeing the snowbound village in winter, and taking long walks through the surrounding countryside in summer always restored his spirits. He would often get up at five o'clock to play the organ at the village church; there were excursions and picnics during the day, and music and dance evenings were held by an informal group of friends who called themselves the Under the Acacia Tree Circle. Janáček was much liked in Hukvaldy; the countryside and the sincerity of its people brought out the best in him. Volatile and outspoken himself, he admired courageous and frank people, and he was prepared to listen to those who could stand up to him.

The 15-year-old Olga frequently echoed her father's feelings. 'Hukvaldy had bewitched us!' she wrote in December 1897 to one of her friends. 'What is its magic? [. . .] Whenever I remember Hukvaldy here in Brno, I always feel so depressed that I cannot live there for ever. Only there, amid sincere people, am I always happy; here there is nothing but hypocrisy.'[31]

By then Olga was almost as tall as Janáček. She was slim, and had inherited her father's features and his olive complexion; like Janáček she was a smart dresser. She had her mother's blue eyes and long, thick, beautiful hair the colour of 'dark gold'. Her feet were tiny and she wore shoes 'just like those for Cinderella'.[32] At her school, she was an outstanding pupil; she had an excellent memory and her surviving letters show wit and style beyond her years. Everyone seemed to love her – she was sweet-natured, generous and sincere. Yet her letters also reveal a strain of melancholy, confirmed by her photographs: there is great sweetness in her face, but a pensive look in her eyes.

Her health was fragile: from an early age she was prone to tonsillitis, and subsequently developed arthritis and pericarditis. Both recurred and although she recovered, she was left with a weak heart and delicate constitution. As a result she missed out on much of the fun of childhood: sports and dancing, both of which she loved, either had to be curtailed or were forbidden altogether.

Janáček and Zdenka adored their daughter, though he was a strict father. Only one thing grieved him, although he tried not to show it: Olga had no talent for music. She had the best piano teacher in Brno but made little progress, and she dreaded her father's music theory lessons. She had a good contralto voice and sang well, but felt no urge to study singing.

Instead, she had an exceptional talent for the theatre: at her college she gave several public performances, reciting Czech and Russian poetry; later she joined an amateur dramatic society, and the Czech press in Brno praised her beautiful, sonorous contralto voice and impassioned delivery. Her parents delighted in her success but did not support her theatrical ambition: her fragile health would not permit that kind of career. They would have liked her to take up teaching, in the family tradition, but because of her health Olga was unlikely to pass the medical. As she was also a good linguist, she began to study Russian and French, hoping to become a private language teacher.

For a few years in her mid-teens, Olga's health was reasonably good. These were her best years: she was allowed to dance again and began to attend balls. At home, everything centred around her: she was a bond between Zdenka and Janáček, as well as a friend, companion, and the kindred spirit they had not really found in each other.

★

Around the turn of the century Janáček was still preoccupied with folk music, and wrote only a handful of pieces. In 1897, apart from the cantata *Amarus*, he composed *Spring Song* for high voice and piano, to a poem by Jaroslav Tichý.[33] This short, exuberant work – originally intended as part of a song-cycle – is Janáček's only surviving solo song; it was performed in March 1898 in the college for girls which Olga now attended.[34]

At the end of the following year Janáček's *Hukvaldy Folk Poetry in Songs*, written in 1898, was performed in Brno; this collection of thirteen folk-songs with piano accompaniment was dedicated to the Under the Acacia Tree Circle. A year later Janáček arranged six of the songs for a mixed-voice choir, specifically for the village singers, as *Songs of Hukvaldy*. Both cycles recall his 1885 visit to his native village. In 1899 Janáček wrote two dances for orchestra, *The Serbian Kolo* and *The Cossack Dance*.

For some years Janáček had also been working on his writing. The treatise *The Composition of Chords and their Connections* was published in Prague in 1887, and his *Singing Teaching Manual* in Brno in 1899. Janáček's treatises and manuals are an important part of his output, and he himself rated his harmony studies highly. But he is not easy to read: his terminology requires an erudite reader, his style is obscure, and he rarely treats a subject in a straightforward way. In the *Singing Teaching Manual*, for instance, he says nothing about voice production, concentrating instead on rhythm, conducting, intonation, dynamics and expression. Nonetheless, the manual's twenty-eight solo songs and three duets, all with piano accompaniment, show how much, all his life, Janáček wanted to instil in future teachers a love of folk-songs, and to ensure they passed it on to their pupils.

The first volume of Janáček's last and most important collaboration with Bartoš, *Moravian Folk-songs Newly Collected* (containing 2,057 songs), was also published in 1899;[35] the second volume appeared in 1901. Some songs were supplied by other collectors, mostly by the invaluable Martin Zeman and his sister Kateřina Hudečková, the folk singer who so captivated the visitors at the 1895 Prague Ethnographic Exhibition. Janáček's preface, 'The musical aspects of Moravian folk-songs', is long, detailed and valuable, despite his idiosyncratic terminology and style. Every Moravian folk-song, he asserts, 'has grown from the cadence of speech'. As he shows, temperament and dialect also influence rhythmical structure. Thus Janáček expands the account of the 'tribal' characteristics which Bartoš began in his edition. Janáček's interest in folk harmonization and authentic instrumental accompaniment is also documented here; many of his observations would eventually find their way into his music.[36]

The third edition of *The Bouquet* – a collection of Moravian folk-songs on which Janáček had collaborated with Bartoš in 1890 – appeared in 1901. Corrections and copious annotations on virtually every page of Janáček's copy make clear how detailed was his study of these songs: he analysed the syllabic structure of their verse, and paid attention to their metrical structure and modulation. He also noted their different forms.

Thus folk music and folk-song were continuing to occupy Janáček's mind, although several of his sacred compositions also date from around this time. In 1901 he composed *The Lord's Prayer* [Otče náš], inspired by eight paintings by the Polish artist Józef Męcina-Krzesz. He also arranged Liszt's *Messe pour orgue* for mixed choir and organ (he frequently looked for suitable works to be performed at the Organ School), and the following year he arranged Grieg's cantata *Olaf Trygvason*, for solo voice, mixed choir and orchestra.

In late 1901 Janáček once again took up *Jenůfa*, in which he brought the atmosphere of a Moravian village vividly to life. The inflexible social order and rigid local customs of the end of the century are portrayed in Preissová's play with great accuracy: the small village community had its own hierarchy, and the relationships, aspirations and tensions within it were the basis for each character's actions and development. Yet after the première of her play Preissová was attacked in the Czech press; although she based *Jenůfa* on two incidents reported in a local paper, the subject was thought improbable and shocking. Country people and village mores tended to be idealized at that time.

Janáček cut about a third of the play in his adaptation, but he retained all the characters and the order of the incidents, as well as the three-act structure. *Jenůfa* is not a reflection of the *verismo* style, a one-act village love, betrayal and murder story. By concluding the opera with a catharsis, Janáček went beyond *verismo*; and his portrayal of the protagonists' development from blind passion to a deeper understanding, forgiveness and love is wholly convincing.

In his version of the story, Laca loves Jenůfa, herself in love with his feckless half-brother Števa, whose child she is expecting. Unaware of Jenůfa's predicament, her stepmother (who is sextoness – Kostelnička – at the local chapel) forbids Jenůfa to marry Števa for a year. She despises the irresponsible Števa and wants to save Jenůfa from the fate she had experienced herself. The spurned Laca, in a fit of jealousy, slashes Jenůfa's cheek with his knife, then flees in confusion and remorse.

Some months later Jenůfa secretly gives birth to a boy; the villagers believe she has gone into service in Vienna. While Jenůfa is asleep (in fact drugged) the Kostelnička – her concern for both Jenůfa and her own reputation overcoming her pride – summons Števa. He shrugs off his responsibilities. Laca also visits and though he still wants to marry Jenůfa, he is shocked to hear of the child. Impulsively the Kostelnička tells him it is dead; she then drowns the baby in the mill-race. Later she tells Jenůfa that it had died while she was delirious. Two months later, at the wedding of Jenůfa and Laca, the tiny body is discovered beneath the ice. The Kostelnička confesses her crime, but is forgiven by Jenůfa as she is led away.

Janáček's natural dramatic talent was nurtured and strengthened by the experience he gained as a folklorist: as his colleague Bartoš had observed, in many Moravian folk ballads the depiction of states of mind and the nature of thought are very reminiscent of classical tragedy. These ballads retain their tremendous dramatic pace because the narrative gives way to action; dialogue is present throughout, and the setting is described briefly but with clarity.[37]

As in such ballads, the dramatic pace of *Jenůfa* is faultless; further cuts that Janáček made in the text are resolved in music. After the discovery of the murdered baby, the action gathers pace. There is uproar before the Kostelnička steps forward; after her confession the tension is resolved and the opera moves to its final phase. It is the depth of understanding that Jenůfa reaches here – and the depth of compassion she feels for her stepmother – which makes the climax so powerful: at last, the Kostelnička realizes the extent of her pernicious pride. 'I have loved myself more than I have loved you,' the Kostelnička admits before she is led away. Thus the catharsis is complete, and so is the moral verdict. It is Števa who is disgraced: no girl, 'not even an honest gypsy', will marry him now. It is Laca, too, who has proved worthy of Jenůfa's love, by standing by her even after public disgrace.

Since Janáček had removed references to the Kostelnička's past, she is frequently portrayed as a harridan. In fact, she is a much respected village *savante* and a counsellor. Nor is she very old. Her reaction to Jenůfa's choice of a partner stems from her own experience: as a young woman she married a reckless husband, and does not wish her stepdaughter to make the same mistake. Thus the opera focuses on Jenůfa; hence the title used for the work outside Janáček's native country.

In spite of her stature, the Kostelnička's fear of Jenůfa's – and her own – disgrace is genuine: in rural communities of nineteenth-century Moravia 'fallen' girls had to endure horrific public humiliation, and they frequently remained social and economic outcasts for the rest of their lives.[38]

The three acts of *Jenůfa* differ in conception. During their writing, Janáček began to question the 'number-opera' convention. In Act 1 there are fewer duets and ensembles than usual; Act 2, written after a long break, is a succession of dialogues, but there are only brief passages where two or more voices are combined. In Act 3 the ensembles are quite sparse.

Among the four principal characters the two female parts are scored for soprano and the two main male roles for tenor; Janáček does not differentiate between Jenůfa's suitors in timbre. His decision was probably also determined by his folklore experiences: the tenor was by far the favourite male voice in Moravian Slovakia – the higher and purer the timbre, the better.[39]

Janáček also changed his approach to structuring the music. He built up sections and often whole scenes from a single motif, repeated, varied and contrasted with others. This does not diminish the variety of expression; and although there is no leitmotif, some melodic figures recur throughout the opera.

Janáček's approach to accompaniment and tone colour also indicated the maturity that his style had now achieved. This approach was based on his observations of old traditions of decorating the melody and bass line in small Moravian peasant bands. Their playing stressed linear rather than vertical thinking; the dialogue of the melody and the background produces strong tension and exudes vitality.

The new type of melodic structure is significant: in *Jenůfa* Janáček abandoned the traditional operatic norm and began to follow his own stylistic code, based on the vigour of the voice part, its expressivity and structure.

The new type of symmetry between the voice part and the orchestra was Janáček's answer to the crisis of the post-Wagnerian opera. Although he was well aware of the importance of the orchestra for some of his contemporaries, his speech melody studies led him in a different direction: to characterize the individual roles convincingly through a logical connection between the emotion portrayed and the melodic shape of the vocal line. In Janáček's operas the orchestra is more restrained, and both the orchestra and the voice parts participate in the dramatic action. For him, speech melodies were now not only the source of types and characters, but also the basis of the entire structure of his music drama.

In *Jenůfa* Janáček also demonstrated his new conception of tonality: its specific character is determined not only by the intervals in diatonic, i.e. major and minor keys, but also by certain intervals within such keys which he changed enharmonically, i.e. in name (for example, C – G sharp, an interval of augmented fifth can become C – A flat, a minor sixth, as G sharp and A flat are, on a modern keyboard instrument, the same note). Janáček's 'chromatic major minor' key therefore consists of intervals of modes which are major in character as well as those which are minor in character, and occasionally their modifications (for example, a minor key which employs an interval typical of a mode which is major in character).[40]

The new ground that had been broken in *Jenůfa* is a testimony to Janáček's originality and a consummate celebration of the richness and power of Moravian folk music. Janáček does not use the Moravian folk idiom merely as a colourist, or simply for structural purposes. The synthesis of many factors that occurred in *Jenůfa* and his subsequent stylistic orientation were dictated by his need for a greater richness and variety of expression in the service of the music's contents. The logic of this synthesis is unique, and its suggestive power inescapable. Although Janáček's future operatic masterpieces differed thematically, the musical language was to remain essentially the same.

★

On 17 April 1902 Janáček wrote to Olga: 'I am working very hard in order to finish the second act before the holidays.'[41] Olga was then staying with her uncle in St Petersburg; her trip was hurriedly organized in order to resolve an alarming situation. In 1900, at a Shrovetide ball, she met a young medical student – the son of her mother's former piano teacher Antonín Vorel – and the two young people fell in love. When Janáček heard of Olga's budding romance, he strictly forbade her to meet the student again; Olga, just as stubborn as Janáček, pointed out that he and Zdenka were engaged when she was barely 15. The young Vorel left for Vienna to complete his studies but Olga continued to meet him whenever he returned to Brno. Soon, though, she heard disquieting rumours about his character and eventually she wrote to him, breaking off relations. In response, Vorel threatened to shoot her during his next visit.[42] In March 1902, the family therefore quickly dispatched Olga to St Petersburg, where she would also be able to practise her Russian. Janáček himself travelled with her, returning to Brno a few days later.

At the end of April Olga fell ill with typhoid fever. She made a partial recovery but in June had a relapse. The Janáčeks immediately left for St Petersburg where Zdenka remained with Olga; Janáček returned to his duties in Brno. But he wrote to Olga constantly, sometimes several times a day. 'I tolerate this wretchedness in my life much less easily than you think,' he confessed. 'Only get well again, my girl. My thoughts are with you.' Olga took a long time to recover enough to travel home. 'I am ready to ask for leave to join you both,' Janáček reassured her. 'It makes no difference whether I live here in a terrible anguish, or there with you two.'[43]

After seven weeks Olga was finally allowed to return to Moravia. Janáček met her and Zdenka in Warsaw to take them back to Hukvaldy, which had always had such a miraculous effect on Olga's health. During the journey her condition deteriorated: she could no longer walk. After her arrival, her heart became weaker, her liver and kidneys were both affected, and she had another attack of rheumatoid arthritis. At the end of the summer she also developed bronchitis, but eventually recovered enough to return to Brno. She never saw Hukvaldy again.

Christmas in Brno was to be her last. Soon she developed dropsy and was in acute pain day and night. She was moved to Janáček's study where she felt she had more air. By then Olga knew she was dying, and she feared the unknown. On 18 January Janáček made a note in his copy of Preissová's play: '18.1.1903, the third week of my poor Olga's fearful struggle with death. It [*Jenůfa*] is finished.' On 22 February, at Shrovetide, Olga asked to be given the last rites.

In the afternoon of that Sunday, the family were sitting around her. During Janáček's work on the last act of *Jenůfa*, Olga had shown great interest in the opera. 'Now she begged him,' wrote Zdenka in her memoirs, ' "Daddy, do play *Jenůfa* for me; I won't live to hear it." Leoš sat down at the piano and played. I could not bear it and ran off again to the kitchen.'⁴⁴

A few more days were spent in leave-taking; many friends and relatives, including the Schulzes who now lived in Vienna, came to say goodbye. Olga's last wishes were written down, including detailed instructions for her funeral. Janáček notated everything she said; the pages of his notebook which describe her anguish and pain during her last three days are the most heart-rending document imaginable. Eventually she became delirious; Janáček notated her last sighs. She died on the morning of 26 February, with the entire household kneeling by her bedside.

Janáček was 'tearing his hair out, shouting "Dear heart! Dear heart!" He still managed to send me to the Monastery to ask them to make the bells toll,' recalled his maidservant, 'and then depression overcame him; he just sat there taking no notice of anything.'⁴⁵ Next Saturday the whole of Brno followed the funeral procession; Janáček placed in Olga's coffin the last page of *Jenůfa*.⁴⁶ After the funeral he locked himself in Olga's room, weeping.When all the visitors had left, Zdenka embraced him and he said softly: 'So we shall carry on living, on our own.'⁴⁷

The Organ School offered him leave but Janáček refused. Suddenly he had aged. Grey-haired, depressed, he carried on working day and night. On 28 April he finished a piece for mixed-voice chorus and piano, *Elegy on the Death of My Daughter Olga*, a setting of a Russian text by M.N. Veverica. But the work that will always commemorate his daughter is *Jenůfa*: on the first copy of the vocal score Janáček inscribed, in Russian: '18.III.1903. For you, Olga, in your memory.'

6

Successes and Obstacles

(1903–14)

IN AUGUST 1903, about six months after Olga's death, Janáček went for a short holiday to the Moravian spa of Luhačovice, some 100 km east of Brno. The picturesque town, which lies in green, pleasant countryside, was small at that time; it was homely yet elegant. Behind the villas on the outskirts peasants were still tending their fields, cordially greeting visitors going for walks in the woods. In the new music pavilion the spa orchestra played popular tunes, while ladies and gentlemen, dressed at the height of fashion, promenaded along the esplanade. Artists and society people alike went to Luhačovice to take the waters, to immerse themselves in mud baths for real or imaginary maladies, to idle and relax.

Janáček's horse-drawn cab arrived in town 'to the distant sound of a little ditty on the clarinet and double bass'. Soon he began to take down more speech melodies: a shepherd's vigorous voice 'rolling through the pure air far and wide'; the mischievous laughter of ladies walking in the woods; gypsies begging at the new bridge. The Mount Velká Kamenná echoed 'with the full fortissimo of the spa orchestra . . . . The effect is indescribably funny when a cow breaks in with its derisive bassoon: "Moo!" '.[1]

He began to feel better; some of his prodigious energy and zest for life returned, despite the terrible void left by Olga's death, and now his profound disappointment at the rejection of *Jenůfa* by the National Theatre in Prague.

Janáček had sent the full score and vocal score of this opera to Karel Kovařovic, the theatre's chief conductor since 1900, who wielded almost unlimited power there. At the end of April 1903 the material was returned to Janáček. 'I regret sincerely that we cannot accept your opera for production,' wrote the theatre's director Gustav Schmoranz. 'We would wish the work to meet with complete success on stage, for your sake as well as for ours, but we are afraid that your work would not have this kind of a success.'[2] There was no

response from Kovařovic; doubtless he had not forgotten Janáček's
sarcastic review of his own opera *The Bridegrooms*, written when
Kovařovic was only 21 and given in Brno in 1887.[3]

Janáček's confidence was crushed; he had spent several years
writing what he believed to be his best work to date. It was in the
room where Olga died,' remembered Zdenka later:

> My husband was sitting at his desk. He took his head in his hands and
> began to weep bitterly. In a fierce attack of depression he blamed
> himself for being no good. I could not bear it. [. . .] I have always
> believed in his mission as an artist, I believed in the beauty and great-
> ness of *Jenůfa*. I embraced his head warmly and, crying myself, I tried
> to console him. Only immense faith in his work could give me all
> those words of comfort and encouragement [he needed].[4]

Eventually the crisis passed; Janáček offered *Jenůfa* to the Brno
National Theatre, whose opera company was in the hands of his
pupil C.M. Hrazdira. The rest of the year brought new projects and
new hopes.

Janáček now began to make more frequent trips to Prague, to see
various novelties at the opera houses and theatres there. One of the
great successes of the decade at the Prague National Theatre was
Charpentier's *Louise*,[5] which Janáček saw in May 1903. It made a
powerful impression on him: Charpentier used authentic street cries
in *Louise*, and painted a true picture of Parisian working-class life.
Janáček, despite his all-embracing interest in speech melodies, did
not approve of quoting them directly in his own music. But
Charpentier was in vogue, and the success of his technique reinforced
Janáček's belief in his own chosen path. He must have also felt heart-
ened by Charpentier's use of prose text.[6]

Setting verse to music involves dealing with regular, symmetrical
lines. Prose text lacks symmetry, and composing to prose usually
results in a more angular type of melody in the voice part. Yet *Louise*
was popular not only because of the daring realism of the libretto, but
also for the lyricism and fluency of the vocal line.

Soon after Janáček had seen *Louise* he contacted the Brno writer
Josef Merhaut. He had read his novel, *Angelic Sonata*, a contemporary
story of an obsessive amateur photographer involved in a dramatic
marital triangle. He sketched a synopsis and did some research, but
Merhaut was not willing to rework his material.

Some two months later 'a novel from life'[7] was suggested to

Janáček at Luhačovice, by one of the spa guests he met there. Kamila Urválková, the young wife of a superintendent of a country estate in Bohemia, was 'one of the most beautiful of women', Janáček remembered with excitement even some twenty years later. 'Her voice was like that of a viola d'amore.'[8]

Contemporary photographs do indeed show a beautiful woman in her late twenties, with an oval, regular face, large, limpid eyes under boldly drawn eyebrows, sensual lips barely suggesting a smile, and a statuesque figure. Invariably she is fashionably dressed, her neck, arms and hands laden with jewellery – though no portrait shows the three fresh red roses that she used to carry wherever she went. This Bohemian belle was being treated in Luhačovice for a heart complaint; it is not clear whether her husband and their small son also stayed there for the duration of her treatment. Not surprisingly, a circle of admirers soon formed around her. There was something intensely romantic and mysterious about Kamila, who had trained as an actress, and she seems to have flouted contemporary social mores to a degree: seeing Janáček sitting at his table alone and dejected, she sent him a bouquet of crimson roses and invited him to join her set. 'Your beauty and the marvel and tenderness of your looks are such as to bring forth a jubilant symphony, one by which you would be celebrated,' wrote Janáček in the copy of his *Hukvaldy Folk Poetry in Songs* with which he presented her.[9] The story of a love affair that she confided in him became an impulse for Janáček's fourth opera, *Osud* ['Destiny'].

This love affair involved Kamila and the Czech composer Ludvík Čelanský.[10] In revenge at its termination by her wealthy parents, Čelanský had pilloried her in a one-act autobiographical opera, blatantly entitled *Kamilla*. Its heroine is a cold-hearted coquette who dallies with a poor, sincere poet Viktor, while also encouraging a rich neighbour to court her. When the latter's affair with her chambermaid is discovered, 'Kamilla' wishes to reinstate Viktor; predictably, the poet has the satisfaction of renouncing her. This vindictive musical portrait was premièred in the autumn of 1897 at the National Theatre in Prague, and clearly was causing Kamila much heartache even after six years. By encouraging Janáček to write a counter-attack, she stood a good chance of having her name cleared.[11]

An intense correspondence blossomed between Janáček and Kamila Urválková for some five months, before it was terminated by her husband. Both she and Janáček used the customary formal address in their letters, dutifully sending greetings to their respective spouses. But photographs were exchanged and frequent allusions made to the time spent together in Luhačovice, and there is an undercurrent of secretiveness in Kamila's letters which would have been unnecessary had their relations been merely polite.

Kamila Urválková was restless and romantic. Her letters to Janáček are signed Tatiana, a name recalling the heroine of *Eugene Onegin*, and supposedly given to her by Janáček. She clearly felt hemmed in by social constraints and the tone of her letters frequently betrays considerable anxiety and an almost desperate desire to live a fuller life.

Janáček also lacked a fulfilling emotional relationship at the time. His daughter had been the last bond between him and Zdenka; after her death the marriage had little to offer either to Zdenka, who grieved deeply and was depressed for a long time, or to Janáček, who grieved no less but whose vitality was irrepressible. Now he found a new soulmate and confidante; his letters and cards to Kamila read almost like diary entries, and they provide a comprehensive account of his life, his ideas and plans.

Although Janáček showed Kamila's replies to Zdenka, she soon suspected that there were other letters; and eventually she found some in his desk. But she had no time to read them: Janáček noticed the missing letters almost immediately, and begged and raged until she returned them to him unread.[12]

Kamila and Janáček planned to meet in Prague at the beginning of October 1903, some two months after their stay in Luhačovice. But on 2 October she postponed the meeting:

> Most esteemed friend, it is impossible for me to come to Prague as I am unwell . . . . I shall probably arrive at the end of this month, but there is no certainty! I cannot make a move at the moment, I am as if in a straitjacket, watched on all sides! I wrote you a letter yesterday, but could not write in detail how I suffer mentally![13]

The letter is full of despair, dark allusions to unkind fate and complaints about terrible loneliness. She thought of Janáček often and wondered if they would meet again in a year's time; she asked him to write to her at a friend's address, and only from Prague, 'from *Brno* it would be *conspicuous*!' Similarly, she would have preferred to write to him at a friend's address, perhaps a family 'he could rely on'.[14]

By then Janáček was already preoccupied with his new opera, though as yet uncertain of its title. 'What of "The Star of Luhačovice," ' enquired Kamila, 'is it already finished? Will you dedicate it to me? At least I shall have a lasting souvenir to remind me of those unforgettable days in L[uhačovice] . . . how fast the time went!'[15]

Besides working on the new opera, Janáček was still revising *Jenůfa* – a work which, as he wrote later, he would bind 'only with the black ribbon of the long illness, pain and cries of my daughter Olga and my little boy Vladimír'.[16] But on 9 October he announced splendid news. 'Yesterday was one of those joyful days,' he wrote in a long letter to Kamila.

Perhaps the 'judge up on high' has turned to me with a smiling face after all? The directorship of the National Theatre in Brno sent for the score of my opera *Jenůfa*. When they were taking it away . . . it was as if they were taking my soul away . . . . I have asked permission to retire from my music teaching job in the Imperial Civil Service, so that I can devote myself entirely to composition and literary work. The times I have looked forward to all my life are now on the horizon. Shall I live to enjoy even happier ones? Will my spirit be capable of yet more brilliant work? I think so – but goodness knows what is going on in my brain. My whole body is on such fire . . . . All in the hands of God and fate! We make our own fate. I know that in this opera [*Jenůfa*] I have painted in black on black; gloomy music – such as was my own spirit.

What I would like now is a fresh, modern libretto, bubbling over with life and elegance – 'the story of a child of our time'. Oh, who will write it for me? I would have plenty of ideas for it – they say that I too can wield a pen – but I am afraid to enter the world of literary folk. And those who offer me their services know nothing but vulgar saloon-bar life. They have no idea that it is possible to find the spirit which infuses life itself, to find it quite nearby, in ourselves, among people so familiar to us, the spirit so enchanting, so piquant, with such surprising phenomena and amazing scenes – they have no idea of it, these literary people, because they don't even know such life.[17]

Even while his correspondence with Kamila Urválková continued, Janáček found a librettist – a young schoolteacher friend of Olga's, Fedora Bartošová. As she taught near Brno, they collaborated largely through correspondence. The first copy of Janáček's own prose scenario was entitled *Fragments of a Novel from Life*, and he sent it to Bartošová in stages; she then put this into verse ('the Pushkinesque kind as used in *Eugene Onegin*', demanded Janáček on 12 November). Bartošová completed her task by Christmas, but further additions and corrections were made in the next few months.[18] Meanwhile, the projected première of *Jenůfa* also occupied Janáček's mind.

By Christmas 1903 – the first without Olga – only the soloists and the chorus had learnt their parts. 'And Prague papers?' asks Janáček ironically. 'You can wait a long time before you read anything there! They ignore everything that concerns Moravia.'[19]

The première was set for 21 January 1904. Josef Malý produced the opera, and the sets were designed by the Slovak architect Dušan Jurkovič (whose work Janáček had admired in Luhačovice). Among the cast were the best singers who could be found in Brno: Leopolda Hanušová-Svobodová as the Kostelnička, Bohdan Procházka as Števa, the director Alois Staněk-Doubravský as Laca, and Marie Kabeláčová – only a few months over 20 at the time – as Jenůfa.

Rehearsals were not without problems. 'Today I am returning quite cross from the first full rehearsal of Act I,' complained Janáček to Kamila on 19 January. First an unpleasant quarrel had taken place between the director and the conductor; later, one of the trumpeters, reprimanded earlier, got drunk and turned recalcitrant. Much patience was necessary to pacify everyone and continue the work: as the style of *Jenůfa* was so innovative, there were more than fifty rehearsals altogether – a unique occurrence in the history of the Brno theatre. Even so, the orchestra lacked the flutes, harp, bass clarinet and cor anglais specified in the score. Small wonder that Janáček had offered the opera to Prague first.[20]

Nevertheless, the première was an outright triumph for Janáček. The theatre was completely sold out; the music was immediately perceived by the audience as entirely new in character. And 'the splendour of the costumes, the singing and the type of decoration used in the violin playing, the dance of the young men . . . all this lively bustle convinced everyone', wrote one critic, 'that a good chunk of our Moravian folk life had reached the stage in all its naturalness and truth'.[21]

The applause was incessant. Janáček, lurking pale and excited in the wings, had to take a curtain call straight after Act I. More curtain calls followed after the remaining acts; Preissová also acknowledged the applause from her box. When the performance finished, Janáček – laden with wreaths – was borne on the shoulders of the soloists, still wearing their costumes, to the Beseda House where a party was given to celebrate.

Reviews were favourable. In *Národní politika* the renowned Prague critic Emanuel Chvála praised the novelty of the libretto and the music, emphasizing also the realistic word setting and the dramatic aspect of the music. Nevertheless, he recommended a greater use of polyphony and a more 'symphonic' developmental method in creating the orchestral sound, an objection also voiced by Jan Branberger in *Čas*; in *Radikální listy*, Janáček's pupil Jan Kunc published a review that amounted to a short analysis.[22]

Kamila Urválková and her husband could not attend the première; she had complained about ill health and frequent 'attacks'. Still, she expressed a passionate interest in every detail, and particularly wanted to know about Janáček's feelings when 'showered and drunk with fame'.[23]

'When you read the reviews,' Janáček warned her soon after the première,

> you will think me a real miracle. But have no fear, it is not that bad! If the reviewer of *Čas*, Dr Jan Branberger, had a dig at me, I know much better than he and could list my shortcomings – which I intend to rectify in *The Glowing Roses* [another provisional title for *Osud*] – in greater detail! One thing is certain. [. . .] They have recognized my dramatic talent and this, at the time of Wagner, Charpentier, Dvořák, etc, etc, is indeed important and most flattering for me.[24]

His confidence now restored, in February 1904 Janáček once again approached Kovařovic: 'I do not base my renewed request . . . on the most flattering reviews . . . I appeal as a Czech composer who cannot get himself a hearing. Because of the Moravian style of the work? So it has been said, mistakenly . . . . Naturally, various corrections were necessary in the score . . . many of the criticisms that had been made have now been disposed of.'[25]

Kovařovic agreed to come to Brno to hear the work for himself; the management sent him nine invitations in all but he could not find the time. This was worrying since the orchestra was 'getting more and more depleted' and the strings had to be supplemented by amateurs.[26] The young Marie Kabeláčová, who had created the title-role, was replaced by Růžena Kašparová whose voice was much smaller. Writing to the actress Hana Kvapilová (the wife of the drama director at the Prague National Theatre) in April 1904, Janáček complained: 'I don't go to the theatre now – I don't want to hear my work in such a broken-down state.'[27]

Kovařovic finally made the trip to Brno the following season but he did not change his opinion. Nor was Gustav Mahler – whom Janáček also invited for the première – able to attend any of the performances.[28] He was too busy in Vienna, though he had at least asked for the piano score with a German translation. This was not available at the time, and there the matter ended.

Undeterred, Janáček now devoted more time than ever to composition. He had retired as a music teacher at the Institute and was on a year's leave on grounds of ill-health. He interrupted his work on *Osud* only for a short trip to Warsaw where he had been offered the directorship of the local conservatoire.

This institution was 'in a state of strife because of the line of study and the language to be used', recalled Janáček later. 'As a compromise could not be reached, the Russians turned to me with the offer.'[29] At first Janáček was full of enthusiasm; internal politics and the necessity of teaching in several languages did not deter him. He met the governors and presented them with his plans, but the following day, 1 May 1904, he missed his appointment with the governor general, and as a result he was not given the post.

Dvořák died the same day. Janáček saw him last in November 1901, after the concert given to mark Dvořák's sixtieth birthday. 'It was getting on for ten years since we had seen each other,' he noted in the margin of a special souvenir programme. 'How he had changed – after a mere ten years. He had aged – so had I, of course. Where are the times of yesteryear! How sad I feel – sorry for the years gone by.'[30] The announcement of Dvořák's death was made at a concert of the Warsaw Philharmonic that Janáček attended; the orchestra decided to commemorate the famous composer by including his *Hussite* overture in the programme. Stunned, Janáček listened to the opening chords. 'Uncertain,' he wrote movingly in 1911, 'I stood up, with others, in an overcrowded hall. Can it [really] be true that he has died?'[31]

Back in Brno, he continued to work on *Osud*, although his friendship with Kamila came to an end. Just before her husband received an anonymous letter from Brno about her suspect conduct, she wrote to Janáček how desperately she looked forward to the summer when she might 'fly out' again. She advised Janáček, who had complained of great fatigue, to take a rest: should his health not improve by the summer, 'that would be very *bad* ! ! !'[32] After this letter there was only a brief card from Janáček, who returned to her – no doubt at her husband's request – her full-size portrait. He never met the 'unforgettable Duchess of Luhačovice' again.

In July 1904 Janáček celebrated his fiftieth birthday. Drinking Moravian wine in the Tebich cellar, Janáček's friends – C.M. Hrazdira, Jan Kunc, the writer Elgart-Sokol and others including František Mareš, K.Z. Klíma and Antonín Průša – talked with great gusto about speech melodies, making up examples. What was Janáček's contribution? 'It was the prophecy of a bold spirit, brief, but expressive like a flash of lightning,' remembered Mareš: ' "The novel of my life is not yet at an end." '[33]

The same year, while working on *Osud*, Janáček completed *Four Moravian Male-voice Choruses* which he dedicated to the Moravian Teachers' Choral Society. This now famous amateur male choir had recently been founded, and soon inspired Janáček to write some of his greatest choral works. Janáček first heard the Moravian Teachers (as they became known colloquially) some time during 1904, and at once sent their founder and conductor, Ferdinand Vach, two choruses – *If Only You Knew* and *The Evening Witch*, both to words by Ondřej Přikryl in the dialect of the Haná district (and probably written in 1900). The latter song is witty, and the effect is augmented by Janáček's use of the Lydian mode (with its raised fourth). The third chorus, *Mosquitoes*, is a setting of a folk text he previously used in *Rákos Rákóczy*; the melodic line is heavily chromaticized. *Parting* is based on a folk text (notated by Sušil), and Janáček preserved the character of the original. The first two choruses were premièred in 1905.

In April 1904 Janáček had considered two further operatic librettos. *The Farmer's Woman* was Preissová's celebrated first play; Janáček returned to the project in 1907 but eventually abandoned it – its theme seemed too close to that of *Jenůfa*. Preissová herself suggested to him her one-act play, *Spring Song*, but Janáček was not inspired by the story of an elderly artist who sacrifices his love for a girl in favour of a younger suitor.

He began casting around for a suitable operatic libretto yet again in 1905. He toyed with the idea of a 'national' opera, based on the fairy-tale *Johnny the Hero*. The story was versified in a folk style by the Moravian writer Karel Dostál-Lutinov, but some scenes were written in too naive a vein, and Janáček soon abandoned the project.

The social changes that had begun the previous year throughout the Czech-speaking provinces of the Austro-Hungarian Empire continued in 1905. The Czechs in Moravia now wished to establish their own university, but in Brno they were still in the minority; Charles University in Prague was the only one open to them. On 1 October the city's Germans, supported by others from throughout the empire, called a rally in protest against the Czechs' request. A counter-protest was held the same day, and clashes with the police and eventually the army followed. A 20-year-old Czech joiner's apprentice was stabbed with a bayonet and later died in hospital. The Czech university in Brno was not to be founded until 1919.

Janáček was distraught, and his immediate response was to compose a piano sonata in three movements, *Street Scene 1.X.1905*.[34] The work's inscription reads: 'The white marble staircase of the Beseda House in Brno . . . . Here an ordinary worker František Pavlík falls, stained with blood . . . . He only came to plead for a university . . . . And was killed by cruel murderers.'

The opening movement, 'Presentiment', is a kind of ballad in E flat minor, with a melancholy first subject circling around the note f'', and in turn forming a part of the second simple, chordal subject. The piece was never described as a 'sonata' in Janáček's lifetime, but the first movement is in a clearly structured sonata form. The second movement ('Elegy', later renamed 'Death'), in the same key, has often been likened to a funeral march; its theme is derived from the first movement's second measure, the 'presentiment' of the title. Dotted rhythms persist throughout, and Janáček consistently develops the melody off the main beats. The movement ends abruptly, and it is not easy to judge the work as a whole since the final movement has not survived. Janáček destroyed it in 1906 after hearing the work at a rehearsal for a concert of music by leading contemporary Czech composers: in a fit of depression he snatched the sonata from the stunned pianist, his former pupil Ludmila Tučková, tore off the finale and burned it on the spot in the stove in the rehearsal room. Later, after a private performance in Prague, he threw both the remaining movements into the river Vltava. 'They did not want to sink,' he remembered. 'The pages bulged and floated on the water like white swans.'[35] Fortunately, Mrs Tučková – forewarned by her previous experience – had made her own copy of the two movements. Janáček did not allow the sonata to be published until 1924.

Janáček's social awareness has sometimes been underestimated outside his native country; some scholars have thought that the evidence of it in his piano sonata and some of his late male-voice choruses was later exaggerated. But at this time, patriotic sentiments and social consciousness often went hand in hand, and it is improbable that a composer of Janáček's background and sensitivity would remain unaware of the changing nature of the nationalist struggle in Bohemia and Moravia. He returned to social themes in October

1906, when he wrote the first of his great male-voice choruses to words by Petr Bezruč. In the meantime, in the early summer of 1906, he completed *Osud*.

This experimental opera, though rarely staged, is essential for a full understanding of Janáček's development as an operatic composer. Its subject – a contemporary life – was a new departure for Janáček; he never returned to a theme rooted as strongly in folklore as *Jenůfa*. The musical language he had developed by then remained virtually unchanged, but in *Osud* Janáček also attempted to create a new style. He was intrigued by the various techniques deployed in operas he had seen during his visits to Prague around that time: apart from Charpentier's *Louise* he admired Puccini, whose *Tosca* he saw in the autumn of 1903. For all its autobiographical slant, *Osud* is thus also Janáček's response to operatic novelties of the time.

The story is set partly in Luhačovice: Míla Válková, an elegant young woman, encounters there the composer Živný, with whom she had once had an affair, and whose son Doubek she bore. When the relationship was terminated, Živný had vented his bitterness by composing an opera, as yet unfinished, in which Míla was pilloried. The couple's interest in each other is reawakened, and they decide to leave together. Míla's mother, who still hates Živný, is so aghast at this new development that she loses her reason.

Four years later, the couple are married and living with their son and Míla's deranged mother. Živný is still obsessed with his unfinished opera. His bitter memories are mocked by Míla's mother; convinced that he is in fact interested only in her family's money, she attacks him. Míla tries to intervene, and in the ensuing struggle the mother leaps from the balcony to her death, dragging Míla with her.

Eleven years pass, and the opera – though still unfinished – is about to be performed. Talking to his students about the work, Živný becomes increasingly agitated, and it is clear that the plot mirrors his own doomed relationship. A violent storm breaks out; a flash of lightning seems to strike the hall and Živný faints. He revives but, half-demented, he intones snatches of music from the opera. The finale, he stresses, is still 'in God's hands'.

Janáček's colourful spa in Act 1 came straight from life. The artists, as well as 'an old Slovak woman, priests, academics, civil servants, daytrippers, schoolmistresses and schoolgirls' would have been typical of the promenaders that he would have met during his daily walks in Luhačovice, and the whole mildly frivolous scene provides a striking background for the unfolding drama.

Some of the main concerns of the opera – the inevitability of love and of its loss and a marriage perhaps destined to be destroyed – are portrayed in Act 2. Živný's text frequently reads like Janáček's own monologue, the uneasy atmosphere corresponding only too closely to his own marriage to Zdenka, which was once more in serious trouble.

Živný is obviously a hero in the Romantic mould, but much in the character of Míla is unclear. Janáček does not comment at all on the stigma that she would have had to live with at the time as an unmarried mother; in Act 2, her distress and guilt are unexplained, as is the age of her son, the pretentiously named Doubek [Oaklet]: in Act 1 he is four, in Act 2 – four years later – he is still only four. And the spectacular deaths of Míla and her mother are probably unique even by nineteenth-century operatic standards, despite the contemporary taste for strong situations. Janáček added the character of the mother while revising the opera; to a degree, she is derived from nineteenth-century operatic conventions, but he went to great lengths to depict her insanity realistically, even studying speech melodies at a Brno mental asylum.[36]

Janáček's telescopic view of the story is fully revealed in Act 3: the hero of Živný's opera, the composer Lenský, is in fact Živný himself, and although Janáček does not always identify with Živný, sometimes he does.[37] An artist, Janáček seems to be saying, rediscovers his life in his work. Janáček does not satirize or condemn 'ordinary' existence and 'normality', but he does contrast them with the realm of creativity.

Janáček does not accord his heroine any special chivalry (although her name obviously derives from that of *Kamila Urválková*). There is no evidence that he saw a performance of Čelanský's opera, or the score.[38] Any parallels between *Osud* and *Kamilla* seem to have arisen spontaneously either from what Janáček heard from Kamila, or from real life.

Osud was not staged during Janáček's lifetime, and there have been only a few productions since his death in 1928. The opera's problematic libretto, and its mannered Czech, have had their share of criticism (though it is surprising how different the text sounds in an intelligent English translation).[39] Although the many echoes, cross-references, parodies and juxtapositions in the opera continue to intrigue musicologists and listeners alike, Czech audiences tend to think the developments of Act 2 bizarre.[40]

The young and inexperienced librettist Fedora Bartošová is not necessarily to blame for all the shortcomings of the text: Janáček revised the libretto several times, but he did not use her new Act 2, dropping her suggestions. She merely versified his scenario, and he was happy with the result: 'Flowing, melodious verse, . . . so new . . . Not only are all the main characters clear, but so also are the episodic ones.'[41] Despite his praise, he restructured her verse even more radically than Preissová's prose in *Jenůfa*.[42]

The music of *Osud*, on the other hand, is among the most lyrical and most passionate Janáček ever wrote, and its voluptuousness was quite new to his work. As in *Jenůfa*, much of the melodic structure is created by repetition and the piling up of short units, but by grouping these melodic units inventively, and by making innumerable variations of simple motifs, Janáček often creates an illusion of a longer, freely flowing cantilena; its intense lyricism is further emphasized by the rich sound of the orchestra. Speech melodies are used too; by now they have become fully integrated into Janáček's style.

Many musical motifs in *Osud* are strongly associated with situations and emotions; various writers have pointed out the opera's monothematicism, the powerful role of the sun in its visual imagery, and the way this is reflected in the music.[43] Examples abound: the waltz in Act 1 is preceded by a brief prelude evoking the sun filtering through the treetops; later on the sun's brightness is described precisely in the stage directions. Many of the spa guests, including Míla, worship the sun; another character, Dr Suda, sings an ode to it.[44] Accordingly, Janáček's 'motif of the sun' (which consists of a combination of his favourite intervals of a second, fourth and fifth) appears several times.[45]

Despite the opera's monothematicism there is a great variety of mood in the music: the stirring opening waltz (whose theme returns several times); the gaiety and parody as the schoolmistresses rehearse a song; the frivolousness and innocence of the numerous, seemingly unrelated, cameos at the end of Act 1.

The scene with Míla's son asking 'What is love?' has perhaps the most lyrical music in Act 2; the speech melodies of the question and answer are dreamily repeated in the orchestra against a spiky ostinato motif, also based on a speech melody.[46]

In the melodic structure of *Osud*, the interval of an ascending perfect fifth appears frequently; neatly, Živný's cry of 'fatum' [destiny, or 'osud' of the title] is set as a descending perfect fifth. And Míla's mother sings the parody of this cry a minor second below.[47]

There are no conventional arias in *Osud*, but the two protagonists are given several monologues. Those of Živný are long, but even the briefest phrases contain some of the most haunting music of the opera (the beautifully shaped 'cizím bolem' [a stranger's pain]; in Rodney Blumer's English version 'bitter memories', Act 3, Scene 2). The part, set exceptionally high, is taxing; in Act 3 the voice soars above the orchestra in an almost manic fashion.

Complex choral scenes are deployed in Act 1 (with a cast of twenty individual characters); Act 3 contains some of Janáček's best male choruses. Dance also plays an important role: the catching opening waltz is suggestive of a spa band, while Dr Suda's ode to the sun in Act 1 is based on a Moravian folk-dance.[48] Other elements of Moravian folk music, such as mirror rhythms and the embellishment of the melodic line at several levels, have by now permeated by Janáček's style.[49]

Instrumental colour is used effectively in *Osud*, especially the woodwind and the brass: an ironic horn call greets Živný's first appearance, and the horns also aptly announce the return of the day-trippers; an oboe accompanies the mother's wanderings, and some haunting music has been given to the violin. By now Janáček was confident enough to write directly into full score.

Although the composer provided very specific stage instructions, staging *Osud* is not an easy task (although cinematic techniques might benefit production). Above all, it is necessary to achieve the right balance between the realistic details and what often seems deliberately *un*realistic in the story.

Osud provides a bridge between *Jenůfa* and Janáček's later operatic masterpieces; the 'golden stream' of music which supposedly flowed from the imagination of the hero of Živný's opera, Lenský ('a short-tempered, lonely man', in some ways modelled on Janáček himself), is one of the most radiant Janáček ever wrote. To paraphrase Živný's words, this opera should no longer fail to please the public taste.

Brno theatre showed a keen interest in *Osud* soon after its completion in June 1906; a producer and a designer were engaged, and rehearsals with the soloists began in the autumn. As the opening of the new Vinohrady Theatre in Prague for November 1907 was announced around the same time, Janáček – once again hoping to succeed in the capital – withdrew the work, submitting it to the Vinohrady in May 1907. By a bizarre coincidence, the designated head of this new opera house was none other than Čelanský, the author of *Kamilla*, but he assured Janáček that *Osud* would be accepted. Yet when the theatre's director Šubert wanted to see the libretto, Janáček suddenly lost heart. The writer he approached to have the problematic libretto rewritten first agreed but then later prevaricated.[50] Brno continued to show interest but Janáček insisted on a Prague première. Unfortunately, Čelanský soon left the Vinohrady Theatre; Janáček revised the work, but many complications followed, including a lawsuit (withdrawn when Čelanský returned in 1913 for a single season). In the end Janáček waited until 1914 when, bitterly disappointed after seven years of frustration, he withdrew the score.

In 1906, the year *Osud* was completed, Janáček continued to travel to Prague to see various productions at the National Theatre: apart from Gluck's *Orfeo* and Beethoven's *Fidelio* he saw Massenet's *Werther*, Wagner's *Lohengrin* and Dvořák's *Dimitrij* (whose libretto he disliked).[51] The opera that particularly struck him was Strauss's *Salome*, which he saw in May that year, only five months after its première in Dresden.

He also continued his folkloristic expeditions, following the foundation in 1904 of a committee for the study of folk-song in Moravia and Silesia. In 1906 he made a field trip to several villages on the river Ostravice near his native region; in 1907 he made two trips, also to north-eastern Moravia. He even crossed over to Slovakia, then ruled by Hungary, and 'escaped the Hungarian *gendarmes* through the Karlovice Pass'.[52]

Some of these expeditions were made from Luhačovice, which he often made his 'headquarters'.

'On his pilgrimage in search of folk-song', we read in a contemporary article,

> Janáček sets out for unknown regions, diverging far from railways so that he may find the people and their poetry untarnished. He hires a gypsy with a small carriage, to which a thin little mare is harnessed. [. . .] If the carriage travels up the hill, Janáček gets down and helps to push. When it runs down the hill, he walks alongside if he wants to reach the valley in full health and all limbs intact. Members of the Luhačovice society have no inkling of all this, when they see him walking on the promenade in a faultless attire which he changes perhaps even three times a day.[53]

During his expeditions on the Slovak side of the border Janáček was enchanted with his finds. 'I have discovered something new in folk music, something quite extraordinary,' he told the Czech composer and critic Adolf Piskáček during a visit to Prague in 1906:

> The best title for it would be 'Nocturnes'. These are strange folk-songs for several voices, and interestingly harmonized. I took them

down during my rambles through the region not explored by other collectors. [. . .] At dusk, after the sunset, girls meet in the backyards; the best singer stands in front of the rest and leads the singing. She intones and the others join in, clasping hands firmly, with an unusual melody which carries over the hilltops, falls into the valleys and dies away beyond the river in the dark forests.[54]

Mesmerized by the beauty of these songs, Janáček arranged them in 1906 as *Folk Nocturnes*, for a female 'folk duet' and piano; they were first performed in 1907.[55]

In March 1907 Janáček published an article describing his field trip to the villages on the river Ostravice. He was particularly interested in the songs' cymbalom accompaniment:

Kotek places the cymbalom on the table, and the tremulous sound of the songs he recalls soon begins to clang in the room. [. . .] How many years he has been playing at dances and at weddings throughout the countryside, both in Moravia and in Silesia! [. . .] In the certainty of joy that here in Moravia, there are some three thousand living folk-songs, folk-songs of pure national style and a variety of types, I cheer up.

But there is more to the article than Janáček's delight in rural music-making. He was already casting around for another libretto, and the piece reflects his state of mind:

Had I wanted to have such a scene from the Silesian 'Meistersinger' on stage, I would have mixed the long chords, whose shaky sound reaches through the hot air right up to the Mount Lysá − chords which pour their music over the sharp Mount Ondřejník, chords as unusual and mysterious as the Slavonic North, towards which rushes the river Ostravice − with the motifs of the people's cries, their chatter, the bellowing of the herd and the angelus of the Frýdlant bells flying right up to us.[56]

The dramatist in Janáček clearly craved a subject for a new opera, now that his style was fully established.

The reference to Wagner is not accidental. In 1885 Janáček had published in *Hudební listy* a short analysis of Wagner's *Tristan und Isolde,* and his conclusions make fascinating reading. 'In harmonic progressions,' he writes, 'Wagner is really in his element.' Yet in the second instalment of the analysis, published the following month, Janáček writes that 'relentless modulations, the real element of progressions, tire us: the composition that cultivates only such progressions strains our spirit.' The article ends on a completely different note: 'Is it necessary to copy this "modern eccentricity"? Must the "modern" drama depend on this exclusive formation of progressions? Is there anything *Czech* in this "Wagnerianism"?'[57]

His quarrel with Wagner continued for some time. On the programme of *Lohengrin*, for instance, which he saw in Prague in 1906, he made the following notes: 'In the speech the moods follow as do the layers. Each mood – makes it own layer. The roar in the orchestra does not suit the situation. This is babbling *plus*, in music what is already in the words.'[58] Clearly, such large orchestral forces did not meet with Janáček's approval, nor did Wagner's aim to provide a commentary on the action in the orchestra; it has been said that Wagner's orchestra becomes the voice of the composer himself perpetually talking. Janáček's orchestra, on the other hand, frequently says what the *character* thinks (in Act 1 of *Osud*, for instance, there is an orchestral interlude before Míla's and Živný's meeting face to face, when the characters remain on stage but are silent). Wagner's operas, which for many years in Bohemia and Moravia were considered the yardstick of musical value, continued to irk Janáček well into the twentieth century.

Meanwhile, his quest for a new libretto continued. In 1906 Q.M. Vyskočil proposed to Janáček his mystery play, *The Soul of the Bells*, but nothing came of this, nor did Janáček pursue his initial interest in *The Mintmaster's Wife*, a historical comedy by the popular Czech playwright Ladislav Stroupežnický. In 1907 he turned to Tolstoy's *Anna Karenina*. Writing directly to a Russian text, he had Russian audiences in mind but although he made some intriguing sketches, only a fragment of the opera survived.

The previous autumn, inspired by a collection of poems by Petr Bezruč, *Silesian Songs*, Janáček had returned to social themes such as discrimination, and the patriotic struggle. Bezruč (the name translates as 'the armless') was the pen name of the Brno post-office clerk Vladimír Vašek (1867–1958), who had been born in a region of Silesia whose Czech population had suffered much social oppression. Bezruč only wrote two collections, but the form and style of *Silesian Songs* (published in 1906) made a strong impact on Janáček: deliberate, strong verbal contrasts, incisive attributes and dialect are frequently used, and words or groups of words are often repeated to drive a point home. His appeal to national conscience to recognize the desperate situation of the oppressed Czechs in Silesia could have hardly found a better advocate than Janáček, whose background was so similar to his own. 'And this is your brother, they say?' Janáček wrote breathlessly to Olga Vašková, the secretary of the Russian Circle in Brno which he had founded in 1898. 'Would he please give me permission to set his *Maryčka Magdónova*?'[59]

Janáček eventually began his 'Silesian' trilogy of male-voice choruses by setting another of Bezruč's poems, *Kantor Halfar*, based on an actual event. Halfar was an assistant teacher in the district of Těšín (his brother, also a teacher, had introduced Janáček to some local songs in 1893). But committed Czech speakers such as Halfar did not win the approval of their German-speaking supervisors under the regime of the notorious Archduke Frederick, nicknamed Marquis Gero.[60] Halfar waited in vain for a permanent post; as result he lost his sweetheart, and finally he committed suicide.

Janáček set each of the three verses of the poem in two contrasting sections. In the opening motif he used his favourite intervals of a second and a fourth; a chromaticized motif accompanies the description of Halfar's misfortunes. The announcement of Halfar's death is a dramatic feat: the tenors are interrupted twice, with the disbelieving basses enquiring: 'Kantor? Kantor Halfar?' By constant juxtaposition of moods and timbres, Janáček enhances the dramatic potential of the text. The work ends in the major, though Janáček fittingly delays the final tonic chord until Halfar is laid to rest.

Maryčka Magdónova, the second of the three choruses, is the story of the orphaned daughter of a miner, who has to care for several younger brothers and sisters. All are hungry and cold, and the desperate Maryčka decides to go gathering sticks in a wood that belongs to 'Marquis Gero'. She is caught and taken to the nearby town by a *gendarme*; to avoid public mockery, she hurls herself into the river Ostravice.

Janáček wrote two versions of this chorus, completing the first some time in the autumn of 1906, and the second, quite different version, the following spring. Retaining the ballad's strophic form, he used several techniques to accentuate the dramatic action. By stressing the heroine's name repeatedly in the refrain, changing and repeating words (at one point, three textual variants are sung at the same time), changing an original question into dialogue, and using different rhythms in the individual voice parts, he greatly speeds up the pace.[61] The first of the trilogy to be performed, it was also the first to bring Janáček international fame. The première was given in April 1908, in the Moravian city of Prostějov (where the work, because of the powerful social comment implicit in it, was likened to 'a Socialist meeting');[62] the same month it was also performed in Paris, during the Moravian Teachers' tour.

The final work of the trilogy, *The Seventy Thousand*, was not written until 1909. Its title refers to the last seventy thousand inhabitants of the district of Těšín, who had not yet abandoned Czech, their mother tongue. One hundred thousand Czechs in the region had been Germanized, the same number had been Polonized. Only seventy thousand remained for whom, symbolically, seventy thousand graves were being dug. Janáček used his favourite technique of 'staggered' parts; an added male-voice quartet speaks for the 'soul' of the oppressed, and it is contrasted effectively with a mercilessly high tenor solo. Like many of Janáček's other choral works, *The Seventy Thousand* is based on a single melodic idea; the quick changes of tonality and tempo aptly convey the mood of accusation, agitation and defiance. Janáček rewrote the original 1909 version in 1913, offering the work to the Moravian Teachers, but their conductor returned the chorus as 'unsingable'. In 1914 it was finally given a première in Prague, by the Prague Teachers' Choral Society; it was an instant success.[63] All three pieces represent an entirely novel direction in Czech choral writing, and still astonish with their vigour.

In 1908 Janáček returned to the piano. Five pieces in his cycle *On the Overgrown Path*, originally conceived for the harmonium, were published in 1901–2 (when Janáček was still working on *Jenůfa*) in a periodical collection for this instrument, *Slav Melodies*. By 1908 seven pieces had been completed, and an enlightened Prague publisher, Bedřich Kočí, suggested the possibility of bringing out a set of Janáček's piano compositions. This prompted Janáček to add a further five; the entire set was finally published in 1911 in Brno.

The first ten brief, intensely intimate pieces show a different side to Janáček – withdrawn, often agonized, with only rare glimpses of quiet happiness. Some are fragile, flickering recollections of childhood and reminiscences of Hukvaldy, others are painful memories of his daughter Olga. Although Janáček was a very good pianist, he never wrote a large-scale work for the instrument; his few solo piano works are perhaps a secret diary, tracing his emotional as well as musical development over the years.

Despite some sustained chords, the five pieces which were completed earliest ('Our Evenings', 'A Blown-away Leaf', 'The Barn

Owl Has not Flown Away', 'The Madonna of Frýdek' and 'Good Night') are equally suited to harmonium and piano; the added pieces, 'Come with us', 'They Chattered Like Swallows', 'Words Fail', 'Such Infinite Anguish' and 'In Tears', all show a definite instrumental style. Written in simple forms, they have clear textures, and the melodic line, reserved largely for the right hand, consists of characteristically short units. Frequent ostinatos and rhythmic irregularities, such as asymmetrical phrase lengths, are derived from Moravian folk music, as are the harmonies. Janáček's piano music has been criticized for its elusiveness, and for being unrewarding to play. Yet this view surely arises from ignorance of the Moravian idiom, as well as from a mis-judged approach to playing. According to the great Czech pianist (and Janáček's last pupil) Rudolf Firkušný, 'Janáček's touch at the keyboard was exquisitely refined, and he sometimes complained that his piano music was played much too roughly'.[64]

The title of the cycle is drawn from Moravian folk poetry, and sug-gests a time gone by. Like Schumann and Debussy, Janáček added titles to the individual pieces only before their publication, when he also arranged their order as it is known today. Some titles are puz-zling, probably because they are personal. In 1912 he wrote to Ezechiel Ambros: 'Let the listener add to the titles of the individual numbers what is appropriate from his own life.'[65]

The titles as well as the contents of the last three pieces in this set, 'Such Infinite Anguish', 'In Tears', and 'The Barn Owl Has not Flown Away', are poignant. The first is a phrase Janáček constantly used when he wrote about his daughter Olga's illness; the hooting of the barn owl in the last number evokes this harbinger of death, which had already hovered around Hukvaldy at the time Janáček composed the piece. The pain of Olga's slow, inevitable end is all too clear in the penultimate number, written after her death. 'Perhaps you will sense tears,' wrote Janáček to the critic Dr Jan Branberger. 'During the hot summer nights that angelic person lay in deathly anguish.'[66]

Of the five untitled pieces in the second series of this cycle only the first was published in Janáček's lifetime; they are even freer in mood than the first series, and their ruminative character recalls his later piano cycle, *In the Mists*. The overall feeling is still nostalgic, and once again Janáček's short-breathed melodic thinking and building by repetition and contrast are evident.

Janáček's next chamber work was inspired by Russian literature. In the autumn of 1908 he completed a piano trio based on Tolstoy's *Kreutzer Sonata*. He rewrote it for a performance given in April 1909 as part of the Tolstoy celebrations, organized by the Friends of the Art Club in Brno, but the work has not survived. The idea was resurrected only fifteen years later as a string quartet.[67]

In 1908 Janáček had also considered another operatic subject, once again a folk drama. When the authors of *Maryša*, the Mrštík brothers, refused to give permission for its adaptation, Janáček unexpectedly turned to a satirical novel by the Czech writer, Svatopluk Čech, *The Excursion of Mr Brouček to the Moon* and (much later, in 1917) its sequel, *The Excursion of Mr Brouček to the Fifteenth Century*.

Janáček was familiar with Čech's work: as early as 1887, during the work on his first opera, *Šárka*, he had published an excerpt from the novel in his periodical, *Hudební listy*.[68] He had since planned several works based on Čech's writings; in 1895 he studied his *Slave Songs* but the projected cantata came to nothing.[69]

The Excursions was, once again, a challenging subject, and Janáček summed up the story of his painful search for a librettist in a *feuilleton* published in 1917:

> On the ground plan of Svatopluk Čech were grafted the thoughts of Karel Mašek, variations by Holý, additions by Dr Janke and witty interferences by Gellner. Mahen has remained the master of his task; Viktor Dyk carved out a motto for the work; F.S. Procházka made his appeal through songs; Dr Max Brod added the twilight of caricature. I could, like the folk-song, ask jokingly: 'Wait, stand still. Count heads, are we all here?'[70]

In 1909 Janáček complained in a letter to Artuš Rektorys that he had been obliged to rewrite the first scene of the opera no fewer than four times.[71] The odyssey continued for five years, even though some of the music had already been written. In April 1913 Janáček finished the second scene, and then, irritated by the problems over the libretto, shelved the work. The composition – and its problems – resurfaced a few years later.

In the years before the First World War Janáček was also repeatedly and seriously ill. He suffered from frequent attacks of laryngitis and bronchitis, and from great pain in his joints. He often sought medical help and tried to find relief at various spas; he was particularly fond of Luhačovice where he was treated for rheumatism, and which he described as 'an annual congress of beautiful women'.[72]

Contemporary diagnoses of his condition varied, and most often it was described as gout. But in 1982 Dr Josef Sajner made a posthumous diagnosis on the basis of Janáček's correspondence and other documents, and diagnosed a chronic infection.[73] Janáček had suffered from especially persistent sinusitis and had been treated for it for decades. To relieve the condition, he had had an operation when he was 39: a tiny metal tube was inserted into the cavity of an extracted tooth, and he rinsed his sinuses through this tube daily. One can hardly imagine how he managed this, and avoided further infection.

In 1906 he continued to make the daily rinses. Sinusitis can be very painful and debilitating: frequent and severe headaches, insomnia, laryngitis and bronchitis were some of the consequences of Janáček's condition, and the infection was obviously carried to other parts of the body. Janáček's painful inflammation of the joints, according to Dr Sajner, was *arthritis infectiosa*. The disease first became evident in 1905, when Janáček complained of 'rheumatism' and pain in his hands even when he was not playing the piano.[74] In 1906 the problem escalated, and he lost his customary vigour.

Two years later Janáček's brother František died, soon after returning from Russia to settle down at Hukvaldy; in 1909 there were illnesses, resignations and even a death among the staff at the Organ School. Janáček, no longer slim, developed minor heart trouble and he also suffered from nervous complaints. That summer he took a special cure, including a strict diet; as a result he suddenly lost a great deal of weight. He was also upset by the gall bladder operation that Zdenka had to undergo unexpectedly. Eventually the 55-year-old Janáček suffered a serious heart attack in Hukvaldy and subsequently decided to have a course of treatment at a well-known Moravian spa, Teplice. But he could not be admitted immediately and so returned to Hukvaldy; on a postcard to Zdenka he complained of an irregular heartbeat. He was recommended to take a lot of fresh air but fewer long walks.

Despite his health problems he worked hard. In February 1910 he completed his *Fairy-tale* for cello and piano, another work inspired by Russian literature. Originally entitled 'The Story of Czar Berendey', it is based on an epic poem of the same name by V.A. Zhukovsky (1783–1852). The Czarevich Ivan is unwittingly promised at birth by his father to the Ruler of the Underworld, Kashchey. When Ivan finally sets out to combat Kashchey, he encounters by chance Kashchey's daughter Marya (who duly falls in love with him). After many trials and tribulations, Ivan and Marya are saved and escape. Although the music does not reflect the story in detail, the two instruments seem to represent the two main characters, and their sound world is among the most poetic Janáček created.

In the opening movement (like the rest of the work, in G flat major), the pizzicato motif in the cello announces the Czarevich against the softly-flowing melody on the piano – the Princess Marya. A dialogue in canon form soon opens between the instruments. The 'love duet' accelerates, running recklessly over spiky ostinatos and off-beats, and briefly returns before the end, with an ostinato scurrying off into the distance. In the second movement, another dialogue develops and this is followed by a broader, lyrical cantilena on the piano. The various themes return and develop, as do the harmonies, and the lyricism is heightened. In the finale, a strikingly 'Russian' theme, based on a major triad, hops and skips in the cello before various short melodic units are piled up, giving an illusion of a broad cantilena. After a brief return to the 'Russian' theme the work ends in the major – an obvious happy conclusion. *Fairy-tale* was rewritten in 1923; the original version was premièred in 1910.[75]

Later in 1910 the Janáčeks moved to a new house.[76] Three years before, the Society for the Promotion of Church Music had bought, at Janáček's suggestion, new premises for the Organ School. The large house on the corner of today's Kounicova and Smetanova Streets, built in 1894, was known as 'the Greek villa', on account of its Neoclassical style. It was quite a walk up the hill from the family flat in Monastery Square, and since Janáček categorically refused to use any of the German-owned trams in the city, Zdenka insisted that, for reasons of his health, they find a well-equipped house with a garden nearer the school.

Eventually Janáček asked the Society to replace the now disused stables in the garden of the 'villa' with a house for the use of the school's director, who would repay the cost in the form of rent.[77] This is how the Janáčeks' 'cottage' came into being. In July that year the composer left the flat where he had written his first four operas, the cantata *Amarus* and the Bezruč trilogy, and where both of his children died tragically young.

The new home brought the Janáčeks much peace. Built to Janáček's own specifications, the house, with four main rooms, was smaller than their old flat but it had electric lighting and a proper bathroom, although there was no gas. The building faced the garden to the north, with an entrance through a small verandah. There was a large salon, with a slightly smaller study behind; between the study and the kitchen was the bedroom whose windows opened on to the verandah. Most of the furniture came from Zdenka's dowry. Fine pieces of embroidery were displayed throughout the cottage, and in the salon stood an old spinning-wheel which Zdenka had inherited from her grandmother. Among the pictures was a Russian icon that Janáček had bought for Zdenka.

Janáček's study was light and quiet, and it was the warmest room in the cottage. In the middle stood an Ehrbar grand piano; between the west-facing windows was a large chest beautifully painted in Moravian folk style by Anežka Uprková the wife of the painter Joža Uprka. Janáček stored his manuscripts in this chest, and Zdenka frequently consigned to it sketches which he had thrown out, thus saving much that might have otherwise been lost. Above it, as was traditional in a country cottage, hung three pictures of saints painted on glass; opposite the windows was Janáček's bed, with a large framed photograph of Olga above. By the window was his desk, with smaller photographs of Dvořák and Olga, and with the Janáčeks' wedding portraits above it; on the wall between the bookcase and the windows hung photographs of musicians who had performed Janáček's works.

Both Janáček and Zdenka took particular pleasure in the garden. Separated from the main courtyard of the Organ School by a low iron fence, with a yellow sand path leading to the cottage, it was full of flowers – irises and lilies-of-the-valley among ferns brought from Hukvaldy – and several lilac trees filled the house with their fragrance each spring. There were a few fruit trees and the Janáčeks grew some vegetables. The garden was full of birdsong: blackbirds, thrushes and finches used to congregate there.

Once the term started at the Organ School 'there was always a lively bustle, laughter and shouting as the students talked before or after lessons. Every now and then some of the professors, especially the ladies [among them], popped over if only for a few words with Madam,' remembered the Janáčeks' maidservant Stejskalová. 'It was busier in the house at that time, there was a good deal more life and happiness.'[78]

The Janáčeks continued to attend concerts and plays, and occasionally met their acquaintances at various Brno coffee houses. Their circle included the painter and photographer J.L. Šichan (who had been Janáček's best man at his wedding), and the physician František Veselý with his wife, the singer and writer Marie Calma-Veselá. They rarely talked about music: 'My husband used to say that he does not want to be bothered with it in company,' recalled Zdenka. These acquaintances were not close friends: Janáček 'had many good acquaintances but he never had a friend, a real friend whom he would love like a brother'.[79] Zdenka also had a circle of female friends, but many evenings were spent quietly at home; in winter the Janáčeks were often 'as if cut off from the world,' Stejskalová remembered. 'There was no telephone, master would not hear of it, and the gramophones, which at that time were only capable of screeching and roaring, used to infuriate him.'[80]

The peaceful atmosphere suited the Janáčeks. 'We used to read, or else I sat at my work and he would pace up and down the bedroom and we talked,' recalled Zdenka. 'He was always full of ideas about what could be done to further the musical life in Brno . . . . There were times when he seemed to be overflowing with the desire to talk about his work. [. . .] I looked forward to those evenings as the most beautiful thing the day could bring me . . .'.[81]

The first work to be written in the new house was a brief cantata for solo tenor, male chorus and orchestra to words by Martin Kurt, *Čarták on the Soláň*, a simple and rather sentimental story. The poet in this 'nocturne' from the Beskydy mountains is pining for the 'pale sweetheart' he had left behind. As he comes up to 'čarták' (an inn) of the title, a smugglers' lair, the strains of the cymbalom are heard and the innkeeper's pretty daughter appears in the doorway. Soon they dance together and, predictably, the poet forgets all about his former love as the starry night falls.

Janáček composed the cantata at the invitation of the Orlice male choir in the Moravian town of Prostějov, for its fiftieth anniversary. Sketching the outline as he read the poem, he adapted the text only slightly. The cantata contains two slow sections, with another in a quick dance rhythm in the middle, and there are two motifs symbolizing the poet's two loves. The first is a descending melody in a mixture of two modes; the choir introduces the second motif, composed of fourths and thirds. As the poet recalls his beloved, the motifs combine, and a frenzied dance follows. The work, completed by February 1911, is among Janáček's least-performed works; it has charm but not the vigour and character of his other choral works.

In the summer of 1911 the Janáčeks visited the Adriatic coast, spending three weeks at the popular resort of Crikvenica, and making a number of excursions throughout the Istrian peninsula. They even experienced a storm at sea, and Janáček – the only passenger on deck – notated the speech melodies of the raging elements. 'What did I look for at this resort?' he later wrote wistfully: 'Teaching thirty, thirty-five or forty hours a week, conducting a choral society, directing concerts, leading the monastery choir, composing *Jenůfa*, getting married, losing one's children – one needed to forget oneself.'[82]

Janáček's health did not improve after this holiday. At the beginning of the winter of 1911 he suffered a particularly bad bout of his chronic infection; his hands, feet, and even his ears swelled up and he could not move for the pain. Regular massage gave him some relief, but he was bedbound for some five months. Even so, he continued to teach in his study at home, and to compose.

In 1912 he found another subject which greatly appealed to him. Svatopluk Čech's poem *The Fiddler's Child* is the story of an old fiddler who dies, leaving nothing but his fiddle and his child. An old woman, keeping watch over the infant, sees the fiddler's ghost at midnight trying to lure the child through his music to another, happier life. Just as he kisses the baby, the old woman drives him away with the sign of the cross. In the morning, the village mayor finds the child dead, and the fiddle gone.[83]

In Janáček's 'ballad for orchestra' the fiddler is still alive when the child falls ill. The character of the old woman is omitted, but the omnipotent village mayor is a strong presence. In an article written for the projected first performance in 1914, Janáček reveals how he instinctively thought in terms of specific instruments for specific themes, without the constant shifting of the theme from one instrument to another. Thus the solo violin, portraying 'the whole character of the old fiddler', is given a prominent role; the moans of the ailing child are expressed by 'the lamenting oboe'; the mayor's steps are 'measured by cellos with the double basses', and 'the bass clarinet spreads fear of him by the same motif'.[84] The shades of mood are well expressed, and the ballad's sound world recalls the voluptuousness of the music in *Osud*. Yet, as the work was considered odd, the 1914 première was cancelled. The score was published on the occasion of Janáček's sixtieth birthday, but the work only received its première in Prague three years later.[85]

Thus Janáček enjoyed very few successes outside Brno after the première of *Jenůfa* there in January 1904. Not a single note of his music was heard at the Czech Music Festival in Prague in April 1904. By 1908 all hopes for a Prague production of *Jenůfa* had gone; Janáček's fourth opera, *Osud*, remained unperformed. And the Bezruč choruses were often considered too difficult to sing. Despite Janáček's characteristic deep involvement in all he did, from his folklore studies to composition, despite the contentment he found in his new home, these were years of increasing self-doubt and bitterness.

Some of this is reflected in his piano cycle *In the Mists*, completed by April 1912. Janáček originally entered the four unnamed pieces in a competition; their collective title has been attributed by Jaroslav Vogel to the 'misty' atmosphere resulting from the use of keys with five or six flats.

After Smetana, in whose work virtuosity and Lisztian grandeur are combined with lyricism, Czech piano music gravitated largely towards the 'lyric miniature'. Janáček started from such miniatures and only slowly progressed to larger concepts.[86] The textures of his piano compositions are sparse, and the writing is economical; the sound is often deliberately simplified and uncluttered. Three-part writing is usually used, the melody is reserved largely for the right hand, and there are many short, rhythmic ostinatos. This style, as the musicologist Ludvík Kundera observed, might frequently give an impression of 'emptiness', yet in a while we feel 'only clarity, plasticity, and respect for every single note'.[87] Despite its deceptive simplicity of sound and form, *In the Mists* is perhaps Janáček's most accomplished work for solo piano.

In the first piece of the cycle, the opening melancholy, chromatic melody in his favourite key of D flat rises and falls stepwise like a timid enquiry; the inevitability of the resigned answer had perhaps been known all along. A chordal motif appears, interrupted by a descending passage, like a gust of wind. A stormy outburst suddenly changes into a defiant peasant dance, but the melancholy dialogue soon returns. Yet, in a flicker of the wind, the mist lifts: as its remains fly over the landscape, the melody changes once more into the major key.

This is also one of the few moments of respite in the cycle. Number 2 similarly begins in a resigned mood; although the main theme asserts itself again later, and the piece ends in the major, there are agitated *presto* runs and halting octave writing in the middle section. A sense of resignation also pervades the last two pieces; in number 3, persistent questioning is finally interrupted by an agitated central part. Motivically all the pieces are related, as are their forms; the final piece has perhaps the greatest melodic, rhythmic and metrical variety of the four. Once again Janáček draws on Moravian folk music when he begins the piece with a phrase that employs one of his favourite devices – repeating part of a motif in a rhythmically displaced version. With their metrical freedom, fragmented harmonies and sudden shifts of mood, so Moravian in character, these four introspective views of an inner world are among the finest in twentieth-century piano literature.

In 1912 Janáček's health problems persisted, and at the end of that year he sought help from several medical practitioners; he could not get dressed without help and could barely walk with a stick. Severe pain in his shoulders often prevented him from sleeping. In 1913 his infection was still being diagnosed as gout, and during the summer, on the advice of his doctors, he went for a course of treatment to the Bohemian spa of Karlovy Vary (Carlsbad). As he was not happy there he soon left for another spa in Bohemia, Mšeno. Here, four days later, he fell ill with erysipelas. Before the discovery of antibiotics, this skin inflammation, accompanied by high fever, was considered very dangerous, particularly when it attacked the face. Janáček spent the following three weeks in hospital but he made a good recovery. Contrary to expectations, he felt much rejuvenated afterwards, and even stopped complaining about his 'arthritis'.[88]

Since that summer he began to take great care of his health. He was under the constant supervision of his distant cousin, Dr Dressler, and was much cosseted by Zdenka. He did not keep to a diet but went for daily walks, and his chronic infection was kept in check by regular massage. At one time he also suffered slight hair loss, but after a successful course of treatment his hair became even thicker and turned a beautiful white that was much admired. 'It shone around the master's head', Stejskalová remembered, 'like a white fire.'[89]

Janáček's sixtieth birthday was now approaching. He had experienced a great deal of disappointment in recent years and, despite putting on a brave face, he was much afraid of illness, pain and death. Even so, between the end of 1913 and the beginning of 1914, he wrote a work brimming with love and warmth: his cantata *The Eternal Gospel*, for soprano, tenor, mixed choir, orchestra and organ.

This is a setting of a rather verbose poem by Jaroslav Vrchlický, whose *Amarus* Janáček had set in 1897. The title is from Revelation 14:6, and the work's theological message is somewhat confused. Essentially, it describes a vision by the thirteenth-century Cistercian mystic Joachim de Fiore, in which an angel brings the Eternal Gospel that foretells the coming of a 'Third Kingdom' – the Kingdom of Spirit, or Love. St Francis of Assisi is to be its 'high priest'.

Janáček divided the poem into three parts with an epilogue; the cantata begins with the 'open arms' motif in A flat,[90] and its grandiose ascent over a soft pedal. A theme in A flat minor follows, full of torment. The beginning is repeated, and the solo violin (representing the Angel) enters with a soft-flowing melody. Only after its climax does the solo tenor, who represents Joachim, begin the story: later the horns take up the motif. The end of the movement is preceded by a jubilant fanfare of three trumpets.

In the second movement, the brief rhythmic figure which accompanies the announcement of the Angel's coming is elaborated; the choir acts as a commentator. The movement builds up to a huge climax, with the opening theme of the first movement repeated twice. This theme is repeated in the third movement as the Angel approaches; when he announces the Gospel, the choir responds with an ecstatic 'alleluia', repeating both his and Joachim's messages. The motivic connection continues in the finale; soon after the return to the opening theme, the unaccompanied tenor declares the coming of the Golden Age, and general jubilation follows.

The cantata was first performed in 1917 in Prague. Janáček's *Eternal Gospel* 'is also a dramatic scene', observed the Czech composer Ladislav Vycpálek, who reviewed the performance. 'Everything is, in a sense, unclear, indefinable by colour but full of ardour, of mighty gestures and apocalyptic ecstasy. It is a strange composition, but somehow intoxicating.'[91]

On 3 July 1914 Janáček celebrated his sixtieth birthday. The Organ School laid on a modest party with presents and speeches; Janáček gave everyone a day off, taking the professors and their wives out to dinner, and they finished the evening off with wine in his garden. Letters and telegrams kept arriving. 'I hate your sixtieth birthday,' wrote the writer Alois Mrštík. 'I would like to have you as I knew you many years ago. But although your hair has turned silver and perhaps quite a few things have changed with the years in your soul, your courage, your verve and your artistic temperament which I admired when you were young, have not left you.'[92] Many well-wishers regretted the fact that Janáček's work had not yet obtained full recognition. Dr Zikmund Janke expressed the hopes of them all when he wrote 'That time will come, it must come!'[93]

Janke was to be proved right in his prophecy of Janáček's imminent recognition. But before Janáček could at long last witness the success of *Jenůfa* outside Brno, momentous events took place. At the time of his birthday party there had been barely a hint of what was to come.

7

Recognition

(1914–1918)

WHEN, ON 28 June 1914, the Bosnian revolutionary Gavrilo Princip shot the Archduke Franz Ferdinand and his wife, no one could have imagined that this event in far-away Sarajevo would change the map of Europe. In Brno a Czech festival had been planned earlier that year for the end of June, and was eagerly awaited by the city's small Czech minority.[1] Janáček was particularly looking forward to the 'Moravian Year' programme, which was to show the city audiences the various folk customs still alive in the country. But on the opening day, 28 June, there was an unexpected delay after the men's calisthenics. When the news of the assassination was finally announced to the stunned spectators, many suspected that the developments would bode ill for the Slavs throughout the Austro-Hungarian Empire. The festival was cancelled immediately.

The Empire declared war on Serbia a month later, and general mobilization was announced in due course. Germany, Russia, Britain and France soon became involved, and other European countries followed. The initial dispute between Germany and the Austro-Hungarian Empire on one hand, and the Alliance (Britain, France and Russia) on the other, escalated into a world conflict.

With Russia on Serbia's side, persecution of Russophiles throughout the Austro-Hungarian Empire soon began. Everyone who had had contacts with Russia or harboured sympathies for the Russian cause before the war was under suspicion of treason; many Czech patriots who had founded Russophile organizations were arrested. Janáček, a staunch patriot, had founded the Russian Circle in Brno,[2] visited Russia several times, and written enthusiastically about St Petersburg and Moscow.[3] Two of his brothers had lived in Russia for many years. Surprisingly, he was now registered as nothing worse than 'politically doubtful'. The Russian Circle had of course to be disbanded; all pro-Russian documents were secretly destroyed and replaced with inoffensive material. Petrified, Zdenka later burned all

Janáček's personal correspondence with friends and acquaintances in Russia and Croatia, without his knowledge. She even concealed the Russian inscription on Olga's grave with trailing ivy.

In the autumn of 1914, during the Russian offensive, the possibility of defeat for the Austro-Hungarian Empire opened a new perspective in Czech politics – the future of Bohemia and Moravia outside the framework of the Empire. Prominent among those who wanted to seize this opportunity was the Moravian-born and Leipzig-educated philosopher T.G. Masaryk. In December 1914 he left for Italy and Switzerland to learn more about the plans of the Alliance; at the beginning of 1915 he decided to stay abroad and organize a campaign for Czech independence. Unfortunately, many political parties throughout the former Crown Lands of Bohemia did not wish to change their established pro-Austrian stance; opportunism prevailed, especially since, after Russia's retreat from Hungary in 1915, the result of the war remained uncertain.[4]

Shortages soon made themselves felt in Brno. The prices of everyday goods quickly rose many times over; some foodstuffs, as well as coal and oil, were rationed. Like everyone else the Janáčeks tried to stock up. Zdenka brought quantities of flour, sugar, rice and other foods, and hid them in the loft of the Organ School. The family silver, glass and china were put in the school's cellar. Later on in the war several large wooden boxes were added, crammed to the top with a collection of folk-songs from Moravia; this was material for which Janáček was responsible, as chairman of the working committee for Czech folk-song in Moravia and Silesia. When the Institute for Folk-song in Austria ordered that all Czech committees hand the material over so that it could be 'safe from enemy incursion',[5] Janáček defied the order: the immensely valuable collection, he declared, was the property of the nation and would remain in Moravia. The Prague committee fully supported him, and all attempts at negotiation by the Institute's directorship in Vienna were resisted.

Despite the momentous changes and developments the war brought, a surprisingly small number of works resulted from it, and only a few were written for large forces; instead, there was a revival of chamber music.

Janáček's spontaneous response to the war was his Violin Sonata, composed in a mood of suspense; he had begun the work as early as summer 1914, 'when we were expecting the Russians to enter Moravia'.[6] He reworked the sonata when the first version was turned down in 1915 by the young Czech violin virtuoso Jaroslav Kocian. Discarding and rearranging some movements and changing others, he only completed the work three versions later, in 1921.

The sonata has four movements, of which both outer ones largely follow (unusually for Janáček) a sonata form. A specifically 'Russian' atmosphere pervades the whole work, and both the main theme of the first movement and the opening theme of the third strongly resemble some motifs in Janáček's sixth opera. *Káťa Kabanová*.[7] In fact, in the first movement, the opening melody on the solo violin, and later the turbulence of the piano accompaniment, recall an operatic scena. In what amounts to a 'development' section, two forms of a brief motif from the exposition are treated. Unexpectedly, the movement ends in the major.

The second (originally third) movement, 'Ballada', was written before 1914 and published separately in 1915 – the only movement that has remained virtually unchanged. Setting it in a rondo form, Janáček – contrary to his customary shortness of melodic breath – greatly develops the folk-like, nocturnal tune of the refrain. The movement is rounded off by a reminiscence of the main theme and the broad-arched cantilena. In the third, quasi-scherzo movement, cutting ripostes from the violin – like biting remarks – are in sharp contrast to the dreaminess of a slower, lyrical trio.

In the finale an expansive tune on the piano is repeatedly interrupted by a tiny, repetitive figure on the muted violin, while the second, *dolce*, subject evokes a different mood. The two juxtaposed motifs soon return in the development section which builds up to a passionate climax: the earlier expansive tune is recapitulated on the violin, with the melody soaring ever higher. Janáček insisted that the accompanying high-register tremolo on the piano was to be played *molto agitato*: this was to represent 'the Russian armies entering Hungary',[8] in September 1914. After Russia's subsequent retreat, however, the war continued for another three and a half years; the sonata ends in a disillusioned mood, and Janáček specifically wanted the last two bars to be played *adagio*.

The sonata is Janáček's third for violin and piano, and the only one which has survived.[9] Following its 1922 première in Brno, and several successful performances outside Czechoslovakia in the 1920s, it has rightly won a special place in the violin repertoire.

War inevitably affected male-voice choirs. By 1916 male choral societies in Bohemia and Moravia were so depleted that their concerts were few and far between. Ferdinand Vach, the conductor of the famous Moravian Teachers' Choral Society, therefore decided to form a women's choir.[10] Janáček was as inspired by this choir as he had been earlier by its male counterpart, for which he had written some of his best male-voice choruses. In 1916 he rapidly completed five works for women's voices: *The Wolf's Tracks*, the three choral *Songs of Hradčany*, and *Kašpar Rucký*, a setting of a ghost story.

In *The Wolf's Tracks* – a miniature drama – Janáček sets to music a poem by Jaroslav Vrchlický, from his *Epic Poems* (*Romances and Ballads*).[11] An old army captain searches in the snow for the tracks of the title, without success; returning home, he spots his young wife in a window, in the arms of her lover. The captain lifts his gun to fire: the tracks have been found at last. Janáček adapted the text slightly: giving, for example, the captain's frenzied query ('Is this kiss to last for ever?') to a solo soprano, he changed the emphasis of the story – instead of stressing, as in the poem, the captain's revenge, Janáček draws attention to the dying lovers' embrace.

The outer sections of the chorus are in C sharp minor (Janáček's 'ominous' key).[12] After a rising major sixth the melody descends and ascends gently, aptly portraying the search; the wolf's tracks are poignantly described by a brief motif hovering around the middle C sharp. The 'search' motif is echoed in the description of the wife's beauty, and the captain's mad jealousy is depicted to great effect; as the sound of gunshot fades, Janáček uses a tenth, the largest interval in the chorus. The work was completed in January 1916 and first performed in August of that year.

Songs of Hradčany is a setting of three popular poems by F.S. Procházka.[13] All three songs powerfully evoke the atmosphere of Hradčany – Prague Castle – which towers above the Czech capital and has always been a powerful symbol of her history.

Golden Lane, the subject of the first chorus, is a short stretch of toy-like houses that still stand along the northern end of the castle's wall; legend has it that they were built for Emperor Rudolf II's alchemists.[14] Procházka contrasts the emptiness of the castle's 'great, gilded halls' with the humble lane, and Janáček illustrates the mood with much sweetness and simplicity. A brilliant fanfare is eventually transformed into a *dolcissimo* in G flat major, the melodic line rising and falling with a Schubertian naturalness.

The second song of the cycle, *The Weeping Fountain*, recalls an allegory which had a clear resonance for Czechs – weeping for the 'dead dream' of their past. The title refers to the Singing Fountain, as it is called, in the Royal Garden of the castle; as the falling stream of water hits the bell–metal from which the fountain is made, the metal emits a curious sound.[15] The piece has solos for soprano (or mezzo-soprano); the 'weeping' or 'singing' of the fountain is suggested by figurations in the flute part.

The Belvedere, a renaissance summer palace in the Royal Garden,[16] is the subject of the third chorus, which meditates on the various events that took place there. This 'poem in stone' was, the poet tells us, built with great love and hence will withstand the ravages of time. Love, he proclaims, is therefore all we need to transform the nation's future. Procházka takes much poetic licence here, but Janáček fully exploits the dramatic potential of the poem; the harp, a regal instrument, is an integral part of the story. Using many of his characteristic vocal devices (contrasting the lines, employing pedal effects and *sforzato* chords followed immediately by *piano*), Janáček builds up a finale in which the poet's prophecy is illustrated with a mighty gradation. Then, as the solo voice rises with the words 'What miracles we might see', the chorus merely whispers: 'My poor land' – an underlying sentiment which would have been clear to all Czechs at the time.

Kašpar Rucký, the last women's chorus from this period, is also set to Procházka's text, which mixes fact and fiction: Rucký was not, as the poet claims, a fraudulent alchemist in the service of Rudolf II but his chamberlain and favourite. After the Emperor's death he hanged himself, but his corpse was executed as if he were alive. Soon, it was rumoured that his ghost haunted the castle; in Procházka's poem, the Devil made Rucký's soul ride for forty nights on a fiery goat, accompanied by one hundred thousand witches and their cats.

Janáček made numerous alterations in the text, sometimes mis-stressing words for parodic effect. Changing the basic metre of the poem, mixing and staggering whole verses, he also deliberately mirrored in the music the popular fairground balladeer style, in which the poet introduced the gruesome story, and the piece sparkles with mischievous humour.

Golden Lane was first performed in Prague in December 1916 and the première of the entire cycle followed some two years later. The last chorus was first performed in 1921, to great acclaim, by the Prague Women Teachers' Choral Society, which had survived the war that brought it into being and continued to thrive. This is when Janáček first heard it. Later the cycle became a great success during the society's tour of Germany.

Janáček had quietly abandoned work on his fifth opera, *The*

Excursions of Mr Brouček, in 1913, over a year before the outbreak of the war. And he had done little to promote his third opera, *Jenůfa*, since its 1904 Brno première.

The Brno Theatre had put on its third production in January of 1911. Janáček had made further cuts and corrections for that, and had made more in 1908 when the opera's vocal score was published in Moravia.[17] But that was all.

Meanwhile his friends continued to campaign on his behalf. In 1911 one of them, the physician František Veselý,[18] privately approached a colleague, with a plea for a production at the National Theatre in Prague; the distinguished pathologist Jaroslav Hlava was the chairman of the theatre's board of governors.

Veselý's petition fell on deaf ears. There was a financial problem, claimed Hlava: the underfunded temple of Czech arts had responsibilities towards a plethora of Czech composers. Hlava was satisfied that the theatre's director and chief conductor Kovařovic was, on the whole, 'receptive towards the younger generation'; from 'a practical standpoint', the board could concede only one or two 'experiments' a year. Hlava's advice to Veselý was to find a Maecenas in Moravia, and to Janáček to write 'something new' – then he would see what he could do for him.[19]

Another possibility might have been to stage the opera at the Vienna Hofoper, only a short distance from Brno. In 1904 Janáček had invited Mahler, then artistic director at the Hofoper, to the Brno première of *Jenůfa* – Mahler had many Czech connections and had shown interest in Czech music throughout his life.[20] A production of *Jenůfa* at the Hofoper, albeit in German, would have been a coup for any Czech composer at that time, bringing prestige to him and also drawing attention to the Czech cause. But, unfortunately, Mahler was unable to attend the première, and there was no further contact between him and Janáček.

Apart from the National Theatre, there had been since 1888 another major opera house, the Neues Deutsches Theater, in Prague. But a première of *Jenůfa* there would have been politically unacceptable for Janáček before Czech independence: the city's Czechs and Germans lived in their own closed cultural worlds, and animosity and rivalry were rife. Indeed, the Neues Deutsches itself had come into being after bitter political quarrels between the two communities: when the Czech National Theatre (built almost entirely by private subscription) was completed in 1881, the city's Germans demanded a state subsidy for their own new theatre. Only when that approach failed did they decide to build their theatre also by private subscription.

The Neues Deutsches's director, the Vienna-born Angelo Neumann (1838–1910), was a clever businessman who was not interested in nationalist polemics. He was responsible for bringing a number of new singers to Prague and for the appointment of conductors of a high calibre (among others, Mahler, Otto Klemperer and Erich Kleiber). Under his directorship the Neues Deutsches (today's Prague State Opera) achieved standards that made it famous throughout German-speaking Europe.

After some initial conflicts between the two houses a tacit agreement was reached with regard to repertory: the Neues Deutsches had first option on all new German operas, while at the National Theatre the Czechs staged novelties from France and Italy; the movement of singers between the houses was carefully monitored. As a city of two cultures Prague therefore had a great deal to offer those who were capable of embracing both. Before the First World War, enlightened enthusiasts fluent in both languages might have seen at the National Theatre Smetana's *Dalibor*, Dvořák's *Rusalka*, Tchaikovsky's *Eugene Onegin* and Chekhov's *Three Sisters*; the theatre's director F.A. Šubert also introduced audiences to the *verismo* operas which were beginning to flourish in the 1890s, such as *Pagliacci*. The Neues Deutsches, on the other hand, offered Weber, Wagner and Richard Strauss, as well as new plays by Schnitzler and Wedekind; Neumann had in fact been staging the entire *Ring* cycle since 1885, and he held the rights to performances of any of the later Wagner works in Prague until 1910.[21]

Therefore, rich as the musical life in Prague was in the pre-war years, there was in fact little chance for *Jenůfa* outside the National Theatre, where the situation was hampered by Janáček's poor relationship with Kovařovic. A composer whose work was stylistically innovative needed friends and allies in Prague. Living and working outside the Czech capital, as Janáček did throughout this life, was a disadvantage.

In March 1913 *Jenůfa* was produced in Brno for the fourth time, and Dr Veselý tried to devise yet another plan to get the opera to Prague. Once again Janáček opposed it. There was the possibility of two of his non-operatic works, *The Fiddler's Child* and *The Eternal Gospel*, being performed there soon, and he declared proudly that that should suffice.[22] In the event they were not performed until some four years later; and in 1914, the great success of Janáček's male-voice chorus *The Seventy Thousand* and the publication of the score of *The Fiddler's Child* made no impact on Kovařovic. The battle for *Jenůfa* did not take a decisive turn until 1915. Chance played a large part in this but Janáček's admirers and well-wishers made sure of using it to the full.

Janáček's ever-faithful friend Dr Veselý had been offered the post of chief medical director at Bohdaneč, a small spa in north-eastern Bohemia; there, his second wife, the singer Marie Calma-Veselá, met the man who was the crucial link. Karel Šípek (1857–1923, real name Josef Peška) was a writer, music critic, translator and, most important, the librettist of Kovařovic's opera *The Dogheads*.[23] Bohdaneč, his birthplace, was where he liked to spend his holidays. Calma soon invited him to a soirée at which she sang several of Jenůfa's arias. Enchanted, Šípek insisted on her auditioning for his friend, the then National Theatre's director Gustav Schmoranz, who was shortly to visit him at the spa. Schmoranz, too, was captivated and promised to intervene, offering Calma the title-role if the production materialized. Hoping for a breakthrough she sent the score to Kovařovic.

After yet another scrutiny of the score Kovařovic stood his ground. He liked Jenůfa's prayer in Act 1, but had many serious objections to the rest of the opera. 'The dialogue', Schmoranz reported to Šípek,

> is [according to Kovařovic] completely faulty. On one hand the composer doggedly follows the principle of reproducing the oral impression of the language as spoken in Moravian Slovakia; on the other, contrary to all the rules of true speech, he makes the singers repeat certain passages in the text countless times. [. . .] [Kovařovic] says that it is a curious mixture of 'novelty' and extreme primitivism (bordering on impotence in composition).

Kovařovic felt that he simply could not 'recommend the work against his artistic convictions.'[24]

The quick-tempered Šípek (whose pen name aptly translates as 'briar') was enraged. His long reply to Schmoranz was not only an indictment of Kovařovic's poor judgement with regard to *Jenůfa* but also of the theatre's limited outlook. Kovařovic, wrote Šípek, had underestimated the subsequent popularity of *Rusalka* and missed a chance to stage *Madama Butterfly* in Prague; the theatre's repertory was uneven and his ensemble variable. No wonder the National Theatre box office 'suffered from anaemia'.

The National Theatre had given Šípek several commissions in the past, and he had much to lose by such vigorous criticism. But he stood by his beliefs. 'If', he pointed out to Schmoranz,

> the Maestro [Kovařovic] heard *Maryčka Magdónova* sung by the Moravian Teachers [Choral Society], he would not have dismissed Janáček as a complete novice. He would not have dared commit the solecism of scheduling the young prophet Jeremiah's opera [*The Old King* by the 26-year-old Jaroslav Jeremiáš], over whose libretto you wrung your hands, while turning down a man of sixty who had composed a tried and tested Moravian folk drama.[25]

By mid-November, the concerted efforts of Šípek, Calma and no doubt also Schmoranz at last began to weaken the obdurate director's resolve. Kovařovic asked Calma (whom he had taught when she was 15) to sing for him any soprano aria from *Jenůfa* that he designated, and he was prepared to have another look at the score.

Everything now hinged on Janáček's agreement to a few changes. This required much tact, and once again Dr Veselý stepped in. Kovařovic was now in principle no longer opposed to the production, and was willing to conduct *Jenůfa* 'in the spring of 1916 *himself*', wrote Veselý to Janáček. 'He has mentioned that he had found some passages very beautiful, especially the final scene . . . . And he said, "Actually, why should I not perform Janáček, even if I do not agree with something [in his score], when I perform modern music with which I do not agree at all!?" ' Once again the score was to be sent to him, and Kovařovic 'would be pleased' if Janáček were to express 'willingness to change a few things'. Veselý trod very carefully: the sections would be *insignificant* . . . Kovařovic has even made changes in Smetana'.[26]

Calma's audition was set for 8 December. Janáček wired a characteristically laconic encouragement: 'Do break through!' Next day, he received an enthusiastic report: Calma had had to sing some arias twice or even three times. 'Kovařovic was *very* happy,' she wrote.

> He has only a few objections – not so much as a composer but rather as an experienced man of the theatre. They are trifles. [. . .] If you agree with these small charges . . . *Jenůfa* would be given for *certain* in the spring. Kovařovic is convinced that he will not harm *Jenůfa* by his suggestions, just as he had undoubtedly helped Dvořák's *Dimitrij* and *Jakobín*. [. . .] For the part of *Jenůfa* he wants me, saying that others would not sing it that well – apparently they have 'fragile' voices.[27]

The delighted Dr Veselý added a few lines:

> If only there had been good relations between you and Kovařovic earlier on, *Jenůfa* could have been performed at the National Theatre fifty or even a hundred times by now. Kovařovic fully appreciates the beauty of the music and its individuality, but as a man of the theatre he requires certain changes, '*so that the work would acquire a greater pace and gain in dramatic impact*'.[28]

Janáček seized his chance: after twelve years of waiting he was not going to waste a golden opportunity. He thanked the Vaselýs in a brief, emotional reply; he felt 'as a prisoner to whom a gate to life and freedom has opened', and he would authorize Kovařovic to make cuts 'as he sees fit'.[29] This he did the same day, and the conciliatory tone is unmistakable: 'Why should I not accept your suggestions for possible cuts? You can be assured that I shall accept them with thanks. Whatever you think appropriate shall be done.'[30]

As the production was scheduled very late in the season, the National Theatre's cautious board of governors was concerned about possible financial loss. Without Janáček's knowledge the magnanimous Dr Veselý offered to underwrite the projected six performances if they were not sold out.[31]

The last hurdle now removed, Janáček travelled to Prague the same month to have a look at the suggested cuts, and to meet Kovařovic. Once again the Veselýs smoothed the path. Calma explained to Janáček some cuts he did not at first understand (and she saved others by suggesting alterations to the text). The composer then joined the couple in their box for a performance of Smetana's *Libuše* which Kovařovic was conducting; during the interval Veselý took Janáček backstage. By then the tension and long-held grudges had gone; Janáček and Kovařovic shook hands, and even attempted an embrace. The reunion ended on a cordial note, and Janáček returned to the box in good humour. 'Done!' he remarked to Calma, terse as usual.

Casting could now proceed, and Calma asked Janáček to enquire whether she should be preparing her role. Although Kovařovic had said that he wanted her for the part, the decision was not his alone: Calma was not a member of the National Theatre ensemble and had not been on stage for many years. Eventually Janáček told her to go ahead and learn the entire part.

A few weeks later it was revealed that the part had been offered to the 29-year-old Kamila Ungrová, a member of the ensemble since

1907, who was unwilling to cede it. The bitterly disappointed Calma accused Janáček of disloyalty:

> . . . it was my Jenůfa that convinced Kovařovic and overcame his many objections about the work being unsingable and so on – and my deep conviction about the beauty of your work helped to defend it and to earn it victory. Now that the main purpose – to get your *Jenůfa* to the National – has been achieved, now that I have stopped regretting the immense amount of work devoted to the study of a role that has become part of my life's blood and soul, I can only express my disappointment, which comes down only to one thing: that you did not or could not find it in your heart to say, 'I want Mrs Calma-Veselá to sing Jenůfa because I feel that no one else would sing it as well as she would.'[32]

It took Janáček, normally a prompt correspondent, over a month to reply; Calma's letter 'cut him to the quick'. He was certain that he had acted 'with honesty', and begged the singer not to blame either him or Kovařovic: the conductor could not have acted differently when it came to casting 'if the production of *Jenůfa* were to take place at all'.[33] In the end, Janáček was obviously not prepared to insist that the role should go to Calma, for fear of jeopardizing the première. The friendship cooled. Janáček did not invite the Veselýs to the première in writing, but did try to make amends in a roundabout way: František Mareš, an old acquaintance of his and Dr Veselý's cousin, was commissioned to convey Janáček's personal invitation verbally. In a long telegram Mareš sent instead,[34] he begged the couple on Janáček's behalf to come to the première and to revive the friendship. The Veselýs wired best wishes, but declined the invitation.

After extensive rehearsals, in which the Czech papers in Prague showed little interest, the première on 26 May 1916 was an extraordinary success – 'probably the happiest day of my life', declared Janáček.[35] Thirteen years after the completion of *Jenůfa* and twelve after its première in Brno, Janáček finally had the satisfaction of hearing his work on the foremost Czech stage; on the eve of the première, *Národní listy* had published an extensive *feuilleton* about the composer.

The casting was exceptional: the Croatian-born Gabriela Horvátová, whose voice, musicianship and dramatic talent had previously made her popular in Prague, created in the Kostelnička the best of her many Czech roles. Kamila Ungrová, as Jenůfa, had been much admired for her interpretation of Smetana. The distinguished young bass Vilém Zítek appeared in the part of the Foreman; Theodor Schütz, Števa in the Brno première, was now the troubled Laca. 'When I remember you sitting with that whipstock on the log before the cottage,' wrote Janáček to Schütz in a letter of thanks, 'well, there is no truer picture of Moravian Slovakia. With your entire appearance, your physique, your strength, your fiery temper, you are a type that has no equal.'[36] Later, however, Horvátová let it be known that both Ungrová and Schütz had voiced many objections to the music, as they had found Janáček's style difficult to perform.[37]

The producer was Robert Polák, a former bass who, between 1900 and 1926, produced some fifty Czech operas at the National Theatre, including new works by contemporary Czech composers. As they had in the colourful Brno staging, the soloists wore genuine folk costumes; Horvátová's magnificently embroidered apron was a gift from Zdenka Janáčková. The auditorium was also ablaze with colour: many ladies wore national costume instead of evening dress, and an anti-Austrian feeling pervaded the air.

Congratulations soon began to pour in. 'Seldom have I left the theatre as enraptured by a work as after Friday's première,' wrote the composer and conductor Otakar Ostrčil. 'You managed to grip the audience for the entire evening . . . . These days, I am continually reliving your work, going over individual scenes, leafing through the vocal score, in short – I am yours . . .'.[38] The composer and music critic J.B. Foerster sent congratulations from Vienna where he was teaching. 'You don't know how pleased I was to receive your letter!' replied Janáček:

> I feel as if I am in a fairy-tale; now I am composing, composing as if driven. I no longer valued my own work – nor my own words. I did not believe that anyone would ever notice any of it. I felt beaten down – my own students started advising me how to compose . . . . I would only smile: there was nothing else I could do. Now I am beginning to believe in my life and its mission.[39]

Articles devoted to Janáček and analyses of his style soon appeared in various Czech newspapers and musical periodicals: almost exactly fifty years after the première of Smetana's *Bartered Bride*, *Jenůfa* was hailed as another milestone in the history of Czech music. Only the musicologist Zdeněk Nejedlý derided the work: 'The old truth has been proven again: life cannot be composed, it must be created,' he wrote. 'Janáček manages to gather enough material but cannot make anything out of it.' To Nejedlý, a staunch supporter of Smetana, the only possible sequence of succession was not Smetana–Dvořák–Janáček but Smetana–Fibich–Ostrčil. Nejedlý thought Janáček's repetitions of certain words almost comical, and Janáček's 'attempts' at duets appeared to him to resemble 'people trying to interrupt each other'. And the 'lifelessness' of *Jenůfa*, he claimed, can best be seen in Janáček's choruses and crowd scenes. '*Jenůfa*', Nejedlý concluded, 'is an old Singspiel in a new habit, and carries in itself all the diseases of this type, against which Smetana put his own type of *cultured* art.'[40] Although Janáček and Nejedlý later met, and attempted to be friendly, Nejedlý's inability to understand Janáček's style continued to provoke Janáček to open mockery in his writings; and Nejedlý's services to the understanding of Smetana, both as a man and an artist, have done nothing to erase the stain of his later treatment of noted performers devoted to Janáček's music.[41]

The score that Nejedlý criticized in fact included over seventy revisions by Kovařovic, including the text. The conductor preferred a full, rich sound and more 'fashionable' orchestration; his idea of an effective ending to Act 3 was a grand canonic finale deploying trumpets and horns. Janáček did not seem to mind: in his letters to his wife he marvelled at the sound of the orchestra, and the account of one of the last rehearsals of *Jenůfa*, by the conductor Pavel Dědeček, supports this view. Dědeček, Janáček's former pupil at the Organ School in Brno, was at the time a member of the National Theatre orchestra; when Kovařovic's re-orchestrated finale was played, he could see Janáček from his music stand, 'and when the mighty gradation, with the showy, high-placed horns, came to a climax, his eyes were shining and he was clearly moved . . . Janáček admired Kovařovic's skill at orchestration, and declared as much to several members of the orchestra.'[42]

It is clear that the composer – almost 62 at the time of the Prague première – was so overjoyed at the prospect of seeing *Jenůfa* at the National Theatre that he was prepared to overlook revisions and changes which he might otherwise have considered interference. His working score of *Jenůfa*, where the cuts are marked, may have been heavily annotated: the cuts are marked and there are remarks such as 'not to hurry!', 'not to be drawn out', 'hold' and '*moderato* not *allegretto!*'. But this did not stop Janáček from writing to Kovařovic that summer with deep gratitude. He asked for permission to dedicate his next opera, *The Excursions of Mr Brouček*, to him; a few days later he sent Kovařovic a photograph inscribed: 'Be my ally even in other works; greater masters than myself are grateful to you.'

In 1917, when a new vocal score of *Jenůfa* was published by a leading Czech publisher, Hudební matice, Janáček sanctioned Kovařovic's version (although the publisher pointed out to him the differences in the finale).[43] Kovařovic probably never considered his revisions to be of a 'creative' nature; in 1918, when Universal Edition in Vienna published the full score of *Jenůfa*, he was paid a flat fee, which he donated to the National Theatre's Widows' and Orphans' Fund.[44] Neither the score nor the vocal score of either edition bears Kovařovic's name, which seems to corroborate the view that he regarded his cuts and revisions as common practice. Some Czech conductors, however, such as Janáček's pupil Břetislav Bakala, thought that Kovařovic had made the revisions in order to justify his earlier, negative judgement. Others suggested, after an analysis of the corrections (some in Janáček's hand), that Janáček had, in fact, participated in Kovařovic's greatest changes.[45]

Although in 1919 Janáček was annoyed to discover that Kovařovic received performance royalties for *Jenůfa* at the National Theatre (1 per cent of Janáček's gross takings), the re-orchestration itself still did not seem to worry him.[46] But in 1923, two and half years after Kovařovic's death, Janáček changed his mind. The theatre's new director stopped the royalty payment to Kovařovic's widow, and she issued an ultimatum: either Janáček paid up, or she would forbid further performances of *Jenůfa* in her late husband's arrangement. Janáček tactically offered half a per cent, but to no avail. Exasperated, he complained to Otakar Ostrčil that Kovařovic's additions were arbitrary and that he was obliged to 'defend his honour as a composer', especially in view of the rumours that Kovařovic had orchestrated the entire score of *Jenůfa*.[47] Although Janáček was willing to accept and occasionally even invite corrections to his scores, he now resented the implication that his own orchestration of *Jenůfa* had been inadequate.

Janáček therefore wrote to Universal Edition and to his Brno lawyer, declaring a ban on performances of *Jenůfa* in Kovařovic's orchestration throughout Czechoslovakia; later that year he claimed that Kovařovic used 'so much red ink' simply because of his long-term negative attitude towards the opera.[48]

As Kovařovic's work was not under copyright, his estate – whose lawyer, to Janáček's further annoyance, was the son of Antonín Dvořák – could not in fact ban performances. Nor was Janáček's own ban feasible. Both parties had to resort to arbitration, and Janáček appointed two conductors to testify for him. Otakar Ostrčil – then Kovařovic's successor at the National Theatre's rostrum – begged to be excused, and Janáček never really forgave him.[49]

Kovařovic's letter, asking Universal Edition for a fee for his revisions (and the right to print and play them), was finally found in 1924. His widow had to drop the case, but in 1926 the National Theatre was still paying her the performance royalty, although out of its own takings; Janáček had no say in the matter.[50]

He was equally powerless with regard to the revisions. The Kovařovic version continued to be played: Universal Edition was the sole publisher of the full score and performance materials, and no other version was published.[51] Only excerpts from the opera in Janáček's version, under Bakala's baton, were heard on Brno Radio in 1941; Bakala used the original Brno parts.[52]

The Kovařovic family eventually reopened the case, and in 1963–4 obtained a ruling according to which Kovařovic's revisions were deemed to be a creative collaboration, and to have played their part in *Jenůfa*'s worldwide success.[53] It was not until 1982, after Sir Charles Mackerras had gradually reintroduced details of the original orchestration, that the opera could be heard according to Janáček's original intentions. Kovařovic's finale was discarded and Janáček's version, with its trombones, restored; extra doublings and sustaining instruments were cut. The Kostelnička's 'explanation aria', which Janáček did not keep in his 1908 revision, was included.[54]

The eight sold-out performances of *Jenůfa* at Prague's National Theatre in 1916 were followed by eighteen repeat performances during the 1916/17 season, and the production unmistakably marked a turn in Janáček's fortunes. Marie Calma and her husband did not come to see the opera, although earlier that summer Janáček had apparently indicated that he now wanted Calma to sing the part of *Jenůfa*, and invited them to a performance in August 1916.[55]

During rehearsals for the 1916 Prague première Janáček found an ardent new promoter of his work in the production's Kostelnička, the 38-year-old Gabriela Horvátová. She had been born in 1877 in the town of Varaždin, north of Zagreb, and considered herself Croatian, although her surname (which she used in Prague with the Czech suffix -ová) suggests Hungarian origins. At 22 she made her debut at the Zagreb Opera, and four years later she arrived in Prague. Rumours about her private life soon created around her an atmosphere of notoriety, admiration and envy – an atmosphere essential to

a diva's success at this time. Yet Gabriela possessed not only temperament and charm but also genuine talent and steely dedication. She
had a powerful voice with an extensive range and excellent technique, and she could effortlessly sing very different roles.[56] She spoke
several languages and soon learnt very good Czech. Prague audiences
fell in love with her Carmen in 1903, and Gabriela settled in the
Czech capital, becoming one of the Kovařovic's leading soloists. She
retained her voice and its flexibility until old age.

A 1916 photograph shows her as a sophisticated woman elegantly
dressed and bedecked with fur; under a large fashionable hat her
handsome face is rather imperious, with dark eyes and thick dark
eyebrows. Her Kostelnička was no ageing bigot bereft of beauty.
From the multicoloured kerchief on her head to her shining high
boots, her tight-fitting bodice accentuating her figure and her hands
defiantly on her hips, this was a full-blooded woman from Moravian
Slovakia in the prime of life.

Janáček first called on Gabriela after her guest appearance in Brno
early in 1916, at Zdenka's suggestion. On his return he admitted,
bewildered, that the diva had received him at her hotel while still in
bed. 'My husband was not used to the free manners of the theatre,'
remarked Zdenka later. 'Despite all his flirtations . . . he was inexperienced in erotic matters . . . . At that time I laughed: "It doesn't
matter, as long as she sings the Kostelnička for you well." '[57]

Before *Jenůfa* was accepted at the National Theatre, the Janáčeks
had once again been living together in relative harmony. Soon after
Janáček began attending rehearsals, he wrote home that 'Mrs Horvátová has an artistic temperament the like of which I have never
seen or heard before';[58] she was 'an angel of virtue, a charitable soul
who would give everything away'.[59] 'I'd seen it all before,' Zdenka
recalled wryly; 'it was the beginning of a new infatuation.' Parting
with Janáček four days before the première, she was seized with terrible anxiety: 'For a moment I felt as if I could see into the future.
[. . .] I knew: Leoš is lost to me.'[60]

During rehearsals Janáček and Gabriela spent virtually all their time
together. When they could not meet they wrote, often several times a
week; sixty-seven letters by Janáček and seventeen by Gabriela
survive. The diva often signed herself either 'Your Kostelnička', or by
her pet name, Jelča.

The Janáčeks' domestic peace evaporated. Janáček insisted that
Zdenka pay Gabriela a visit in Prague, and the two women assessed
each other 'without illusion'. After the première, at a celebratory

dinner in a fashionable Prague hotel, Janáček sat at the head of the table with Gabriela, who shone with 'her success, her emerald jewellery and her vivacious . . . almost venomous mood'.[61] The Janáčeks' friends were shocked by his behaviour; the 50-year-old Zdenka, in her modest, wartime black dress, was sitting further down and could barely suppress her tears. Eventually, in order to reassure Zdenka, Janáček declared that *Jenůfa's* success was due solely to Gabriela. But the following day Zdenka heard that his courtship of the diva was the talk of Prague. The Janáčeks returned to Brno in an icy atmosphere.

Janáček still maintained that his relationship with Gabriela – 'the only possible Kostelnička'[62] – was nothing but 'a fusion of souls'.[63] He often stayed at Gabriela's Prague flat, and was happy for Zdenka to read his correspondence with the singer. But soon after the Prague première their attraction developed into an affair. An unsigned note in one of Janáček's speech melody notebooks, in Gabriela's bold handwriting, even seems to indicate that the diva wanted to bear him a son; it is impossible to say whether the note was written in earnest or in jest, or whether Gabriela encouraged Janáček's fantasies.[64]

While Zdenka was spending time in Vienna, looking after her aged father, Janáček continued his trips to Prague to see Gabriela. On her return, Zdenka was soon on the verge of a nervous breakdown. Gabriela now wrote to Janáček daily; on one occasion, Zdenka unsuccessfully tried to snatch his reply as he was writing it; in response, Janáček sent for the senior consultant at the Brno lunatic asylum to assess her mental condition.[65]

By now, in the third year of the war, prices were rocketing and the Janáčeks also began to quarrel about money.[66] On 10 July 1916 Janáček returned from another trip to Prague in a foul mood. According to Zdenka he then began 'to reproach me that I was his misfortune, that I had ruined his life, that I was the obstacle to his creative power . . . . He humiliated me terribly.' That night Zdenka, then 51, took an overdose of morphia.[67]

She came to in St Ann's hospital, where she was hospitalized for over a week. Embarrassed and worried that her suicide attempt might be reported in the press, Janáček sent for Zdenka's lawyer brother who managed to suppress all mention of the affair. Not a word was spoken between Janáček and Zdenka as to the reason for her desperate step but later she always claimed that she had decided to take her life 'so that he could be free'.[68]

Janáček then left for Luhačovice, where Horvátová was to join him. As she had to break her journey in Brno, he insisted that

Zdenka – to whom he wrote daily from the spa – invite Gabriela to stay with her. Zdenka obliged; in the hospital she had changed – as if she 'had hardened'.[69]

Janáček and Gabriela made several short trips from Luhačovice; still working on the role of the Kostelnička, she studied the costume, deportment and even facial expressions of a renowned folk singer – the best possible model for the role.[70]

Returning to Brno, she then accompanied the Janáčeks part of the way to Bohdaneč, where they were to visit the Veselýs. Throwing herself in Calma's arms, Zdenka told her everything. 'The confidences that Mrs Janáčková poured out to me as soon as she arrived . . . made clear to me the depth of her misery,' wrote Calma later.

> If Janáček is sometimes portrayed as a sensitive, emotional man, it is either a deliberate, hypocritical attempt to disguise his true colours, or a failure to fathom the depths of so complex a personality. One could write an interesting, [even] enthralling novel about him. But would that help his cause? His contribution to the arts is so great that it outweighs any flaws in his character.[71]

There were angry words later on, when Janáček and Dr Veselý spoke privately: Veselý talked 'openly, perhaps too openly as a friend and as a physician'.[72] Ignoring everyone, Janáček insisted on making a detour to Prague to see another performance of *Jenůfa*; afterwards, the Janáčeks dined with Gabriela and her husband, the manufacturer Bedřich Nolč.

Back in Bohdaneč, Janáček refused to stay with Zdenka on his own, and insisted that Gabriela share their hotel room for the night. By dawn, when Gabriela finally left the room, Zdenka was physically sick; Janáček, who had spent the night on the couch, followed the singer to her room.[73]

After a few calmer days in Brno, Janáček 'could not bear being without Mrs Horvátová', and asked Zdenka to invite her to stay with them.[74] A certain amount of social decorum had to be maintained and Janáček therefore spent the nights in Zdenka's bedroom; Gabriela stayed in his study. But Janáček apparently could not stop himself from openly declaring his passion; in her memoirs, Zdenka described other unpleasant scenes that followed.[75] During the day Janáček and Gabriela were often out together for long periods of time, returning only for meals; in the evenings Zdenka had to accompany them to the theatre, where the audience 'watched our box more than the stage'.[76] Eventually the distraught Zdenka sent a telegram to her brother in Vienna, asking for help. Gabriela left Brno the following morning, but before her departure she hung her framed photograph in Janáček's study, between his portrait and Zdenka's. Janáček then had his bed moved from the cottage to his office at the Organ School. Soon there were more scenes, and in the end he admitted his infidelity. Relieved that everything was now out in the open, he then suggested moving back to the cottage.[77]

Zdenka could have sued both Janáček and Horvátová, which would have had serious consequences for Janáček especially,[78] but both she and her brother dismissed the idea: in Brno a lawsuit and divorce would also have meant social disgrace for her. Zdenka decided to stay. According to the law of the time, even one night away from the marital home without Janáček's permission would count as desertion, and she had no way of supporting herself – since the age of barely 16 her entire life had revolved around him.

The couple carried on as before; Janáček even began to confide in Zdenka about details of his relationship with Gabriela. Later that year he claimed that Gabriela had been pregnant with his child but that she had miscarried. Even Zdenka did not take this, or plans for another pregnancy, seriously.[79]

At Christmas 1916 Gabriela's husband received an anonymous letter from Brno; Janáček suspected Zdenka. Angered, she impulsively suggested divorce and Janáček immediately agreed. Zdenka, who had not seriously meant this, was frightened, but Janáček insisted. Eventually she took legal advice; among her conditions, she demanded Janáček's pension.[80]

In January 1917 a private agreement was finally reached out of court, with the help of two lawyers who were also family friends. Janáček, then almost 63, undertook 'to keep the peace and quiet of the home' and not to hurt Zdenka's feelings; Zdenka also agreed to keep the peace. Janáček continued to take his meals at the cottage and to provide for Zdenka; she was guaranteed continuation of her marital status.[81] Court proceedings would only take place if the agreement was breached. The agreement therefore did not amount to divorce and was not even legally binding, but Janáček never realized that, and happily signed it.

The quarrels and scenes stopped but in all other respects the marriage was over. The situation was insoluble; as Gabriela also had many useful social contacts, Janáček consulted her on all his plans, and in Prague she often accompanied him on the many official visits he had to make. 'A composer's life with her could be a happy one,' he wrote to Kovařovic on 28 July 1916, less than three weeks after Zdenka's suicide attempt.[82] Whatever Zdenka's faults, it seems patronizing to dismiss her, as Jaroslav Vogel has done, for 'lacking – in spite of her goodwill – the understanding necessary for the wife of a genius'.[83] Perhaps Gabriela's husband possessed the understanding necessary for the husband of a prima donna, for Janáček's relationship with her continued for another year or so. Meanwhile, Zdenka was not even sure if she still loved Janáček. She turned for comfort to her faith, which she had almost lost after her daughter's death.[84]

Marie Calma-Veselá did eventually sing the part of *Jenůfa* at the National Theatre in May 1920, four years after the première – at a fortnight's notice, and with a single rehearsal. In 1965, aged 84, she maintained that she had been badly directed, to the point of bursting into tears while rehearsing. Although she was happy with her performance, she admitted that she had been 'frightened at her own courage'.[85] Despite a full house, the critical response was lukewarm, and Janáček did not come to see her. In a brief note he wished her success, and stressed that he had no say in the 1916 casting.[86] He simply glossed over the problem. Although he had suggested to Kovařovic a young soprano from Brno,[87] he would not do the same for Calma whose efforts had helped to convince the conductor of the validity of the score.

In 1924, at the time of Janáček's seventieth birthday, Calma published a short article on the battle for *Jenůfa*. From her introduction it is clear that she felt embittered by inaccurate accounts of the events in the press at the time; her husband's part had never been properly acknowledged before his death in 1923, not even by Janáček himself. Janáček responded immediately. He regretted being unaware of Veselý's underwriting the production but insisted that Kovařovic would have refused to assign the role of *Jenůfa* to Calma: 'If the work depended on your performance, he would have thrown it out without any hesitation.'[88]

Although Calma continued to promote *Jenůfa*, and took the score to Paris,[89] she now rarely met Janáček. In 1965 she told her interviewer that she loved Janáček's music 'but not him'. When she died in 1966 a manuscript of memoirs in verse, *The Voice of the Gong*, was found among her papers. Bitterness pervades the few pages devoted to *Jenůfa*, and the chapter ends with the words: 'As a human being Janáček was always a stranger to me.'[90]

The Prague production of *Jenůfa* in 1916 also brought Janáček into contact with Max Brod, the man who introduced him to the world. Brod was 32 at the time, and belonged to a minority within a minority – he was born into a middle-class Jewish family, and his mother tongue was German, the language of the country's rulers. In this he was not untypical of educated members of the Jewish community in Prague, even though by the 1880s many Jews in Prague had begun to identify with the Czechs.

The linguistic duality prevailing in Prague at the time extended to every sphere of life: there were primary and secondary schools, as well as a university and an engineering college for each language group. Opera and theatre, art and music schools, newspapers, bookshops and even clubs and civic organizations also existed in two versions, Czech and German. In such a divided community the Jews occupied a delicate position.

Brod's literary heritage was German but he was fluent in both languages, and brought to the world's attention not only Kafka (whose mother tongue was German), but also two Czechs, Janáček and the great humorist Jaroslav Hašek (1883-1923). His enthusiasm and generosity were extended to many artists. Today, much of his own work is overshadowed by that of the writers and musicians he promoted.

He was a small, bespectacled man, with a dignified air. A childhood ailment had left him with a curved spine and a permanently raised shoulder, but he made 'an unforgettable impression on all who came within his sphere',[91] and he had phenomenal success with women. As a contributor to several German newspapers Brod was a familiar figure at Prague's concert halls and opera houses. He was a gifted pianist, and he also studied composition with a pupil of Dvořák's, Adolf Schreiber.

Brod was a great admirer of the German composer Max Reger, and in 1913 members of the celebrated Bohemian Quartet asked him to look after Reger during his visit to Prague. The quartet's second violinist was Dvořák's son-in-law, Josef Suk. Some three years later Suk suddenly wrote to Brod, urging him to see a performance of *Her Foster-daughter* (as *Jenůfa* was, and still is, known in Czech) by Janáček, a newly discovered composer from Moravia. Suk had met Janáček during the dress rehearsal earlier in the year, and had also recommended the production to Richard Strauss during his visit to Prague in October. Although Strauss missed Act 1, and thought Janáček's technique 'somewhat mannered', he found a great deal to admire.[92]

Brod took Suk's advice. As the performance was virtually sold out he could buy only a standing-room ticket. He could barely see the stage but the music brought tears to his eyes. On 15 November 1916 his enthusiastic essay, 'The good fortune of Czech opera', was published in the Berlin theatrical weekly, *Schaubühne*; the translation was published in several Prague and Brno newspapers.

Janáček thanked Brod in a brief note; the critic responded with an invitation. Janáček wasted no time: a few days later, early on a Sunday morning, he turned up in Prague. 'He showed his hand immediately,' wrote Brod in his autobiography; 'everything depended on my translating *Jenůfa*.' Years later, Brod still remembered much of what Janáček had said:

> During [my train] journey I could not sleep, I thought only of you the whole time. And since six o'clock this morning I have been walking around your house, saying to myself; if this Brod will translate *Jenůfa*, everything will be all right. If he refuses, I'll remain where I was. Everything will be as before, I shall not break through.[93]

Janáček's openness touched Brod deeply. 'When I saw him sitting in front of me, completely devoted to his work', he wrote, 'I felt: this is the kind of man that God wanted . . . . I have postponed all other work and promised to translate *Jenůfa*.'[94]

Janáček's instinct was right. Czech was spoken by only a few million people; German, on the other hand, was spoken throughout Austria, Germany and part of Switzerland, and was also read by educated people in bordering countries. At this time, when Vienna was the artistic capital of Central Europe, the quality of translation would be crucial for wider recognition.

In fact, the translation must have been first suggested to Brod by his lawyer, Dr Jan Löwenbach,[95] a copyright expert, and also a great admirer of Janáček. He did not want to attempt the translation himself, but he tried to interest the German music publisher, B. Schott Söhne, in *Jenůfa*, and sent the firm Brod's review. Brod was already negotiating with Universal Edition in Vienna but its directorship wanted to see a satisfactory German translation before deciding whether to publish it. Schott, in Mainz, on the other hand, expressed interest on seeing Brod's review, even before the score of the opera had arrived. Their representative was invited to the next performance of *Jenůfa* that autumn, and Janáček was prepared to wait for the best offer. In the end Schott's representative never came to Prague; Universal Edition's director, Emil Hertzka, knew Janáček from the

Central Committee for Folk-song, and was keen on a production in Vienna. Brod was to send him the translation of each act as soon as it was finished; the German text was to be written by hand into the existing Czech vocal score, and this was to be submitted to the management at the Hofoper. In the event, the final decision to publish the score was only reached after further developments.

In March 1917 the Neues Deutsches Theater in Prague was putting on two one-act operas: *Florentine Tragedy* by its chief conductor, Alexander von Zemlinsky,[96] and Julius Bittner's *Hell's Gold*. Universal Edition was Bittner's publisher, and three weeks before the world première of this double bill a special party of four illustrious Viennese gentlemen visited Prague: the director Emil Hertzka, the Hofoper's conductor Hugo Reichenberger, Bittner, and another critic, Richard Specht of the *Illustriertes Wiener Extrablatt*.[97] A special matinée performance of *Jenůfa* was hurriedly scheduled for the same day. Bittner and Hertzka shared a box with Brod but both were so critical that Brod, fearing the worst, eventually stormed out of the box.

Yet the following morning Hertzka offered Janáček a publishing contract. Although he had remarked earlier that surely no European audience would tolerate a depiction of such a savage act as infanticide, he was now convinced that Janáček's opera was the most important Czech stage work since Smetana's *Bartered Bride*. 'But the work also belongs among the most individual and most valuable novelties in opera,' he wrote to the Hofoper's director Hans Gregor. 'Although there have been offers from three leading theatres to produce a German version of *Jenůfa*, I would welcome it with great pleasure if the work could first be heard in the German language in Vienna.'[98] Reichenberger also wrote to Gregor: a somewhat 'brutal' plot nevertheless 'made an extraordinarily rapturous impression; the music is the work of a first-class natural talent . . . a 'Czech Debussy'. Reichenberger was convinced of its success with Viennese audiences and musicians alike.[99]

Despite his recommendation, and Hertzka's conviction that the proposed première would 'contribute to the desired unity of our nations',[100] staging *Jenůfa* at the Hofoper would not be to everyone's liking. Following the death of Franz Josef I in 1916, the Austro-Hungarian Empire was disintegrating. The young emperor Karl tried to make concessions to various minorities, especially the Czechs: for them, the première of a Czech work at the Hofoper would constitute a gesture of goodwill. But German-speaking nationalists would not be pleased: the war was going badly for the Empire, and many

Austrians wanted to strengthen their alliance with Germany and did not want to be conciliatory towards the Czechs. Several months passed before the première was finally scheduled.

These were turbulent times. At the beginning of the war Janáček taught at the Organ School without any pay, and later for a mere third of his salary. Most of the time the Janáčeks survived on a small pension; whatever Janáček made on *Jenůfa* and other works was barely enough to cover his travel and other expenses.[101] The school's subsidy had been stopped, and many students could not afford the fees. Food became scarce, and in the autumn of 1917 the school was without fuel. Finally, the Olomouc archbishop, in response to a plea from Janáček, sent a wagonload of beech logs; Janáček himself chopped the wood.[102]

Earlier in July the composer, now 63, had visited Luhačovice as usual; there he met the woman who held him under her spell for the rest of his life, and who was to inspire many of his most famous works.[103] Kamila Stösslová was 25, married and had two children. She was of medium height and curly-haired 'like a Gypsy'; she had an olive complexion, big black eyes under heavy eyebrows, and a sensuous mouth. As the Janáčeks' maidservant Stejskalová recalled, Kamila had a peculiar habit of always holding something in her hand – 'a scarf, a hat, or perhaps even a stick which she used to wave about'.[104] She was uncomplicated, good-natured and happy; her charm is well captured in her early photographs. Only her voice, apparently, was 'shrill [and] strident'.[105]

Janáček was immediately struck by Kamila, and soon sent her some flowers; in an accompanying letter he wrote: 'Please accept these few roses as proof of how infinitely highly I think of you.'[106] When his train left Luhačovice a few days later, he 'wept bitterly and then, in a depressed mood, brooded until . . . Brno'.[107] He was touched by the Stössels' happiness: this was his 'most beautiful stay ever at Luhačovice'.[108]

Kamila's husband David, who was in the army but had been invalided to the home front, soon helped to supplement the Janáčeks' wartime rations, when even flour was scarce; the Janáčeks reciprocated with fruit from their garden. ' "An ox-eyed Hera" like Mrs Horvátová', thought Zdenka when the Stössels came to stay in August 1917; although surprised that Janáček had befriended these 'downright Jewish types', she had to admit that the Stössels brought with them 'action and laughter'.[109]

Zdenka soon found out that Janáček had confided in Kamila about Gabriela Horvátová. 'My husband', Zdenka commented wryly, 'made this young person, whom he had just met, the judge of our affairs.'[110] But when Kamila heard Zdenka's side of the story, she showed such concern that Zdenka was won over, especially since Kamila seemed to have a surprising influence on her husband: when Zdenka told her how much Gabriela's photograph in Janáček's study irritated her, Kamila asked Janáček for it, and took it home. 'What I, our friends and lawyers could not manage was achieved in a trice by this clever, cheerful Jewess,' observed Zdenka.[111]

Kamila was 'not particularly intelligent, and she knew nothing whatsoever about music', recalled Zdenka.[112] But she possessed an unfailing feminine instinct. Her early postcards – reproductions of paintings, which amused Janáček – have just the right touch of non-committal coquettishness: a timid youth standing by a girl at the spinet, a portrait of a sad girl entitled 'Did he forget?' and so on. 'Your postcards', Janáček wrote to her, 'are . . . like a song without words.'[113] At the end of August Janáček again confessed to her: 'When so much binds me to Mrs Horvátová, you will appreciate that it is impossible to tear it out of one's heart . . . .'[114]

Tongues wagged in Luhačovice after Janáček's departure, and Gabriela soon found out about 'his' Kamila and was not pleased. Later in the year, however, Janáček resumed his correspondence with the diva. 'You don't know, dear heart, how I must count every *kreutzer*,' he complained in December 1917, irritated by the wartime hardships. 'The household expenses used to cost me 224 crowns a month, now they cost 600!'[115] The Janáčeks' maidservant used to travel right up to the Czech border to scrounge for provisions, and everyone had to barter. 'Today I had a sensible student at the school,' Janáček reported. 'He came to sit an examination and paid the fee with a sugar loaf!'[116]

On 12 December 1917 Janáček at last completed the second part of his fifth opera, *The Excursions of Mr Brouček*, which he began in 1908. 'As I was writing the last bars, I was sorry that I was about to finish,' he declared to Gabriela. 'I shall not write another opera.'[117] The work had emotionally exhausted him: 'It was necessary to put the whole of Act 3 in order in my mind, in one breath,' he wrote to Kamila a few days later.[118]

The Excursions of Mr Brouček is Janáček's only comic opera. Svatopluk Čech (1846–1908), on whose two novels it is based, was a lawyer by training, a prolific, widely-read writer of both verse and prose who had also edited a number of key Czech journals. A skilful storyteller, he switches from Brouček's account to his own observations, to the narrative and back again, and the reader's interest is kept continuously alive.

Janáček's chief problem with *Brouček* was finding a suitable librettist to convert the text of the novel into verse. In less than a year following the inception of the project Janáček negotiated with six potential candidates; some turned him down, others presented unsuitable scripts. In March 1910 he wrote to his friend Artuš Rektorys (who had helped to secure the rights): 'I am going to stick as faithfully as possible to Svatopluk Čech's *Brouček* – let all these other poets of ours leave me in peace.'[119] He then arranged the libretto, extracting dialogue from the novel and changing indirect speech into direct; he also added new characters where he needed more material.[120]

He revised *Brouček* after the acceptance of *Jenůfa* in 1916, inserting several new episodes based on the work of another batch of librettists. The story of the libretto's genesis has some almost comic aspects to it. Janáček's friend Dr Zikmund Janke, for example, worked on the first scene and was asked for additions to a revised libretto; in the end his sole contribution was two lines. František Gellner, Janáček's most helpful librettist in the first part of the opera, died before the project was finished. Jiří Mahen, a well-known Czech playwright, misunderstood Janáček's instructions and flew into a rage when he discovered that his work had been for nothing. Another playwright, Viktor Dyk, was very helpful until he was arrested for defying war censorship. In the end Janáček did most of the work himself.[121]

At the beginning of 1917 the opera contained a single *Excursion*; in March that year, after completing the epilogue, Janáček suddenly decided to set Čech's second Brouček novel, *The New Epoch-making Excursion of Mr Brouček, This Time into the Fifteenth Century*. The libretto for this part was arranged by F.S. Procházka (who had done some work on the first act epilogue, later discarded),[122] and Janáček completed the music in a mere seven months.

In his version of the story Mr Brouček, a middle-aged Prague landlord, is staggering home from the inn he frequents when he encounters Málinka, the Sacristan's daughter. She is annoyed with her sweetheart, Mazal, an impecunious painter and Brouček's tenant. Trying to make Mazal jealous, she declares that she will marry Brouček, who agrees, even though Mazal mocks him. When the Sacristan wants to hold Brouček to his promise, our hero sobers up and insists that he will only marry 'on the moon'. Mysteriously transported there, he discovers to his horror that the lunar folk disdain food and drink: they live off the scent of flowers and devote themselves to the arts. The poet Starry-Eyes, curiously resembling Mazal in appearance, bemoans his unrequited passion for Etherea, a moon

maiden. She becomes infatuated with Brouček and whisks him off
on Pegasus to the Temple of Arts. Starry-Eyes and Etherea's father
Moongrove set off in hot pursuit, armed with a butterfly net and a
volume on aesthetics.

At the Temple of Arts Brouček becomes an object of great interest.
Etherea makes passionate advances to him, but just as Wonderglitter,
who presides over the Temple, is about to bless this unlikely union,
Etherea's father arrives and she runs off. Buried in flowers and deaf-
ened by lunar song, Brouček dreams of roast pork with sauerkraut
and dumplings. On waking, he eats a sausage he has in his pocket;
the delicate moon-dwellers are shocked. Exasperated, Brouček then
destroys Etherea by blowing at her and makes his escape on Pegasus.
At dawn, he is found, drunk, near the inn and carried home.

Next evening, there is a heated discussion at the inn about secret
passages under Prague Castle; on leaving, Brouček finds himself in a
subterranean tunnel to the past. As he tries to get out of the treasure
chamber, the Author interposes, bemoaning the lack of exalted
national characters on which to base his story. Meanwhile, Brouček
has gone back to the fifteenth century, with Prague under siege.
The Mayor of Prague (who strongly resembles the Sacristan) invites
him home: the Protestant Czechs, branded by the rest of Europe as
heretics, will need good fighters for the forthcoming battle against the
Pretender to the Czech throne and an invading army of Crusaders.
The Mayor's daughter and his guests ask Brouček's opinion on politics
and religion and soon discover that he is a coward. In the ensuing
battle the Hussite army wins, but the Mayor is killed. As the men
return, Brouček tries to escape. He is taken for a spy and, in spite of
his protests that he is a son of the future who has not yet been born, he
is condemned to be burnt to death in a barrel. Back in the present, the
innkeeper investigates groans coming from his cellar. Brouček is
found in the barrel; he claims to have liberated Prague almost single-
handed, beating the Crusaders to a pulp. But it must remain a secret,
he adds, looking warily around.

Even listeners not familiar with the opera's historical background can easily recognize the archetypal bourgeois represented by
Brouček, and laugh at him. The moon-dwellers – the gossamer
Etherea, the lyre-strumming Starry-Eyes and Wonderglitter's retinue
of impossibly affected artists – can all be recognized as disciples of
Aestheticism, even if audiences outside Janáček's native country are
unaware that these caricatures were directed at the Lumír school of
poetry in Bohemia.[123]

Much of *The Excursions* takes place in the historic parts of Prague with which Czech audiences are familiar, and this knowledge can greatly intensify the impact of the story. The Vikárka inn – Mr Brouček's erstwhile headquarters – survives, standing on the site of the old chapter-house refectory within the precincts of Prague Castle. Below the castle lies the Little Quarter where Mr Brouček lived. Mayor Domšík's house is the oldest Gothic house in Prague, the House of the Stone Bell.[124]

In the second part of *The Excursions*, despite Brouček's fantastic dream, further minute historical details and contemporary references are skilfully woven in,[125] and this is where problems may lie for producers and audiences outside the Czech Republic. Both Čech and Janáček are dealing with Czech patriotism here, but Czech audiences would never conceive of the self-indulgent, platitudinous Mr Brouček as 'almost a tragic figure', as has recently been suggested in Britain.[126]

Brouček exemplifies the mediocrity of the Czech bourgeoisie, and not only in the 1880s. It is the tendency of the Czechs to adapt too readily to any set of circumstances, no matter how unprecedented or bizarre, that is lampooned in the second part of *The Excursions*. Brouček shirks any responsibility or involvement – anything that may threaten his easy life. He is not only a coward but also a weather-vane, always ready to side with the winner. In the end, he is hoist with his own petard. Janáček makes his own view of Brouček clear in his *feuilleton* about the opera: 'We see as many Broučeks in our nation as the Russian sees Oblomovs,' he wrote in December 1917, shortly before the Czechs openly demanded independence. 'I wanted to make us feel disgusted by such a man . . . to smother the Brouček in each of us . . . . Let us not suffer for the character of the Broučeks as much as others suffer for the Oblomovs.'[127]

The Excursions is not easy to stage, and the episodic nature of the work might be well served by cinematic techniques. Nevertheless, in spite of its rapid, mosaic-like sequence of scenes, *The Excursions* has a firm structure, reinforced by the appearance of several characters in other guises. This unifying principle is underpinned by the recurrence of certain themes, and a technique based on a rondo and sets of variations.

As in Janáček's two previous operas, the vocal style of *The Excursions* is determined by speech melodies, and Janáček strove hard to match the stress patterns of the Czech language by irregular rhythmic groupings. Yet examples of mis-stressing can still be found throughout the opera,[128] and one gets the impression that, despite Janáček's theory, the text was sometimes fitted to existing or preconceived melodic lines. Moreover, colloquial Czech has occasionally been retained, not always to advantage, and even the grammar has sometimes been influenced by some of the Moravian dialects. And, as a result of Janáček's cuts, the meaning of the text is sometimes blurred.[129]

Janáček makes frequent use of seconds, fourths and fifths in *The Excursions*. Along with his constant striving for better declamation goes the widening of the intervallic range. Thirds and sixths are used in greater measure as the opera progresses; wider intervals, such as a leap of a ninth, are used whenever Janáček needs to portray heightened emotion, the moon-dwellers' exalted manner, or Brouček's hunger pains.[130] Brouček's dream of the Czech national dish of roast pork, sauerkraut and dumplings is projected with sly humour: as he calls out his order to the innkeeper, a tritone (the interval of an augmented fourth, 'diabolus in musica') is used, since the idea of eating flesh is perceived as devilish by the fastidious moon-dwellers.[131]

The 'moon theme', which first appears in the bassoon in the introduction, reappears in Act 1 of Part I virtually as a leitmotif, but the moon's comings and goings over Prague are portrayed by a decidedly Moravian mirror rhythm. A variant of the 'moon theme' also neatly appears in Part II, as Brouček tries to convince the Hussite warriors that he has come back from Turkey (the land of the crescent, or half-moon).[132] A dance element is also stressed in the opera – there are several infectious waltzes and polkas, and the waltz in Act 1 of the moon excursion is almost ecstatic.

The 'burlesque quality' which Janáček strove for comes through strongly, but the score also includes several patriotic hymns. Janáček wrote new tunes for several Hussite chorales in the opera, and he also incorporated the famous Hussite battle hymn, 'Ye who are God's warriors', as the men go off to battle.

'My head is empty,' wrote Janáček at the beginning of December 1917, shortly after completing *The Excursions*. 'What now?'[133] This was a familiar state of mind whenever he completed a large work, but there was little time for contemplation: *Jenůfa* was finally scheduled at the Vienna Hofoper for February 1918, and there was much excitement about the possibility of productions elsewhere.

After the 1916 Prague première Gabriela Horvátová showed the score to the celebrated Czech soprano Emmy Destinn.[134] Incarcerated by the Austrians during the war at her castle in south Bohemia, as a suspected spy, Destinn was nonetheless allowed out to give concerts throughout the country and to visit Prague; she expressed interest in the opera but hesitated to commit herself. 'Would you not like to create the role of Jenůfa?' Janáček finally enquired in December 1917:

A woman who goes through entire purgatory, the whole range of human suffering and who, in the end, dazed by the vision of divine goodness and justice, forgives those who had wanted to stone her, forgives even the one who killed her baby . . . . I know that you would bring this conception of Jenůfa to life . . . . Prague would certainly experience a day never to be forgotten.[135]

Destinn was touched; Jenůfa, she replied, was 'a rapturous role, in the realm of the deepest human emotion, and worthy of every sacrifice on the part of the artist who would create her'.[136] She would try. But she needed time: she was accustomed to singing in Italian and, apart from Smetana, the Czech repertoire was largely new to her.[137]

Hertzka thought even this response sensational. 'What an event that would be,' he wrote to Janáček. 'Perhaps Miss Destinn could also give guest performances elsewhere.'[138] Destinn's Jenůfa and Horvátová's Kostelnička would be a formidable combination: after the Vienna production, other European capitals – perhaps even New York – would surely beckon.[139]

Meanwhile, Janáček continued to correspond frequently with both Gabriela Horvátová and Kamila Stösslová. He invited Kamila and her husband to spend New Year in Brno with him and Zdenka, but after a few days in Prague at the end of December, he also wrote to Gabriela with great warmth. 'Among your words . . . "let me be as I am" impressed themselves in my mind deeply,' he remarked, referring to a recent conversation. 'These words are a gateway to your soul: I see you through them and like you as you are – although I have often felt anguished and sad. That is why I have showered you with kisses and would smother you with them!'[140]

In January 1918, after 'a sunny day' with the Stössels, Janáček related to Gabriela the problems Kamila had experienced since their happy summer in Luhačovice the previous year: loss of business and property, and illness in the family. 'I do not wish for anything like that to visit me,' he wrote:

And yet I have always longed for a family. Notes – they are my family now. They have their little heads and legs, they can run, frolic, bring out tears yet also joy. It is difficult to catch them, and to understand them . . . [. . .] At least they will not forget me, will not renounce me: 'we are Janáček's'. It this not pleasure enough?[141]

A few days later he mentioned to her the Stössels' mouth-watering contributions to the Janáčeks' wartime diet. 'Goose liver today, enough to fill a pot,' he wrote. 'I have brought home bacon and butter from the Stössels. Some venison, already skinned. And here a rabbit hopped our way, with a piece of bacon tied to its foot.'[142] From Janáček's next letter to Gabriela it is not difficult to surmise what the diva had been thinking. 'How foolish your last letter was,' Janáček rebuked her. 'I have no more thoughts of conquest now . . . . You were my only, but also the last riotous, jubilant shout of sensual delight.' The Stössels were 'good people' and there was 'no need to malign them'.[143]

That month, *Jenůfa* was finally in rehearsal at the Vienna Hofoper but there were still problems during the last stages of the translation: the conductor Reichenberger wanted Brod to render the libretto in an Austrian regional dialect, preferably Tyrolean. Keen to avoid an unintentionally comic effect, Brod vigorously defended his original translation, but in the end he had to make some concessions.[144]

Yet another development soon threatened the première. On 29 January, with just over two weeks to go, three members of the Imperial parliament questioned the minister in charge of state theatres. They wanted to know why nine non-German operas were scheduled to be performed at the Hofoper between 22 January and 3 February; now, they objected, a new work by some Czech, whose plot and music were inspired by Czech nationalism, was to be produced at great expense, and was being heavily promoted. This was nothing but a blatant provocation of Vienna's German population, and the minister must intervene.[145] Eventually the Court itself intervened: in an effort to discourage chauvinism, the young Emperor Karl and his wife decided to attend the première, and the posters bore the legend 'By Supreme Command'.

Maria Jeritza sang the role of Jenůfa and Lucie Weidt was the Kostelnička; Janáček was disappointed that Brod's recommendation of Gabriela Horvátová for the role was not taken up. 'You are a different type of Kostelnička,' he wrote to her, 'the right one!'[146] He attended several rehearsals, and although the daily six-hour return train journeys to Vienna utterly exhausted him, he even lent a hand with rehearsing the dances in Act 1.[147]

Although he frequently complained about his tempos being 'drawn out', after the first dress rehearsal he was transported. 'You cannot imagine what I am experiencing here!' he wrote to Gabriela:

The splendour of the colours – a hundred and fifty folk costumes – the marvellous, deep stage . . . . The mill and the distant view of the magnificent hilly landscape. All in brilliant sunshine, enough to make the audience perspire. The conscripts, with the stable-man from the mill on a garlanded horse – yes, this is the decor I longed for in Prague, in vain.[148]

The première on 16 February 1918 was a major social event, even though the Imperial couple did not in the end appear (the opera's distressing plot was thought unsuitable for the pregnant Zita). Janáček was very nervous: the auditorium was packed with nobility and high officials, and representatives of the Strassbourg and Zagreb operas were also present, as well as friends, colleagues and well-wishers. He had also been upset by Preissová's attitude: since *Jenůfa*'s success in Prague the writer had been claiming (and receiving) a percentage of Janáček's royalties and, expecting him to be paid tens of thousands in Vienna, she had pursued him there.[149]

Janáček insisted that both Zdenka and Gabriela attend the première. Since 1916, Zdenka had only seen Gabriela once, by chance. Now, fearing more misery, she invited the Stössels for support.[150] In the end, to her great relief, Gabriela only came for the dress rehearsal; on the day of the première she could not be released from an engagement in Prague, and Janáček welcomed Zdenka 'almost warmly'.[151] Gabriela only sent a gushing telegram: 'With you, [and] your genius until death and today, Kostelnička.'[152] In the end she never saw the production, although Janáček invited her three times.[153]

At the première Janáček shared his box with Brod. 'After each error on stage, and each wrong tempo,' reported Brod, 'Janáček relieved his feelings by poking me in the ribs. By the end of Act I probably my entire left side was one big bruise.' The direction and production were 'confused', wrote Brod; the Kostelnička, who should be 'a regal figure, a sort of Deborah, a *savante* whom the entire village regards with respect and who accordingly appears in her Sunday best (it is a holiday), carrying a beautiful lace shawl', had appeared 'in a soiled working dress, quasi "realistic" . . . with a pitchfork on her shoulders. I looked at Janáček at that moment. His face was distorted with pain; he was crying.'[154]

This account has found its way into much Janáček literature, but Janáček's own account of the rehearsals does not fully support Brod's recollection. Although Janáček did indeed regard the Kostelnička as a regal figure, and had very definite ideas on how she ought to be portrayed, his letters to Gabriela from Vienna are consistently full of praise for Lucie Weidt who created the role there. 'Mrs Weidt's acting is excellent – following the director's instructions,' wrote Janáček on 12 February, hinting only slightly at the producer's different conception of the role. Weidt, a soprano, did not have Gabriela's 'silken, dark voice, fitting the plot so well', but there were moments 'when one trembled'.[155] 'You are the Kostelnička-aristocrat, Weidt is a rugged one,' wrote Janáček to Gabriela on 18 February.[156]

Maria Jeritza, in the opera's title-role, was ideally suited to portray a Moravian peasant beauty. After a sensational début in Vienna she was chosen by Strauss to create the title-role in his *Ariadne auf Naxos* (1912); her voice was big and warm, and she was also admired for the energy of her acting style. 'I have at last heard and seen Jenůfa in my opera,' wrote Janáček on 20 February 1918.[157]

The première was a great success; Janáček had to take twenty curtain calls. Later that day he was to meet his friends and well-wishers at the Hotel Post where he was staying; on his way there he fainted, but he soon recovered and sat among the guests 'glowing with happiness'.[158]

The reviews were generally favourable. The greatest understanding for the opera's new style was expressed in the *Wiener Tagblatt* by Max Kalbeck (Brahms's biographer and the first translator of Smetana's *Bartered Bride*). At the influential *Neue Freie Presse*, Julius Korngold thought the work effective in parts, even though Janáček, in his view, lacked melodic invention. Richard Batka, writing for the *Fremdenblatt*, was the least perceptive critic: although he had worked in Prague for many years, he was a confirmed Wagnerian.[159] Yet despite the general success, the opera was taken off after a mere ten performances, and was not staged at the Hofoper again until 1925.

The publication of the German version of *Jenůfa* in 1918, by Universal Edition, greatly contributed towards Janáček's recognition outside his native country; the German première was to follow in November that year in Cologne, conducted by Otto Klemperer.[160]

Meanwhile the war continued and the political future – especially after the momentous November 1917 revolution in Russia – seemed black to Janáček.[161] On 29 March 1918, Good Friday, he completed his 'Slavonic orchestral rhapsody' *Taras Bulba* – a work which perhaps best reflects his reaction to the First World War and other political events that took place around that time.[162] Janáček was greatly attracted by this seventeenth-century Ukrainian legend, full of passion and heroism. It had been written down by Nikolai Gogol, and the composer's reasons for choosing it seem to be similar to Gogol's own. It was to be, as he wrote to Gabriela, his 'musical testament'.[163]

Janáček first read the legend in March 1905; he made notes and dated passages as he went along, but he only began to write the rhapsody in 1915, before the defeat of the Russian armies; in celebrating Russia's defiance, Janáček made no reference to the rivalry common between Slav nations.

Although he completed a sketch by 1916, there were to be many improvements before the score reached its final shape. The rhapsody is made up of three parts, 'The Death of Andriy', 'The Death of Ostap' and 'The Prophecy and Death of Taras Bulba'. In the first part, the Cossack army, led by Bulba, besieges the town of Dubno; Bulba's son Andriy rescues the beautiful daughter of a Polish nobleman with whom he is in love. In the ensuing battle Andriy sides with the Poles but, meeting his father face to face, is shamed and accepts death by his father's hand. In the second part, Bulba's other son, Ostap, is taken prisoner; tortured by the Poles, he calls out for Bulba who unexpectedly appears in the crowd. In the third part Bulba is captured after a punitive expedition against the Poles, to avenge Ostap's death. Sentenced to death, Bulba rejoices in seeing his warriors escape; before he dies he has a vision of his people's invincible spirit.

The piece was originally conceived as a cyclical concertante work, with solo violin, viola and cello, and only later reworked as a large-scale orchestral piece.[164] In its final version, much of its programme is reflected in the instrumentation: soon after a melancholy theme, portraying Andriy's divided feelings, bells and organ depict the enemy praying for help. After fragmented rhythms in the woodwind, a heartbreaking melody on the oboe paints a passionate scene of Andriy with his beloved, with cymbals indicating a raging battle outside; Taras himself seems to appear in the descending, *fortissimo* motif of the trombones. In the second part, after a brief, shimmering figuration on the harp, the striking ostinato in the strings creates powerful suspense. Ostap's cry and Bulba's appearance are portrayed by a high solo clarinet over a *fortissimo* tremolo in the strings, and the blare of trumpets. The finale is particularly vivid, bringing together echoes of the battle, a frenzied Polish dance and far-away fanfares. In the dying Bulba's apotheosis of indomitable Russia, bells and organ combine with the orchestra in a soundscape of great majesty and power. Throughout the work Janáček continued to develop and refine his montage technique, creating large blocks of sound from small units of varying density, a mosaic of solos, orchestral and poly-melodic layers (but not true polyphony). The work was an immedi-ate success both in Brno (1921) and Prague (1924).[165]

Earlier in the spring of 1918, Janáček was constantly trying to ward off depression and loneliness. On 15 April he wrote to Kamila Stösslová:

> You have no idea how low my spirits are. To live like *this*, so isolated, so introverted, without any fondness for [my] world and my sur-roundings – I cannot keep it up for long. Despite all the fame and great success I feel like one of the most unhappy people, as if exposed to ridicule . . . . I benumb and deaden myself by doing nothing but work; I throw myself into difficult tasks, to forget the *human being* who is also part of me . . . . Such is my fate.[166]

A week later he wrote to Gabriela: 'Yesterday I wrote you a tender, yearning letter. Do not wonder at it, and let no one wonder: this is the lot bestowed by nature on us ardent and inflamed composers.'[167] This particular letter has not survived, and although Janáček and Gabriela soon met again, two months later their correspondence broke off: it transpired that the diva had also been having an affair with the conductor Vincenc Maixner. During an unpleasant scene in his flat Maixner told Janáček that Gabriela 'had been and will be his mistress'; Janáček then terminated the relationship in writing. He never knew that Gabriela returned his letter, and that Zdenka inter-cepted and indeed kept that letter and the reply Gabriela sent with it.[168] He only wrote to her once more, ten years later. Addressing her formally, he congratulated her on the completion of twenty-five years with the National Theatre.[169]

In 1938 Gabriela insisted that Janáček was her 'artistic, sacred love . . . and I was his'.[170] And in the mid-1960s Gabriela, then almost 90, denied any involvement with Janáček and even made light of his passion for her. But Janáček, she told her interviewer, was very diffi-cult to get on with: 'He was very individual, not one person but five or six people rolled into one and you did not always know which one you were talking to . . .'.[171]

After his affair with Gabriela had ended, Janáček began writing to Kamila Stösslová several times a week. It is clear from various allusions in Janáček's letters that a loan to help the Stössels start a new business venture was discussed during his visit in May 1918.[172] By then Janáček's finances had taken a turn for the better. In June 1918 he wrote to Kamila that a publisher had been found for *The Excursions of Mr Brouček*; Janáček's royalties were to be 16 per cent of the retail price, with an immediate outright payment for the first edition – some 5,000 crowns, or fifty times Janáček's small teaching salary.[173]

Meanwhile the Stössels were sending further provisions and Kamila continued to correspond with Zdenka. After a brief meeting in Luhačovice in July 1918 Janáček repeatedly invited the couple to Hukvaldy, extolling to Kamila the beauty of his birthplace. In vain: he was not to see her again until November, when the Stössels came to Brno to stay.

By then a whole new world had opened up for Janáček and his countrymen. On 8 January 1918, after the Czech members of the Imperial Council and the assemblies from all the Czech provinces had demanded an independent state,[174] President Wilson submitted a programme to the American Congress, declaring his support for the principle of self-determination for the nations within the Austro-Hungarian Empire. At the end of May, in Pittsburgh, the Czech philosopher T.G. Masaryk and the representatives of the Czech and Slovak émigrés in the USA agreed to form an independent state of Czechs and Slovaks. Their right of self-determination was accepted by the French government in June, followed by Britain in August and the USA in September. Wishing to keep the monarchy intact, the Austro-Hungarian Empire began to negotiate an armistice. The end of the war was in sight; after a general strike in Bohemia in October, Masaryk, Eduard Beneš and the Slovak General Štefánik formed a provisional government in Paris, and submitted a declaration of independence to the US government.[175] The new state of Czecho-Slovakia (as it was spelled then) came into existence on 28 October 1918, thus ending almost three centuries of Habsburg rule for the Czechs, and a millennium of Hungarian domination for the Slovaks.

In Brno everyone had been eagerly awaiting the great day. When Janáček heard the news, he 'jumped up like a young man' and immediately began to make far-reaching plans: 'what would need to be done in the musical life of Moravia, what a future there would be for the Organ School and the theatre. We listened to what he said as if it were gospel, in which a new, wonderful future was opening for us.'[176]

8

The Indian Summer Begins

(1918–1924)

'A NEW EPOCH is coming, a springtime for the nation,' Janáček observed in 1918, soon after the foundation of the Czecho-slovak Republic.[1] The new state was roughly the size of present-day Austria and Switzerland together, with a population of about 13 million. There was an astonishing creative surge in its first decade, and a tremendous sense of optimism.

In November 1918 Janáček completed his first post-war work, the patriotic male-voice chorus *The Czech Legion*. Setting a poem by Antonín Horák, he exploited techniques developed in his Bezruč trilogy and echoed the Czech national anthem; despite poetic licence and a certain naivety in the text the work attracted much attention at the time.

Early in 1919 Janáček worked on his song-cycle *The Diary of One who Disappeared* – the first work inspired by Kamila Stösslová with whom he was now deeply in love. His feelings may not always have pleased her: judging by Janáček's letter of 27 July 1918, she did not want to see him in Luhačovice that summer, although she was staying there. 'I wanted to pay my respects to you,' protested Janáček, 'and in return you humiliated me in front of the servants. Surely I have never offended you that much!'[2] When his niece Věra reported how Kamila cried over 'Zdenka's fate', and 'boasted' of having managed to keep Janáček 'at arm's length', the composer was enraged – but not with Kamila.[3]

She continued to correspond with Zdenka that summer but not with Janáček, who became dispirited as a result. By September he had even lost for a while the desire to continue working on *The Diary*. A familiar obsessive tone reappears. 'I have done nothing to you, wanted nothing from you,' he mused. 'I am only writing to you because of the memories of the most beautiful stay in Luhačovice in 1917. I have nothing but memories now – well, I live in those.'[4] Kamila was then staying with her children at her mother's house in the small south Bohemian town of Písek; before long, Janáček sent another confession there:

> I write to you because I have no one else to whom to send these few lines, so that they may be read, and yet not read, because they remain unanswered. [. . .] It is as if I were talking to myself, pitying myself, consoling myself. [. . .] My thoughts keep stopping at you. That I told you only one thing, that you are beautiful. Yet it was not only your looks that made me do so, but rather your nature, that good, open nature of yours.[5]

The Stössels finally visited the Janáčeks in November 1918, after several invitations; Kamila subsequently thanked the couple in a letter which shows sincerity though little sophistication:

> Once again we thank you for your hospitality it was all very good and I cannot begin to describe to you how much we enjoyed it. What pleased us most were your contented faces how happy I am that the sun's rays again warm everything in your house a little more than when I saw you last. Only now have I felt in your house as if I were your daughter be very happy and healthy the rest will come by itself . . . .[6]

The Stössels returned the Janáček's hospitality in February 1919, a few days after the death of Janáček's sister Eleonora. The composer needed a break. 'Dying is a terrible thing,' he remarked to Kamila. 'I looked at it with terror.'[7]

A month later he announced that he had finished 'those songs about the gypsy'.[8] In fact, he had begun working on *The Diary* in 1917, soon after meeting Kamila for the first time in Luhačovice. 'Regularly every afternoon, a few motifs for those beautiful verses about that gypsy love come to my mind,' he wrote to her in August of that year. 'Perhaps a nice little musical novel will come out of this . . .'.[9]

The 'beautiful verses about gypsy love' – *From the Pen of a Self-taught Peasant* – were twenty-three anonymous poems written in a dialect from Valašsko. They were published on two successive Sundays in May 1916 in a popular Brno daily, *Lidové noviny*, where Janáček – a subscriber and regular contributor – came across them. According to the newspaper, the poems were the diary of a farmer's son; his parents had discovered them in his room after his mysterious disappearance, and they had assumed that the poems were folk-songs copied out by him. Their true meaning – the description of his romance with a gypsy girl – became clear only during a subsequent legal enquiry.

This kind of subject-matter was far from new at the time. But many details seem to have been inverted here. The stock nineteenth-century image of a fallen girl has been replaced by that of a fallen *man*, lamenting the loss of *his* virtue; Zefka, the Moravian Carmen, has a baby son by the young farmer who only then elopes with her, embracing his voluntary exile among the gypsies with joy. And in 1997 the 'folk poet' turned out to be an obscure Czech writer.

Ozef [Josef] Kalda, born in Valašsko, worked for a while as a railway official in Prague; he was posted to the provinces after publishing a story in which he pilloried his employers, and soon afterwards abandoned his declining career for literature. He was a prolific writer and explored many genres, but the Czech literary establishment saw him as a provincial, a member of a 'cowpat school' of literature.[10]

The assertion that the author of the verses was an uneducated peasant had never been taken seriously. A hoax was widely suspected, and possible culprits were heatedly discussed.[11] But no one thought of attributing the raw – and, for its time, daring – eroticism of the cycle to Kalda. In fact, scarcely three weeks after it had been published, he had written to a literary friend that he had allowed himself 'that little *eskamotage*' [sleight of hand].[12] Unfortunately, this letter lay buried among his friend's family papers for over eighty years; only its chance discovery by a local historian finally confirmed him to be the author of the cycle.

Why did Kalda pretend that his skilfully told story was the work of a country youth? We shall never know. Aged only 50, he died a few months before the première of *The Diary*, and he was never to enjoy the fame Janáček's setting would have brought him.

Janáček clearly identified Kamila with the gypsy enchantress of the story; in 1924 he confessed: 'And that black gypsy girl in my *Diary of One who Disappeared*, that was especially you.'[13] No doubt the dénouement – the young farmer's flight to a new life with his beloved – also had a special appeal for him. Nevertheless, the work went through many revisions. Although in March 1919 Janáček announced to Kamila that he had finished it, more work was still to be done; on 25 June he wrote once again that 'the black gypsy' was completed.[14]

Late in 1919 *The Diary* was finally put away in the painted chest in Janáček's study, where other unperformed works languished, and it was then forgotten. Over a year later it was discovered by Janáček's pupil, the conductor and composer Břetislav Bakala. He arranged the papers according to their various stages of composition; his friend (and Janáček's lawyer) Jaroslav Lecián then checked through the tenor part. A week later they performed the cycle for Janáček, who revised the punishingly high tessitura for the tenor and made the soprano Gypsy into a mezzo.[15]

On 18 April 1921 *The Diary of One who Disappeared* was successfully premièred in Brno; by the autumn it was published. Bakala's copy bore a dedication: 'As a souvenir for your having pulled it out of the chest . . . November 23, 1921.'[16]

Janáček invited Kamila – whose picture, with her hair loose, he wanted on the cover of the score at first – to the Prague première in December. As usual, she was diplomatic: 'It is impossible for me to come to Prague since my husband has not arrived . . . . If you took your wife perhaps I could come even without my husband [but] as things are, it is impossible.'[17] *The Diary* was a great success in Prague; Berlin, London and Paris premières soon followed.[18]

The Diary is not a song-cycle as we know it: it is in effect a dramatic cantata, composed for tenor, mezzo-soprano, piano accompaniment and three women's voices offstage, with rudimentary stage directions. Janáček set all the poems virtually in full, allocating the 'silent' poem (number 13, depicting the seduction) to the piano and linking the original numbers 10 and 11. Unlike any song-cycle written before, it tells a story, rather than depicting moods and impressions.[19]

The cycle is monothematic in origin, with much word painting; the melodic structure is based on fourths and seconds, on the pentatonic scale, and speech melodies. The words are beautifully set, perhaps because the style is clearly inspired by folk music (though only one song, number 20, is strophic, and particularly reminiscent of a lighthearted folk song).

Throughout *The Diary*, the piano writing is influenced by Janáček's vocal style – the piano doubles, imitates or anticipates the voice, with the vocal motifs compressed and rhythmically displaced. In the final song the piano suggests an orchestral accompaniment; the 'mute' number, with the powerful dynamic rise and fall of its ostinato motif, is a miniature drama in itself.[20]

Kalda portrayed the young man's initial fear of his awakening sexuality – a latter-day Schubertian journey – in the style of the best Moravian folk poetry, and the sincere, spontaneous tone is rendered vividly in Janáček's setting. It also shows how Janáček embraced important stylistic trends in European music, developing his own unique brand of each style: his 'impressionistic' music is, in fact, rooted in Moravian folk music, while his 'expressionism' evolved from his speech melody studies. The pithy yet intensely lyrical music of *The Diary* looks forward to his next great opera, *Káťa Kabanová*. But the form of *The Diary*, in which Janáček subverted the conventions of a traditional song-cycle, was dictated by his need to find a vehicle for his innate dramatic talent.

Janáček's stage directions in the score of *The Diary* are basic but clear: the work is to be performed in semi-darkness, with reddish lighting to heighten the erotic mood; Zefka is to enter and leave unobtrusively, and the three women's voices sing offstage, almost inaudibly. Did Janáček intend it to be fully staged, rather than merely wanting to enhance its expressiveness on the concert platform? The first performance on the theatre stage took place in 1926 in the Slovenian city of Ljubljana; in 1928, the director of the municipal theatre in the south Bohemian city of Plzeň also wanted to stage the work, and asked Janáček to orchestrate it. The composer answered immediately: 'I like your idea of a staged performance. We'll do it.'[21]

These plans were never fulfilled. Although a staged performance of *The Diary* was given at this theatre in 1943, the score remained unchanged. Nor is it certain that orchestrating it would be an improvement.[22]

Before *The Diary* was rediscovered, Janáček had already completed the orchestral *Ballad of Blaník*, which he originally called 'The Knights of Blaník'. This work is based on a poem by Jaroslav Vrchlický[23] and is a modern version of the old Czech legend which was also the inspiration for Smetana's final tone poem in his cycle *Má vlast*. The Blaník Hill (near Vlašim, south-east of Prague) has great historical importance for the Czechs: according to the legend the knights of the title are asleep inside the hill, and they will arise to come to the aid of the Czech nation in its hour of greatest need.

Janáček wrote the *Ballad* in his favourite key of A flat minor, while also exploring a whole-tone effect. In Janáček's setting, the hero, the young man Jíra, is suggested in the main theme by its high range, and the melodic line is reminiscent of a shepherd's song from the Valašsko region.[24] But it is as the hero approaches the Blaník Hill that Janáček uses the whole-tone scale.[25] Jíra's surprise at seeing the knights is followed by a noble chordal *maestoso* on the harps (the knights' motif);[26] this is later varied, then it peters out, and the structure becomes unclear. For Jíra's awakening, Janáček quotes the first theme, which returns frequently in the finale, as does the knights' motif; he also introduces a theme strongly reminiscent of the apotheosis of Russia in the finale of his orchestral rhapsody *Taras Bulba*. Layers of sound are built from these various themes, with their fragments and variations; the resulting jubilant mood then gives way to a minor key, with a solo clarinet describing Jíra's disillusionment – he is now an old man. After returning to the opening sequence and the knights' theme, the work ends in a stately mood, following a splendidly resolved closing cadence.

The topical theme of the poem – swords being turned into ploughshares – clearly appealed to Janáček, but the *Ballad* does not belong among his key works. At its première in Brno on 21 March 1920 it had a mixed reception; the performance was not helped by the standard of the orchestra.[27]

After the war ended Janáček also set about various tasks he wished to complete. 'I would like to finish my life's work,' he wrote in November 1918 to his friend, the writer Jan Herben.

> (1) Ten thousand songs lie in my care as chairman of the working committee for Czech folk-song in Moravia and Silesia . . . . The first volume has already been prepared for publication. (2) The musical institute where I have communicated my musical beliefs, the Organ School, is to be taken over by the state. I have carried the burden and the worries of this institute for thirty-six years – and I would like to (3) push the burden out of my mind so that I can uninterruptedly devote myself to composition . . . .[28]

One of Janáček's chief aims was the transformation of the Organ School into a conservatoire. His efforts were continually frustrated and, much to his displeasure, several members of staff sent a petition to the ministry of education not to appoint him director. 'I have devoted my entire life to the idea,' he complained bitterly to Kamila, 'and now they hatch plots to repay me in this fashion.'[29] The new Brno Conservatoire – then still a private institution – was founded in September 1919 by merging the Organ School with the music school of the Brno Beseda Club, and Janáček did in fact become its first director. 'Who would want to teach finches to sing? Who would want to teach anyone to compose?' he wrote, somewhat paradoxically, in a *feuilleton* published shortly afterwards. 'Do not obscure the brightness of its [creative] process with foreign work, do not stifle it with an alien atmosphere. The field of *exploration* is the only field of *learning*.' The new institution was also to contribute towards the preservation of the nation's heritage by continuing research into speech melodies. '*At this modern Conservatoire,*' concluded Janáček, '*we want to contribute to collecting material for a dictionary of the living Czech language.*'[30]

Later that year Janáček tried to engage for the Conservatoire various Czech musical luminaries – the violin teacher Otokar Ševčík, the violin virtuoso Jan Kubelík and the soprano Emmy Destinn (now using the Czech version of her name, Ema Destinnová). But the negotiations came to nothing. Nor was Janáček appointed to the new board of governors at the National Theatre in Prague; two other composers, J.B. Foerster and Vítězslav Novák, were chosen instead. 'The threads binding me to Prague are being broken,' Janáček declared to Kamila in April 1919, adding defiantly: 'I was self-sufficient before, I shall be self-sufficient now.'[31]

On 22 March 1920, despite various intrigues, the Brno Conservatoire finally became a state institution. This was the culmination of 'thirty-nine years' work' on Janáček's part.[32] Yet his directorship was not renewed: the post went to his pupil, the 37-year-old composer Jan Kunc. And as all the Czech state conservatoires had to offer an identical syllabus, Janáček's theory of harmony – which he had been teaching at the Organ School since its foundation – was excluded from the course of the Brno Conservatoire. Nevertheless, in September 1920 Janáček was appointed professor of the composition master-class at the Prague Conservatoire, but resident in Brno; he and Zdenka were granted free tenure for life of their 'cottage' in the garden of the Brno Conservatoire.

Thus Janáček was still able to teach and could also devote more time to composition. He was glad of the free time, and seldom admitted how much it grieved him that he no longer headed the new Conservatoire. As the former Organ School, it had been his pride and joy – he had chosen every piece of furniture in the building, and had personally supervised every aspect of the school's day-to-day running. And the students, as he used to say, were his family. Thanks to Janáček they had free tickets to the opera, and to concerts at several music societies. Many students came from poor families, and Janáček would frequently provide not only money for fees and sheet music but also clothes and shoes, especially during the war.

Nevertheless, he had always been a strict teacher, feared even by his best pupils. In his harmony class, for instance, Janáček would ask: 'What do you see when you look at this chord?' If no one could provide the answer he wanted, Janáček would complain furiously: '*Ja,*

Jesus Maria, I have nothing but idiots in my class!' and storm off home to calm down.[33] Today Janáček's theoretical writings are rarely studied, although his ideas are of interest and relevance. But while too individual and creative an artist to be an ideal teacher, he inspired much affection. 'I remembered that I played a *Slavonic Dance* by Dvořák very slowly,' recalled the famous Czech pianist Rudolf Firkušný, whose mother first took him to Janáček in 1917. On hearing his future pupil, then barely five, Janáček 'screamed "No!" and rushed to the piano to play the music at the right tempo. He also played the last movement of Beethoven's "Moonlight" Sonata, a revelatory experience for me,' remembered Firkušný. 'For the first time, I heard what great piano playing sounded like. [. . .] I soon found out what people close to him had known all along – that under the forbidding outer shell of that stormy genius there existed a kind and generous human being.'[34]

The Brno Conservatoire remained a hive of activity, as did the Janáčeks' cottage; music-making never ceased and visitors continued to pour in. Janáček was also briefly on the board of directors of the Brno Opera, but soon resigned.[35] Fortunately, the post of the new artistic director went – at Janáček's suggestion – to the Moravian-born František Neumann, who had worked mostly in Germany and Austria, but had always kept in touch with Czech musical life. Neumann began his appointment with a new production of *Jenůfa* in August 1919; Janáček was to entrust him with the premières of many of his later operas.

Neumann's arrival enabled Janáček to solve another problem in the musical life of Brno. For many years he had tried to establish a combined tradition of concerts and opera in the city, but his attempts had been thwarted: Brno could not afford to maintain a permanent symphony orchestra, nor was the orchestra of the Czech opera house encouraged to give regular concerts. Now, Janáček insisted that Neumann's contract should stipulate that he give concerts with the theatre orchestra during the opera season. Thus the players were able to explore a larger repertoire than before; the standard of playing improved and before long a new artistic community grew around Neumann, including a whole generation of indigenous Moravian composers. At last, Janáček was able to see the city's musical life developing along the lines he had always wanted; the Brno opera house (known as the City Theatre) became an operatic platform second only to Prague in the Republic.[36]

During the first decade of the newly-founded Czechoslovakia

Prague remained the country's cultural centre, growing quickly into a truly modern metropolis. Janáček visited the capital frequently during 1919, while negotiating the publication of his works with the Hudební matice publishing house. He also attended meetings of an advisory committee for music and national monuments, of which he became a full member a year later. His visits became even more frequent in 1920, when *The Excursions of Mr Brouček* was finally staged at the National Theatre.

Janáček had been negotiating this production with Kovařovic since the end of 1917, but it had been continually postponed. Wartime shortages of materials for the sets and costumes did not help; moreover, there was a dearth of suitable tenors for the title role, with its dizzying tessitura.[37] It was not until November 1919 that Otakar Ostrčil, recently appointed dramaturg at the National Theatre, was asked to make a critical assessment of the opera. By then Kovařovic was seriously ill; when Ostrčil produced a favourable report he was entrusted with the production,[38] and orchestral rehearsals began in January 1920.

Janáček was looking forward to the première in April that year,[39] and he invited the Stössels to join him. They had visited the Janáčeks in Brno the previous Christmas; since the summer of 1919 Janáček had been wearing a ring engraved with Kamila's name, which she had given him in exchange for his. David Stössel was trying to rebuild his antiques business and, much to Kamila's chagrin, was often away from home. 'I have to wear black all the time,' she wrote to Janáček, half in jest, in February 1920, 'since I am constantly in mourning for my husband.'[40]

Zdenka, who was also going to attend the première, was afraid of 'looking like Cinderella' next to Kamila.[41] Before the Vienna première of *Jenůfa* Janáček had written to Kamila to say how much he would welcome her presence at the Hofoper, so that Zdenka would have 'someone to lean on'.[42] Now, with a deplorable lack of tact, he suggested that Zdenka should pose as Kamila's mother 'who had passed on everything beautiful to her daughter'.[43]

The Excursions – produced by Gustav Schmoranz, with stage design by Karel Štapfer – was given a run of ten performances. Many of the singers were among the pillars of Kovařovic's ensemble: both the small, stocky Mirko Štork, well suited to the role of Brouček, and Miloslav Jeník, as Mazal/Starry-Eyes/Petřík, were outstanding tenors; the 29-year-old soprano Ema Miřiovská played the triple role of Málinka/Etherea/Kunka.

The mixed reception the opera received was a bitter disappointment to Janáček. Four years before, after one of the sold-out repeat
performances of *Jenůfa* in Prague, he had written triumphantly to
Zdenka: 'I believe I have dealt a heavy blow to Smetana's importance
as a composer. I would compose a different *Libuše*.'[44] Now, on
the afternoon of the première of *The Excursions* Janáček was 'very
depressed', recalled his pupil, the composer Osvald Chlubna; after
the performance, only a few close friends gathered to celebrate with
Janáček in an almost empty beer cellar. 'The Prague artistic community and critics still did not want to take notice of Janáček,' observed
Chlubna.[45] Some two weeks later Janáček remarked bitterly to
Kamila: 'It is my lot always to be vindicated in everything only
through struggle.'[46]

True to form, Kamila did not attend the première after all. 'My
gloomy mood was interrupted by your news,' responded Janáček 'I
smiled bitterly and said not a word.' Once again he 'hardened and
grew cold' towards Prague. 'I was dreading the performance,' he
complained to her, 'especially since at the dress rehearsal the theatre
was filled to the last seat and everyone listened to the entire work
with an icy coldness! What kind of people were they!? And yet this is
my best work, and no doubt will please more as time goes on.' As the
opera unfolded, the audience warmed up and eventually 'burst into
an ovation', he reported. 'The newspapers called me the [country's]
foremost dramatic composer − but with what reluctance! I spent a
fortnight in Prague, but believe me, I felt as if I were in a foreign city:
no one ever noticed me anywhere. [. . .] Not a word in the periodicals! [. . .] Everyone kept stubbornly silent.'[47]

Why was *The Excursions* not a success in Prague? Although it is difficult to perform, Ostrčil rehearsed it devotedly.[48] And, incredibly,
Janáček even encouraged him to make 'colourful' orchestral changes if
necessary.[49] Ostrčil declined to do that: certain changes had to be made
in the vocal parts (which were too high for the singers) but he tried his
best 'not to harm the spirit of the work'.[50] Even after the première
there was correspondence between the two: Janáček worried about
the instrumentation, suggesting changes in the chorus, stressing certain
tempi, and remarking on the length of the ballet on the Moon.[51]
Ostrčil was firm on the first point: 'As far as orchestral changes are concerned, Maestro, you will have to decide for yourself . . . . Kovařovic
makes orchestral changes left, right and centre. He made changes even
in [Smetana's] *Má vlast* . . . . I, on the contrary, am against such changes,
on principle.'[52]

The male singers were far less loyal. Václav Novák (as the publican Mr Würfl) let it be known that he was not 'a bawler'; others also reproached Janáček, belittling his style. 'Believe me, I have never experienced more bitter moments than during the dress rehearsal [of *Brouček*],' Janáček wrote to Novák on hearing of these objections. 'It seemed to me as if I were openly hated by you for my work. And that is naturally painful.' Nonetheless, he later went out of his way to assure the singers of his gratitude for their 'outstanding, unique and exhausting' performances.[53]

The critics praised some aspects of the opera but also expressed doubts. 'If Janáček's orchestra is up to the grotesquerie of the lunar environment,' declared Miloš Kareš in *Tribuna*, 'it fails completely in the second part, when the composer more often hits a serious note.'[54] And while Janáček's libretto for *Jenůfa*, said the reviewer of *Národní listy*, was 'a complete, rounded drama, already tried out as far as its stage effect is concerned', *The Excursions* had been created 'from the fragments of scenes very diverse in character, difficult for a musical composition', and its dramatic effectiveness remained 'a question which only further experience can answer'.[55] Only Dvořák's biographer, Otakar Šourek, gave the work full marks: to the 'rich spectrum of his musical expressiveness' Janáček had now added 'a new, hitherto unknown tone, the more surprising in that it is successful: humour – tough, unsparing, caustic humour, revelling in ridicule and caricature'.[56] Ostrčil remarked ironically that the critics 'danced between praise and rejection, to avoid harming themselves';[57] on reading the reviews Janáček commented: 'Why do they puff it up in such a learned manner? If I have written such music and so much of it that everyone who has eyes and ears can genuinely laugh, I have already fulfilled my task.'[58]

In fact, the première of *The Excursions* may have come too late. In 1917, Janáček's jubilant tone in his *feuilleton* about this opera[59] – prompted, no doubt, by the success of *Jenůfa* – was in tune with the general atmosphere before Czechoslovak independence. By 1920 the new republic was established; presenting Brouček as 'a warning' was perhaps now less necessary than Janáček had thought; indeed, his anti-hero may have seemed obsolete.[60] As early as 1915, Karel Šípek [Josef Peška] – the librettist, writer and translator who had done so much for the Prague première of *Jenůfa* – had written to Marie Calma that the text Janáček had sent him was 'impossible':

A mere sketch, without an exposition, assuming that everyone knows Čech's *Brouček*. [. . .] Anyway, is the material worth it? Has it not aged?

Isn't its very premise flawed? The lunar literary dream could have been dreamt by Čech, but not by a Prague beer-imbibing bourgeois. Thus the psychology of dream[s] is in fact being slapped in the face. Does Mr Janáček also live partly on the moon?[61]

Certainly Janáček's dramatic construction and stage requirements were extremely ambitious, and contemporary opera houses lacked the machinery necessary to do them justice. *The Excursions* was not seen in Czechoslovakia again in its entirety during Janáček's lifetime. The moon adventure was staged on its own in Brno in 1926, and contemporary critics in fact thought that omitting the fifteenth-century part did no harm. *The Excursions* was also the only Janáček opera which Max Brod did not translate into German: war is 'glorified' in one scene, and this went against Brod's pacifist beliefs. Yet in 1960 Brod 'almost regretted' his decision: 'The music of *Brouček* is particularly impassioned and individual; I made a heavy sacrifice . . .'.[62]

In January 1920, even before *The Excursions* was in rehearsal in Prague, Janáček had begun work on his sixth opera, *Káťa Kabanová*. 'The chief character . . . is a woman, soft by nature,' he confided to Kamila. 'A breeze would carry her away – let alone the storm that gathers over her!'[63]

This was not the first Russian subject that Janáček had considered for an opera. In 1907 he thought about Tolstoy's *Anna Karenina*; in 1916, considering the same author's posthumous novel, *The Living Corpse*, he sketched the score of the first scene.[64] In 1918 three Slavonic subjects were suggested to him by Václav Jiřikovský, the young assistant director of the Brno City Theatre; one of these was *The Thunderstorm*, written in 1859 by the Russian playwright A.N. Ostrovsky (1823–86).[65]

There was no Czech subject that appealed to Janáček at the time and, according to Jiřikovský, he acquired the relevant books immediately. When he returned to see the director, he was 'taken so strongly' with *The Thunderstorm* that he talked about it as if completely convinced by its suitability. It was the play's 'raw earthiness' that attracted him most, although he had doubts about some character traits and situations. By November 1919 he was negotiating for the rights to the Czech translation of the play.[66] Jiřikovský perhaps takes too much credit for awakening Janáček's interest in Ostrovsky soon after the Vienna première of *Jenůfa*. He also claims that – in order to reinforce it – he had the play specially put on in March 1919. In fact, there is no evidence that Janáček considered *The Thunderstorm* before 1919.[67]

His inspiration for the character of Káťa was the heroine of Puccini's opera *Madama Butterfly*. Janáček loved this opera, which he first saw in 1908 at the National Theatre in Prague.[68] In 1919, after seeing a performance in Brno, he recalled how touched and excited he was when he used to travel to see it: *Butterfly* was 'one of the most beautiful and most sad operas'. Inevitably, he now likened 'the small, dark-haired Butterfly' to Kamila. *Káťa Kabanová* also reveals his growing love for her. During their initial meeting in 1917 he was touched by her 'great, measureless love' for her husband, and these memories were awakened as he worked on the opera. 'When . . . I saw your tears – the child in your arms, your husband at the front – your grief, your suffering, your despair poured into my vision of *Káťa Kabanová*,' he confessed in 1928. And on the title-page of the vocal score he gave her the same year, he reported a conversation with a friend many years before: like 'a miracle', Kamila had always been on his mind. 'My Káťa grows in her, in her, in Kamila! It will be one of my most tender works.'[69]

Unlike *Jenůfa*, and *The Excursions of Mr Brouček*, *Káťa* was written quickly: fifteen months after he first mentioned the opera to Kamila, Janáček announced that he had completed it. 'I don't know whether they will call it *The Thunderstorm* or *Katěrina*,' he added. 'Against *The Thunderstorm* is the fact that another opera by that title already exists; against *Katěrina*, that I write nothing but "female" operas! [. . .] The best thing would be to give, instead of the title, three asterisks.'[70] In the end Janáček settled (on the advice of Gustav Schmoranz) for a diminutive of the heroine's name, Káťa, rather than the more formal Katěrina.[71]

Ostrovsky was a leading exponent of Russian Realism in the nineteenth century; a Russian Balzac, a sharp-eyed chronicler of the Muscovite merchant class, he wrote some fifty plays, of which *The Thunderstorm* has remained the most popular, especially with Russian audiences. It has been said that Ostrovsky's plays lack technique, and that their plots have little finesse. But his style is rich, idiosyncratic and full of local colour.

The original Russian title of the play, 'Groza', may be translated not only as thunderstorm, but also terror, and the play has often been seen as a political allegory: the 'black hole of provincialism' which it depicts, the dreariness of life in the vastness of Czarist Russia, was thought to reflect a regime nearing its end. Despite her eventual suicide, the heroine represents an element of hope: she stands up to the world of rigid mores and set values, defying prejudice and hypocrisy.

Janáček's change of title shows a different perception of the story: in his hands, the original, relatively strong heroine became rather submissive. Working hard on the score in February 1920, the composer told Kamila how he repeatedly reminded himself that Káťa had an extremely gentle disposition: 'I am afraid that she would melt, indeed dissolve, if the sun shone on her fully.'[72] He also dispensed with several of Ostrovsky's peripheral characters; combining some roles, and reducing others.[73] It was Káťa who carried the psychological interest of the story. He did not stress the symbolism inherent in the original title, nor did he exploit the potent imagery usually inspired in Russian music by the river Volga.

The plot is simple: a young, tender-hearted woman with a vivid imagination is married to a weak husband (Tichon) with an overbearing mother (Kabanicha). In the provincial town where Káťa lives, Boris – recently arrived from the capital – is the only person capable of understanding her unexpressed longings. She is irresistibly drawn to him, succumbs and, racked with guilt, eventually takes her life. Of all Janáček's operas, *Káťa* alone can be seen as pure tragedy.

As he wished to avoid the difficulties he had experienced with the librettists for *Mr Brouček*, Janáček adapted *The Thunderstorm* himself. He made heavy cuts (indicated in his copy of the play), moving the material around, inventing some lines, and working out many of the verbal details during the actual composition. Instead of retaining Ostrovsky's ground-plan of five acts, Janáček cast the opera in three, each with two scenes; the last two scenes of the final act correspond to the play's last two acts. The situation in each act is therefore clearly mapped out: the events before Tichon's departure for a business trip, Káťa's subsequent affair with Boris, and the ensuing débâcle.

Káťa's transformation in Janáček's hands has been much discussed. In Ostrovsky's original, her rebelliousness is unmistakable: 'If I really get to loathe this place, no power on earth will stop me,' she tells Varvara in Act 2. 'I'll jump out of the window, I'll throw myself into the Volga. If I don't want to live here, I won't; I don't care what you do to me.' Janáček cut this outburst: it would not have fitted in with the extreme gentleness and sweetness of character which he ascribed to Káťa. Instead, he stresses her religious feelings, her conscience and, even before her affair with Boris has fully developed, her excessive feelings of guilt – of which she eventually dies.

Faced with Káťa's fragility and tenderness, one sometimes wishes someone *would* rescue her; she even dismisses swiftly any chance of building a new life with Boris – perhaps because it would have to be based on a lie and betrayal. Hers is clearly a gradual process of disintegration. Káťa also speaks of her need for public confession, and her desire to suffer, long before her affair is consummated. Moreover, her religious ecstasy in Act 1, Scene 2 hovers perilously close to the sexual. Yet references to Káťa's not-so-latent masochism have largely been avoided by performers and producers; indeed, they have been frowned upon, especially in Janáček's native country.

Kabanicha – possibly the worst mother-in-law in operatic history – has not retained in Janáček's libretto even a glimpse of the coarse sense of humour Ostrovsky allowed her; Dikoj, writhing at her feet, is another character tinged with masochism. And both men in Káťa's life are clearly weaklings. Only Varvara – a mover and shaker in the opera – offers hope. She and Kudrjáš alone break free, leaving behind the 'realm of darkness' as they escape to the capital and a new future.

Janáček employed in *Káťa* all the techniques he had developed in his earlier works – speech melodies, a characteristic melodic structure, varying rhythms, a specific type of harmony and distinctive orchestration – to powerful effect. From small speech-based motifs, he created music of immense melodic wealth and lyricism. And although Janáček's melodic thinking is not based on long, broadarched tunes, the great sweetness of music in *Káťa Kabanová* is in no way hampered by his habitually short-breathed phrases.

Surprisingly, Káťa is not associated with any specific musical theme. Instead, Janáček uses a combination of techniques, portraying the changes in her states of mind with remarkable sensitivity. First, we hear a characteristic *type* of music (frequently in the same key, B flat minor) even when Káťa is not actually singing. In Act 1, Scene 2, 'Káťa's music' is heard between Kabanicha's ordering Tichon to instruct Káťa how to behave in his absence, and Tichon's reply; a symmetrical four-bar motif, scored for viola d'amore, begins one bar before his response. Káťa therefore 'speaks' even when she is silent. At the end of this scene, one bar before Káťa breaks down, Janáček gives the motif to the flute while Tichon sings his order, once again preparing the listener for the dénouement. Similarly, in Act 2, Scene 1, Káťa's cry of 'Misfortune!' is preceded by several bars marked *pianissimo* and *dolcissimo*; based on a motif from the prelude, the music clearly expresses Káťa's gentleness. Varvara, on the other hand, has been given a theme which recurs throughout the opera – a lilting, teasing tune which unmistakably evokes a Russian folk-song, as does Kudrjáš's 'waiting song' before their rendezvous in Act 2, Scene 2.[74]

Káťa's part is also characterized by smaller intervals, extended only during periods of emotional turmoil (for example, in Act 2, Scene 1, the rising augmented seventh as she asks Varvara 'Have you really gone mad?'; meeting Boris, her 'Why, don't you see?' is sung to a falling octave, just before she finally raises her eyes and looks at him). In contrast, Kabanicha's vocal lines are frequently angular and composed of large intervals, consonant with the speech of an angry person.

The harmony also contributes to characterization; as the various motifs grow and are varied, new and expressive harmonic changes occur: whole-tone harmony is juxtaposed with diatonic harmony, and keys oscillate between major and minor.[75]

The overture to *Káťa*, unlike those of Janáček's other operas, uses material from the rest of the work. The powerful, doom-laden theme on the timpani and trombones (its eight notes consisting of an interval of a rising perfect fourth, with each note repeated four times) recurs several times. This 'fate theme', as it is often somewhat simplistically called, is heard again at the end of Act 1 and in both scenes of Act 3. The 'Russian' or 'troika' theme with its tinkling bells, which reappears towards the end of Act 1, signalling Tichon's climatic departure, also derives from it.

Janáček's use of thematic material in *Káťa* is masterly. Some themes are used throughout an act – the 'sigh of the Volga', for instance, is announced in the storm scene in Act 3, reappears in a wordless chorus version during Káťa's suicide scene, and is last heard as the act closes. Themes and motifs are contrasted and ingeniously played against each other, and the mood is powerfully evoked.

Although orchestral colours do not always blend well in *Káťa*, and the writing of individual parts shows some awkwardness, Janáček's characteristic sound had largely developed by then. The composer never had much patience with the limitations of instruments, nor with musicians' objections to his demands; and he often bemoaned his inability to notate clearly the image he had in mind. In *Káťa*, new, intriguing sounds leap out from almost every page; the instrumentation includes viola d'amore, and sleigh-bells reinforce the opera's Russian atmosphere.

A fortnight before Janáček claimed to have completed the opera, the Janáčeks only just avoided another domestic upheaval. When Zdenka's mother died in Vienna during the devastating 1918 influenza epidemic, Zdenka's father begged her to take him back to

Brno. She found him a room with one of her friends; in 1920 he moved closer to the Janáčeks' cottage.[76] Zdenka would have liked him to move in, but dared not ask her husband; instead, she broached the subject through Kamila. 'I can hardly believe that Zdenka could write to you along those lines,' Janáček replied in February 1921.

> Why, she knows only too well that while I am working, both she and Mára [the Janáčeks' maidservant] are afraid to enter my room. [. . .] If an intrusive fly were to buzz about the room, I wouldn't stand it. If unaccustomed steps or rustling around were heard in the next room, it would disturb me. Disturb?! I would explode, incensed, I would be angry, unbearable. In creative work it is – I tell you frankly – as if a mother were about to give birth and someone were to prevent her, impede her in a natural act. [. . .] This is not [just] about her father: it's about me, my whole being, my entire activities, my work, all my scant happiness, [my] hard-won domestic peace and quiet: it is not a question of physical comfort – but of my entire mental equilibrium.[77]

After this outburst, Kamila advised Zdenka to have her father to stay while Janáček – still not reconciled with his father-in-law – was on holiday in Luhačovice.

At the end of 1921 Janáček made what he considered a sound investment: from his brother's widow he bought a small four-room house in Hukvaldy, with a garden and some land.[78] The house became a source of great joy: Janáček referred to it jokingly as his 'estate'.[79] Yet while at Hukvaldy that Christmas he felt very much alone; avoiding people, he was already planning his next stay at Luhačovice, when he might see Kamila again. 'Perhaps you will listen to reason when a sick man begs you,' he pleaded, clearly trying to wheedle her into meeting him.[80] A more cheerful letter followed, with a drawing of the house which he hoped she would see one day.

It is difficult to detect exactly what Kamila's feelings for Janáček were. She was happily married with two children and she certainly did not wish to compromise herself. On the other hand, her husband was often away and at times like that she may have welcomed Janáček's continuous attention. It was also to the Stössels' advantage, financially and in other ways, to cultivate his friendship. Just before Christmas, Kamila reminisced about the past: 'I would never have thought we would correspond for so long,' she confessed. 'And that we would be such good friends.' Janáček re-read her letter many times. 'I am glad I have a friend,' he replied. 'That one can have a friend without the world pointing a finger at one. How difficult it is to understand! Everywhere people look only for filth and vice. Well, let us set an example!'[81]

In the immediate post-war years, much of Central and Eastern Europe was in turmoil; and Czechoslovakia was, in the early 1920s, still suffering from post-war shortages. An atmosphere of nervousness prevailed, and in Prague the situation reached an ugly climax at the end of 1920: November saw three days of anti-Jewish and anti-German riots, and a general strike followed in December. In 1923 the anarchist-inspired assassination of the Czech minister Alois Rašín rounded off the difficult post-war years. Prague began to breathe again; as the economy stabilized, the newly-founded Czechoslovakia began to flourish.

Known as the First Republic (1918–38), the country had a developed legal system, a self-sufficient economy, and an independent culture. As there was no longer any need to use subterfuge against oppressors, a new morality developed. Democracy was, for the Czechs and the Slovaks, an entirely novel phenomenon.

The country's capital, Prague, embraced and reflected developments elsewhere in Europe; with the Viennese influence now gone, there were strong ties with Germany and France. Radio Prague started regular transmission in 1923; the streets blazed with the new colours of posters and advertisements, new architecture gave the fast-growing city a modern look, and Praguers began to enjoy themselves.

And what about Brno, situated a mere hundred kilometres north of Vienna? Before Czech independence Janáček was not fond of the city. 'On the whole, our town has a rather bad reputation,' he remarked ironically in 1903. But after the foundation of the Republic his attitude changed, even though the German element remained fairly strong in Brno. 'Gone was my aversion to the gloomy town hall, [gone] my hatred of the [Špilberk] hill, in whose bowels so much misery had resounded at one time, [gone] my disgust for the street and [the masses] teeming in it.'[82]

Yet no operatic subject associated with the city suggested itself to him.[83] Instead, in his seventh opera, *The Cunning Little Vixen* (1922–3, known to Czech audiences under its original title, *The Adventures of the Vixen Bystrouška*), Janáček turned to the Moravian countryside. Like *The Diary of One who Disappeared*, the opera's origin is closely connected with the Brno daily, *Lidové noviny*, to which Janáček began contributing again after a gap of several years.[84]

In 1920 the paper published a series of 200 charming line-drawings by a Moravian painter, Stanislav Lolek.[85] Rudolf Těsnohlídek, the paper's law correspondent, was persuaded to write an accompanying text, and the resulting serial was published in fifty-one instalments between April and June, under the title *Bystrouška*.[86] It told the life-story of a vixen, caught as a cub and reared by a forester; much to the chagrin of the forester's wife, the vixen gradually decimates the population of the henhouse. Later she escapes, turns a badger out of his sett, and marries the fox Goldenstripe, with whom she rears a family.

Janáček's maidservant describes in her memoirs how she brought the serial to his notice: the composer heard her laughing aloud at the latest instalment, in which the Vixen was pictured walking with her suitor, the Fox, and coyly carrying a flower. Intrigued, Janáček looked at the picture and smiled at the text; Stejskalová immediately suggested that the serial would make a wonderful subject for an opera, especially for someone like himself who understood animals and liked to notate their cries. For them on Janáček is thought to have begun collecting the remaining instalments as they came out (although there is an almost complete set in the Janáček Archive). The following year the text was published as a novel.

Těsnohlídek was summoned to discuss the project with Janáček soon after the composer had decided on the subject, but only wrote one song for him (at the beginning of the Act 2 inn scene).[87] Janáček adapted his own libretto from the novel, following it fairly closely in the first two acts; the third act was assembled from various episodes in the book. In his version, the marriage celebration concludes the second act; in the third, the Vixen is shot by the poultry dealer Harašta, and the Forester has a dream in which he recognizes one of her cubs as the spitting image of its mother.

Of all Janáček's operas, *The Vixen* has invited the most diverse interpretations: on one hand, it has been promoted as an entertaining opera for children; on the other, it has been ranged among Janáček's 'tragic' operas.[88] Much has also been written about Max Brod's translation of the original title into German, *Das schlaue Füchslein* (in English *The Cunning Little Vixen*), under which name the opera has become known outside Janáček's native country. Brod based his translation on the assumption that the Vixen's name, Bystrouška, was made up from the Czech feminine adjective *bystrá* (shrewd, sharp, quick-witted). Although the name *could* also refer to the Vixen's sharp ears, the more usual Czech interpretation would indicate her cunning.[89] In the English rendering of Brod's translation the traditional perception of the fox as the wiliest of animals is thus reinforced.

This view of the fox goes all the way back to antiquity, but neither Těsnohlídek's story nor Janáček's opera is a classic Aesopian fable or pure satire: it is a parable. There is no cloying sentimentality, nor are the animals in *The Cunning Little Vixen* caricatured: whenever they assume human manners, it is to satirize human foibles.[90] Nevertheless, Janáček clearly saw the Vixen as a symbol of pure femininity, and a free spirit.

The libretto moves between the animal and human worlds, between lighthearted parody of human situations and the tragedy of loss; Janáček's view of humanity in this opera is neither entirely benign nor completely cynical. The two contrasting worlds, from youth to old age, are juxtaposed within the single realm of the countryside, and the music bridges the gulf between them. The mythic, the tragic and the comic are intermingled in the opera; and by the reappearance of the Vixen's daughter in the finale Janáček clearly wanted to emphasize the cyclical nature of life.

The internal structure of the opera differs from Janáček's earlier stage works: the pairings of the characters, and their relationships with each other, are no longer analysed in depth. Instead, Janáček draws bold outlines and abbreviates the story substantially. The cartoon-strip origins of the novel, with its juxtaposition of images, are probably reflected in the combination of different forms within the opera: Janáček used not only operatic dialogue, song, chorus and ballet but also mime, and there are orchestral preludes and interludes as well as wordless singing. In every one of his stage works, Janáček tried – and perfected – new techniques; by the use of mime and dance, for example, he enabled the animals in *The Vixen* to comment on the action even when the character concerned does not sing.[91] And although the animals, like most of the humans in the opera, conduct their dialogue in a broad, rather comic local dialect,[92] their observations on and response to human behaviour are comprehensible only to the audience.

The episode portraying the Vixen in captivity in the Forester's farmyard is relieved by many moments of pure comedy. When the Vixen enters farmyard politics, the characteristics commonly attributed to the individual animals are exploited to the full. The preening, chauvinistic Rooster is portrayed as an agent of capitalist Man, with the subservient Hens busily laying eggs. The Vixen herself, adopting the mask of a revolutionary, gives a speech in literary Czech whose clichés have a hilarious, unmistakably pseudo-Marxist tone.[93] Janáček clearly delighted in setting the scene; his views of

Communism are obvious from one of his notes (written in a typically terse style):

> [. . .] When a house is being built [a workman] steals a door handle
> when it suits him – albeit after dark! [Off] to the forest to gather kin-
> dling – and take a tree.
>   To use up the pasture, he drives in a herd of goats.
>   And at all times: [he shows] a genial face!
>   No enterprise – the dark shadow of communism.[94]

In the inn scene (Act 2), the trio of ageing friends (the Forester,
the Schoolmaster and the Parson) has often been analysed, although
some of the labels applied to them – from all-out establishment
figures to bitter hedonists – sound rather pompous for inhabitants of
a Moravian village. Still, as they drink, play cards, tease each other
and fantasize, a whole fabric of social conventions, restrictions and
prejudices is disclosed. But the mockery is kindly. Although Janáček
created in *The Vixen* a work of much greater depth and wisdom than
the original cartoon or the subsequent novel, the landscape is a gentle
one – without the towering peaks and fathomless gorges of his other
stage works.

The Vixen is characterized as a rebel, though in Act 2 her courtship provides the opportunity for a mild parody of contemporary
mores. But not everything is comic: the growth of her love is movingly portrayed. In Act 3, her rebelliousness is stressed again: as she
outwits the would-be poacher, her 'To club, to kill, just because I am
a Vixen?' is repeated no fewer than six times. Yet her death is not the
axis of this act, and no one dwells on it.

Instead, Janáček's finale is full of wisdom and optimism. The
Forester, now in the autumn of his years – as was Janáček – recognizes
that life is a process of perennial renewal, of which death is also part.
As the opera closes, he drops his gun in wonderment. Yet Janáček did
not insist on any particular interpretation: 'Let everyone work out for
himself what he will,' he wrote to Brod in 1925.[95]

Long before he wrote any of the music, he was quite clear about
the shape and nature of the work. As usual, news travelled fast in
Brno: on 26 April 1921 *Lidové noviny* announced that Janáček had just
completed *Káťa Kabanová*, and less than three weeks later the paper
sent its reporter, Adolf Veselý, to interview the composer about his
new opera. Janáček was forthcoming: 'In my *Vixen* there will be dramatic action,' he insisted. 'And then the animals! For years I have lis-

tened to them, memorized their cries; I am at home with them.'[96] Two weeks later the paper published another of his occasional *feuilletons*, in which Janáček wrote that he was already 'collecting a suitable company for the Vixen Bystrouška'.[97]

Nevertheless, during the rest of the year he was still busy with the final corrections to *Káťa*. The Brno première, on 23 November 1921, was 'a decided success', as he wrote to Kamila, and the opera was also accepted by the National Theatre in Prague.[98] Janáček continued 'tidying up' *Káťa* even after its première, partly in response to various suggestions by Max Brod, who was working on the German translation.

Janáček's method of composition had always been somewhat haphazard. By *Káťa* he had long been composing mostly into full score but not in any particular order, setting whatever part of the libretto stimulated his imagination, and revising all the time. He used a variety of pens, pencils and inks, and his script was hasty and difficult to decipher; his corrections, made by scratching out errors with a penknife and writing on the thinner, scraped paper, were often illegible. He also specified unusual time-signatures and many double sharps and double flats. To produce a readable copy from his sketches he used several copyists, including his pupils. As even those familiar with Janáček's working methods sometimes misinterpreted his intentions, he would often make further changes. Vocal scores and orchestral parts were made from this copy and, inevitably, there were many mistakes and spurious passages in the vocal score of *Káťa*, made by Janáček's pupil Břetislav Bakala.

In 1922, when Janáček's publishers, Universal Edition, were preparing the orchestral score for publication, they were bewildered by all these problems; moreover, Janáček seemed incapable of coping with proofs, and the first printed orchestral score was teeming with mistakes. Yet the 'greatness of *Káťa*, as Sir Charles Mackerras wrote in the preface to his new edition of the score in 1992, 'shone through the mass of errors of notes, phrasings and dynamics . . . played more or less uncorrected for years'.[99]

Janáček did not begin writing the music for *The Vixen* until 22 January 1922, according to the date in his autograph score. He first mentioned the new opera to Max Brod: 'Wish me luck with *The Vixen Bystrouška*!' he added in a postscript to an undated letter (probably from mid-December 1921). Yet in January 1922 Janáček complained to Brod that his head was 'like a burnt-out shell. I don't know what to sink my teeth into. I fiddle about with folk-songs; I read Einstein the while. But his relativity of time and space is unsuited to sound.'[100]

It was not until February 1922 that Janáček mentioned the new work to Kamila. 'I have begun writing *The Vixen Bystrouška*. A merry thing with a sad end: and I am placing myself at that sad end. And so I fit in there!'[101] This self-identification suggests that Janáček was beginning to contemplate the inevitability of ageing and even death: he was approaching 68 at the time. 'I am experiencing sad moments,' he remarked in the same letter. 'Why do bygone thoughts try to press forward to the light? I had no time for such thoughts before: that was life. Some violent change is hatching in the body, in the blood.'[102]

Kamila was much on his mind. Sending her the published vocal score of *Káťa*, he confessed that he had always put her photograph in front of him by the score as he composed;[103] it is obvious that by now the emotional bond was also a tremendous source of inspiration. Kamila, as so often before, was diplomatic: she wanted a dedication so that 'I or my children could have something as a souvenir of you'.[104] Yet a month later Janáček reproached her in his briefest letter: 'Can't you even say thank you for *Káťa*?[105] 'You must forgive me,' replied Kamila two days later; she had written but forgotten to post the thank-you letter. 'I am often so at odds with the whole world . . . . So forgive my negligence and accept my thanks today. I would like to see it. Perhaps it is also my fate.'[106]

As work on *The Vixen* continued, Janáček's mood improved. He had 'no time to think of *himself*', he wrote to Kamila in March 1922,[107] but he had not seen her for a while and kept trying to arrange a meeting. Kamila did not respond until the summer: she was angry with Janáček, as she finally wrote in August, because of a comment he had made about her fickleness. 'You know only too well why I do not want to come to your house,' she continued. 'I have still not forgotten the last time. Why cause someone else pain without a reason? I already thought that I should no longer be writing to you. But as the old saying goes, "Old love never becomes rusty", although there is no love between us only mere friendship . . .'.[108] Thus Kamila slips from one mood to another, binding Janáček to her even more closely, as is apparent in his next letter.

Believe me, I need your twittering and your scrawls like a drought needs rain, the dawn the sun, the sky its stars . . . . You are that little star which I look for every evening. Do not wrong Zdenka. Both of us are always pleased to see you. Do not wonder that she is needlessly a little jealous. She knows that you are always on my mind.[109]

And in another letter, still from Hukvaldy, he added: 'So long as my little sun will shine for me, I will compose! Should it go out, that would be the end.'[110]

The Prague première of *Káťa Kabanová*, set for 30 November 1922, was entrusted to Otakar Ostrčil. Although both the soloists and the conductor were enraptured by the work,[111] further correspondence between Janáček and Ostrčil followed, with the composer pointing out corrections, the right tempi and so on. The Stössels were invited for the première but yet again Kamila sent her apologies, as her husband would be away.

Janáček had looked forward to the première, which was to be 'beautifully staged',[112] but not all the reviews were favourable. The *Národní politika* reviewer criticized Janáček's compression of the play into three acts, and while conceding that 'dramatic power and characterization' were his strongest assets, he thought the music 'rather thin', particularly the melodic invention. 'It is only impressionism,' he wrote, 'a mood and only a mood.' The orchestration he considered 'evocative', but Janáček's chosen path was too individual and could not become the basis for a school. 'Czech opera,' concluded the reviewer, 'has only one heritage and one way forward: Smetana.'[113] Although the *Národní listy* critic found the music imposing, albeit impressionistic, the most common description of Janáček's characterization as 'like mosaic' did not please the composer. 'So much malice!' he remarked in a letter to Otakar Ostrčil, even though he himself had criticized the acting.[114]

Only some newspapers in Prague (both Czech and German) were enthusiastic; the *Lidové noviny* critic, the composer Boleslav Vomáčka, praised the opera as 'an entirely modern work . . . unique of its kind in the world literature of music'.[115] In April 1923, after a première of *Káťa* in the Slovak capital, Bratislava, Janáček wrote to Kamila: 'This is where they have staged my work most beautifully. Better than in Brno, better than in Prague. I have become fond of Bratislava. In Brno they hate me, in Prague they envy me, but in Bratislava they really like me.'[116]

In November 1922, before completing the first version of *The Cunning Little Vixen*, Janáček wrote a short but impressive choral work, *The Wandering Madman*, a setting of a poem by Rabindranath Tagore. Janáček had heard the Bengali thinker and poet recite some of his poetry in Prague in June 1921, and immediately fell under his spell. Four days later he published an enthusiastic *feuilleton* about Tagore, illustrated with several speech melodies. 'It seemed to me as if a white, holy flame had suddenly sprung up over the heads of the thousands present,' wrote Janáček in awe. '[It was as if] he did not speak; the sound was rather like the song of nightingale, smooth, free of consonantal roughness.'[117]

Janáček's text is taken from Tagore's collection *The Gardener*, about a man's lifelong search for a stone which could turn iron into gold. Asked one day by a country boy about a gold chain around his neck, the wanderer remembers with surprise that it was originally made of iron. He must have found the magic stone and thrown it away without realizing its power; his quest must start anew.

Janáček set the ballad in his favourite ABA form, with the boy's question separating the parts of the wanderer's quest. The work opens in E flat, with a baritone solo declaiming the story on a single note; later Janáček used his now customary technique of staggering the choral parts or setting them against each other. After an impassioned gradation the soprano presents the boy's question in a short solo. The public derision of the madman is described in a masterly passage: a motif of laughter, clearly based on a speech melody, is preceded by powerful chords in the entire choir. Following the return of the opening single-note motif, and the final gradation, the soprano is heard for the last time, set again the low B major chord of the basses.

The Czech translation is in free verse form; it irregular prosody gave Janáček an opportunity for matchless setting, an entirely realistic stylization of spoken Czech. The musical and verbal accents are virtually identical: the metre and the rhythm of the opening baritone solo, for example, stem from the syllabic lengths as well as the accentual aspects of the text, and the 3/4 time of the entire first part is dictated by the predominance of three-syllable words.[118] The work is demanding for the performers: the vocal compass spans three octaves (from a high B in the tenors to the low B of the basses in the final chords).

By November 1922 the Brno City Theatre had made an early bid for the performance rights for *The Cunning Little Vixen*, but Janáček completely rewrote the work during the following year, finishing it by 10 October 1923; the Brno première was not held for over a year. Janáček had mentioned to Kamila in October 1922 that three weeks of work on *The Vixen* had 'exhausted' him, but it seems that, on the whole, composing the opera caused him no serious anguish.

1. The church in Hukvaldy, Janáček's native village

2. The village school, where Janáček was born in 1854

9. Kamila Stösslová and her husband David in 1917,
when Janáček first met them

10. Janáček's cottage in Hukvaldy, which he bought after the First World War

11. Two of Eduard Milén's designs for *The Cunning Little Vixen*: the Mosquito and the Badger

12. A caricature by Oldřich Sekora of the performers in the Brno première of *The Makropulos Affair*, with Janáček in the middle of the bottom row

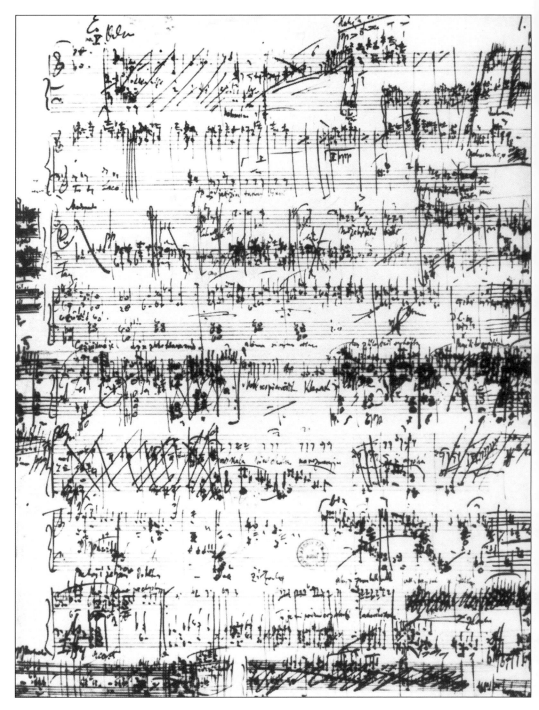

13. Part of the piano score sketch of *Jenůfa*, in Janáček's hand

14. A drawing of Janáček by
Eduard Milén

15. Max Brod in a 1909 drawing
by Lucian Bernhard

16. The Janáčeks and the Stössels in 1925

17. Introduction to *From the House of the Dead*, in Janáček's hand

The 'field work' was fun: throughout 1922 Janáček wrote several *feuilletons* about birdsong – pieces about thrushes, hens, a cockerel and even crows.[119] And during the summer he observed the habits of a family of foxes in a forest near Hukvaldy. A party was made up to follow the stream in the Ondřejnice valley up to the Babí hora. 'And . . . as if to order,' wrote the gamekeeper Sládek in his memoirs,

> the vixen's family emerged from the burrow and began to show off and play around. Janáček started twitching with excitement until finally he frightened the foxes away. 'Why couldn't you keep still? You could have gone on looking!' Completely exhilarated and happy, Janáček just brushed the rebuke aside: 'I saw her! I saw her!'[120]

The composer loved animals, and had been notating animal cries and bird song for many years. As well as dogs, the family kept a few pigeons, a goldfinch and three hens. 'He talked to the hens as to children, they looked at him, answered something and he understood,' his maidservant later recalled. 'In the evening, when he sat down in the garden in his armchair to read the paper, he rapped on the table, like a schoolmaster at school, [and] the hens came running at once, jumped up . . . and kept him company.'[121]

In his copy of the novel, Janáček made many notes, including dialogue, the order of events and so on. Not all the doublings have materialized; the composer noted down 'sparrow-schoolmaster' and elsewhere 'schoolmaster-fox'. In the end, the Schoolmaster was coupled with the Mosquito, the Badger and the Parson were also paired, but the Fox has no human double. Another parallel, between the Forester's wife and the Owl, tends to be ignored in productions of the opera.[122]

As in Janáček's previous operas, the melodic line is largely based on speech melodies. From these also stems the vigour of the music in general; the states of mind expressed in the speech patterns are in turn reflected in the intervallic range. Although this is frequently composed of Janáček's favourite intervals (fourths, fifths and seconds, typical of Moravian folk-song), larger intervals appear whenever anger, fear, indignation and so on are indicated in the text; perhaps the most obvious is the gradual widening of the range in the Vixen's 'To club, to kill', in Act 3.[123] Instrumental motifs are often varied melodically and augmented rhythmically, and used to accompany the vocal lines in which the same intervals are echoed.[124]

The motivic development is also sometimes based on principles observed in Moravian folk-song, with the melodic line in the second part of a phrase beginning a minor third up, and the intervallic range widening.[125] Moravian folk-song is also echoed in the modal mood of the Act 3 Foxcubs' song, with its Lydian (augmented) fourth, although the text of this nursery rhyme in fact refers to a town in Bohemia.[126] Folk texts are used for the entrances of the poultry dealer, though the music is Janáček's.

To encourage the correct declamation, Janáček frequently groups the notes in threes, fours, fives and even sevens, which helps the rhythmical flow. Although the syllabic length is not always correctly observed, a convincing representation of spoken Czech, as well as the local dialect, is achieved.

Further characterization is added by the voices used; with the exception of the Badger and the Mosquito, most of the animals' voices are high and largely female (the Vixen is a soprano, the Fox and the Dog mezzos). Most of the humans are males, with a complete range from tenor to bass.

The ephemeral Terynka, the girl about whom the men fantasize, never appears in the opera. Some of the smaller animals' and insects' roles are written for high children's voices, a novel approach at the time;[127] at the Prague première, Janáček wanted the Rooster, Hen and Dog sung by 'girls about fifteen years old'. The chorus, which had been used to such good effect in *Osud* and *The Excursions of Mr Brouček*, is deployed here too: at the end of Act 2, all the forest animals join in a joyful wedding celebration.

As in other works of Janáček's last decade, the tonality in *The Vixen* is based on modes, which he altered further. He also expands his harmonic range by using, for example, the chords of the seventh and the ninth, with further alterations; these are based on any degree of the scale, and the music often borders on polytonality. The so-called *sčasovka*, Janáček's own term for a short rhythmical figure, is frequently used, and folk rhythms are also heard.[128]

The Cunning Little Vixen also resonates with echoes of Debussy. Janáček was familiar with Debussy's music before 1912, as is clear from an example he quoted that year in his *Complete Harmony Manual*.[129] Although he could not have heard much of Debussy's music, it made a strong impression on him: 'Throughout Franz Liszt and Debussy,' he wrote, 'harmony has acquired a shining chordal colour such as might have been teased out at sunset on the surface of the sea.'[130] From 1919 – when Debussy's works were regularly performed in Brno – he began to study them systematically.[131] Thus Debussy's influence is apparent in the harmony based on fourths, pedal notes and muted orchestral colours.[132] But, like other composers in whom Janáček was interested (such as Puccini), Debussy was less an influence than a stimulus.

In the summer of 1923 Zdenka's father – then in his late eighties – fell seriously ill. He and Janáček had not been on speaking terms for some forty years, but now Emilian Schulz wanted to make peace. Janáček promised Zdenka he would see him, but procrastinated. Finally, he was sent for: the dying man was calling for him all the time. Janáček 'came round immediately', wrote Zdenka movingly in her memoirs, and 'when he saw what remained of Papa, he turned his face, ran to the window and wept. [. . .] They embraced. Papa told him in gasps how he had always followed his success with pleasure, even though they were not on good terms.'[133] Now reconciled, the two men said goodbye. Yet, as Janáček habitually avoided family funerals, he did not attend his father-in-law's interment either.

Although Janáček began contemplating another opera, *The Makropulos Affair*, almost immediately after completing *The Vixen*, he suddenly turned to another medium, the quartet. His First String Quartet (in reality the second) was inspired by Tolstoy's novella *The Kreutzer Sonata* (1891), composed by 28 October 1923 and revised by 7 November 1923.

The story's hero, Pozdnishev, believes he has married for love but realizes his mistake within days. Both partners find themselves trapped in a marriage without any real affinity for each other, and their feelings alternate between passion and hatred. When Pozdnishev returns from a business trip to find his wife dining alone with her violinist lover, he stabs her, mortally wounding her; the musician escapes. After only a short term of imprisonment, the guilt-stricken husband now wanders the world, unable to find peace.

Tolstoy's novella, in which he ascribed to music the power of corrupting morality and indeed encouraging adultery, took Europe by storm after its publication. These days it is often dismissed as a rather pathetic, misogynistic product of his old age, but it must have struck a powerful chord with Janáček, who had long felt trapped in his own marriage. His music portrays the feelings of all three characters in the story, particularly those of the wife. Nevertheless, the text merely provided a starting-point for him. Although some scholars have perceived the piece as programmatic in origin, one can almost sense the individual characters entering and leaving the stage, and hear their scenas develop: a born dramatist, Janáček – tracing the outline of the story with a structure of motifs and themes – clearly conceived even his chamber music in terms of drama.

The composer must have read the novella before 1908, when he wrote a piano trio based on it (in honour of Tolstoy's eightieth birthday). The revised version was performed in Brno at a chamber concert in April 1909,[134] and was occasionally played right up till 1922. A year later, having adapted it as a string quartet, Janáček destroyed the trio material. Although, apparently, not much of the original survived, it is argued that the quartet was written rather too quickly for the composer not to have incorporated earlier material, and that the adaptation was not especially extensive.[135] Yet the First Quartet is no mere transcription – its mature style firmly belongs to Janáček's last, glorious decade.

The quartet has four movements. In the opening Adagio in E minor, a brief two-bar motif on the first violin strongly resembles the offstage 'sigh of the Volga' in *Káťa Kabanová*. This motif alternates with a broader melody introduced by the cello (its melodic line based on the intervals of the fifth, second and fourth), which hurries along lightly. As the melody broadens, a new motif is introduced on the violin against the ostinato triplets on the viola, and develops into the broken chords of the *Vivo*: the plot thickens. The movement ends with a hesitating echo of the opening motif.[136]

In the second movement, a scherzo in A flat minor, the viola's opening dance-like melody recalls a polka.[137] When a new, startling motif is introduced on the viola, *sul ponticello* [played near the bridge], utter mystery, anguish and perhaps even guilt are suggested. A broader, soulful melody follows; passion, energy and resolution can all be heard as the movement develops, yet it closes on a quiet chord of A flat minor after both themes have been briefly recalled.

Marked 'lightly, timidly', the violin and cello duet in the third movement clearly evokes the wonderful theme of the variations in Beethoven's 'Kreutzer' Sonata; in Tolstoy's story this is performed at a crucial point – a concert given by Pozdnishev's wife and her violinist admirer. Janáček combines several of his favourite techniques in this movement: staggered parts, ostinatos and rhythmic diminutions of themes and their parts, as well as figurations played *sul ponticello*, thus creating rich layers of sound by seemingly simple means. Duple and triple time alternate, as do the 'sul ponticello', and 'naturale' passages. After the agitation of the middle section, the mood changes again in the following *Andante*, and one can almost hear questioning and gentle pleading. The opening motif returns but, as the movement closes, the dream seems to have faded.

The muted opening theme from the first movement returns several times in the finale, sounding almost like a chorale; it is interspersed with a melancholy melody that Janáček marked 'jako v slzách' (as if in tears). Suddenly, a passionate lament appears on the viola, over broken chords on the second violin, and a multi-layered structure is again built from various themes and their derivatives. As tension mounts, the intervals broaden and the melodic line is chromaticized. The opening theme is again hinted at but quickly superseded by descending octave leaps, marked repeatedly 'zoufale' (in desperation). Both themes reappear; the motifs and figurations intermingle until the opening theme of the quartet returns, played *fortissimo* and 'feroce' (ferociously). In the concluding bars, contrasting it with the variation of the 'lament', Janáček marked the phrase 'slavnostně, jako varhany' (in a festive manner, like the organ). The tragedy has reached its climax; the work ends with a faint echo of the opening motif.

Writing excitedly to Kamila Stösslová after a rehearsal at which the Bohemian Quartet gave a 'magnificent' performance of this work, just over a year after it was completed, Janáček declared that he had had in mind 'a poor woman, tormented, beaten, battered to death'.[138] While Tolstoy, it can be argued, marginalized the heroine's voice, Janáček – speaking on her behalf – transformed the narrative.

Yet, at a time when Janáček's desire to portray powerless heroines was growing, his marriage was far from happy – as the troubled Zdenka confided to Zina Veselá, the wife of the reporter Adolf Veselý. 'I thought: poor devils, both of them,' recalled Mrs Veselá in an interview many years later. Accompanying her at the time to a performance of *Káťa Kabanová*, Janáček impressed upon Mrs Veselá that he had wanted an oppressed woman as a subject for *Káťa*. 'He did not have to look far, I thought,' Mrs Veselá told her interviewer wryly. 'I have been pondering why that marriage of his was so unhappy. I think that it was simply out of boredom. Zdenka was a virtuous wife, always the same voice, the same walk; she was insipid, always the same. His heart was aflame with his belated success, and he also longed for success in his personal life.'[139]

Among Janáček's unexpected late successes was the Berlin première of *Jenůfa* in 1924.[140] The director of the Berlin State Opera, Max von Schillings, came to Prague in February 1922 to conduct the Czech Philharmonic, managed to see the opera the day before the concert, and was very impressed. Although Prague musical circles tried to interest him in other Czech operas, it was *Jenůfa* he chose, to Janáček's delight.[141] Travelling to Berlin for the première in March 1924, he visited Frederick the Great's summer residence at Sans Souci, and the Czech cemetery: 'places of deathly silence'. In contrast, the atmosphere in the State Opera was 'jubilant'. An extra dress rehearsal was arranged for Janáček's benefit, and tears ran down his cheeks as he listened to the superb rendering of the opera under the baton of Erich Kleiber.[142] 'I have heard an exemplary performance of my *Jenůfa* here,' he declared in a *feuilleton* about the visit;[143] on his return to Brno, he thanked the conductor in an especially warm letter. 'You gave my work several supreme moments, filled with the brilliance of the sun . . . . You really brought the end of each act to an elemental climax. It is your *Jenůfa* that can be seen from afar – not the one in Prague, nor the Vienna one!'[144]

Celebrations in honour of Janáček's seventieth birthday began in Brno on 13 January 1924, when his *Taras Bulba* was played, along with Josef Suk's *Ripening* (Suk's fiftieth birthday also fell in 1924). Many of Janáček's works were played throughout the year both in Czechoslovakia and abroad. Only the Prague National Theatre failed to acknowledge his anniversary – no Janáček opera was included in the 1924 programme.

As July approached, Janáček wanted only to escape his well-wishers – and to see Kamila again. At the end of June, he finally arrived, at the Stössels' invitation, for his first visit to the small town of Písek in southern Bohemia, where they now lived. The three days he spent in their house were 'without a shadow'; there was much laughter and fun, and in his first letter to Kamila on his return to Brno Janáček again bemoaned the 'merciless passage of time'.[145] With her 'raven black hair undone', her habit of walking barefoot indoors, her spontaneity and vitality, Kamila continued to hold Janáček spellbound, and his letters now became open declarations of love: '. . . you are beautiful, exquisite, [judging by] what else I have glimpsed,' wrote Janáček in his next letter. 'And your eyes have a strange depth, they are so deep that they do not shine . . . . But enough now of my ravings,' he added, only to declare his feelings openly a few lines later: 'Kamila, if it weren't for you, I wouldn't want to live.'[146]

Despite his age, Janáček was still full of vigour. 'He did not feel old,' recalled his maidservant. 'Even at seventy he held himself erect, his eyes sparkled, he spoke quickly and with animation, his sight was good . . . [and] he was so full of ideas and interested in life that many a young person could not equal him.'[147] On 3 July 1924, Janáček enjoyed a quiet day at Hukvaldy, having escaped the celebrations in Brno. But a few friends were in the know and caught him at home on the eve of his departure. As they talked, singing could suddenly be heard in the courtyard of the Conservatoire: members of the Foerster choral society had come to serenade him. Janáček went out to the porch to thank them, and suddenly announced defiantly: 'In ten years' time I shall be standing here again.'[148]

His wish did not come true. Only four years were left to him, but they brought another spate of works whose originality, depth and vision still continue to astonish audiences worldwide.

9

The Unbending Spirit

(1924–1927)

Tᴇɴ ᴅᴀʏs ᴀꜰᴛᴇʀ Janáček's seventieth birthday, a long article about
him appeared in the *New York Times*. 'Janáček is now 70 years
old,' wrote the American journalist Olin Downes:[1]

> white-haired, but singularly vigorous . . . a very full-blooded person-
> ality whose dominant tone is that of fresh idealism and a great pleasure
> of living . . . . He waited long for success, which did not come to him
> in any considerable degree until *Jenůfa* . . . was given in Prague in 1916
> and thereafter in a number of European cities. His happiness in his
> present circumstances and his success is naive and without any pre-
> tense. Correspondents run out to see him, there is a succession of
> visitors of high and low degree, and Janáček is frequently taking the
> train to Vienna or Prague or Berlin to hear his operas performed.[2]

This enthusiastic article was published after the announcement
of the American première of *Jenůfa*, scheduled for the 1924/5 season
at the Metropolitan Opera; as the only contemporary American
account of Janáček's views and tastes in music, it is crucial. Naturally,
speech melodies were discussed and the composer showed Downes
his notebook, though he stressed that he 'never used these motives in
their literal form', and 'never used popular melodies'. And no one
had influenced him, he told Downes emphatically, though he
admired 'Chopin and Dvořák most'.[3]

They also discussed Mussorgsky and Charpentier. Janáček first
glanced through the score of *Boris Godunov* rather coolly around
1910, but now told Downes that he had heard the opera for the first
time the previous year, and 'admired it very much'; he still valued
Louise (though he was now 'tiring' of it). His disapproval of Wagner
was unremitting: 'It is not only that he is too symphonic, and that the
orchestra usurps the stage,' he explained, 'but that his system of
motives [= leitmotifs] is at once too detailed and too inelastic . . . .

[The leitmotif] has not sufficient resource and flexibility within itself to reveal the constantly changing emotions and motives of the character that the composer attempts to portray.' And Debussy's *Pelléas et Mélisande* had 'too much speech and too little song'. 'Melody cannot be replaced in music,' insisted Janáček, 'and I prefer a better balance of symphonic style and musical diction than Debussy believed in. In certain places in my operas the orchestra takes a musical phrase from the singer and expands it. The phrase is absolutely truthful, and the instruments, in such instances, carry out its implications as no human voice could.'[4]

During that particularly happy summer of 1924 Janáček quickly wrote one of his sunniest works, *Mládí* ('Youth'), a suite for wind sextet. The first impulse for this piece can be traced back to 1923, when Janáček attended the International Society for Contemporary Music (ISCM) Festival in Salzburg; although he was the oldest composer represented there, his Violin Sonata aroused much interest. It was Janáček's first encounter with contemporary chamber music at an international event: during his two days at the festival he heard, among others, works by Prokofiev, Szymanowski, Walton, Bliss, Roussel and Stravinsky.[5] Roussel's *Divertimento* was performed by an outstanding Parisian wind ensemble, the Société moderne des instruments à vent, and repeated at their concert in Brno in April 1924. A month later – casting his mind back to his Queen's Monastery days and his fellow choristers[6] – Janáček wrote the *March of the Bluebirds*, for piccolo, 'bells' and tambourine (or piano), for his copyist Václav Sedláček, a flute/piccolo player in the Brno Opera orchestra. Even this miniature work went through preliminary stages: Janáček's comments and musical sketches in a *feuilleton* about his March 1924 trip to Berlin make it clear that the swiftly moving opening tune of the piece recalls the fifes and drums of the Prussian army sweeping through Brno during the 1866 Austro-Prussian War, when he was at Queen's.[7] The same tune opens the third movement of *Mládí*; perhaps the composer had been thinking of writing a larger work for some time.

The suite, originally entitled 'Young Life', was written during a mere three weeks at Hukvaldy. 'While here I have composed a kind of reminiscence of my youth,' Janáček confided to Kamila in July 1924.[8] Keen to hear the piece played during his jubilee year, he first offered it to the director of the Prague Conservatoire, Dr Jan Branberger, to be performed by his students. But the projected performance never took place. *Mládí* is not an easy work; its fresh and often jocular tone belies the technical demands it makes on the players, for Janáček also wanted to try out the virtuosic possibilities of a wind ensemble. During rehearsals for the work's Brno première, he made a number of changes, possibly as a result of the performers' suggestions.

Of the four movements of the suite, the outer ones are for the most part fast, predominantly in rondo form, while the middle two consist of a slow movement and a fast scherzo, with a slower trio section; in the second movement Janáček combines rondo form with variations. The main motif of the opening Allegro explains the work's title: its repeated descending thirds are said to derive from the speech melody of the Czech saying 'mládí, zlaté mládí' ('youth, golden youth'). The wistful motif moves from one instrument to another, alternating with another motif in the minor. After several changes of mood the first theme reasserts itself; once the horn (marked 'con splendore') has repeated the opening theme, the movement ends in a rushing codetta.

A pensive motif opens the second movement, with another variant appearing later; this variant is rounded off with a descending *dolcissimo* run on the horn and the bassoon. The overall mood is melancholy, interrupted only twice by a brief, agitated *Più mosso*.

In the scherzo, the lively symmetrical main theme, on the piccolo, ascends and descends playfully; this is a modified version of one of Janáček's sketches included in his Berlin *feuilleton* (with off-beat chords in the accompanying instruments).[9] And the graceful pace of the first sketch (reminiscent of the 'great flautist', Frederick the Great) is twice echoed in the trio, although the tune has been moved to the oboe.

The main theme of the first movement reappears in the finale, and its new motivic variants are developed in the joyful second idea. Further variations follow before the tempo slows down and the ideas are recapitulated; the wistful sigh of 'youth, golden youth' is repeated several times. When the pace quickens, the horn once again pauses musingly, this time in unison with the flute, before the piece ends boldly in a breakneck *stretta*.

Mládí is deservedly popular: the instrumental combinations are superbly calculated, as are the alternating dark and lighthearted moods. The première on 21 October 1924 was nevertheless a failure: the oboist managed to right a sudden fault in his instrument, but the key the clarinettist needed most often stopped functioning and he was forced to leave the corresponding note out. As soon as the performance was over, the agitated Janáček rushed on to the platform, loudly addressing the audience: 'Ladies and gentlemen, that was not my composition! Mr Krtička was only pretending to play, he was not really playing at all!'[10] Fortunately, the Prague première – almost exactly a month later – was a great success; the work was published in January 1925.[11]

Although the Prague National Theatre made no effort to produce any Janáček opera in 1924, *Jenůfa* had a short run at the suburban Vinohrady Theatre.[12] President Masaryk had expressed a wish to hear the work, but could not attend because of illness. Thus Janáček's birthday celebrations passed without so much as a word of congratulation from any of the country's leading statesmen.[13] A request for an official gesture was eventually made in October by Brno University. But Janáček's often critical view of Smetana, the most revered Czech composer, was well known, 'and although [Janáček's] former pugnaciousness had abated,' the Chancellor Dr Říha commented in an internal note, 'he still manifests this attitude openly'. If, the Chancellor went on in a carefully worded summary of the situation, the President were to send Janáček his personal congratulations, the Smetana camp (headed by Janáček's chief detractor, the Smetana scholar and critic Zdeněk Nejedlý), 'would surely be taken aback' and 'might perhaps comment in various ways'.[14]

The division of Czech composers and writers on music into rival factions, and their frenzied support of their idols, frequently astounds dispassionate observers. But it has to be remembered that, for the Czechs, music had long been the best, and sometimes the only means of expressing their creativity. For some two centuries, before the break-up of the Austro-Hungarian Empire, the Czechs had no internationally acclaimed writers or painters, but plenty of musicians to be proud of; after the foundation of the National Theatre in 1881, opera in particular was fundamental to Czech nationalism.

Inevitably, preference for one composer over another was rarely a matter of personal taste alone: it had become a question of political allegiance. Dvořák was seen by the opposition to associate with prominent 'conservative' *staročeši* ('Old Czechs'), though in fact very little is known about his political affiliations; Smetana belonged to the 'radical' *mladočeši* ('Young Czechs'), a movement also supported by Janáček.[15]

Personal interests also played a part in the alignments: Nejedlý had been rejected by Dvořák's daughter Otilka, who married the composer Josef Suk instead; and as late as 1948 Nejedlý, then Minister of Culture, continued to display hostility towards Suk, as well as towards notable performers of Janáček's music.[16] Thus there is a whole agenda hidden between the lines of Chancellor Říha's cautious note.

Prague nevertheless celebrated Janáček's birthday with several concerts, two of which were organized in November and December by the Hudební Matice Society and the Czech Philharmonic Orchestra; Janáček's piano, chamber and choral works were heard at the first concert.[17] The society's representatives – the composer Boleslav Vomáčka and the writer and critic Dr Jan Löwenbach, with the Czech Philharmonic's Moravian-born conductor Václav Talich – sent the President an official invitation, summing up the composer's achievements and his importance to Czech culture. 'Janáček's personality and work do not belong only to the art of music,' they emphasized:

> Czech culture has in Janáček a unique and unrepeatable phenomenon. It is through him that the culture of Moravia speaks most eloquently at the present time, and that is why the Prague celebrations are to be an expression of homage and appreciation paid by the Czech public . . . to the entire Moravian culture. Like Smetana in his time, Janáček, too, experiences his own time with great intensity, feels the pains and longings of today and expresses them in his works. Whether he is inspired by political, social or ethical motives, Janáček always finds for his works an expression of immense emotional depth and achieves a spontaneous, strong dramatic effect.[18]

The letter is an outstanding example of how deeply some contemporary Czech musicians felt about the cultural significance of Janáček's music, and indeed more generally about the role of Czech artists from Moravia within the Republic. Nor was their wish for the President's personal congratulations to Janáček an expression of social snobbery: the Moravian-born Masaryk was a scholar and philosopher by profession, and was thus unique among Europe's heads of state. He represented for the Czechs and Slovaks their highest moral and cultural authority.

Masaryk eventually promised to attend the second concert, by the Czech Philharmonic and the Prague Teachers' Choral Society, on 8 December (which included the cantata *The Eternal Gospel*, male-voice choruses, and the tone poems *The Fiddler's Child* and *Taras Bulba*). Janáček commented happily on the outcome to his sister Josefka: 'So my celebrations end in a dignified manner. [. . .] Well, I have won late but I have still won!'[19]

At Christmas 1924 Janáček once again took up work on a symphonic project that had germinated in March 1923, during his trip to the city of Bratislava. He was then much taken with the Slovak capital, where he saw a new production of *Káťa Kabanová*.[20] 'A beautiful old town,' he wrote to Kamila Stösslová, 'the swift Danube. During the holidays I fancy a cruise down the Danube as far as the mouth – or at least until Belgrade. Would you like to come along?'[21] But the cruise never materialized. And although Janáček started working on the projected *Danube* symphony – perhaps to rival Smetana's tone poem *Vltava*, celebrating the river of that name in Bohemia – some two months after returning from Bratislava, he was soon preoccupied with other works and other events. 'One day,' he wrote in his 1924 autobiographical notes, listing works in progress, 'perhaps in 1925, when my mind is at ease, the work will ripen quickly as if in the sun.'[22]

Yet by August 1926 the symphony was still far from ready, despite Otakar Ostrčil's desire to give its première with the Czech Philharmonic the following year. Writing to his wife from Hukvaldy, Janáček complained of making mistakes; to Ostrčil he replied briefly that the river was no longer very tempting, and hence he was 'not in a hurry' to finish the work.[23] Whatever the reason, he did not look at the sketches again until his last stay at Hukvaldy in 1928.

The work clearly did need final revision. The four movements that have been preserved are more or less continuous drafts; the first movement is fragmented and the material of the second is undistinguished, although the remaining two are animated. Janáček finally deleted about a third of the original material, and reversed the order of both the middle and the outer movements. A realization, made by his pupil Osvald Chlubna, was performed in 1948; another version, by Leoš Faltus and Miloš Štědroň, was premièred in London in 1993.[24]

Janáček's comments regarding the work's programmatic origins are not enlightening. In his autobiography, he mentions Insarov's poem 'Lola' in connection with the second movement (Janáček's idea was that the prostitute of the title, fallen on hard times, drowned herself in the Danube). But he also copied into the score of this movement extracts from a Czech contemporary poem by Pavla Křičková, 'The Drowned Woman' (whose protagonist, a young girl, drowns herself for shame after being seen bathing).[25] Nor is the piece a musical picture-postcard of the famous river, although Janáček was at first so enchanted with the Danube's 'light green waves'. Perhaps the wealth of ideas in his mind somehow worked against the piece.

The musical sketches Janáček included in his 1924 autobiography suggest that once again he was thinking in terms of definite instruments ('I know that the bassoon jumped up and . . . rippled the surface of the Danube').[26] The atmospheric timpani chords which he also mentions ('the tremolo with the four timpani') are heard several times in the second movement; the soprano and oboe *vocalise* of the third movement is imitated by a viola d'amore.[27] Thus the orchestration is the most remarkable aspect of this unfinished work; typically for the soundscape of Janáček's late works, outer voices are given prominence in the texture.

Earlier in October 1924, Janáček's seventieth birthday celebrations continued in Brno with two concerts of his choral and chamber works, several of which had not been heard before in Moravia. Astonishingly, Janáček's superb male-voice chorus *The Seventy Thousand*, which had so impressed Olin Downes in Prague, did not receive its Brno première until 11 October 1924; *Czech Legion* and *The Wandering Madman* were also new to Brno. At another concert on 19 October, given by the Beseda Philharmonic Society, Jaroslav Kvapil conducted the cantatas *Our Father*, *Amarus*, *Čarták on the Soláň* and *The Eternal Gospel*, most of which were also being heard in Brno for the first time. And on 13 December the Bohemian Quartet gave the Brno première of the First Quartet.

Yet even in Brno 'Janáček was still not fully appreciated,' wrote Jaroslav Vogel. 'The concert of cantatas drew only a small audience, and an orchestral concert planned [for 27 November] by the Moravian Composers' Club, at which František Neumann was to have conducted some early works, including the Suite for strings, *Dances from Lašsko* and the overture to *Šárka*, had to be cancelled for lack of interest.'[28] This concert eventually took place on 2 December; in Janáček's own words, his celebrations in Brno had been 'beautifully rounded off'.[29]

During the 1924 autumn season the Brno audiences also had an opportunity to see three of Janáček's operas: *Káťa Kabanová*, a new production of *Jenůfa*, and on 6 November the première of *The Cunning Little Vixen*, all conducted by the devoted Neumann. Janáček was delighted with the production of *The Vixen*; during rehearsals he would laugh, watching the cast 'crawling on all fours', recalled Božena Snopková, who created the Fox. Greatly entertained at seeing her, in one scene, bringing the Vixen a rabbit in her teeth, he presented Snopková with a pheasant; when she demurred, he assured her slyly: 'You know, foxes like pheasants.'[30]

The sets were imaginative, the main roles were sung by the best Brno singers, and as usual Neumann conducted with the utmost dedication to Janáček's idiom. 'They say,' recalled the Janáčeks' maid-servant Stejskalová, 'that when, at the dress rehearsal, they finished playing the end of the third act, where the Forester dreams about the young Bystrouška [and] instead catches the Little Frog . . . the master wept and told the producer Zítek, standing beside him: "You must play this for me when I die." '[31]

Janáček's fresh celebration of life was warmly received by the Brno audiences; they knew the tale from the instalments in the city's popular daily, the forest of the story lay close by, and they were familiar with the amusing Líšeň dialect used in much of the opera.[32]

The musical establishment, on the other hand, remained sceptical. Even Vladimír Helfert, who had been Janáček's one-time passionate adversary but was now his dedicated promoter (and future biographer), thought *The Cunning Little Vixen* lacked dramatic action. 'From the musical point of view the new work is a testimony to Janáček's admirable creative freshness,' he wrote in his review. 'The score is rich, with delicately and cunningly rendered colour; the elementary rhythmical pulse complements the melodic line which is rather more developed than we are used to in Janáček's work.' But from a dramatic point of view the work suffered owing to the subject matter: 'The action is too disparate, unfocused. The simultaneous positioning of the animal and human worlds on stage casts shadows not only on the scenic representation but also on the entire work. The episodic portrayal of the human characters gives an impression of disunity, and it would only be in the work's interest if these characters could be cut, and the work became an opera solely from the animal world. Then the ingenious and fresh music would be rendered more valid.'[33]

A month after the Brno première of *The Vixen*, *Jenůfa* was given its American première at the Metropolitan Opera, New York.[34] It was a remarkable development: the Met's notoriously conservative director, Giulio Gatti-Casazza, rarely mounted an opera he did not know. Maria Jeritza, the triumphant *Jenůfa* of the Vienna production, sang the title-role; the sets were built under the supervision of Czech artists, and the exquisitely embroidered folk costumes were made in Moravia. Yet already before the première, Olin Downes was doubtful of the opera's success: 'Whether the theories and dramatic style of Janáček will make as strong an impression in America as they have in his own country and in parts of Austria and Germany is to be seen.'[35]

His misgivings were well founded: *Jenůfa* did not appeal in New York, in spite of the colour and attention to detail. Wilhelm von Wymetal's staging was too literal; Jeritza, dressed in a richly embroidered gown and a large, elaborate bridal headpiece, towered over the rest of the cast. The influential English music critic Ernest Newman, then working in New York, savaged the work in a notorious *Evening Post* review: 'A more complete collection of undesirables and incredibles has never before appeared in opera.'[36] In the *Herald Tribune*, Lawrence Gilman was similarly caustic: 'There is nothing seriously the matter with *Jenůfa* except the music.' Pointing out what he considered to be parallels with Mussorgsky, he added: 'But Janáček lacks what Mussorgsky had so abundantly – the power of musical invention.' Although Janáček's music had 'all the preliminaries and accessories: honesty, feeling, psychological insight, theatrical skill', the composer lacked 'the ability to write music that in itself, as a pattern of tones, is eloquent, expressive, memorable. . . . Hearing it once, one has no wish to hear it again.'[37]

The reviews effectively ruled out further productions of *Jenůfa* at the Met for another fifty years.[38] Yet Jeritza sent Janáček an enthusiastic letter of congratulations on 'a wonderful performance'. Janáček himself reported to Kamila Stösslová that it had been 'an immense success',[39] although the Prague music journal *Dalibor*, at the time the unofficial mouthpiece of the Smetana camp, eagerly reprinted the unfavourable New York reviews. Later, Janáček was given a full account of the première by his one-time pupil, František Rybka (then choirmaster and organist at Pittsburgh Cathedral). Rybka was enthusiastic about the production, chorus and soloists, especially the Kostelnička of the Hungarian contralto Margarete Matzenauer, a distinguished Wagner singer. But he was critical of the orchestral playing, and especially of the tempos.[40]

Nor was the production a success from a financial point of view. Janáček's royalties amounted to a paltry $100; Jeritza confirmed that this was, by the Met's standards, extremely low. Recent research shows that the fee per performance was actually $250, to be shared between the composer and his Berlin publisher, Universal Edition. Although a cheque for $1,500 (for the six performances) was in fact sent as early as April 1924 to the publisher's Berlin agent, nothing is known of the fate of Janáček's share, $750 – then a considerable sum in Czechoslovakia, and positive riches in Berlin, collapsing as it was under inflation.[41]

Meanwhile, Janáček's seventieth birthday celebrations in Prague continued: after the première of his First Quartet in October and the concert of chamber and choral works in November, an orchestral concert followed in December at the Art Nouveau Smetana Hall, and Janáček was twice invited to the President's box.

There were many parallels between the two men: both grew up in the Moravian countryside, where their experience made them acutely aware of poverty as well as social and linguistic discrimination. Both went to school in Brno and studied in Leipzig and Vienna, and both were Russophiles. They had first met in 1919, along with other members of the Consortium of the National Theatre in Brno; Janáček recorded the compass of the President's voice, and notated a few of his words.[42] He may have asked Masaryk to accept the dedication of *The Excursions of Mr Brouček* on this occasion (a year later the President accepted a copy of the vocal score);[43] in 1920 Janáček dedicated to Masaryk *The Ballad of Blaník*, whose première marked the President's seventieth birthday.[44]

Yet, surprisingly, during Masaryk's first official visit to Brno in 1921 Janáček was not on the list of guests the President met, although he was among the invited representatives of cultural life in Moravia. And not a single note of Janáček's music was heard during the President's visit; one does wonder whether these lapses were accidental.[45]

Janáček's notes from his conversation with Masaryk during the December 1924 concert make interesting reading. The centenary of Smetana's birth was celebrated that year, and the President was very interested in learning about the contribution the Czechs had made to the general development of music in Europe.[46] In an article published in March 1924, Janáček himself had discussed Smetana's creativity and praised his achievements. At the same time, he asserted his own position in the history of Czech music: 'Where [Smetana's] work stands there is no room for anyone else. But he casts no smothering shadow. Every composition can grow alongside him, freely and with the same verve.'[47] Masaryk also asked for Janáček's views on his chief detractor, Zdeněk Nejedlý; Janáček's single, brief remark was telling: 'He has been torturing me for years.'[48]

Throughout his celebratory year Janáček was frequently complimented on his youthful looks and remarkable vigour. 'What does it matter that they tell me all the time how young I look,' he wrote to Kamila Stösslová from Hukvaldy a day after his birthday. 'Why don't they ask instead for whom my heart aches, and give me a remedy? I would drink it, not only a spoonful three times a day but all the time.

You don't understand this, and that is good.'[49] Kamila eventually
replied in a long letter:

> It is good that I do not understand that spoonful of medicine. So long
> as I do not I am happy. If I did my gaiety and my whole life would be
> gone. It would seem to me as if you had picked the head off some
> flower and it [still] stands but how? I would not survive that as I love
> my husband so much that I would lay my head down for his life.
> Perhaps he himself does not know how much I long for him[,] prob-
> ably as much as you do for me. I write rather sadly but I [re]read your
> letters and so I sense your love for me. And I am sorry when someone
> suffers . . . . So be very cheerful as this is what I wish. For it is beauti-
> ful that you have those memories of me that is enough and the main
> thing is that [they are] so pure. I never thought that I would be corre-
> sponding with a man, I resisted you [and] did not want to talk to you.
> But fate wanted otherwise so we must leave it to fate. It is better that
> you are already old, had you been young my husband would never
> allow it.[50]

'How could one not want you when one loves you?' wrote Janáček
a week later.

> But I know that I shall never have you. Why should I pluck that
> flower, that family happiness, why override my respect for you, whom
> I esteem as no other woman in the world? Would I then be able to
> look your children, your husband and your parents in the eye? Could
> I then step inside your house? You see, we rave about paradise, about
> heaven, and we never reach it. So I too rave about you and know that
> you are unattainable heaven. [. . .] Fortunately it is I alone who burns
> – and you are safe.'[51]

In response to this ardent epistle, Kamila teasingly fanned the
flames:

> The [town] fair is over, I bought you a gingerbread heart there which
> all but burned with ardour. Afterwards I went for a bathe and do you
> know what happened? The heart got soaked and floated away . . . .
> Last night I had a dream about you when I woke up I could not
> believe that I could dream I was your wife. [. . .] Will you please burn
> this prattling that I write to you. Anyone would think I was sixteen,
> and had no common sense.[52]

Back in Brno, Janáček could not put Kamila out of his mind; his letters recalling the details of his visit are unambiguously erotic:

When you came in the morning and during the heat even in the evening with your black hair undone – it was like a cloud . . . and when you bent down, I did not see yet I could imagine – but I will say it, why, it is only a dream, it was the undulation of your surely beautiful breasts. Surely, surely beautiful ones. A dream, or reality?[53]

A month later, in Luhačovice, he mused about his life. 'I poeticize it to make it more bearable,' he wrote to Kamila. 'Had fate united us, who knows whether I would be in need of [my] art, whether it would awake in me at all? Whether I would not see the whole world in your eyes, which regard me so sincerely?'[54]

By November 1924 Janáček had had enough of celebrations. 'Believe me,' he declared to Kamila, 'there wasn't a single moment when I wasn't thinking of you . . . . Will anyone understand this love of mine for you? Will they be able to imagine it as so pure? [. . .] No, I would like to have all of you and kiss you passionately! [. . .] But there are limits,' he continued, with unaccustomed solicitude for his long-suffering spouse, 'you are happy with your family, and here at home is a wife who has already suffered enough'.[55] Later in the month he touched on the subject again. 'You would soon learn how to become a composer's wife. But it is a bitter role.'[56]

The Stössels attended the December gala concert in Prague, and Kamila thanked Janáček in her habitual half-humorous tone. 'Once again I am back on my old track from which you derailed me for a few beautiful hours . . . . You stood [there] like a victorious Napoleon. Mind they don't deport you to the island of St K[amila]! That would be fun, wouldn't it?'[57] The composer was pleased that he could 'show Kamila off' in Prague; there is no mention of Zdenka attending the concert. But Janáček was now more attentive and generous towards her, often bringing her small gifts from his trips; she was flattered but for the most part resigned to the pain caused by the ever-widening emotional gulf between them.[58]

The year 1924 also saw a number of newspaper articles devoted to Janáček, and two books. Max Brod's biography, *Leoš Janáček, Leben und Werk*, completed the previous year, was immediately translated into Czech and published on Janáček's seventieth birthday.[59] In Brno, the *Lidové noviny* reporter Adolf Veselý brought out a commemorative volume of Janáček's autobiographical notes.[60] This is a wonderful if somewhat haphazard collection of Janáček's recollections of his childhood, studies, trips abroad, and comments on life and art, written in his typically elliptical, epigrammatic but often poetic style. 'The inner life is for the composer the barrier against naked naturalism in his work,' Janáček declared in the final pages; his own creativity stemmed from 'the special emotional warmth, my inherited intellect and blood', and the majesty of nature which surrounded him in his youth. 'Emotion maketh the composer,' he concluded, 'not the store of education but that of the emotions.'[61]

On 28 January 1925 Janáček received an honorary doctorate of philosophy from the University of Brno; he was overjoyed but almost ill with stage-fright before the ceremony: although he liked to be fêted, he hated officialdom and pomp. Pale and moved, he wept during the celebratory speeches, remembering his parents. He was deeply gratified by the title, and for the rest of his life he never failed to put 'Dr. ph' in front of his signature.

Throughout the year, Kamila's infrequent replies to Janáček's often impassioned letters seemed enough to sustain him; he usually wrote several times a week, confiding in her about his work, projected performances of his music, his plans and even his financial affairs: he had 'no secrets' from her.[62] Kamila was generous and hospitable by nature, but she and her husband were well aware of Janáček's increasing prestige and growing wealth: since 1924 his income from performances of his works and from state prizes had enabled him to add continually to his land at Hukvaldy, and he was now spending a fair amount on furnishing his cottage there. Although it is uncertain whether David Stössel knew of Janáček's declarations to his wife, he had no reason to doubt her fidelity: Kamila was adamant that she would not attend social events with Janáček unless accompanied by her husband, nor would she receive Janáček in her home alone.

For his part, Janáček was unaware that his 'pure' friendship with Kamila could be causing his wife emotional distress. Their marriage existed only in a formal sense: the composer continued to take his meals at their house but slept in his study at the Conservatoire, across the courtyard. 'Everyone must come to their senses,' he commented to Kamila in January 1925;[63] as he was supporting Zdenka, he felt he had the right to insist on emotional freedom.

He was not to see Kamila again until March 1925, during a stopover from Prague. 'After six months, again a contented mind,' he wrote to her on his return to Brno, 'albeit only for a few hours!'[64] In April he spent a few days at Hukvaldy, planting 5,000 trees in his burgeoning forest and working on a new piece. 'While here, I have composed a piano concerto, "Spring",' he reported to Kamila. 'There is a cricket in it, little flies, a deer, a wild stream – and, well, a man.'[65] The *Concertino*, as the work was later named, may therefore be programmatic in origin, as Janáček himself suggested cryptically in a *feuilleton* published in 1927.[66]

In the first two movements, the work is a dialogue between the piano and the horn, and the piano and the clarinet respectively; in the final two movements the piano is joined by all the instruments or their various combinations. In the opening movement the fierce, percussive first theme is followed by a *rubato* run and a chromaticized conclusion; in keeping with the concertante character of the piece, Janáček wanted the piano part to be played by heart. A rhythmic figure from this theme gives rise to further motivic development, and continues in the 'sulky motif' of the horn: this is the hedgehog of Janáček's *feuilleton* 'beside itself with anger'.[67]

The piano's percussive nature is again emphasized in the second movement, with its persistent chordal motif; the clarinet's symmetrical tune, and later its trills, depict Janáček's squirrel, which he observed chattering, then moaning 'in a cage' (though eventually 'it turned around and danced to amuse the children').[68]

The first theme of the third movement, on the piano, also derives from the clarinet tune; the other instruments answer in alternate chords (with the owls' eyes staring 'insolently out of the strings of the piano'). Then the busy day in the forest is over: the clarinet runs, like tiny cantilenas, evoke a calm, nocturnal mood (*Poco meno mosso, Lento*), and the initial theme returns after a brief piano cadenza.

In the finale, Janáček remarked, 'everything seems like the penny that people quarrel about in fairy-tales'.[69] The strings begin the dispute, against the descending runs of the piano, and events get under way in a brisk, relentless tempo. The clarinet, horn and bassoon interrupt, as does the piano in two brief solo passages; the quarrel is repeatedly and even joyfully picked up, gradating in the concluding *Presto*.[70] Although there are only six accompanying instruments in the piece (two violins, viola, clarinet, French horn and bassoon), and the full ensemble is not heard until the end of the second movement, the work is sometimes conducted; Janáček's choice of accompaniment shows that he was well aware of trends in contemporary music, especially that of Hindemith.[71]

The *Concertino* was premièred both in Brno and Prague in 1926, by the excellent young pianist Ilona Kurzová-Štěpánová;[72] it is dedicated to Jan Heřman, in gratitude for his superb performances of Janáček's *Diary*, *On the Overgrown Path* and Piano Sonata. Janáček's letter to Heřman reveals that the impulse for the work might in fact date from his youth. 'I have a feeling it is like an echo of the time when I was struggling with the piano,' concluded Janáček.[73]

Following another happy stay at the Stössels' at the beginning of May (after a concert of his works in Písek), Janáček eagerly planned another meeting with Kamila later in the month. '*The Cunning Little Vixen* is growing miraculously at the Prague National Theatre,' he wrote, trying to entice her to the première. 'Within a week her fur will be like red gold.'[74] Janáček attended several rehearsals but once again he was exhausted. 'My doctor has ordered me quite seriously to un-harness myself from work,' he reported to Kamila, 'if I am not to fall seriously ill.'[75] This was not the first time: in 1917 the librettist Karel Šípek had written to Marie Calma that Janáček was in danger of 'a mental breakdown, if he does not abandon composition for a while.'[76]

Since Kamila sent her excuses, Zdenka joined Janáček a day or so before the première. During an evening out with friends she enjoyed herself, and was congratulated on her looks and elegant dress. On their return to the hotel in the small hours, Janáček 'suddenly rushed towards me, wanting to kiss the hollow of my throat. I pushed him away and said, outraged: "How dare you?"' Without a word, he left the room; Zdenka quickly went to bed and feigned sleep, 'incensed and offended that after all that had happened, he approached me . . . without apology, without permission, as if I were a thing with which he could do as he pleased.' Coming back to their room, Janáček persisted, pleading with the protesting Zdenka. 'I wronged you, I wronged you terribly,' he agreed. 'But you could have long seen that I would have liked to make amends. In Brno I was afraid, since I know you to be a pure and proud woman. Here it's easier for me.' Zdenka objected, saying that she had earned her relative peace of mind, but Janáček insisted 'more and more passionately'. In the end, 'without joy, in tears', and feeling somewhat humiliated, she suc-cumbed. 'In the morning I was awoken by his kisses. He was happy, radiating tenderness, saying things that I have long, long forgotten hearing . . . . He was as beguiling as he used to be, he enraptured me.' After all their unhappy years together, Zdenka seems to have fallen in love all over again. Still somewhat embittered, she reproached Janáček for the nine years they had lost. 'Nine years, nine years,' he repeated, rapt in thought, 'what a pity.' On leaving Prague, the Janáčeks passed by Gabriela Horvátová's house. Turning to her husband, Zdenka said triumphantly: '"And yet I have won." He nodded, solemnly and sincerely: "Yes, you have won." '[77]

The première itself was a disappointment. 'I have been looking forward to it for months,' Janáček grumbled to Kamila, 'and it did not come out as I had envisaged.'[78] Ostrčil conducted, the sets were by the painter Josef Čapek (brother of the playwright Karel Čapek), and Emil Burian excelled as the Forester. But since the producer changed the ending, letting the Forester die, Janáček's insistence on an open interpretation of the final scene came to nothing. 'What Mr Pujman decided to make of it – the Forester in his death throes etc. etc. – was dreadful,' Janáček complained to Brod.[79] Nor were his foxcubs and chickens sung by children as he had requested. Instead, Ostrčil – having failed to find a suitable children's ensemble – used the shortest members of the theatre's chorus, thus unleashing 'monsters' on the stage. The composer only calmed down after seeing another performance of the opera in Brno.[80]

In June, he told Kamila that Zdenka and he were reconciled: 'That is why she is different now, she does not see everything in such a gloomy light. She remembered how you took the photograph of that Prague hag down from the wall!'[81] This was the picture of Gabriela Horvátová, Janáček's erstwhile 'last shout of sensual delight'[82] who, he added, 'tried to ingratiate herself with me in Prague; they say she is divorced now'.[83] But he was not interested in renewing that friendship; it was Kamila who was 'for almost ten years a solace in the most sorrowful moments of life'.[84]

A kind of double emotional life ensued. 'Life in our house was beautiful now,' recalled the Janáčeks' maidservant. Janáček and Zdenka 'went everywhere together, the master confided in her about everything . . . . She simply blossomed in these circumstances, was interested in his every move, read a lot and dressed up.'[85] The couple nevertheless separated for the holidays, and Janáček stayed as usual in Luhačovice where memories of his reluctant muse continued to feed his imagination.

He wrote to Kamila that Zdenka had happened to read one of her earlier letters: 'She did not suspect you, but she was probably upset that spiritually you are closer to me than she is . . . my friendship for you is – as you will know – deep. I need it so that I can live contentedly, live happily. That is why we will all come to an understanding.'[86] Once again he recalled his first meeting with her at the spa in 1917, and how he 'lay in wait' when, with her hair 'like a black mane', she stepped out in the evening on to the balcony of her apartment.[87]

Holidaying in Luhačovice in 1925, Janáček also engaged in a lively correspondence with Max Brod, about the translation of *The Cunning Little Vixen* into German. Janáček had great confidence in Brod, who had already translated *Jenůfa* and *Káťa Kabanová* for Universal Edition; Brod also advised Janáček on the best contacts in Prague and abroad and undertook some negotiations on his behalf.

Brod's translation of *Káťa* – by no means an easy commission – was very successful. But when he first saw the libretto of *The Vixen* early in 1923, his response was cautious; perhaps because, as he said, he was not familiar with the world of animals. He then made it clear to Janáček that his translation would be in the nature of an adaptation: the libretto was 'very poor and unclear', and major changes were needed for the work to succeed on the German stage. Brod took great pains 'to liven up the action', begging Janáček to let him have 'all the freedom' he wanted.[88]

For Brod, the Vixen was 'a symbol of youth, wildness and nature'. Since Janáček's cuts had obscured the symbolism of the novel, Brod's answer was to simplify matters, in order to make the plot 'comprehensible and dramatically focused'.[89] The composer suggested that Brod's ideas should be 'joined' with his, and was willing for Brod 'to work it out' so that the original Czech text could be amended in the German edition. He nevertheless insisted on keeping the original ending as well as the children's roles.[90] Interpreting Janáček's attitude as complete liberty, Brod then introduced a number of modifications to both the characters and action. Janáček protested, and once again Brod pleaded for complete freedom. The composer relented, though remaining adamant about the final scene.

Brod's version was only performed once in Germany during the composer's lifetime (in 1927, in Mainz). The production folded after three performances; one dares not to speculate as to whether this failure was attributable to Brod's changes. In his biography of Janáček, Jaroslav Vogel voiced the objections of Czech musicians: praising Brod for his great service to the composer's work, he nevertheless characterized his interventions in *The Vixen* as 'a complete lack of understanding'. They wholly altered 'not only the sense' but the 'basic character of the majority of the scenes', so that they were no longer in keeping with the exact mood of the music.[91]

On his return from Luhačovice in July 1925, having not heard from Kamila for a while, Janáček could not shake off his loneliness. Learning that she had corresponded with Zdenka, though, he cheered up at once, and left for a month at Hukvaldy.[92] He did not even return to Brno for Zdenka's sixtieth birthday on 30 July; on that very day he announced to Kamila that he was composing a set of nursery rhymes. 'It will be merry,' he added. 'Something to laugh at.'[93]

Humour in contemporary music was in fact very much on Janáček's mind at the time. In September 1925, accompanied by Zdenka, he attended the Terzo festival di musica da camera in Venice, held under the auspices of the ISCM, and felt compelled to express his misgivings about a number of works performed there. 'Never before have I heard a more vulgar and theoretically feeble composition than Louis Gruenberg's *The Daniel Jazz*,' Janáček declared in his *feuilleton* published in November; of itself, as he emphasized, music could communicate neither love nor hatred, grief nor gaiety. 'There is neither jest in it nor irony, neither satire nor humour nor joviality; neither burlesque nor banter, neither travesty nor a mask. And yet how much one longs for gaiety in music nowadays!'[94] His own approach was different: 'A kind of whirlpool of laughter flows from a collision of double images.'[95]

Janáček's criticisms did not stop there. In the *Serenade*, op. 24, Schoenberg had 'latched only on to Viennese mandoline or guitar strumming', while Stravinsky, who performed his own Piano Sonata, did not know that 'the rules of composition . . . follow the rules of human thought'.[96] Janáček's own First Quartet was in competition with Hindemith's *Kammermusik* no. 2, Ravel's *Tzigane*, Honegger's Cello Sonata, Vaughan Williams's Three Rondos, quartets by Szymanowski and Korngold, and works by Roussel, Malipiero and other Italian composers. And it was well received. 'My quartet will go on from here to Rome, Paris, London,' Janáček announced jubilantly to Kamila. 'I have won!'[97]

Zdenka, at first, was delighted with this trip: throughout her married life she had longed to travel but, apart from a holiday on the Adriatic coast before the First World War, Janáček had always been against the idea. He was exceptionally thrifty, and considered foreign travel far too extravagant (although he himself frequently travelled throughout Czechoslovakia and attended premières of his works in Austria and Germany). Moreover, he disliked the lack of home comforts, was incapable of planning an itinerary for himself, and felt helpless when dealing with foreign trains and hotels.[98]

There were many vicissitudes in store for the Janáčeks during this particular trip, from accommodation problems in Trieste (inadvertently, Janáček had not booked a direct route to Venice) to a missed concert (and dinner) in Venice itself. And after the performance of

his quartet at La Fenice theatre, while attempting to get to the stage
to take a bow, Janáček could not find the way and repeatedly found
himself outside in the street. But the splendour of the city clearly
touched his heart. 'A city in which kings should reside; even the
kings of the spirit,' he wrote reverently in his *feuilleton*. Only its
cuisine failed to meet with his approval. 'Italian food!', he reflected
wryly, writing to Kamila on his return to Brno. 'Out of hunger one
eats everything.'[99]

Shortly after his return to Brno Janáček suffered a serious attack of
shingles. He was in great pain for eight weeks, and often in very bad
humour. But by the beginning of November 1925 his health had
improved, and he was looking forward to the première of his first
opera, *Šárka*, thirty-eight years after its composition. Having substantially modified the work in 1888, he then abandoned it, but the great
success of *Jenůfa* in Prague in 1916 had prompted him to revise it in
1918–19; in 1925 he made further revisions.[100]

Janáček did not change the overall structure of *Šárka* in 1918, only
cutting a little in the choral passages; the changes affected largely the
solo voice parts, though their accompaniment was left intact. Yet the
difference in the vocal style is immense. A detailed comparison of the
1888 and 1918 versions was made in the late 1980s.[101] The 1888
version was written when Janáček had barely begun his speech-
melody studies; thirty years later, he 'unhitched the voice from the
orchestral accompaniment. Its part became speeded up, irregular . . .
moved over a wider range, and made use of a greater variety of
rhythms . . .'.[102] Against the more or less regular phrases of the
accompaniment, the voice, poised above the orchestra, expresses
the emotions in a reasonably realistic stylization of spoken Czech.

Janáček thought highly of his first opera; he was unable to entice
Kamila to the 'pretty' Brno production, but reported that it had gone
well.[103] He was eager for a Prague production, but the National
Theatre showed no interest; Otakar Ostrčil considered the work
merely 'an interesting retrospective', and the Brno production 'an
act of piety' towards Janáček. Janáček's long-standing friendship
with Ostrčil cooled; the composer was peeved and disappointed,
while Ostrčil rightly maintained that *Šárka* had not been commissioned by the National Theatre, and that he could not be blamed for
preferring to stage Janáček's more recent works.[104] Brod protested
about the theatre's attitude in the *Prager Tagblatt*; in 1928 he and
Janáček discussed the possibility of a German translation. Yet in the
end even Brod was sceptical.

On 5 December 1925, less than a month after the première of *Šárka*, Janáček announced to Kamila that he had completed his eighth and penultimate opera. *The Makropulos Affair* is based on the play of that name by the Czech writer Karel Čapek, which Janáček had seen in Prague in December 1922 (under Čapek's own direction).[105] The young playwright was already enjoying considerable success in Czechoslovakia and was soon to make his reputation abroad: two of his best-known plays, *R.U.R.* (*Rossum's Universal Robots*, 1920) and *The Insect Play* (1921, written with his brother Josef), were staged in London in 1923.[106] Always on the lookout for new material, Janáček was immediately attracted to *The Makropulos Affair*. He made a note of the event in his diary,[107] but only mentioned it to Kamila almost three weeks later:

> They have just been giving *Makropulos* in Prague. A woman 337 years old, but at the same time still young and beautiful. [. . .] And do you know that she was unhappy? We are happy because we know that our life isn't long. That is why it is necessary to make use of every moment, to use it accordingly.[108]

Makropulos deals with longevity; by coincidence, G.B. Shaw's *Back to Methuselah* also appeared in 1922. Shaw's 'metabiological Pentateuch', which the playwright considered his masterpiece, postulates that increased lifespan would bring increased wisdom and happiness. Čapek – although a follower of relativism – came to the opposite conclusion, and in his preface to the play dismissed any connection with Shaw; he had had the idea for several years, though at first he had intended to make it into a novel.[109] He regarded his play as a comedy and, surprisingly, thought it unsuitable for operatic treatment, although one of the characters is a prima donna, and another a budding diva. When Janáček approached him in 1923, the playwright answered humbly that the text of his '*conversational*, fairly unpoetical and over-garrulous play' might not suit the composer, whose music he valued highly. Instead, he suggested that Janáček devise his own version, in which 'a 300-year-long life and its sufferings would be the pivot and centre of a more suitable framework'.[110] Yet to his sister Helena Čapek grumbled: 'That old crank! Soon he'll even be setting the local column in the newspaper. It's good that he is not asking me to help him with it . . . . I don't have the time, and even if I had, I wouldn't want to do it.'[111]

Undeterred by legal complications – the play's film and musical rights had already been sold for the next ten years – Janáček took a copy of the play to read during his summer holidays in Slovakia. On his return he learnt that there would be no problem with setting the play in Czech. He was free to make whatever changes he wanted; he would, Čapek wrote flatteringly, 'surely make something great' from the play.[112]

The story harks back to a glorious period of Czech history, the reign of the last Hapsburg emperor and king of Bohemia, Rudolf II (1526–1612). Under his rule, Christians and Jews, Protestants and Catholics, believers and non-believers lived in relative peace and mutual tolerance. His court – the last imperial court based in Prague – attracted some of the foremost musicians and painters of the day; as a highly intelligent would-be scientist and philosopher, Rudolf also had a strong interest in astronomy and alchemy, and the royal castle was brimming with genuine scholars as well as charlatans.[113]

In Čapek's play, a Greek physician from Crete, Hieronymus Makropulos, is commanded to devise an elixir that will give the emperor an extended lifespan – 300 years, in fact. The potion is first tried on the physician's daughter, the 16-year-old Elina, who immediately falls gravely ill. Makropulos is imprisoned; understandably, Rudolf does not try the elixir. Unconscious for a week, Elina later recovers and flees from Prague, taking the secret of the formula with her. In time she becomes a celebrated singer, but loses interest in people and in love – she has seen so much that nothing really matters to her. As she has retained her great beauty, she continues to attract men, leaving behind a trail of broken hearts and deserting twenty children altogether. Moving around the world, she continuously changes her name, but keeps the same initials: Elina Makropulos becomes Eugenia Montez, Ekaterina Myshkin and Ellian MacGregor. By 1922 Elina is 337 years old and, as Emilia Marty, has returned to Prague; Čapek's play and Janáček's opera both begin at this point.

Weary of life, the famous diva now becomes involved in a long-standing lawsuit about which she seems surprisingly well informed. Its resolution hinges on the discovery of a will, in which the illegitimate son of 'Ellian MacGregor' is the named beneficiary. But Marty's main interest lies in recovering an ancient Greek document she knows to be kept with the will. In addition, Albert Gregor and Jaroslav Prus, rival claimants to the estate, both become besotted with Marty; Prus is persuaded to bring her the document in return for a night with her. In the end, Marty reveals her identity, explaining that her desire to recover the 'magic formula' contained in the document was born out of her fear of imminent death. Now, feeling she has lived too long, she offers the secret to Krista, a stage-struck young singer. But Krista refuses, and burns the document as Marty dies.

Although Janáček was clearly gripped by the play, in 1926 he told the Brno reporter Adolf Veselý that *Makropulos* was 'rather a difficult job, I rewrote the libretto three times before I got what I wanted'.[114] He made large cuts but did not change the setting (though he indicated special lighting effects), and retained even the minor characters. He often improvised, reducing the dialogue and making further cuts during the revisions. On the other hand, he made only small changes to the lines in his adaptation but repeated some words and lines for the sake of rhythm and emphasis. This is particularly noticeable at the end of Act 3, where the chorus echoes Marty's monologue.

Janáček employed in *Makropulos* his by now customary ground-plan of three acts; with no scene changes during any of the acts, there are no instrumental interludes. Act 1 is nevertheless sandwiched between one of Janáček's longest overtures and extended curtain music. Conversely, the orchestral music opening and closing the other two acts is succinct.

In keeping with Čapek's 'conversational' play, there are no genuine arias or duets in *Makropulos*, not even among the lovers – only mono-logues, narrations and dialogues, especially in Act 2. Nor are there any strophic songs, while choral writing has been reduced to an off-stage male chorus in the final scene.[115]

Marty's extended scena constitutes much of the final act; the climax affirms the cyclical nature of the opera. In the earlier scenes the words intersperse a continuous stream of instrumental music, but in the finale the prose comes in more regular units; the voices and orchestra are integrated, and the symphonic style is in perfect balance with the musical diction. 'I pride myself on the third act,' Janáček later told an interviewer: 'What a climax, what a precipice! This is what I felt. This is what I had wanted. I worked on it for about a year. I carried it about in my head, kept thinking about it – but then, what speed! I wrote like a machine!'[116]

As in his previous operas, Janáček made use of speech melodies in *Makropulos*, setting not only Czech but also snippets of German, Latin, French, Spanish, Greek and even English. In short phrases, and in words with equal syllabic length, with standard stress on the first syllable, Janáček often gives a credible representation of contempo-rary spoken Czech. Yet there are some minor transgressions from the norm – either as a result of Janáček's need to develop the portrayal of the character's state of mind, or due to his own staccato accent. And as elsewhere, one sometimes gets the impression that the text was fitted to a preconceived melodic line.[117]

Although Janáček compressed the play skilfully, there are some minor inaccuracies which give rise to possible misunderstanding. And unnecessary idiosyncrasies have somehow crept into Čapek's text: grammar and syntax are sometimes incorrect, and words from Janáček's dialect are used. The characters also sometimes rapidly change from one form of address to another. Once again one wonders whether Janáček made such changes in order to fit preconceived instrumental lines, or whether these textual errors were made in the heat of creative effort and escaped Janáček's notice during later revisions.[118]

Many writers have also tried to account for the differences in Marty's age, which occur in both the libretto and the vocal score (first 337, then 327); it would seem that these are plain errors, probably left uncorrected during the composer's lifetime due to misplaced reverence.[119]

As he did in his other works, Čapek (who was, and still is, much loved by the Czechs), portrayed in *Makropulos* a wide spectrum of characters, from all walks of life, and employed different modes of contemporary speech, including a typical Prague accent.[120] His examination of longevity and its implications has an ironic aspect; essentially, the play is a thriller. Janáček, on the other hand, saw the protagonist's predicament as tragic. Thus his adaptation of the text entirely altered not only the way Marty is perceived, but the very character of Čapek's modish play.

His most substantial change was the ending. In Čapek, Marty laughs cynically as she watches the document burn, and shows no fear of her approaching death; Janáček has his heroine collapse while she is murmuring the opening words of the Lord's prayer (*Pater hemon*) in her mother tongue.

In the play, the wounds which Marty inflicts on her suitors and her offspring have a comic effect; in the opera, Marty's tremendous allure is highlighted instead, starting with her imperious entrance in Act I. The part is written with great flair, and it calls for a genuine singer-actress – the diva's emotional compass ranges from adolescent feelings to motherliness, from tenderness to rage, and from passion to her famous 'icy coldness'.

Krista, on the other hand, is at first a breathless, infatuated *ingénue*, and there is a slightly comic aspect to her behaviour even in Janáček's shortened text. Yet in the finale she carries a lot of the emotional weight. When she holds the document, she faces a Faustian dilemma: one wonders whether the sorry tale is about to begin all over again. But Krista has matured – through her own tragedy (her boyfriend Janek's suicide, though we hear nothing of her actual reaction to it), and her compassion for Marty. Although the heroine dies, redemption – which, with compassion, is the cornerstone of most of Janáček's stage works – reconciles the audience to the tragedy. And the fact that Marty dies voluntarily no doubt reflects Janáček's changing outlook on death, which he had always greatly feared.

The nature of the characters is suggested by Janáček's choice of voice types: inevitably, Marty is a dramatic soprano, while Krista is a mezzo, as are two other female roles. Four of the male roles are tenors (in Gregor's case, Janáček actually wrote 'tenor' in his copy of the play). As in *Káťa Kabanová*, most of the males in *Makropulos* appear feeble; only Prus is shown as a shrewd and strong contender for Marty's favours, aware of his power.

Two themes run throughout the opera; it is often held that the first, a group of four chords of equal time value, derives from the Czech speech inflections of the word 'Makropulos'.[121] Another theme, a fanfare for offstage horns, trumpets and drums, first appears in the overture, and later recurs, perhaps evoking Marty's childhood at the Prague court of Rudolf II.[122] Other distinctive themes are linked to particular characters or subjects. The lawyer Kolenatý and legal matters are characterized by a succession of alternating fifths and a rising fourth. Another theme, in Act 1, is associated with Marty – descending stepwise from the fifth note of the scale to the first and followed by a leap of a minor seventh, it is scored for viola d'amore and glockenspiel.[123]

Word painting and various characterizing devices are also used. In Act 1, the violins imitate Kolenatý's hasty scribbling (illustrating the stage direction 'K. scribbles irritably in his papers'); in Act 2, Marty's derisory gossip about a 'squealing' prima donna is accompanied by a flute flourish in a high register, and Janáček also used 'Spanish' elements such as syncopated rhythms and castanets; a xylophone announces a knock on Marty's bedroom door in Act 3.[124]

Once again Janáček used fourths and fifths as standard building devices in the melodic line of *Makropulos*, but rising and falling thirds are increasingly often employed, perhaps mirroring the largely conversational nature of the text. As in his other operas, the characters' varying states of mind are successfully portrayed by widening the intervallic range; this is particularly noticeable with Marty. The men, by contrast, often recite on a single note – for example, Kolenatý in the summary of the court case, and Vítek, Hauk and Prus elsewhere.

As in Janáček's previous operas, modal inflections also appear in *Makropulos*: a Lydian modality dominates the tonality of the opera's catharsis, and in its very conclusion (*Grave*), the impact is reinforced by a tonal change from the Lydian mode in B to A flat major – a kind of progression often skilfully used by folk musicians in Moravia.[125]

Janáček's well-established technique of introducing and preparing the speech motifs in the orchestra, or echoing them, is evident throughout *Makropulos*. The scoring is characteristic: the unusual – and haunting – combinations include a high-pitched child's drum (set against the tremolo of the violins in the 'Makropulos' theme), and a viola d'amore (in 'Marty's' theme).[126] Percussion and brass also play prominent roles.

Janáček began working on *Makropulos* on 11 November 1923. Dates on his autograph score clearly document his progress: by 15 August 1924 he had already completed the first version of the first two acts. Act 3 took longer, and often lay heavily on Janáček's mind; the first version was completed in February 1925.[127] Yet when he finally finished the opera, he was full of pity for his heroine: 'Poor 300-year-old beauty! People took her for a thief, a liar, a heartless animal. They called her a beast, a slut, wanted to strangle her – and what was her fault? That she was doomed to live too long,' he wrote to Kamila. A familiar thought-process – typical of Janáček's habitual *horror vacui* – ensues: 'Three years' work is at an end. What now?'[128]

Yet by the end of March 1926 he had written a new male-voice chorus, *Our Flag*, a setting of a poem by F.S. Procházka, and by April 1926 he had also completed one of his most stirring works, the orchestral *Sinfonietta*. The previous year he had heard, in Kamila's company, a military band playing rousing fanfares in a Písek park; later he wrote some fanfares of his own, in response to a request for music for the Sokol Gymnastic Society festival, and soon Janáček's 'pretty little Symfonietta with fanfares' was growing movement by movement.[129] The work is dedicated to the Czechoslovak Armed Forces,[130] and the original title – on which Janáček insisted during his lifetime – was 'Military Symfonietta'; for the Prague première he named the individual movements 'Fanfares', 'The Castle', 'The Queen's Monastery', 'The Street' and 'The Town Hall'. Thus the work is also a tribute to Janáček's adoptive home town, which he only began to love after 1918: 'I prided myself on [the town], I belonged to it,' he wrote in 1927. 'And the blare of the victorious trumpets, the holy peace of the Queen's Monastery hidden in Úvoz, the shadows of the night, the breath of the green hill and the vision of the secure growth and greatness of the town arose in my Symfonietta from this recognition, from my Brno.'[131]

In the majestic opening fanfare, parallel fifths are used; a Moravian mirror rhythm (on the bass trumpet and timpani) appears at its close. This is followed by another fanfare, also with a mirror rhythm at its close, and its speeded-up variant; the rhythmic flow is sustained by frequent repetitions. The following jubilant *Maestoso* strongly resembles the speech melody of a folk song from Valašsko;[132] the movement, scored entirely for brass (nine trumpets, two tenor tubas and two bass trumpets), ends with a canonic imitation.

Frequent repetitions and changes of tempo also appear in the second movement. A dance-like tune on the oboes is heard first, followed by a lyrical *Meno mosso*; a seemingly new tune on the horn is derived from an earlier motif, and provides material for a gradated development. Janáček used many of his favourite techniques in this movement: persistent ostinatos in the accompaniment, juxtapositions of motifs on various instruments, and modal inflections; in the following *Maestoso*, the trumpet fanfare is made up of his favourite intervals of fourths and seconds.

One of Janáček's most lyrical themes, a brief cantilena on the strings, opens the third movement. Over a low pedal in the tuba and bass clarinet, and against the arpeggio figurations on the harp, it develops, moving from one instrument to another. A syncopated figure then appears three times on the trombones (*Con moto*), followed by a fast motif on the flutes and piccolo, like a gust of wind before a storm. After another section, with a brief return of the yearning melody and its variants, the motif is finally taken up by other wind instruments in the formidable *Prestissimo* ('it's got to be like the wind,' Janáček said irritably to the protesting principal flute player before the première).[133] But the storm passes, and the movement ends with a brief reappearance of the *dolce* theme.

The fourth movement is a kind of scherzo; once again the main theme – repeated no fewer than fourteen times – has a modal character, and a Moravian mirror rhythm also reappears. All further motivic development throughout the movement is organically derived from this theme.

A chorus of three flutes begins the last movement with a variant of the fanfare from the fourth movement. After a solo motif on the flute, against swift figurations on the cello, the music intensifies; soon after the change of tempo, no fewer than twelve trumpets in unison repeat the very first fanfares. This is Janáček in full cry: persistent trills in the rest of the orchestra embellish the festive sound, and the work ends with a brief coda whose powerful modal cadence resembles the conclusion of his tone poem *Taras Bulba*.

Although some writers claim that the *Sinfonietta* was conceived as a suite, the first movement (*Allegretto*) is only a short intrada. Nor is the piece a full-blown symphony; 'a modern symphonic fresco' is perhaps the most fitting description.[134] The *Sinfonietta* requires large orchestral forces and makes great technical demands on the players, but its tremendous vitality makes it a thrilling work.

By 1926 Janáček's reputation was spreading throughout Europe: *Jenůfa* had already been performed in some seventy opera houses. None of his operas had reached London, but an invitation to visit the city came that very year from Rosa Newmarch. In the first three decades of the twentieth century she was the most highly regarded woman writer on music in England: she wrote programme notes for the Queen's Hall, translated various studies and published books on Tchaikovsky and Sibelius. She did much to promote Russian music: she met renowned critics and musicians such as Stasov, Glazunov, Rimsky-Korsakov and Chaliapin, and subsequently gave lectures and published articles and libretto translations. Shortly before the 1917 Revolution, when access to Russia became difficult, Mrs Newmarch turned her attention to the cause of the Czechs and Slovaks.

Janáček had known of her work since *The Musical Times* published her analysis of *Jenůfa* in 1918; in April 1922 he invited her to Brno to see *Káťa Kabanová*. There was a strong affinity between them: Mrs Newmarch had visited Czechoslovakia three times, and responded instinctively to the Slavonic character; her perception of Janáček's music was extraordinary. They communicated in Russian, but she understood Czech well.[135] On her return to England she gave two lectures on Czech music, particularly Janáček's, and organized a concert at which *The Diary* was performed.[136] That December she published an article on Janáček and his speech melody theory, and 'the battle for Janáček' began in earnest: in 1923 she was instrumental in putting *The Fiddler's Child* on the programme of Symphony Concerts at the Queen's Hall, and in 1925 she reviewed the Prague performance of *The Cunning Little Vixen* for *The Times*.[137]

Among the members of the committee she formed to promote

Janáček's London visit were Ralph Vaughan Williams, Sir Henry Wood, and Sir Adrian Boult (whom Janáček had met in 1925 in Prague), as well as directors of the Royal College of Music and the Royal Academy of Music. Janáček was delighted by the invitation; clearly, he viewed the trip as a promotional exercise and an opportunity to discuss the possibilities of staging his operas in England. Mrs Newmarch knew better. 'We have not as yet any national or state opera-house in which repertory operas are given,' she responded, 'and I do not think anything will be sufficiently established to venture on novelties for several years to come . . . . Much influence, favouritism and money would be needed to get a new work performed . . . . No, I am afraid we must be content with small beginnings.'[138]

A concert of Janáček's chamber music was therefore arranged; at her own risk, Mrs Newmarch hired the 600-seat Wigmore Hall. Janáček suggested the programme: First Quartet, Violin Sonata, *Fairytale* for cello and piano, the wind sextet *Mládí* and the *Concertino*. He diligently studied the map of London, and was very interested in the Thames, which he saw as 'the artery of London life'.[139] His visit was announced in *The Times*, and over 1,200 posters were printed.

After numerous organizational difficulties, the composer finally set off on 28 April with Jan Mikota, his secretary and interpreter throughout the trip;[140] arriving in London two days later, they stayed at the luxurious Langham Hotel. Rehearsals began in earnest on 1 May; Adila Fachiri, granddaughter of Joachim, played the Violin Sonata, and other well-known musicians such as the oboist Leon Goossens participated. There was a whirl of social events: dinner with Sir Henry and Lady Wood; a reception at Claridges; Sunday afternoon at the Woods' country house, and much sightseeing (including the London Zoo, where Janáček notated some of the monkeys' cries). Another reception took place at the School of Slavonic Studies, with some of Janáček's vocal music on the programme;[141] the composer also met the extremely helpful Czech Ambassador Jan Masaryk, son of the President.

Socially the visit was a great success, but its promotional effect was marred by the fact that the concert coincided with the General Strike on 6 May. 'The workforce is seething with unrest,' Janáček reported to Kamila Stösslová; he believed the strike was 'incited by Russian bolsheviks and Germans'. 'Today they shot one chauffeur in the street . . . . But London is so big that round the corner no one knows about it,' he concluded.[142]

There was no public transport; some of the musicians had to walk to the hall (Leon Goossens took three hours), and no programme notes were available. And the *Concertino* – in Janáček's view the best piece on the programme – had to be cancelled as Janáček took a strong dislike to the pianist, Fanny Davies, and her interpretation.[143] Nor was the concert reviewed, although the programme, particularly *Mládí*, was well received. On his return journey Janáček rested for two days in Holland; both on the ferry and on the Dutch coast he enthusiastically notated the sound of the waves. But his supposedly 'iron nerves' had suffered as a result of the trip, as he later confided to Rosa.[144]

'A path has been made clear for *Jenůfa* for next season,' Janáček claimed on 7 May 1926.[145] Yet hopes of bringing his first masterpiece to London soon foundered. In September 1926 Rosa reported on a letter she had received from the arts patroness Mrs Courtauld. Because of heavy losses – particularly on Strauss's *Elektra* – only one new opera could be performed at Covent Garden in the forthcoming season, and Puccini's *Turandot* had been chosen. 'It always takes three or four years longer for music to reach us in England than in Continental towns,' complained Rosa. 'I will watch chances for you . . . I will do all I can. But to capture Covent Garden is like trying to storm the gates of Heaven – or perhaps Hell would be nearer the mark.'[146] A performance of *Taras Bulba*, under Henry Wood, took place in October that year, and there were plans to perform the *Sinfonietta* (of which Rosa was the second dedicatee). But the correspondence petered out and Janáček and Rosa Newmarch never met again.

Janáček was the second major Czech composer to visit England but, unlike Dvořák, he never became popular with English audiences in his lifetime; *Jenůfa* only received its Covent Garden première in 1956, and then not in Czech.[147] In his *feuilleton* 'The sea, the land', published in June 1926, Janáček put forward his views on England and the nature of contemporary English musicians and audiences; it was the sea, he believed, which cast its implacable influence over everything, 'wearing down and raising up the banks of human character – and also shaping the artistic character: the English, the northern character'. The players' technique was correct, but greater emotional warmth was wanting. 'Something set a limit to it. . . . The sea.'[148]

A few days after returning to Brno at the end of May 1926, Janáček set off again, this time to attend a dress rehearsal and performance of *Káťa Kabanová* in Berlin, under Fritz Zweig.[149] Zweig was one of several German musicians who assiduously promoted Janáček's work during the composer's lifetime, and he clearly understood Janáček's idiom. 'Káťa comes down to the fateful rendezvous,' Janáček wrote in his *feuilleton*. 'The ingenious conductor invested her trembling steps with a stagnant silence both in the orchestra and on the stage. . . . And how the storm in the third act raged in the orchestra of ninety-five players! Such productions dazzle. They throw open the gates of the world for the work.'[150]

The audience included many of Janáček's supporters: the conductor Erich Kleiber, the composers Franz Schreker and Arnold Schoenberg, and the soprano Maria Jeritza (the first Jenůfa in Vienna and in New York). Kleiber's 1924 Berlin production of *Káťa* had launched the opera's international career; another renowned conductor, Otto Klemperer, had introduced *Jenůfa* to Cologne in 1918 and *Káťa* in 1922.

Zweig, Kleiber and Klemperer all had Czech connections: Klemperer's father was born in Prague; Kleiber's parents had married in the Czech capital, and although he was Viennese by birth, he spoke perfect Czech. Zweig was born in Moravia; his wife, Tilly de Garmo, was a prima donna at the Neues Deutsches Theater in Prague, where both Kleiber and Klemperer had served their apprenticeship, and whose staff Zweig was later to join.[151]

On 11 July 1926 a memorial plaque was unveiled at Janáček's birthplace in Hukvaldy; after a weekend of celebratory speeches, lunches and concerts, he left for his annual stay at Luhačovice, looking forward to having a rest. But that summer the weather was so bad that there was nothing to do but work; within three weeks the composer wrote the *Glagolitic Mass*, his first large-scale cyclical composition for voices and orchestra, to a liturgical text in Old Slavonic.[152]

As director and teacher at the Brno Organ School Janáček had been involved with liturgy for many years, and had even composed a Latin Mass with his pupils; his upbringing and early musical background made him well versed in liturgical texts. Yet the *Glagolitic Mass* is not written in a traditional ecclesiastical style, and there has been much speculation about its purpose: some scholars regard it as a musical celebration of the ancient Slavonic text, others interpret it in purely literary terms, without considering its liturgical aspects. In fact, Janáček wanted to 'add [his] work' to the millennial anniversary of the two Greek missionary brothers who brought Christianity to Moravia. 'The whole atmosphere of Cyril and Methodius! This is what was missing here,' Janáček later told an interviewer.[153] Although it is not certain whether he had discussed the missionaries with Archbishop Prečan, the work's dedicatee, Janáček later emphasized in his *feuilleton* about the *Mass* that he wanted 'to show faith in the certainty of the nation not on a religious basis, but on a moral one; a basis of strength which takes God as its witness'.[154]

Despite the precise historical reference there is no tendency towards archaism in the *Glagolitic Mass*. As in most of his work, the basis of the music in the *Mass* is a process of considering the sound and meaning of the individual words. A fanfare-like introduction opens the work; the speech melody of the opening words of the ensuing Kyrie, 'Gospodi pomiluj' ('Lord, have mercy') can immediately be recognized, and the vocal line is introduced as well as echoed by the strings. A solo soprano part is accompanied by rising and falling figurations on the strings and the bassoon.

Small bells open the Gloria, and here the solo soprano is set against figurations on the harp and viola; once again the melodic line derives from the speech melody of the text, and there are many changes of tempo, indicating passages of differing character. The solo soprano returns in the *Moderato*, against the characteristic ostinatos in the woodwind and the violas; the horns and organ are set against each other. A tenor solo is introduced in the *Maestoso*, interspersed with the invocations of the bass and the chorus. Full orchestral forces, including powerful timpani, are summoned up in the closing Amen.

The main vocal theme of the Credo, sung by the chorus, immediately conveys a sense of deep, steadfast faith; the following Amen skips along almost joyfully. Later on, a tenor solo is preceded and echoed by a brief but poignant trumpet solo before Janáček returns to the opening rhythm. The main motif of the Credo returns three times; a tender orchestral *Andante* then accelerates before a stormy, chromaticized organ solo takes place. The chorus returns, eventually repeating the main motif *pianissimo*; after tenor and bass solos, the section finally closes with another Amen.

The soft, feathery sounds of harp and celesta open the Sanctus; later on, a solo violin, in a very high register, has a calm, unearthly quality. In the ensuing *Con moto* Janáček employs timpani, bells and cymbals, to powerful effect; all the solo voices appear in the *Meno mosso*, with the alto and tenor in a brief, harmonious respite, and the movement closes with a joyful Hosanna.

In the short Agnus Dei, an ostinato motif on muted strings (and later in the woodwind) is soon followed by a beautifully structured and developed three-bar main motif in the chorus, its cadence deliberately unresolved; the two motifs alternate. Later on, all the solo voices are deployed in repeated invocations and the cadence is only resolved after the return of the initial ostinato, before the final chorus.

A frenzied organ solo follows, with a persistent chromaticized ostinato pedal. This section is unprecedented in Czech sacred music: from a simple motif Janáček creates music of tremendous power and great beauty; marked *fortissimo* throughout, it accelerates into the *Prestissimo*, slowing down only in the majestic closing chords. A brief orchestral Intrada concludes the work, its dance-like motif in the brass and brisk ostinatos leading to the final assertive, triumphant major. 'I shall write a merry Mass,' Janáček told his wife in 1926,[155] and the tone is certainly far from supplicatory: beneath the flesh and bones of the religious text lies another, larger world. 'The balmy breeze of the Luhačovice woods was always incense to me,' wrote Janáček in his *feuilleton* about the *Mass*. 'The church grew for me into the gigantic size of a mountain and the sky vaulted into the misty distance.' Yet Janáček's pantheism is combined with an acute feeling for Czech history: 'The candles are the tall pines in the forest, and somewhere in the ceremony, I see the princely vision of St Wenceslas.'[156]

Nevertheless, various speculations as to whether he had finally embraced religion were briskly refuted: 'Not an old man, not a believer, you callow youth,' he responded in his usual terse style to the otherwise well-balanced analysis of the *Mass* by the Czech musicologist and pianist Ludvík Kundera.[157] Despite his advancing age Janáček did not seek the comfort of faith, and was not going to abandon his agnosticism: 'Only when they convince me,' he often remarked wryly towards the end of his life.[158] Although he grew up in a religious atmosphere, demanded that his children say their prayers, and always happily celebrated Christmas and Easter, he had developed a strong dislike for all churches, to the point that he avoided entering them. Yet he was not hostile to Catholicism. 'Why should I secede from the Catholic Church? The Catholic Church has done me no harm,' he remarked in 1924.[159]

Thus Janáček's overall attitude to religion is not at all straightforward. The *Glagolitic Mass* is an ecstatic celebration of life; Ludvík Kundera's son, the Czech writer Milan Kundera, thought it more an orgy than a mass.[160] Yet perhaps it also portrays the pain of longing for God in those who have lost faith, and have found nothing with which to replace it.

Janáček's next work, the *Capriccio* for piano left hand and wind

ensemble, was written between June and October 1926, simultaneously with the *Glagolitic Mass*. It owes its origin partly to a tragedy
of the First World War: Janáček was approached to write it by the
Czech pianist Otakar Hollmann who had lost his right hand in
action. Although Janáček initially refused (as he wrote to Kamila,
'It's hard for the one-legged to dance!'), he was sympathetic to
Hollmann's plight: on 11 November 1926 he reported that the
Capriccio (originally to be entitled 'Defiance') was finished.[161] He
had not written it, he declared, just for the sake of producing a composition for the left hand; further exploration of the genre he had
found in the *Concertino* was clearly one of the strongest motives.[162]
Nevertheless, the *Capriccio* remained for a long time among Janáček's least performed works. This is at least partly because of its
sound world and its technical demands – the wind ensemble
includes flute, two trumpets and three trombones, of which the first
and second trombones have difficult parts, with figuration at breakneck speed.

The first movement (of four) opens with a fast, march-like theme
on the piano, accompanied by the trombones. Later on, the piano
echoes this introductory theme, following it with its inversion. In the
middle section, a trumpet cadenza introduces a dialogue between
two themes, before the return of the opening motif and the trombone ostinato; the movement ends with its anguished echo.

The piano also opens the second, slow movement; a simple halting
melody and its frequent interruptions, marked *dolce*, are played by
the left hand on both staves; this construction in opposite motion is
followed by a folk-like compression of the melodic line. A brief
diminution figure, so characteristic of Janáček, continually disturbs
the main melody. A flute makes its first appearance in a recitative-
like entry; once again the motifs mingle in the middle section, until
the trombone motif returns and the opening melody resignedly
closes the movement.

In the main theme of the third, scherzo-like movement, the gro-
tesque humour, irony and mockery are portrayed by the tenor tuba;
unusual instrumental combinations (such as muted trumpet against
glissandi on the piano) are also used. Later on the trumpet shines
brightly in the repetition of the main theme, but the trombone motif
prevails, distorted – in Vogel's words – 'into a grimace'.[163] The movement closes with the *pianissimo* of the brass.

The flute opens the finale, and once again its melodic line is composed of Janáček's seconds and fourths. The overall mood is joyful:

the brass soon enters with gusto (*Maestoso vivo*) and a turbulent piano cadenza, with its chromatic runs of triads, recalls the orgiastic organ solo in the fourth movement of the *Glagolitic Mass*. The trombones return, but the flute theme, now on the piccolo and underpinned by the trumpets, takes over and the work ends in a triumphant D flat major.

At the end of this prolific year Janáček also completed his definitive version of *Nursery Rhymes*.[164] Like *The Cunning Little Vixen*, *Nursery Rhymes* is based on excerpts from the children's supplement of *Lidové noviny* – short humorous verses with drawings by popular artists such as Josef Lada (best known outside the Czech Republic for his illustrations of Hašek's comic masterpiece, *The Good Soldier Švejk*) and the children's book illustrator and caricaturist Ondřej Sekora.[165] Janáček's original version consisted of eight pieces for three women's voices, clarinet and piano, and the work was first performed in that form in October 1925.[166] It was then re-scored for nine voices and ten instruments, and now comprises eighteen numbers and an instrumental introduction.

The vocal line of the rhymes (in Czech, in a Moravian dialect and in Ruthenian) often deliberately imitates a children's style of reciting, with intentional mis-stressing (numbers 6, 9 and 11); in number 4, perhaps also recalling the world of children, contrasting voices respond to one another, as children might do at play.[167] There is also much motivic imitation. Janáček frequently employs the intervals so characteristic of him (seconds, fourths and fifths) but his use of downward thirds sometimes pinpoints the mocking style of the rhyme (numbers 5, 13 and 14). In number 10 ('An old hag making magic'), the text is masterfully characterized by a descending whole-tone run; in number 12, larger intervals such as sixths are used for characterization.

The main vocal motifs are repeatedly used in individual instruments, although the chordal, percussive nature of the piano is stressed in the overall structure, as are the figurations or runs on the flute and the clarinets. Unusual instruments such as the ocarina and a toy drum are also used for characterization, and different structures are often juxtaposed to good effect. Numbers 3, 4, 6 and 7 have brief instrumental conclusions; the extended, dance-like, instrumental conclusion to number 19 rounds off the whole piece – a Czech 'counterpart to [Stravinsky's] *Pribaoutki*, *Cat's Cradle Songs* and other similar works'.[168]

During 1926 Janáček saw Kamila only three times, but sent her some sixty letters and postcards. As always, he confided in her about everything; occasionally she was also the recipient of what he called 'peevish' or 'heartbroken' letters, whenever the intervals between his missives and her infrequent replies grew too long for his liking.[169]

His comments about his experiences and the performances of his works are often telling, and occasionally quite blunt;[170] although Kamila was not a music lover, he continued to invite her to concerts and performances of his operas. And both he and Zdenka invited the Stössels and their children to spend their summer holidays with them at Hukvaldy that year. But once again Kamila's husband was too busy, and she preferred to stay at home in Písek.

This time Janáček took offence, reproaching her for making excuses. Later that summer he met Kamila's husband and brother in Luhačovice, but without Kamila he felt very much alone there. 'I'm withdrawing into my shell which has no windows,' he wrote to her bitterly. 'No one to talk to. . . . Memories – [they are] like a wilted flower.'[171] Several bouts of ill health during the year contributed to his melancholy state of mind. 'I know I will wear myself out,' he predicted on return to Brno.[172] Yet work seemed to be the only cure.

In October 1926 the Neues Deutsches Theater in Prague wanted Janáček to attend its performance of *Jenůfa*; Janáček duly invited the Stössels. After some hesitation, the couple accepted, and Janáček insisted that Zdenka accompany him; she guessed he wanted her to meet Kamila again. When, after a business meeting in Prague, he telephoned the Stössels' gallery, Zdenka was astonished to observe his face change completely on hearing Kamila answer. 'Such a enraptured, wistful expression as I have never seen on his face before.'[173] The two couples met in the evening but Kamila did not want to see the opera, and suggested they all meet afterwards at a restaurant. The Janáčeks were dumbfounded; only much later did Kamila tell Zdenka that Janáček 'was looking at her in such a way that she was afraid to go to the theatre'.[174] The following day Janáček – the first client at the Stössels' new antique shop – purchased a painting from them, 'for luck', as Kamila said. Returning with Janáček to Brno, Zdenka knew something was amiss.

The Brno première of *The Makropulos Affair* was given a month later, but Janáček did not invite Kamila.[175] 'You went "your own way" in Prague,' he reproached her, 'and that hurt at the time.'[176] *Makropulos*, he nevertheless went on, was an 'unthought of' success, with its spectacular costumes: 'In Act I some sort of greenish fur as a lining. Those pearls and long gold earrings. In Act II a white fur coat, a long train, in [Act] III a dress of gold, as if [made] out of gold scales.

What a spectacle!'[177] Karel Čapek attended the première and, completely forgetting his earlier misgivings about Janáček setting his play to music, 'simply glowed, drinking mutual toasts with the Maestro,' recalled his sister Helena.[178] Soon, *Makropulos* was to be shown in Prague, Janáček reported to Kamila. 'So you will come to see that "cold one",' he added. 'You will perhaps see your own photograph.'[179]

Zdenka also attended the Brno première; during the interval one of the friends who came to congratulate Janáček at his box began to talk enthusiastically about the music. Suddenly, Janáček blurted out in his staccato accent: 'And that's what I wrote with such a stupid wife, if you please.' The visitor tried tactfully to make light of his remark, but Janáček meant it. Zdenka, though stricken, decided to let it pass.[180]

Universal Edition published the vocal score just a few days before the première, with a German translation by Max Brod. While working on it, Brod had nevertheless wanted 'to clarify' several passages in Janáček's occasionally hastily adapted text. The composer protested vigorously;[181] later he conceded some points, but clearly felt disgruntled.[182]

Plans for a Berlin production were afoot within a month of the Brno première. By then Janáček set out further objections to Brod's translation in a lengthy letter: claiming he had been made aware 'from several quarters' that the translation of Act 3 was too free, he listed altogether fifty-two discrepancies, underlining in red six to which he took particular exception.[183]

Brod – a skilled writer – was taken aback. Eventually he yielded to eleven of Janáček's demands, and these changes could still be made in a separate German libretto, to be published later. But the vocal score had to remain unchanged. Relations with Brod cooled; Janáček was convinced that the adaptation harmed not only him, but also Čapek, whose text inspired the opera.[184]

In March 1927 Janáček was invited to Prague to take tea with the President Masaryk. This was an honour but the occasion was by no means a private affair – several hundred people were usually present, among them many well-known artists.[185] Then, as their Brno cottage was being redecorated, Janáček – encouraged by Zdenka, who wanted him out of the way – planned to spend a part of Easter with the Stössels in Písek. Several eager letters before the visit show how much he yearned for a rest and a change of scene.

On his return he wrote to Kamila with unambiguous passion:

I know that I would be consumed in that heat which must not blaze up. On the roads I would plant oaks that would endure for centuries; and on the trunks I would engrave the words that I have shouted in the wind . . . . To no one, ever, have I said them with such compulsion, such ruthlessness. 'You, Kamila! Look back! Pause!' And I also read in your eyes that something united us in that gale and heat . . . . I would have wished the road to be endless; I waited without tiring for the words you whispered: what would I have done if you were my wife? Well, I think of you as if you were my wife. Just thinking that is not much, yet [it is] as if the rays of hundreds of suns flooded me . . . . Do with this letter, with this declaration of mine, as you wish. You can burn it, or not.[186]

Whatever had actually passed between them (and Janáček frequently invested Kamila's actions and words with unintended significance), clearly the friendship was now moving forward: from April 1927 until his death sixteen months later Janáček sent Kamila some three hundred letters, writing almost daily and sometimes several times a day.[187] Yet even after reading all the letters it is still difficult to chart the development of their relationship; the composer comments on many of Kamila's responses, but at her express wish he burned most of them after reading.[188]

Kamila's initial reaction to Janáček's written declaration of love was, apparently, 'great anxiety',[189] and both of them did their best to keep their friendship from prying eyes. Yet to him the bond meant everything: 'Oh, do love me,' he implored her in the same letter:

In the thought that I have you, that you are mine, rests all my joy in life. I know that my compositions will be more passionate, more rapturous . . . . Oh, Kamila, it is hard for me to calm myself. But the fire you've set alight in me is necessary to me. Let it burn, burn in a flame, the desire to have you, to have you![190]

Never before had he experienced such deep emotions, he assured her a few days later. 'How blissful I feel to have declared my love for you, that I have experienced declaring love to someone. It has never happened before, not even with Zdenka.'[191] Gone was the memory of his passionate courtship of his teenage bride more than forty-five years before. Yet although Janáček used the Czech intimate form of address, 'Ty', Kamila rigorously continued to address him as 'Maestro'.

Constantly recalling minute details of their walks together and her daily routine in Písek, he was anxious for her to visit Brno soon so that they could see each other again. 'Write one letter [saying] how you look forward to Brno so that Zdenka can read it,' he suggested. 'She is surprised at my not getting any letters from you!'[192]

With her husband often away on business, no doubt Kamila *was* lonely at times; yet although she wrote to Janáček how much she was 'looking forward to seeing you all again', she was in no hurry to set off.[193] When Janáček finally implored her to sign at least one letter 'your Kamila', his request had serious repercussions: Zdenka – tidying up his study at the Conservatoire – found Kamila's reply.

One of the cupboards was open, with a few letters scattered about. Putting them in order, Zdenka noticed Kamila's signature. Feeling 'as if stabbed in the back', she read the rest: 'That cannot be what you ask,' Kamila reportedly wrote, adding 'so here goes: Your Kamila – at least that has now come true for you.' Dumbstruck, Zdenka thought: ' "At least that." I knew my husband too well not to guess that that wouldn't be enough for him and that he would [now] launch a fierce attack. And that he wouldn't give up until he achieved everything.' When Janáček missed the letter, he dashed home, enraged. 'Give me back the letter you have stolen from me,' he demanded. Zdenka refused: 'As your wife I have a right to keep it. You wouldn't give me back a letter like that.' She then reminded him of what had happened between them after the première of *The Vixen* in Prague, reproaching him for lying about his revived love for her. 'He answered casually: "Oh, it just came over me when I was lying beside you." We said no more about the subject. But inside me everything changed,' recounted Zdenka later. 'I realized the complete pointlessness of my life, that until its end I would always have to struggle with my husband's infidelities, that nothing would cure them, neither my love, nor the fact that I had tried to understand him . . . not even old age – nothing'.[194]

This confrontation led Janáček, too, to evaluate their unhappy marriage. 'So, peace [at the moment],' he wrote to Kamila on 21 May:

About the house Zdenka is quite exemplary. I wanted to have children, after the death of my two poor little ones – she didn't. At night I am in my study, in the morning I come [back to the house], have breakfast, read the papers – and start working. [When] I come back from the post office, we have lunch; a little bit of everyday talk. I go back into my study, towards evening I walk for an hour and a half; supper, [and then] I play – with our little dog! And off I go to my study for the night. [. . .] Is that meant to be the joy of life? I, by nature a passionate person, naturally . . . need a soul in whom there would be warmth of feeling and compassion. You crossed my path by fate – and ever since, I have inside me something to caress, something to cheer me. Is there anything wrong in it, am I therefore a bad person? I ask myself these questions; am I really to live a life embittered at every moment because of my wife's hard nature? [. . .] I am happy that this love for you blossomed forth. [. . .] Only you know that, and therefore you know me as no one else does. To everyone I am just a smiling person, [but] would I tell anyone how this Janáček, recognized throughout the world, really lives? Condemn me if you will. If I have gone over the top – forgive me . . . . You are far from me and yet the nearest in my heart.[195]

A few days later he declared: 'I respect Zdenka for the suffering she has had, and wish her no harm. But I need freedom of feeling . . . . I have become attached to you and to the end of my life nothing will tear me away from you.'[196]

10

The Final Masterpieces

(1927–1928)

IN A POSTSCRIPT to yet another confession to Kamila, Janáček mentioned his forthcoming opera, *From the House of the Dead*: 'You are, in
my new opera, under the name Aljeja: such a tender, sweet creature.'[1]
He had started the work in February, after a happy stay snowed-up in
Hukvaldy. 'I don't know what work to begin,' he had written to her
then. 'One is within reach, but everyone in it is in fetters.'[2] Yet apart
from two brief references, even Kamila heard no more about the work
until Janáček had nearly completed the first version.[3]

Meanwhile, their friendship developed further, despite a near rift
at the end of May, when Kamila accused Janáček of neglecting her
older son Rudolf during a school trip to Brno; the mortified composer never forgot the incident.[4]

He was much preoccupied by a need to explain his feelings for
Kamila to his wife. When he tried to do so, 'There [was] peace at
home [for a while]: Zdenka burnt the letter. There was nothing in it
apart from that *Tvá* [yours]: I said that I forced it out of you . . .', he
wrote to Kamila.[5] In a postscript next day he reported: 'Zdenka is
not taking it tragically: nor is there any reason to.'[6] He planned to
write to Zdenka from Hukvaldy, where he was to stay early in June:
'I want for once amicably and without anger, calmly to explain to her
my relationship with you.'[7]

In fact, Zdenka *was* taking the situation badly: she had been
suffering for some time from thyroid problems and decided to
undergo an operation, then generally regarded as dangerous. In view
of her age, she considered her chances of survival scant, and sincerely
hoped for a 'discreet, decent death'. She wrote her will and returned
a brooch Kamila had once given her, dismissing her friendship as a
lie: she never wanted to meet her again.[8]

During these valedictory preparations, Janáček left for Hukvaldy.
Writing to Kamila on 8 June, he commented on the long-planned
letter to Zdenka:

It was an open confession: I think she will understand it. She had imagined more than is at all possible. For between us, after all, there is only a beautiful world, but one in which the beautiful, these desires, these wishes, that *Tvá* and all, all is just made up! I told her that this made-up world is as necessary for me, for my life, as air and water. I told her that the vision of you has released me from the clutches of that disgusting H[orvátová], and how for eleven years you have, without knowing it, been my guardian on all sides. I told her how in my compositions, where[ver] pure emotion, sincerity, truth and ardent love give out warmth, you are the one through whom my touching melodies come, you are the Gypsy with the child in *The Diary of One who Disappeared*. You are the poor Elina Makropulos, and you are in my latest work as the lovable Aljeja. I told her that if the thread that binds me to you were broken, so too would the thread of my life be broken. I think that she will understand all this, and especially this eleven-year conundrum of ours!'[9]

Did Zdenka understand? This is what Janáček actually sent her on 13 June:

1. By the bright memory of my father and my mother I swear to you that Mrs Stösslová is an honourable wife and mother. Do you believe this now? 2. I ask you once and for all to leave off this spying, this suspicion of my feelings. I am tormented by the concealment of a perfectly ordinary sympathy, the hiding of an ordinary feeling of friendship. Will you believe once and for all in my mission in life which needs freedom of feeling, freedom which in no way detracts from my feeling for you? To these two questions give me at once a simple answer.[10]

The situation was complex: while Janáček's and Kamila's friendship was indeed platonic, the erotic basis of his feelings for her had always been unmistakable. Thus 'perfectly ordinary sympathy' it was not, as Zdenka's intuition had told her long ago.

And what did Kamila's husband make of a letter Janáček addressed to him two days later? 'Dear friend,' wrote Janáček,

I have been corresponding with your wife for eleven years. For eleven years we have had a pure friendship, have talked about what causes us pain, what we desire; in my greatest compositions, where[ver] there is most pain and love, there your wife has been the inspiration of my celebrated melodies. This pure bond of friendship has saved me from much evil in my life. I have implored her to be my protector until the end of my life, [and] as proof to sign only once [with] the word *Tvá* [Yours]. This she did, just the once. Surely you believe that behind that *Tvá* there is no betrayal either on my part, or on Mrs Kamila's! [. . .] By suspecting me and your wife, my wife has committed an unheard of discourtesy. I do not know how I shall come to terms with her. After all, I have also let her know what I am writing to you! I implore you to stay my good – indeed better – friend, and I implore your wife to continue corresponding with me.[11]

David Stössel's reaction to this letter is unknown. Perhaps he did not think it worth responding. In fact, he had nothing to lose by encouraging Kamila to keep in contact with Janáček: to see her more often, the composer was only too willing to keep visiting the Stössels' antique shop.

Zdenka's operation, though extremely painful, was successful. Janáček telegraphed his congratulations from Hukvaldy, but followed this with a letter, demanding that Zdenka apologize to Kamila for offending her.[12] Stopping over in Brno before his trip to Frankfurt, he visited Zdenka in hospital; during their conversation he suddenly asked her: 'Do you believe I have an intimate relationship with Stösslová?' Zdenka replied that she did not think so, and Janáček visibly relaxed.[13]

She only found out later that on his way to Frankfurt Janáček had stopped over in Písek for two days;[14] references in his subsequent letters to Kamila indicate that at that time he also lent money to the couple, who were reportedly in financial difficulties.[15]

The Frankfurt concert on 30 June (part of the fifth ISCM Festival) was a great success – the *Concertino*, played by the excellent Ilona Štěpánová-Kurzová, was extremely well received, as Janáček diligently reported to Kamila. On the way back (probably 5–6 July), he stayed with the Stössels again,[16] returning to Brno 'cold [and] reserved'.[17]

After a few weeks back in Brno, he was off again, this time to Luhačovice, elated at the prospect of seeing Kamila again. 'In [all] my life I have not experienced more beautiful moments than those this afternoon,' he wrote in a note sent to Kamila's pension on 20 August:

I knew you emotionally so deep, so honourably saintly, so sensible, so genuine, strong, quiet, devoted, that I stand before you as before a vision which only the good Lord could have sent me . . . . How warming were your words, how warm was your little hand which, for the first time, did not draw away. I cannot go to sleep until I tell you that you are more precious to me than my life.[18]

After Kamila's departure Janáček stayed another week in Luhačovice, writing to her daily. Yet even after two weeks in his company Kamila was still keeping her distance; by 1 September Janáček nevertheless began to refer to her as his 'wife'.[19]

Desperate to see her again, he travelled to Písek on 8 September for a chamber concert which included his First String Quartet.[20] But he made no mention of the performance in the letters written around that date; everything revolved around Kamila: 'I see and know more and more that without you I wouldn't want to live!' he declared after the visit.[21]

Janáček and Zdenka then spent a fortnight together in northern Moravia, visiting friends and relatives, and awaiting delivery of two paintings he was buying from the Stössels. By then Zdenka sensed that Janáček did not want to be alone with her; and he could not stop talking about Kamila. Being told the friendship was innocent, and that he 'no longer needed a woman' was no help: predictably, Zdenka thought the statement directed at herself.[22]

Restless and edgy, Janáček went on many excursions and long walks, and wrote frequently to Kamila; Zdenka was full of foreboding. Meanwhile, Kamila scarcely responded; Janáček complained about her silence and about her 'dry' tone. Yet his enchantment continued; even the tremendous success of his *Sinfonietta* in Berlin (29 September, under Klemperer), and the possibility of *Jenůfa* and the *Sinfonietta* in Moscow were overshadowed by the memory of his holidays with her in Luhačovice ('the most beautiful and merriest of all').[23] To remind Kamila of him during his absences, he bought her a special album in which he planned to record his thoughts, as well as some music, during his visits to Písek; the first entry was made on 2 October 1927, immediately after his Berlin trip.[24]

We shall never know what Kamila herself thought of their time together: none of her letters from that period have survived. Whatever she may have discussed with Janáček, she certainly did not want it read by prying eyes; and whether she responded to Janáček's feelings or not, she remained a tremendous source of inspiration. Half way through October, he confessed to her: 'I am feeling melancholy again today. I am finishing a big work – probably my last opera . . . .

And I always feel sorrow when I am parting with those whose lives I have been living for as much as two to three years. And you understand my pain and also my sorrow.'[25] Somehow, Kamila's spontaneity always managed to keep pain and sorrow at bay, at least for a while.

In Janáček's second letter to her that day, he announced that he had just completed the first version of *From the House of the Dead*: 'A terrible title, isn't it? But now the work with my copyist! I would rather shift gravel!'[26] On 21 October 1927 Janáček described his day to Kamila: 'In the morning working from 7.30 until 12; in the afternoon until 4. Post the letter at noon, in the afternoon go hopefully to the post office [Kamila wrote to him *poste restante*] – but there is nothing.' As Janáček's nomination for a state prize for *The Makropulos Affair* became public knowledge, he tried to impress on Kamila how much more she meant to him than any wordly distinction: 'If [only] "our state" were to say to me: "Marry that charming girl called Kamila. And be happy with her!" That would be the honour, the state prize which would please me most.'[27] On 30 October he wrote in a darker vein: 'Here at home I have been given some "serious" talking to.'[28] Although he added that 'the crisis had passed', and Zdenka herself later declared that she did 'everything in her power' to keep calm and avoid scenes, the discord continued undiminished.[29]

In November, Janáček escorted Kamila and her mother to a performance of *Jenůfa* in Písek, by a south Bohemian company. 'It pleased me a great deal [to hear] the effect *Jenůfa* had on your mother,' he commented later. 'I value that knowledge more than all that journalistic outpouring.'[30] As always, the pain of separation was unbearable: 'When I was leaving I could not open the carriage window to take one more look at you. And it was as if suddenly all those nice things fell into an abyss.'[31]

Later that month Janáček described to Kamila meeting Pietro Mascagni and his wife, after a performance of *Aida* which the Italian composer conducted in Brno:

> Only now do I know how happy I am to have you. You quiet, devoted, soft-natured soul. [Mrs Mascagni,] loudmouthed . . . kept interfering with what they were doing on stage. When the producer had had enough, he took the lady into the auditorium and they shut the door on her . . . . How she banged![32]

But he got on well with Mascagni, who promised to return next spring to hear *The Cunning Little Vixen*.[33]

Janáček continued to report to Kamila on all his activities, and on performances of his works; on 5 December, the première of the *Glagolitic Mass* was to be broadcast from Brno, and he advised her to listen to it 'somewhere where they have a large wireless – a six-valve one.'[34] Kamila, for her part, amused him by chatting about her household and visitors, and occasionally scolding him playfully.[35] As the Stössels had now bought a piano, Janáček wanted to teach Kamila to play; on 16 November 1927, the great composer instructed his reluctant muse, at great length, how to play a Bohemian folk-song with one finger.[36]

Many of Janáček's letters suggest that Zdenka was still suspicious and jealous, and that she was still making unwelcome comments. 'You shouldn't have got upset,' he tried to pacify Kamila towards the end of November. 'True, it upset me too – but I soon calmed down. I know that [Zdenka] herself will bring about – what we are content to leave quietly to fate [that is, their divorce]. If it happens – it will fulfil only what is predetermined. That is why I am so resigned to fate. Thus everything rolls forward, no one can stop anything . . .'.[37]

Janáček was now clearly considering a divorce, and was convinced that Kamila was also beginning to think along the same lines: 'Your letter was serious. I felt it after the first reading . . . . I feel that a thought is ripening in you – as in me – into a decision.'[38] He did not chastise Kamila when she admitted that she crossed out certain passages in his letters. 'You do well to "ink out" those sinful bits,' he wrote. Whether Kamila was prudish, as some writers think, or simply a very private person, she certainly took care to eliminate anything she believed incriminating.[39]

Janáček's passion fed on everything, and in his imagination he saw Kamila everywhere; he described to her the *Glagolitic Mass* as a private nuptial mass, and his 'cathedral':

> I have set it in Luhačovice . . . . Where else could it stand but there, where we were so happy! And that cathedral is high – it reaches right up to the vault of the sky. And the candles burn there; they are the tall pine trees, and at the top they have lighted stars. And the little bells in the cathedral belong to the flock of sheep . . . . Two people enter that cathedral, they walk ceremonially . . . . And these two want to be married. [. . .] You, priest, come at last! Nightingales, thrushes, ducks, geese, make music![40]

He was still feverishly making adjustments to *From the House of the Dead*, and this 'black' opera was giving him a hard time: 'It seems to me as if I were gradually descending through it lower and lower, right down to the most wretched people of humankind.[. . .] You are . . . the ray of light which gives me the will to persevere in my work.'[41]

As Janáček had recently immortalized Kamila in two *feuilletons* extolling her generosity to some gypsy children, and was now frequently seen with her in public, Zdenka's jealousy grew day by day. But he brushed her feelings aside: 'Well, everyone has his or her sorrows,' he wrote to Kamila. 'But it is necessary to suffer for love. To endure it while it is possible . . . . And one is bound and restricted by so many chains . . . close to you I do not feel that I am being restricted, that is how free I feel . . .'.[42]

We shall never know what had really occurred during Janáček's walk with Kamila the previous April when 'it seemed that the earth would split open' as he declared his love for her.[43] But his letters to her suggest a kind of courtly love on his part, with the most intense pleasure stemming from desire rather than fulfilment. And, imbued with such passion, they sometimes seem like a private journal written in order to sustain him – which he valued too much to destroy – as well as an outlet for his erotic fantasies. 'We shall have to think up something so that we won't have to burn [the letters],' he suggested to her, 'and yet write what we want and what we feel.'[44] Without Kamila, 'so distant, desired and unattained', he would not have 'a [single] bright moment . . . I would have only work – and . . . oppressiveness.'[45] And while he was finishing *From the House of the Dead*, his 'perhaps greatest work', he was agitated to the point where 'my blood almost felt like spurting out'. Zdenka, it seems, was unable to understand this kind of intensity. 'When I would like to cheer – I have to keep silent. But that's nothing, on top of that poison is dripped into my blood.'[46]

After another stay in Písek Janáček wrote to Kamila from Prague, where his First String Quartet was performed at a commemorative concert.[47] He made it clear how happy he had been with her: 'Now I know that you are my soul! And I only worry that you might fly away from me – you know, I would be left a poor wretch.'[48]

Back in Brno, he proudly announced to her: 'The heart is good, kidneys clean. Anyone would take me for about sixty! Well, I am still fit for life – and perhaps a little for my lady, my Kamila?'[49] By now he had a standing invitation to stay at Písek whenever he liked, and was already eagerly planning another visit in the New Year, for he badly needed a rest.[50] 'You said that during the first two days I was not the same person as in Luhačovice,' he responded dejectedly on 16

December. 'Oh, in my mind I was the same: but sometimes one is drained like a well to the very bottom. But wait a while – and there will be fresh water in it again! And in my profession it often happens like that!'[51] Fortunately, *From the House of the Dead* was nearly finished; only the fair copy of the last act was to be completed. 'Then a load will fall from me!' declared Janáček. And since some local enthusiasts were planning to stage operas in Písek, he intended to send vocal scores of several of his operas to Kamila. Some were to include an open confession: 'On certain books of music I shall write who was in my soul when the notes swarmed out of it, and that for these notes one must credit not only me, but you as well, my Kamila.'[52]

Can we assume that the letters from Kamila that have not been preserved were much more revealing than those which survived? 'Your last but one letter was the most heartfelt I have ever received . . . in my life,' Janáček avowed on 18 December. 'I could not take my leave of it for a long time, until finally last night. I would have put my hand into the flames and still snatched from them what was nice in that letter . . . . On Tuesday I shall await a warm letter again. Before you send it, place it on your heart, won't you. Then put your mouth to that '/', won't you?'[53] Yet his next letter still stresses the platonic nature of their relationship. 'Between us there is only pure emotion: the kind that ignites regardless of what blazes up from it.'[54]

That Christmas Kamila planned to send Janáček the gift of a tie, but superstitiously did not want to give him a tie pin lest it 'puncture' their friendship. 'But how shall I repay you? I will swamp you in music,' he declared.[55] 'And when you have your Christmas meal,' he entreated her the following day, 'remember that you are taking the first morsel for me; and I shall do the same for you . . . . I am finishing one work after another, but strangely, I am not thinking about a new one. That is because I am doing the sweetest work – remembering you.'[56] Despite Zdenka's touching efforts to prepare his favourite festive dishes and create a pleasant atmosphere, Janáček recounted to Kamila an unmistakably erotic dream: 'It was nothing but Kamila! And your "yes, yes, yes", how many of [your yesses] have I counted, without end!'[57]

He sent her a special gift: the scores of four of his operas. 'And what else did you get apart from those four operas?' he asked, somehow suspecting that Kamila's husband had not spent the holiday with her. 'Why, is a father not capable of staying a while with his [own] children?'[58] As it transpired, Kamila had fallen ill with bronchitis on the 28th, and had indeed spent the holiday alone with her children (her husband was away on business as usual). Anxious about her health, Janáček immediately planned a trip to Písek. 'But no preparations in our heaven,' he commanded.[59] 'Lay the fire and that's it. And if you are not completely well, stay in bed. I will manage to get to you from the station and could at least nurse you for a couple of days . . . . So long as you are ill I would just caress you.'[60]

After a pleasant Christmas, the Janáčeks spent New Year's Eve together at home. But New Year's Day was 'the worst . . . in my life,' recalled Zdenka in her memoirs. At breakfast, Janáček announced his intention of going to Prague in a few days, and then to Písek; unwisely, Zdenka asked him whether he had to make a detour to Písek every time he visited Prague. 'He thumped his fist on the table so that the crockery bounced,' recollected Zdenka. 'I thought that he would throw it all at my head. Enraged, he shouted: "You do nothing but suspect me!" '[61] Everything came out: 'That I don't understand him, that he only feels happy at the Stössels', that here at home it feels sad, that he could have spent all of Christmas [in Písek] but out of consideration for me had stayed at home . . .'.[62] As he was getting dressed, he asked the weeping Zdenka to bring him the new, bright red tie from Kamila; taking the pin Zdenka had once given him, he pointed out: ' "Look, a tie from Stösslová and a pin from you." Yes,' Zdenka later remarked bitterly, 'he really succeeded when he created that symbol. That's how he would have wished it: both her and me, both of us together, me as housekeeper and confidante, she as mistress and "muse".'[63] Blustering, Janáček continued to reproach Zdenka who ran out of the house in despair. Eventually she found a church where she calmed down. On returning home she asked Janáček whether she could come to Písek with him; all parties could then talk everything through. 'He looked at me terrified and blurted out: "They would throw you out." "Is that so? I knew you wouldn't agree, because what you are trying to make me believe is not true." '[64]

A veritable storm followed; a visitor, come to wish the couple a happy New Year, fled in terror. No one at the Janáčeks' could eat or rest that day. At dusk, Janáček sat down at the piano and finally Zdenka asked him gently: 'Look, does it have to be such hell all the time?' Janáček burst into tears, once again reproaching her for ruining his New Year's Day. Desperate to pacify him, Zdenka 'knelt down beside him, tried to talk him out of it, begged his pardon'.[65] Eventually, both calmed down somewhat. As she tried to rest, Zdenka suddenly felt unwell; she wanted to cry out but could only manage a moan. Janáček came running to her, clearly afraid. 'He sat

beside me and said: "This can't go on, this must come to an end." '
He wanted to stay with her that night, but Zdenka refused.
'Crestfallen, worn-out, in low spirits, we parted that ugly day . . .'.[66]

'I hope you had a better first day of the year than I did,' Janáček
complained to Kamila in a letter begun earlier that day. 'I do not have
the words today to tell you all I have been through. On one hand I
see myself, wretched, on the other I see [Zdenka], unable to control
herself.' In the evening he added a postscript: 'So, dear soul, calm
again after the storm. I kept the peace through self-denial. But I
know and she knows, too, that this kind of agitation cannot ever
be repeated.'[67] The next day he was reflecting: 'Perhaps now, while
finishing this opera of mine, I too am agitated. I need peace, self-
control, and I cannot restrain myself.'[68] By 3 January, his revisions to
Act 3 of *From the House of the Dead* were finished; on the 4th, he
wrote Kamila a brief note: 'So, my beautiful girl, see you [soon]. The
opera [is] finished. The work [is] finished. Now I only want to see
you and have [a few] joyful moments.'[69]

On 6 January he was in Prague; the following day he met Gustav
Holst though, sadly, no detailed report of their conversation has been
preserved. And during the two days in Písek which followed, his
relationship with Kamila obviously moved forward: [Your agree-
ment] 'that you want to profess publicly that you are my only love –
for that a most happy fellow thanks you.'[70] The letter in which
Kamila allegedly expressed this wish has not survived; from Janáček's
letter to Max Brod, a week or so later, it is clear that Janáček, too,
wished to declare his 'spiritual' love for Kamila in public, in order to
clear their names of any hint of scandal.[71]

Brod and Janáček did not meet until 21 January when, at Brod's
insistence, Janáček and Kamila attended the Prague première of *Káťa
Kabanová* in German, at the Neues Deutsches Theater. Three days
before the performance Janáček sent Brod the following letter:

> My *Káťa* etc. are not just musical inventions. Tell me, could one ever
> disclose that my ideas have crystallized through a particular person?
> Has any writer ever disclosed any such thing? With painters it is no
> secret. [But] has any composer done it? Would it be taken amiss if
> this spiritual, this artistic relationship were made known to the
> public? It is certain that the permission of the person bound [to me]
> would be necessary. She approves, for both she and I see [this as] a
> defence from being accused of another kind of relationship . . . this
> spiritual relationship has already lasted thirteen years, and has never

exceeded the bounds, even though it is based on friendship. It is incredible, but true. I am aware of the psychological aspect of the propensity for a motif to draw from real life experiences. The apperception of that motif is accelerated, it acquires certainty, freshness. In my music it is evident! Through this kind of composition I have grown and matured . . . .[72]

We do not know what Brod, a confirmed womanizer, made of this admission. Clearly, Janáček was convinced that his relationship with Kamila stimulated his imagination, and his erotic yearnings obviously did help him to attain a state of heightened creativity. Even mundane events in Kamila's life often inspired the portrayal of some of his heroines, although the actual events and emotions, and his sexual drive, were sublimated. This impression is reinforced in his letter of 12 January: *Káťa*, he wrote to Kamila, was also *her* work: 'You were to me that warm atmosphere in which, in my thoughts, you were always present in all those parts of the opera where expressions of love occur . . .'.[73]

The performance of *Káťa* received a 'fabulous' review in *Lidové noviny*.[74] Yet the royalties, for a period of five months, totalled a risible 240 crowns. Janáček resolved that these should go to Kamila, although he perceived how reluctant she was to be seen with him in Prague: 'Into the café – you did not want to go with me, in the theatre – you hid yourself,' he accused. Embarrassed at her leaving the theatre without him, he tried to impress on her that the whole company 'guessed at our relationship'.[75] Yet Kamila may well have wanted to avoid public speculation about their friendship: Janáček's niece Věra reportedly knew of the Stössels' financial difficulties, and tried to warn Janáček that the couple might want to exploit him.[76]

Zdenka, now often ill, began to hate Kamila, and was convinced that the Stössels were inciting Janáček against her. '[Kamila] seemed to me more dangerous than Mrs Horvátová,' she asserted. 'That one was a moody, fickle actress, this one a clever businesswoman.'[77] What lured Janáček to Písek was not, in Zdenka's view, his need for inspiration, but his 'ageing masculinity'.[78]

Undeterred, on 29 January Janáček announced to Kamila that he had begun work on a new string quartet, which was 'to describe musically' their correspondence; the piece, which became one of his most famous works, was to be called *Love Letters*.[79] 'I think that it will sound delightful,' he declared, cheered by her most recent letter:

Why, there have already been quite a lot of those dear adventures of ours! They will be the little fires in my soul and they will set it ablaze [to create] the most beautiful melodies. Just think! The first movement I have already done at Hukvaldy. The impression when I saw you for the first time! Now I am working on the second movement. . . . Oh, how I am looking forward to it! In this work I will always be only with you! No third person beside us. There will be plenty of yearning, as there, in your house, in that heaven of ours! I shall love doing it! You know, don't you, that I know no other world than you! [. . .] And when you write 'I am for ever only yours', you open heaven to me![80]

The quartet took shape at breakneck speed. 'I am writing the third of the *Love Letters*,' Janáček reported on 8 February. 'Let it be . . . very cheerful and then dissolve into a vision which would resemble your image, transparent, as if in a mist. In it there should be a suggestion of motherhood.' This train of thought – imagining Kamila pregnant – seems to have preoccupied Janáček much as a similar idea did many years before, during his relationship with Gabriela Horvátová. 'Today I wrote down in music my sweetest desire,' he confessed to Kamila in his second letter that day. 'I am battling with it, the desire wins. You are giving birth. What fate in life would that little boy have?'[81]

Janáček was now clearly pressing Kamila to bring things to a head. 'You have no idea what an impression your letter of yesterday made on me!' he wrote. 'How will you reply tomorrow? Will you again avoid a direct answer?'[82] He even decided against going to Vienna for a performance of his *Sinfonietta* on 12 February.[83] 'What will you do so that a step back can never never be taken?!' he asked; the letter, with its spelling errors, clearly shows his agitated state of mind. A postscript reads: 'Your letter brought me to seventh heaven! May I stay there, and you with me!'[84]

Although gossip about their relationship continued, Janáček wanted Kamila to accompany him to the dress rehearsal of *The Makropulos Affair* at the Prague National Theatre on 28 February, before spending another three days together in Písek. Meanwhile, work on the quartet continued apace. 'Today I have succeeded in the movement "when the earth trembled". That will be the best one,' Janáček declared on 18 February. 'Well, it was an astonishingly beautiful [time]. And it was truthful. Only the prettiest melodies can fit it. I only hope I succeed in bringing off the last movement. That will be like my anxiety about you.'[85] The last movement was, in the end, to portray 'a great yearning – and, as it were, its fulfilment'.[86] The title was to change, too: 'I have entitled the piece *Intimate Letters*,' he announced to her on 20 February. 'I do not deliver my feelings to the tender mercies of fools.'[87]

But by 23 February he had not heard from Kamila for several days; anxious, he made a trip to Písek between rehearsals for *The Makropulos Affair*, and from his letter of 26 February it is plain that his temper almost got the better of him. 'In my memory [I hear] those serious, beautiful words "You would destroy me!" And on top of it your tears and my sorrow that I was capable of causing you pain, although the image of the burning album only flashed through my mind,' he wrote to Kamila. 'I know it would be cruel to destroy that witness of our beautiful days. Never, never will it occur to me again.' The reason for his outburst seems to have been jealousy: he felt that even the local shopkeepers were not impervious to Kamila's allure.[88]

Despite Janáček's earlier worries, rehearsals for *The Makropulos Affair* went well. 'Mrs Kejřová, who is playing the 300-year-old woman, has movements like you,' he reported to Kamila. 'That lady looks [just] like you, with her gait and her whole appearance.'[89] Nevertheless, he felt that the impression the opera made was not 'pure', not good enough for *her*, at any rate: 'costumes and stage sets are missing, mistakes made, things repeated. It would be too much for you to imagine that which is missing and to overlook what still has to be corrected . . .'.[90]

At the première, in Janáček's own words, 'success mounted to unprecedented storms'.[91] There were presents from guests and well-wishers, and after the performance the thirty-strong company gathered to celebrate in one of Prague's best-known restaurants. Kamila did not attend but Zdenka did: Janáček insisted that she should, especially as the next day Otakar Hollmann was to give the première of the *Capriccio*. The Prague visit was something of a professional triumph: Janáček also succeeded in obtaining a substantial government subsidy for the publication of various editions of folksongs and further research. While gathering material for his meeting with the Minister of Education and other highly placed officials, he had been studying, among other collections, Sušil's famous *Moravian Folk-songs* (1835), making a number of notes and excerpts on his customary small white cards. On the back of the last he jotted down: 'Béla Bartók, but for the Slovak songs from which he has drawn, his work would be dry.' By then Janáček had heard Bartók's music at several concerts, and the two composers had met three times and talked at length; Janáček was always biased in favour of all things Slavonic, but he rightly perceived that Slovak folk music was one of Bartók's primary sources.[92]

Among those who wanted to meet Janáček in Prague was Gabriela Horvátová. By now his once passionate attachment to her was completely forgotten; when he heard that Horvátová planned to visit him while he was sitting for the well-known Czech photographer J.F. Langhans, Janáček responded sarcastically: 'Apparently she will be celebrating her twenty-fifth jubilee in the theatre in Prague . . . . Indeed for her work as a singer she deserves that the theatre remember this anniversary. But it did not remember . . . . She herself thought up this celebration!'[93] Later he felt that perhaps he should congratulate Horvátová for her creation of the Kostelnička: 'I don't know whether I will do it,' he wrote to Kamila, 'whether my recollection of her disgusting life will not supersede my purely artistic recollections. I fear she would make public use of the letter, and I don't ever want to be linked with her.'[94] He could not forgive Horvátová her affair with Maixner: 'For trifling with me she became completely dead to me,' he confided to Kamila the next day.[95]

During their visit to Prague the Janáčeks had met the Brods whose own marriage now existed only in name. Janáček was pleased that the wives had met; Mrs Brod, he reported to Kamila, told Zdenka that 'she puts up with everything, with artists there's no other way'.[96] Soon, he was planning further meetings and holidays with Kamila, in Luhačovice and Hukvaldy; she had put on quite a lot of weight, and he joked playfully about the gossip their outings in Luhačovice would excite: 'There will be talk, won't there? That is why we have to be there, so that we can confuse their conjectures even more.'[97]

He continued to press her about an open declaration of their feelings: 'Have you told your husband that you love me?' he was soon asking. 'Zd[enka] knows that I love you, and that I will love you till the end of my life. [. . .] Kamila, since there is a serious reason for it, we shall speak openly; we shall confess . . .'. A more cautious statement followed. 'We shall not broadcast it, but in certain circumstances and face to face with certain people we cannot conceal the fact.' Incredibly, he suggested telling 'those who are closest to us'.[98]

At a concert in Písek on 4 March Kamila was obviously delighted with her reception as Janáček's official muse. Yet her next letter to him was not what one might have expected at this stage, given Janáček's own impassioned tone:

It was very nice[,] they were very pleased that I came, I sat next to the Mayor . . . . Everyone asked me whether I had been in Prague and asked after you. I was surrounded on all sides[,] it gave me great pleasure . . . . As for Luhačovice I cannot as yet say anything definite today[,] as I don't know how it will be with the children. It cut me to the quick when you wrote that your wife suffers on my account[,] perhaps she too could be given a little love. [. . .] I make no claims on anything at all. But she is your wife and has claims on everything. [. . .] What can your wife think when you say that we are bound together[,] do you know what that means? You have given me no pleasure this way. It is your outspoken character[,] it's all the same to you even if you wound.[99]

Two days later David Stössel visited Janáček in Brno, to ask for a reference to enable him to obtain Czech citizenship – the entire family was still regarded as being domiciled in Poland, his father's native country.[100] 'I told him, completely calmly, what binds me to you,' Janáček wrote to Kamila. 'The conversation ended without [any] greater excitement.'[101] As Stössel was acutely aware of the danger of being repatriated, no doubt Janáček's 'bond' with his wife was not uppermost on his mind; Janáček, for his part, was only too happy to do anything in his power to keep Kamila in Czechoslovakia. Meanwhile, the gossip about their relationship reached new heights in Brno: people 'laughed, pitied, maligned, informed me what was happening', recalled Zdenka.[102]

The fair copy of the Second String Quartet, *Intimate Letters*, was now finished, and Janáček was busily planning further trips to Prague, detours to Písek, and a fleeting visit to Hukvaldy in April. 'In May Berlin perhaps. [. . .] July [in] Luhačovice and you in Hukvaldy,' he suggested to Kamila. 'August also there; lots of visitors. Perhaps the [High] Tatras. September – Italy perhaps.'[103]

Yet now he seemed to want to postpone the ultimate in their relationship, 'so that that day, that night of ours may come unexpectedly,' he daydreamed. 'So that we may be able to say, God, has that happened? Is that possible? Are we still here in the world? Is it not a golden fairy-tale? Is it not only a dream, only that raving of ours?'[104]

This was Kamila's reply:

I really don't know what I would have done during this bad weather if it were not for your letters . . . and I find myself thinking of you all the time even if I don't want to. [. . .] On reading your letter today I thought so much about everything in the past[,] about everything I have lived through and I was happy. You remind me of it when you write how your life was before and how it is now. And what about mine[?] I have not known anything else[,] have not longed for anything else[,] and my life just went by without any love and joy. But I always went along with the thought that it had to be so. Now I think that God was testing you and me and when He saw that we are good[,] that we deserve it[,] He has granted us this joy in life. [. . .] I steered clear of everything[,] did not look for anything and only you who have known me all these years [know] that this really is the truth. Anyone else would just smile [and say] how is it possible[,] yes, it is possible[,] you are much dearer to me than if you were young. I assure you that my life is pleasant that I don't wish for any better. And this is your doing alone. For that I also thank you . . . .[105]

Had Janáček's constant blandishments finally won Kamila over? Or was she capable of responding to his outpourings in a suitably romantic vein, in order to keep the friendship of someone so influential and well-to-do? Was he really devoted to *her* or to an imagined, ideal Kamila? From his last letter it is obvious that the relationship had not been consummated; and throughout their correspondence one feels that Janáček was often all too ready to dramatize situations. Kamila *was* warm-hearted and generous in spirit, but had always kept her distance, committing herself to nothing that could taint her reputation – even in the letter just quoted she still used the formal form of address. Or was the correspondence maintained on two levels, Kamila's 'innocent' letters being preserved, while Janáček burnt those which were more revealing?

We shall never know; one can only conclude that Janáček's 'spiritual' bond with Kamila was essential to him and that, both as man and artist, he *needed* a quest for love; between 14 March 1928 (the date of Kamila's revelatory confession) and 26 July 1928 (his last letter to her from Brno), the composer was to send her another 112 letters. Yet this kind of 'pure' inspiration he claimed to have found in Kamila had been familiar for some five hundred years: when the great fourteenth-century Italian poet Petrarch fell for Laura (like Janáček's Kamila a virtuous married woman), he fully understood the sexual nature of his obsession, and sought to sublimate it. Laura became a symbol of all love, earthly and spiritual; Petrarch's unrequited passion – and perhaps even Laura's untimely death – clearly stimulated his creativity, and the idea of Petrarchan love soon took hold of the popular imagination.[106]

But for many of Petrarch's followers it became merely 'a refinement of adulterous sensuality'.[107] Perhaps Janáček's passion for Kamila as the source of all wisdom and all love was part of this legacy: like any Petrarchan lover he whipped himself into a frenzy at Kamila's merest frown, and went into ecstasies at her approval. And no matter how often he stressed the 'purity' of his feelings, the erotic nature of his attraction is pretty clear even in his early letters. In the Second String Quartet, *Intimate Letters*, Janáček celebrated his and Kamila's emotional life together as he saw it; although all of his emotions were sublimated, love is undeniably the subject-matter of this work.

Three of the work's four movements begin at a leisurely tempo. The first theme of the opening *Andante*, on the violins, descends and rises stepwise over a sustained trill in the cello; the viola soon enters with an eerie melody, originally envisaged for viola d'amore,[108] and this is later repeated on the cello. A new, more tender motif (*Con moto*) then appears on the first violin. This is developed and gradated until a variation of the eerie theme is introduced (*Allegro*); Janáček increasingly employs triplets on the strings against the rocking ostinatos of the lower voices. Another, lyrical theme (*Meno mosso*) emerges after a brief return of the first and second themes; all themes are reintroduced and variants of the first theme employed as the movement speeds on, only to come to a halt in the closing, joyous *Grave*.

The second movement opens in B flat minor; as in the first movement, there are many changes of tempo. The first, meditative, questioning theme on the viola (later marked *dolcissimo espressivo*) is developed for a considerable length of time, the intervals widening and contracting over the ostinato figurations in the accompanying voices. The movement accelerates, slows down and picks up speed again before the *Andante* from the first movement returns, in another guise. In the following brief *Adagio*, a new, *flautato* figure of descending sextuplets on the second violin sounds like a sudden flight. A new theme is then finally introduced on the first violin (*Presto*): this simple, dance-like tune later appears in the major, the sudden shift of mood perfectly in character, and the motif is developed, varied and gradated before the main theme reappears. As the theme moves canonically from one instrument to another, the first chordal theme from the opening movement suddenly emerges (*Vivo*), this time pitted against the second theme of the present movement, on the viola. The *flautato* briefly returns before the first theme re-emerges on the first violin, against quick interjections from the second violin. Marked *fortissimo*, the theme slows down as the movement closes in a pensive mood.

A gentle, rocking theme introduces the third movement (*Moderato*), once again ending with an upward, questioning interval. This material is developed further; in the following *Adagio*, a tender, warm but rather timid motif on the first violin is played over a pedal in the lower voices. After a brief chordal passage, the second theme is heard: passionate, broad (marked *Largamente*), it develops over the arpeggios on the cello and figurations on the viola. After several changes of mood and tempo (*Presto – Adagio – Presto*), a variation of the first theme appears, skittishly repeated in a fast, rhythmically displaced version. As the movement nears the end, brief sections of *Allegro* and *Andante* alternate; the melody soars ever higher, over a trill on the viola, and both the opening and the second theme of the movement are recapitulated. The movement closes with a victorious, repeated cadential flourish on the violins, over a descending figure on the cello and another trill on the viola. By mixing, piling up and compressing simple motivic material, Janáček creates textures of surprising complexity.

The fast *Allegro* of the finale opens with one of Janáček's most memorable themes, in A flat minor – impetuous, defiant, yet not quite free of anxiety; its regular structure and melodic line (repeated a minor third up as it develops) recall a folk-dance. This theme, on the first violin, is then varied and developed as the melody moves higher up the scale before it reaches, after several high-pitched trills, the calm, chromaticized *Andante*, its motif repeated canonically in the upper three voices over a sustained bass. A kind of chorale (*Andante*) is heard after further variations; the ensuing *Con moto* is followed by a mere three-bar *Maestoso* before another of Janáček's most memorable, impassioned motifs emerges, and is developed up to a sudden *dolce* (*Molto meno mosso*). The second theme follows on the first violin (in the major, and based on the opening theme). A new, pizzicato motif in the following *Andante* is soon taken up by the first violin – a dreamy echo of a waltz, perhaps, the memory strengthened as the motif is repeated on the viola. After the ensuing *Adagio*, nothing prepares us for the sudden *furioso* (marked *fff sul ponticello*), with a cadenza *ad libitum*; the waltz-like tune is then echoed on the viola. Following a chordal passage, a canonic development of the material related to the first theme finally prepares the recapitulation: the first theme soon returns, now in the major. As the movement hurries on, the pizzicato motif is taken up by the first violin in an augmented version, and the finale ends with an emphatic cadential close – weakened somewhat by the final E flat within a D flat major chord, thus strikingly at odds with the overall joyous mood.

At first Janáček had hoped that the celebrated Bohemian Quartet might give the first performance of *Intimate Letters*, but the players would only be able to rehearse the piece during their summer vacation, so on 13 April he also gave the music to the Brno-based Moravian Quartet.[109] In the end the public première was not held until six weeks after his death.[110] Yet Janáček did hear the work – the Moravian Quartet played two movements for him privately at his house on 18 May, and the whole work on 25 May 1928. The piece – one of the most exciting twentieth-century quartets – was published ten years later by the Hudební Matice publishing house.

Meanwhile, a performance of the *Glagolitic Mass* had been planned in Prague for 8 April, but further corrections to the score had first to be made with the conductor, Jaroslav Kvapil. An extra rehearsal was necessary, otherwise 'hell will break loose', Janáček wrote to Zdenka on 22 March.[111] But he was delighted to hear from the Swiss writer William Ritter, who 'greatly extolled' the *Mass*, proposing that it be performed annually at a number of significant historical locations in Moravia. 'What doesn't he want to do with it! That wouldn't occur to our people, oh no!'[112] Janáček's music was still regarded by many as controversial: during the performance of his *Sinfonietta* in Dresden on 16 March, 'some clapped, others whistled,' he reported to Kamila. 'But the first group won.'[113]

Amid these reports, he made time to advise Kamila to talk her son out of joining a Communist physical training society: 'He won't hear anything good there!' he warned her, underlining the entire sentence. 'We need peace and honest work here at home, not fire and murder!' Here, in a nutshell, is Janáček's unchanged view of Communism, whose policies he had already dismissed elsewhere with a similarly acerbic stroke of the pen.[114]

He had been looking forward to seeing Kamila at the Prague concert of the *Glagolitic Mass*, and was despondent to hear that she was 'not well enough' to come. She only changed her mind after his long, imploring letter: 'I shall miss you very much,' he pleaded. 'At a nice moment [like this] someone I love so much will not be standing beside me, so what's this stupid glory for[?]'[115] In the end Kamila arrived in Prague on 7 April, and spent four days with Janáček: she accompanied him to concerts and outings, among others to the Villa

Bertramka in the Prague suburb of Smíchov and the Karlštejn Castle near Prague; the couple even went to the races at the fashionable Velká Chuchle. To Janáček, this was heaven, and parting from Kamila left him 'drowned in tears';[116] he did not even go to see a performance of *The Makropulos Affair* at the National Theatre on 11 April. Thanking her for everything, he now demanded: 'You must devote yourself entirely to me.'[117]

Yet Janáček was far from alone with Kamila during those four days; David Stössel (whom he had also invited to the concert) had joined them on the excursion to the Bertramka, where they were also accompanied by the director of the Czechoslovak Mozart Society.[118] Kamila also had errands of her own while Janáček attended rehearsals. But she may have persuaded her husband not to join them for the Karlštejn trip. 'Now, when I know that you saved Karlštejn for us,' Janáček acknowledged on 11 April, 'I place a higher value on everything. Without that day how much sadder it would have been!'[119]

In the photograph taken at the Bertramka, Kamila – overweight, with a double chin and wearing a distinctly unflattering hat – seems a far cry from the dashing, seductive woman of thirty-four in the double portrait of the Stössels and the Janáčeks taken in September 1925, only two and half years earlier. But to Janáček she had lost none of her charm: 'I'm glad that Kamila is as plump as a *majolenka* [village beauty],' he commented, still dreaming of the ultimate.[120] 'Oh, let us allow the greatest joy to come by itself; let it come as if it were blind, as long as it finds us: unexpectedly, suddenly, naturally,' he fantasized on 13 April. It will be as beautiful as that time when the earth trembled, as when you cried out: "I have never experienced this until now!" [. . .] With holy calm I await that most blissful moment. It will come!'[121]

He was delighted to have spent so much time with Kamila, but he still returned to Brno rather disgruntled: at the performance of the *Mass* he sat with the Stössels opposite President Masaryk, who was there with his daughter Alice. The Masaryks left immediately afterwards, without inviting Janáček to the presidential box; some saw this as a rebuke for Janáček's openly showing off his mistress.[122]

A visit to Prague, where his edition of *Moravian Love Songs* was about to go to the printer's, gave Janáček another excuse for a detour to Písek between 23 and 25 April. 'Kamila, twenty years of work are concluded with this,' he wrote of *Love Songs*, sounding as if he were settling accounts: 'Everything, everything [is] concluded! I am even coming to an end with my operas.'[123] The visit – a mere day and a half – brought him much happiness: 'So you told me that you love me!' he rejoiced on returning to Brno. 'I have said it to you countless times, your [saying it] once outweighs mine . . .'. He had now decided on a dual role for Kamila: 'In company we have to belong to one another, whether you are my irreproachable daughter or my delectable young wife.'[124]

As Zdenka later recounted, Janáček – always parsimonious – now became downright stingy with her housekeeping allowance; she could only suspect that his visits to Písek were costly.[125] Yet, despite Zdenka's obvious distress about Janáček being 'completely bewitched', one cannot always sympathize with her. 'Even when one disregards race,' she commented later, 'Mrs Stösslová's reputation in Písek was not of the best, and Leoš compromised himself greatly: his age, his name, his honorary doctorate obliged him to live a respectable life . . .'.[126] The situation was as insoluble as ever, and it now also clearly aroused the resentment of someone in Písek: Zdenka began to receive anonymous letters. 'Apparently you are receiving parcels through the post every moment,' Janáček complained to Kamila, exasperated. 'Apparently I am sending you a whole garden! But I am giving something for something, and I am giving less than I receive.'[127] Although it was impossible to find out who the anonymous 'villain' was, Janáček was convinced that the writer knew Kamila and her house well.[128]

Hoping no doubt to please Kamila, he totted up for her the future royalties from *Intimate Letters*, which he planned to give her. But Kamila was 'very hurt' by his calculations: 'Why, if one always has to calculate the likely value [of things],' she replied, positively offended, 'I'd rather have nothing . . .'.[129] She was also to receive royalties for another performance of *Káťa Kabanová*, which was to inaugurate the Exhibition of Contemporary Culture in Brno on 26 May.[130]

On 1 May Janáček began to feel exhausted: 'I am overworked and I don't have . . . that sweet relaxation beside you! How hard it often is for me to endure it, this love far beyond the hills!'[131] The extension at the Hukvaldy cottage on which he had then embarked was 'coming on fast', and Janáček looked forward enormously to having a rest: 'As soon as I have finished tidying up the opera here, I shall go there at once. I really feel it is high time to put down my pen . . .'.[132]

On 6 May 'a load fell off' Janáček's mind: he finally completed the last of the two plays enacted by the prisoners in Act 2 of *From the House of the Dead*, and the final revisions to the opera had now all been made. Despite his delight, the familiar emptiness soon set in. In addition, hopes for the first foreign première of *The Makropulos Affair*, in Berlin, were dashed – scheduled for May, it was cancelled at the last moment when Barbara Kemp, wife of the Intendant Max von Schillings, refused to sing the part of Marty.[133] Still, there was much to rejoice about: Bruno Walter was to conduct *Taras Bulba* at the Leipzig Gewandhaus in the autumn, and Henry Wood was to pre-mière it in London.[134] Janáček's investments were growing, and there were further plans for lectures and performances.[135] But all the while he longed only for Kamila; the tone of his letters becomes more and more erotic:

> Oh, my little sun is still so high! But one day I will go there, to that place where it sets, where it is so near that I could catch it in my hands. And I will catch it and make up a bed for it and will not let it go, even when it would burn, cry, sigh and thrash itself about! No, my little sun, I won't let you go, until you set in that black night[,] and rest until the morning![136]

On 18 May he described breathlessly the Moravian Quartet's private rehearsal of *Intimate Letters*: 'They played the first and third movements for me! And, Kamila, it will be beautiful, unusual, un-restrained, spirited, a composition outside all the usual conventions! [. . .] I think that together we shall triumph! It is my first composition to spring from directly experienced emotion. Until now I composed only about things remembered, [but] this composition, *Intimate Letters*, was composed in fire. The earlier compositions only in hot ash.'[137] The players were 'bowled over by it,' he reported after the private première on 25 May. 'Universal Edition are interested . . . I shall invite them for the main rehearsal on 11 June.' Surprisingly, he dithered about the dedication: 'Either: *Dedicated to Mrs Kamila S.*, or *Dedicated to Mrs Kamila Stösslová*, or *Dedicated to Mrs Kamila Neumannová S.*,' he suggested, since Neumannová was her maiden name.[138] In the end Kamila herself decided on '[to] Kamila S.J.'[139]

By now Janáček no longer 'made excuses' to Zdenka that Kamila was merely an inspiration; and she was convinced that any resistance on Kamila's part was a clever ruse, in order to arouse Janáček's passion. Afraid of the developments to come, Zdenka wrote to Janáček's sister Josefka, asking her to make him aware that the Stössels' friendship might be feigned, and that they probably wanted to make use of him.[140] But Josefka gave her short shrift; when she threatened to send the letter to Janáček, the petrified Zdenka thought it best to let him know herself.

When Josefka forwarded Zdenka's 'slanderous' letter, at first Janáček did not bother to read it. 'I will tell my sister in good time what you are to me,' he explained to Kamila, 'that you have been and are my consolation in the bitter moments of life. . . . that letter apparently said that anyway you will leave me one day, and soon! So you know what [Zdenka] looks forward to . . .'.[141] When he finally read the letter, it put him in 'an extremely serious mood', as he observed to Kamila. 'I never suspected until now how Zdenka sees me. Only in her letter to my sister did she show herself to me as she really is, and how cruelly she slanders me . . . . How she offended, insulted even my elderly sister! She must not come to Hukvaldy any more.'[142]

Planning another brief visit there on 14 June, to oversee the work at the cottage, he continued to dream about Kamila. But her next letter was a blow:

> Dear Maestro[,] we have come from the consultant[,] [my] hands [and] legs are shaking. It is all over[,] mama has cancer[,] she has got five or six months to live[,] the end might come within three months. On Monday she will be operated on[,] they will take water from her. I am already ill myself . . . . Now I am writing to Luhačovice that I cannot go. If I don't write[,] don't worry[,] you know what grief I suffer.[143]

This letter changed all Janáček's plans. On 3 June he was expecting the German producer Gustav Hartung who had asked him to write incidental music for Gerhart Hauptmann's play, *Schluck und Jau*; now, upset by Kamila's news, he felt no desire to commit himself to Hartung's offer. 'My thoughts have stopped,' he confided to her, 'they won't go on.'[144] Convinced that Kamila needed him (her husband was away on business), Janáček wanted to see her as soon as his busy schedule allowed, 'either 12 June or 20 June'; he offered his cottage 'for recreation' whenever she wanted.[145] In another letter, written the same day, he proposed to go alone to Luhačovice at the end of the month, and return on 12 July; he would then bring Kamila to Hukvaldy so that she could have a rest.[146] Feeling extremely isolated and still upset about Zdenka's letter to his sister, he was again contemplating divorce.[147]

On 5 June, nevertheless, he continued writing the music for *Schluck und Jau* (planned as an open-air production at Heidelberg

Castle during the summer). Calm was restored at home: Zdenka was duly informed of Kamila's mother's illness, and Janáček's 'holy duty' to give Kamila every support.[148] Yet another disappointment soon followed, during the Prague Conservatoire visit in Brno that June. Six concerts had been arranged for the occasion: two of orchestral music, two of chamber music, and two matinées of organ and orchestral music; there were also two operas, Novák's *The Imp of Zvíkov* and Stravinsky's *Mavra*. Novák, the artistic director of the Prague Conservatoire, had seven works on the programme, Josef Suk and J.B. Foerster three each; other Czech composers, including those from Moravia, were also represented at this mini-festival of contemporary music.[149] Yet only one of Janáček's works was performed – the piano cycle *In the Mists*. 'You'll gather how they bring them up, these promising young people,' he complained bitterly to Kamila,

> from the fact that neither the Rector [Novák], nor the director, nor the conductor [Pavel Dědeček], whom I helped to get a position, still less of course the pupils, knew, during a stay of more than a week, that some sort of composer lives here – who has surely rendered some sort of service to Czech music. As if I didn't exist in Brno, either socially or musically.[150]

Janáček begged Kamila in several letters to let him know the instant she needed him, but all the while he hoped that everything would somehow sort itself out, and that she would come to Luhačovice as originally planned. 'If your sister would be kind enough to take over caring for your mother for a while, then you could get away,' he wrote on 8 June. 'The doctor said to me, just go if it will give you pleasure. [But] what is to give me pleasure without you! [. . .] I feel from your letter that you too are secretly, timidly, longing to be there,' he concluded, his wishful thinking only too apparent.[151]

The following day Brno suffered a heatwave; at the Janáčeks' it was like 'a furnace': 'In the morning the copyist finished Act 3 by 10 o'clock; part of Act 2 still remains to be looked through . . .'.[152] That day Janáček also attended the laying of the foundation stone for the Masaryk University in Brno (he had completed a piece for the occasion, for male voices, on 2 April):[153] 'They sang my [piece] fairly well. I stood [only] some five steps from the President. "High" society all round me. . . . In the evening I went to the theatre and then to have a look at the illuminations in the town.'[154]

Having bought at the Exhibition some furnishings for 'Kamila's' room at the Hukvaldy cottage, Janáček constantly planned further improvements and continued to hope that they would meet in Luhačovice. He also suggested that Kamila's son Otto should come with her: the locals, he remarked, 'would think that he is "our" son'.[155] Kamila, visiting her mother at the sanatorium on 9 June with the family, was trying to put on a brave face: she 'cheered everyone up' but 'felt terrible' herself. Her mother's prospects were not good, she admitted two days later; full of anxiety, she clearly needed a break:

> I still can't get used to the idea that one day I may be alone. That's why I'm not thinking about Luhačovice . . . . I just long for peace and I'll find it only at your place in Hukvaldy . . . . Otoušek [Otto] is lonely[,] no wonder since she brought him up. I'm glad that school will be over soon[,] I'll take him with me. He also needs a rest[,] he's weak . . . .[156]

By mid-June Janáček was at last at Hukvaldy, alone. 'How well I feel here in the sun; in that pure air, in this lovely quiet!' he enthused to Kamila. 'Br! Brno!'[157] Nevertheless, four days later he was back in town, having missed en route the long-announced concert of his cantata *Amarus* in Kroměříž: the welcoming party had failed to spot him at the railway station, although he was looking out of the carriage window. 'I didn't make a move. The [conductor] blew the whistle, [and] I fell back on my seat, laughing,' he related to Kamila. 'You can see from that what sort of mood I am in. I wouldn't be able to stand the music-making and that drivel before and after.'[158] In addition, he had come back with a cold, an upset stomach, and lumbago.

On 20 June, the copyists at last finished work on *From the House of the Dead*. Three days later Janáček spent two days at the Stössels', also making an excursion with them to nearby Zvíkov. Back in Brno, and packing for his Luhačovice trip, he was glad to have diverted Kamila for a while. Although she made it clear that she could not come to Luhačovice, she responded warmly: 'It is so sad here at home [now], but I have been so happy . . . that I could forget everything.'[159]

Janáček's next letter was prophetic: 'I have finished all my work as if I had no reason to return to Brno . . . . Everything seems to be hurrying to its end of its own accord. It is as if I were no longer going to pick up a pen here.'[160] Two days before leaving for Luhačovice, he was still trying to persuade Kamila to join him. He even suggested writing to her mother's doctor on Kamila's behalf, in order to find out 'the unvarnished truth' about Mrs Neumannová's state of health – perhaps hoping that if she had, say, another two months to live, Kamila could have a week's break in Luhačovice. On his last day in Brno, he found some satisfaction: 'The leader of the Bohemian Quartet . . . came to see me – about *our* quartet *Intimate Letters!*' he wrote. 'They will play it in Holland first. People are already talking a lot about this work of *ours*, and [saying] nice things. That gave me a lot of pleasure the whole day.'[161]

In Luhačovice, Janáček avoided his fellow guests, retired at half past eight – 'my Kamila's hour' – and took his meals at a vegetarian restaurant where he used to eat with her the previous summer. There were no letters from Kamila until 4 July, and she was not pleased with Janáček's maudlin self-pity: 'I have read your letter several times and it grieved me how you grumble about the whole world,' she chastised him.

> Is everything really so hopeless with you? Were you happier before? Even *you* know how to embitter one's life. Are you just a small child that can't do without a dummy? [. . .]There is time for everything, for joy and for sorrow. I am losing heart but you even more so . . . . Why do you take it so tragically[,] maybe you will be with me so long that you will grow tired of it . . . .[162]

Janáček calmed down a little. 'Yes, I need great strength for what awaits me this year,' he responded. 'I am gathering it in Luhačovice, and perhaps I will get rid of these rheumatic pains from all that sitting and – from that joyless life at home. Forcefulness and defiance, movement and change, that's the way I like to live.' Yet even embracing Kamila was still only a fantasy: 'Oh, if only you would let yourself be hugged just once! And you always escape just like a slippery little fish!' He realized his complaints must have seemed tiresome: 'You ought to have said that I write not like a man – but like an old woman! That's what you wanted to say, isn't it? It is true, I am a silly child.'[163]

On 8 July he outlined two plans to Kamila: either a week in Luhačovice together and then 'as long as you want' at Hukvaldy; or Kamila could travel to Hukvaldy via Brno, stopping for a day to see the Exhibition of Contemporary Culture with him.[164] When Kamila remained undecided, he reproached himself at length for his earlier 'irritated' letters. Everything seemed somehow connected with her: 'Today in the reading room about six young ladies and students surprised me,' he recounted on 16 July. 'They wanted my autograph . . .

and they were all Jewish! [. . .] That is how it is when I burn with love for my dear dark [lady], said to be Jewish! But we have our god who does not recognize religious differences, the god of love!'[165]

Janáček had gone on a diet at the spa, and had lost a great deal of weight. He also took hot mud baths and enjoyed his invigorating hot and cold water treatment. Yet on returning to Brno he felt utterly tired and listless, and hardly left the house: with no news from Kamila, he suffered.[166]

Both Zdenka and the Janáčeks' maidservant noticed how unwell he looked. 'I used to look at him with anxiety,' recalled Zdenka, 'as he barely dragged himself round our garden. One day I could not help myself and told him not to gamble with his health so.' Then, not knowing where the thought came from, she added: 'One day you will get pneumonia and that will be the end.' Nodding his head, Janáček simply said quietly: 'Yes, yes.'[167]

At last news arrived from Kamila: 'After great grief and suffering I am letting you know that my beloved mama died on Tuesday [17 July], they brought her [home] to me on Wednesday and her funeral was on Friday. I can't write any more[;] till we see each other on Friday [27 July] or Saturday in Brno. I want peace and that I shall find only with you.'[168]

Full of sympathy, Janáček responded immediately: 'On Monday 30 July at 10 a.m. we shall leave [from Brno], we shall be at Hukvaldy towards evening. There you will calm down, you will have a rest,' he reassured Kamila on 23 July, suggesting the next day: 'Let your husband look after the Písek household a little more this time.'[169]

When, still upset, he told Zdenka about his plans, she knew it was 'the beginning of the end': 'I could have shouted with pain when I thought that she would now live with Leoš in our cottage at Hukvaldy for several weeks – yet aloud I [only] asked when I should get his luggage ready for him.'[170]

Before leaving Brno, Janáček needed to see to various important tasks: 'I have burnt your letters which refer to what only the two of us know,' he announced to Kamila on 24 July. 'The other letters I have put away in the safe. Take good care of my letters, too; also that album. It is not for curious people.'[171] He planned to take his *Danube* symphony and *Schluck und Jau* with him, but his main concern was to make Kamila's stay as pleasurable as possible. Once again he wrote lovingly, though combining childlike naivety with self-centred desire: 'We shall remember the beautiful evenings in the Písek heaven. Let us transfer that heaven into the Hukvaldy cottage, too. It will fit in there; we shall make a whole little heaven for ourselves. We shall be happy like no one else on earth.'[172]

The following few days at the Janáčeks' were peaceful, though Zdenka hardly slept. Kamila, her husband and their son Otto finally arrived in Brno on Sunday 29 July; their other son, Rudolf, remained in Písek. Lunching at home, Janáček praised Zdenka for her excellent roast veal. 'Oh God, what use was it to me!' recollected Zdenka. 'He got dressed in his new light silk suit, put on his cap and merrily left.'[173] Janáček went with the Stössels to an exhibition of paintings by Joža Uprka, and then to the Exhibition of Contemporary Culture. When he returned that evening, Zdenka saw he was not in a good mood and guessed why: he had expected Kamila alone.

He was to leave with the Stössels for Hukvaldy next day at noon. The Janáčeks' maidservant Stejskalová resolutely refused to carry his luggage to the railway station,[174] and Zdenka advised Janáček to take a taxi. Ready to go, he picked up the third act of the *From the House of the Dead*, which he wanted to look over at Hukvaldy, and put it in his briefcase. 'Then he closed the piano,' recalled Stejskalová. 'He stood over it deep in thought, and when I went by he said quietly: "I have everything ready, but it seems to me as if I were not coming back".'[175]

Zdenka waited with him on the porch for the taxi, 'keeping her feelings in check with all her strength'.[176] Suddenly Janáček drew closer to her:

"Today is your birthday?"
"Yes."
"You forgot my birthday this year."
"I didn't but I thought you didn't care for my good wishes."
He held out his hand: "I wish you all the best."
He had no idea what a harrowing mockery it was. [. . .] I could not speak. All of a sudden the taxi rattled up. [. . .] He held out his hand again and tried to kiss me. Meanwhile at the station the other one was waiting. I ducked my head:
"Must it be?"
"It can and it must."
He kissed me brusquely and left.[177]

Stejskalová takes up the story:

Čipera [the Janáčeks' dog] began to bark at the car, the mistress ran out to call her back. The master was already in the garden, he took the

mistress by the hand but she sobbed, broke loose and ran home . . . .
At last the car started and the master in his light suit and white cap disappeared from my sight. I returned to the kitchen. The mistress
appeared calm, as if nothing interested her but the apricots from our
garden which she was about to bottle.[178]

The two accounts tally. But reports about Janáček's and Kamila's
stay at Hukvaldy vary considerably; there were few or no witnesses,
and the discrepancies that emerge have been repeated in various
biographies. On the other hand, Janáček's entries in Kamila's album,
in which he had been recording events since October 1927, are
dated.

The Stössels' arrival at Hukvaldy was noted by a local woman,
Otilie Krsková, who occasionally looked after Janáček's cottage.
According to her recollections, published in 1948,[179] David Stössel
left soon afterwards. Kamila and her son Otto moved into the upstairs
bedroom of the cottage that Janáček had had built and decorated for
her; the composer stayed in the two ground floor rooms, one of
which was a bright study, with a large harmonium.

The first two days passed happily, with Janáček working a little but
also taking his guests for daily walks in the countryside. On 1 August
they went by carriage to the pretty town of Štramberk, where they
visited Janáček's friend Dr Adolf Hrstka to see his folklore collection;
as Hrstka reported later, Janáček was 'full of good humour' and
planning further works.[180] The Swiss writer William Ritter and his
adopted son Josef Ritter-Tscherff had been staying at a local inn,[181]
and Janáček promised Hrstka that he would bring them to Štramberk
the following week. The party also visited the nearby National Park
on Kotouč Mountain, where Janáček was keen to show Kamila a
statue of him which had been erected there in 1927. On 2 August
Janáček sent a card to Zdenka: 'Arrived safely. Cheerfulness in the
house. [. . .] That's how it should be. The money arrived.'[182]

'That "cheerfulness in the house, that's how it should be" stung
me,' Zdenka later commented bitterly. 'It was also a reproach that my
household was sad, that I did not know how to be cheerful . . . and it
told me how unnecessary I was and how joyful it was without me.'[183]

Yet all was not harmony at the Hukvaldy cottage. Kamila's son
Otto later recalled that his mother was 'packing [their] suitcases' virtually every day, annoyed at Janáček's playing the harmonium late
into the night.[184] Janáček's entry in Kamila's album seems to confirm
that she wanted to leave; as many of his friends and colleagues knew,

he was in the habit of hammering the same chord or tune repeatedly when composing. By Sunday, 5 August, peace was restored; Janáček added a codicil to his will in the album, by which the interest on a sum left to the University of Brno,[185] as well as the royalties from *Káťa Kabanová*, *The Diary of One who Disappeared*, *From the House of the Dead* and the Second String Quartet were all to go to Kamila.

From here onwards, versions of what happened next differ. In an article published in 1928 Robert Smetana reported that on Wednesday, 8 August, Janáček, Kamila and Otto Stössel went for a walk to Babí hůra, a hill in Janáček's forest; on the way back they picked up their laundry from Otilie Krsková's mother. But neither Smetana nor Krsková give any mention of the events which have found their way into all subsequent biographies: that Kamila's son Otto, who was about 11, got lost while they were out walking, that Janáček tried to find him and, dashing up and down the hill, got overheated, eventually taking off his coat and sitting down on a bench. The boy turned up but Janáček meanwhile caught a chill, developing serious complications the next day. Accounts by Adolf Vašek (1930) and Janáček's niece Věra Janáčková (1940),[186] who claimed to be quoting the testimonies of local people, date the expedition as Monday, 6 or Tuesday, 7 August; Marie Stejskalová's version includes a rainstorm – apparently the entire party got drenched on their way back to the cottage, and Janáček immediately felt unwell. Charles Susskind reports that Josef Ritter-Tscherff could not recall any child staying at the cottage at the time;[187] Zdenka was later told that the boy stayed on his own at the local hotel.[188] Moreover, in Janáček's entries in Kamila's album there is not a word about any missing child, nor of any expedition or an illness of any kind until 10 August, when he recorded sweating during the night.[189]

Medical reports exist from Thursday, 9 August when, as most biographers concur, Janáček sent a note to the Hukvaldy doctor, Emil Franta, asking him to come and see him. Influenza with laryngitis and mastoiditis were diagnosed, as well as an irregular heartbeat, partly due to Janáček's long-term heart problem. Dr Franta and his colleague from the neighbouring town – who confirmed that the influenza and chill had now turned to pneumonia – insisted that Janáček go to hospital, as did the Hukvaldy mayor. Janáček resisted until Friday, 10 August, but that morning he felt much worse, and was taken by car to a sanatorium in Moravská Ostrava, the nearest big town.[190] Still in good spirits, he arrived at the sanatorium with a high temperature (104°), and the earlier diagnosis was confirmed by X-ray.

His condition deteriorated, though by Saturday he had rallied after adrenalin injections and even attempted to do some work on a score. But the end was in sight. His breathing became difficult, he was coughing, and his heart showed signs of failing. Repeated injections failed to stimulate the heart, and eventually Janáček refused further medication. The doctor spent the night at his bedside;[191] about 2 a.m. on Sunday morning, 12 August, Janáček wrote his last will in Kamila's album, in pencil (though Jaroslav Vogel mentions 'some additions on a separate scrap of paper',[192] and Charles Susskind states that Janáček 'reiterated the terms of the codicil he had written into their album').[193] Two nurses suggested a visit from the priest, but Janáček refused, declaring 'You probably don't know who I am.'[194] He became feverish, his consciousness slipping away; he was then given a sedative and fell asleep at 9 a.m. He died exactly an hour later.[195]

Meanwhile in Brno, Zdenka – keeping her end up – decided to have a good time, and on Friday, 10 August went out drinking with friends at the ever-popular Exhibition of Contemporary Culture. They all enjoyed themselves so much that Zdenka made another date for the Sunday. That morning, she received a telegram from Kamila: 'Maestro seriously ill, come immediately, sanatorium Dr Klein.'[196]

Zdenka wanted Janáček's cousin, Dr Dressler, to come with her; on her way to the Dresslers', she ran into tenor Stanislav Tauber.[197] As soon as Zdenka was out of earshot Tauber was approached by a funeral parlour employee who had seen them, and told Tauber of Janáček's death. Tauber went up to the Dresslers' flat; when Zdenka herself answered the door, he asked to see Dr Dressler, a long-standing friend, but Zdenka guessed what had happened. On returning home, she found a telegram from the sanatorium, confirming the distressing news. As Dr Dressler could not accompany her, Zdenka begged Tauber to come with her. The journey took several hours by train, and Zdenka, Tauber reports in his memoirs, 'described to me all the troubles of her disorderly marriage. [. . .] She was at last resigned to the present situation. [. . .] "What was I supposed to do when he told me that she inspired him, that he needed her?" '[198]

In Moravská Ostrava, they went to the sanatorium first; the doctor who had stayed with Janáček until the end told them that Kamila had brought him to the hospital 'in a hopeless state', and that Janáček had insisted his stay be kept secret.[199] Kamila, apparently, also had a check-up and an X-ray at the sanatorium, at Janáček's expense.[200] Aware of the approaching end, the doctors then asked Janáček whether his wife should be summoned. As Tauber recalls, the physician – lacking all discretion – repeated Janáček's answer to Zdenka. 'It was shattering and its effect [on Mrs Janáčková] naturally the same.'[201]

Tauber, Zdenka and the funeral parlour employee then visited Kamila at the Hotel Imperial where she had moved, taking Janáček's belongings with her. Tauber describes how the anguished Zdenka begged him not to leave her, and in the end he promised to speak to Kamila on her behalf.[202] They were hoping to obtain from her the keys to Janáček's desk and safe, so that his will could be found, and funeral arrangements made according to his wishes.

Appearing unexpectedly in the foyer, Kamila 'came running to me,' recalled Zdenka,

> grasped my right shoulder and asked: 'Are you angry with me?' I pushed her away after that absurd question: 'Leave me alone, you have stolen my husband from me and destroyed him.' She started wailing: 'It isn't my fault, I didn't have an affair with him.' 'Keep quiet, this is not the right time to speak about such things, I am not asking you.'[203]

When Zdenka asked for Janáček's keys and belongings, 'Mrs S[tösslová] categorically refused to hand them over,' Tauber reports. According to Zdenka, Kamila declared that Janáček had handed them over to her, and that she 'must be present' when things were being sorted out.[204]

The two women then retired to discuss the situation in Kamila's room.[205] As Zdenka later recounted, Kamila swore on her husband's love and her children's happiness that she 'never had an affair with my husband, that he never so much as kissed her hand'.[206]

> I reproached her that she knew how much I loved Leoš, that apart from him I had nothing in the world when my children died, that she knew how much trouble I had been through and yet she took him away from me without mercy.[207]

The argument, says Tauber, was 'very counterproductive'.[208] When Zdenka started lamenting her dead husband, Kamila 'suddenly opened her handbag and began taking out the keys, my husband's gold watch with a chain and his completely plundered wallet.' Zdenka next asked about the Universal Edition royalties – a considerable sum of 33,000 crowns – sent to Janáček at Hukvaldy; of the 15,000 he and Kamila had taken to Moravská Ostrava, Kamila had paid 4,000 to the sanatorium. As for the remainder, 'the Maestro gave it me as a present,' Kamila maintained, 'so that I could buy something with it for myself.'[209]

The 'loud wrangling' came to a head in the street, reports Tauber; there he spoke to Kamila privately:

> . . . I asked Mrs S[tösslová] to divulge whether the Maestro, in what he wrote in bed a short while before his death, had voiced his last wishes about his funeral. Apparently not, that was something quite different. When my pleas did not help, I declared that I would go and fetch a policeman. That helped. She even showed me what the Maestro wrote . . . .[210]

Kamila then insisted that Zdenka come to Hukvaldy with her for the rest of Janáček's belongings, and the party set off in a hired car. 'The two ladies sat at the back, I with the driver in front,' recalls Tauber:

> Nothing separated us, so that like it or not we were forced to hear their conversation. I was ashamed of them. The driver commented critically on the dialogue several times . . . .[211]

Among other things, Kamila was 'glad that everything was over,' Zdenka related later. 'Be glad that he has already died, at least you will have some peace,' she reportedly told her, and later threw into Zdenka's open handbag the gold ring Janáček had once given her.[212]

At Hukvaldy, Zdenka asked Kamila to tell Janáček's sister Josefka the news. Kamila then produced the keys for Janáček's desk, in which she and Zdenka found the keys for Janáček's desk in Brno and another wallet, containing 7,000 crowns. 'So they have spent 11,000 crowns in a fortnight,' Zdenka commented bitterly; before Janáček left for Hukvaldy, he had given her only 600 crowns for a month, for herself and the maidservant.[213] Although Zdenka and Josefka met, they parted acrimoniously; moreover, as Zdenka decided to have Janáček's funeral in Brno, many people, including Josefka, never forgave her for not having him buried at his birthplace.[214]

At 10 p.m. the party were back in Moravská Ostrava; a car carrying Janáček's coffin, already closed, then left for Brno, stopping in front of Zdenka's hotel for only a few minutes. After a sleepless night, Zdenka visited Kamila again early next morning, reproaching her once more for enticing Janáček. It was then that Kamila reportedly showed her a leaf from her album, according to which Janáček bequeathed her the royalties for several of his works.[215] Kamila only allowed Zdenka a glimpse; then, withdrawing the album, she said: 'What you give me, you give me.'[216] Tauber himself was unwilling to disclose Zdenka's comments to him – not that he wanted to take sides: he had never been fond of her.[217]

Further complications ensued in Brno over Janáček's funeral service;[218] only the following day could Zdenka finally look at Janáček through the glass cover of his coffin. Seeing that his face was 'contracted in a sullen expression, angry', she could not help thinking: 'You hated dying, you have been wrestling with death.'[219] Exhausted, she only succumbed to tears the day before the funeral on 15 August (which had been the Janáčeks' daughter Olga's birthday).

Crowds waited in and outside the church, which was packed with flowers. After the religious ceremony the coffin was taken to the city's theatre where Janáček was laid in state in the foyer. When the orchestra, under František Neumann, began to play the Forester's Farewell from _The Cunning Little Vixen_ – which had so moved Janáček when he first heard it – Zdenka 'jumped up [from her chair], exclaimed "Little Vixen!" and was about to faint.'[220] Stejskalová, 'who was at my heels everywhere that day, like a faithful dog,' managed to catch her; Zdenka barely remembered the rest of the ceremony.[221]

Many prominent public figures attended the funeral, including the composer Otakar Ostrčil, the composer and conductor Oskar Nedbal and Max Brod. The speakers included the Lord Mayor of Brno, the composer Boleslav Vomáčka, the Vice-Chancellor of the Masaryk University in Brno Dr Jaroslav Kalláb, and the director of the Brno Conservatoire Jan Kunc; Brod spoke on behalf of 'the hundreds of thousands of German listeners who have enjoyed the works of Janáček's musical genius'.[222] Finally, before Janáček was carried from the theatre where so much of his music had been heard, the Beseda Choral Society and the City Theatre orchestra, conducted by Janáček's pupil Jaroslav Kvapil, performed the first part of Dvořák's _Requiem_ – with Stanislav Tauber among the soloists.[223]

The city of Brno had given Janáček a place of honour in the local cemetery; František Neumann spoke for the last time at the graveside, moved to tears.[224] After a brief religious service, the Czech national anthem completed the ceremony and, to the sound of horns, the coffin was lowered into the grave.

It did not remain there long: two days later, after Zdenka had voiced her objections, the coffin was dug up and moved to the family tomb. Only a few guests accompanied Zdenka this time – the Lord Mayor and his wife, František Neumann, and some friends and pupils. Thus, after five days' wandering, Janáček was finally laid to rest.

Janáček's last opera, *From the House of the Dead*, was first performed in Brno on 12 April 1930, over a year and a half after his death. Of Janáček's nine works for the stage, it is the shortest. At first it may well seem to be the bleakest: its characters – who range from a Russian 'gentleman' to an illiterate Tartar boy – are inmates of a Siberian prison camp, and the stench of death pervades the story. Writing it, Janáček felt as if he were 'descending . . . right down to the most wretched people of humankind'.[225]

Janáček's choice of the subject and its treatment represent a radical departure for someone who had once been accused of composing only 'female' operas.[226] With only one female character (a prostitute, a mere vignette), there is none of the erotic charge evident, for example, in *Káťa Kabanová* and *The Makropulos Affair*. The work does not even have a single protagonist; it is, in essence, an ensemble opera, with a number of vividly drawn characters, including those described in the stories told by the inmates.

Once again inspired by Russian literature, Janáček wrote the libretto himself, after Dostoyevsky's *Memoirs from the House of the Dead*. The novel, which brought the writer fame, was originally published in serial form between 1860 and 1862, and presented as the memoirs of a Russian aristocrat. In fact, the experiences were those of Dostoyevsky himself: in the early 1850s, imprisoned for his membership of a revolutionary circle, he served four years in the prison camp of Omsk. In effect, the work is reportage: Dostoyevsky described in the individual chapters his impressions of the camp and the conditions there, his fellow prisoners and their crimes, religious holidays and other festivities, the prison hospital, the animals in the camp, and so forth. He found compassion even in such a dismal gathering of discarded humanity and this, along with the rich stock of the prisoners' stories and the intense emotions shown by them, was undoubtedly a powerful stimulus for Janáček, who made compassion and redemption the cornerstones of his operas.

'Opera . . . is surely a misnomer when applied to *The House of the*

Dead', wrote Rosa Newmarch, the English musicologist and Janáček's ardent advocate, in 1931.[227] As in Dostoyevsky's novel, there is no plot: its three acts, of which the last is divided into two scenes, consist of a series of tableaux. Physical violence and murder abound in Janáček's operas, but here similarly terrible deeds are portrayed in retrospect, once their perpetrators had been removed to the living hell of the penal colony: we do not see them being committed, nor do we see the characters mature.

Janáček first referred to the novel in an open letter to Max Brod, published on 13 February 1927.[228] Later that month he sketched a preliminary scenario in his diary; other preliminary material exists but no draft libretto.[229] Janáček worked directly from the Russian edition of the book, marking those passages which interested him and making copious annotations. Although he owned a copy of the novel in a Czech translation, the text in the opera does not correspond to this edition: Janáček translated the Russian text into Czech himself. He extracted dialogue, adding some phrases from the indirect speech and inventing others; he often transliterated rather than translated, and even kept some words in the original Cyrillic. Some of these transliterations must have been intended for the sake of local colour, but Janáček later tried to eliminate the Russian words, although he never succeeded completely.[230]

Act 1 opens in the prison courtyard, on a winter's morning. The inmates argue and bait an eagle with a broken wing, admiring its defiant spirit. A new arrival, the 'gentleman' and political offender Gorjančikov, is brought in; the Commandant orders him to be flogged. As the prisoners work, Luka Kuzmič, a Ukrainian, tells the story of his revolt against another brutal Commandant. Eventually, he stabbed him to death; as a punishment, he was flogged nearly to death. Gorjančikov is brought back, weak from his hundred lashes.

Act 2 takes place in summer, on the banks of the river Irtysh. Gorjančikov had befriended Aljeja, the Tartar boy, and offers to teach him to read and write. It is a feast day, and the prisoners celebrate. Skuratov tells his story: he loved a German girl, Lujza, but she was forced to marry a wealthy middle-aged watchmaker. Skuratov shot him, was caught and sentenced. Some of the inmates, still in fetters, perform a show for the camp's entertainment: an 'opera', *Kedril and Don Juan*, and a pantomime, *The Miller's Pretty Wife*. Afterwards, as Gorjančikov and Aljeja drink tea, one of the prisoners attacks and injures the boy.

In Scene 1 of Act 3, in the prison hospital, the feverish Aljeja –

who can now read and write – expresses his admiration for Jesus and his teachings. The dying Luka Kuzmič argues with another prisoner. Šapkin tells his story of life as a vagrant and robber. Šiškov tells his story of the perfidious Filka Morozov who slandered Akulina, a rich merchant's innocent daughter. Šiškov married the dishonoured girl; on his way to the army, Filka finally begged Akulina to forgive him. When Šiškov discovered that she still loved Filka, he drove her to the forest and cut her throat. As the story ends, Luka Kuzmič dies; Šiškov recognizes him as his former rival Filka, and curses him. An old prisoner blesses the body: 'He too was born of a mother.'

In Scene 2, the half-drunk Commandant apologizes to Gorjančikov for having had him flogged. An order has arrived for Gorjančikov's release; he and Aljeja say goodbye. As Gorjančikov leaves, the prisoners release the eagle, whose wing has now healed; watching it fly away, they sing of freedom, before the guard orders them back to work.

Janáček's autograph score is dated 18 February 1927, the date on which he probably started working on the opera in earnest.[231] From October that year, when he nearly finished the first version, his progress and the strain his 'black' opera caused him are charted in his letters to Kamila. And, as in some of his other works, he identified the most tender creatures in the opera – Aljeja and Akulina – with her.[232]

Although Janáček changed and to a degree distorted Dostoyevsky's intentions, his treatment enriched his source.[233] He largely followed Dostoyevsky's order of events, but cut down the number of characters by combining them.[234] Employing his dramatic instinct to great advantage, he also moved some around: for example, he put parts of Aljeja's story – which Dostoyevsky leaves in a single section – into Acts 2 and 3.[235] Some events are paralleled: in Act 1, a reported event of flogging and an actual one (Gorjančikov is brought back just after Luka Kuzmič describes his own punishment); in Act 2, the eagle – wounded at the time of Gorjančikov's arrival – is released as Gorjančikov leaves. Surprisingly, Janáček's Don Juan in the little 'opera' in Act 2 does not seem to be the character we know from other Don Juan stories; according to recent research, Janáček may have originally intended to use Don Quixote.[236]

The text, with its mixture of Czech, Russian and even Ukrainian words, is at times so condensed as to appear fragmentary. But the deeper connections are made apparent in the characters' monologues (an important feature of all Janáček's operas, though here some may seem disproportionately long).

The music of Act 1, as harsh and unrelenting as the grim atmosphere of the prison camp, is offset by much of Act 2, with its summer's day outdoors, the feast and the show, all of which bring light relief; some of the most lyrical music of the opera is heard in Skuratov's touching tale. Act 3 is yet again a complete contrast; while the music of the hospital scene is appropriately feverish in character, after the wonderful night music (for solo violin and clarinet, then flute and bass clarinet), Šiškov's monologue is relatively restrained. And the abrupt ending of Act 3 is quite different from the glorious apotheoses of some of Janáček's earlier operas; it has been suggested that this might have been Janáček's response to Berg's *Wozzeck*, which he had passionately defended in an interview early in 1928.[237]

Much of the music in the overture to *The House of the Dead* can be traced to Janáček's Violin Concerto, drafted probably by February 1927;[238] he then used some of the haunting music from the overture in Luka's monologue in Act 1. However, as in his other operas, Janáček does not necessarily associate particular thematic material with a specific character or situation; he varies and transforms it as the relevant situations or emotions require. Thus the theme used throughout the section devoted to Skuratov in Act 1 is also heard in the coda, although by then the action has long moved on. And the 'Skuratov' theme does not appear at all in his long monologue in Act 2; this is based on an entirely different material with a modal flavour.

Among two themes that are used consistently, the dissonant chords which open Act 1 are also heard, for example, while Gorjančikov is flogged, and at crucial points of Luka's monologue; Janáček constantly varies the orchestration.[239] This theme also recurs in Act 3 (in Šhapkin's story and at the height of Šiškov's monologue); it returns in the major in the interlude between scenes 1 and 2, and as Gorjančikov and Aljeja part. In Act 3, the prisoners' chorus extolling freedom is foreshadowed in the prelude to this act.

Although the work's texture is chamber-like in character, and the outer voices are often widely spaced (high piccolos and low trombones), the sound is frequently quite clamorous. As someone who never quite left behind his childhood infatuation with kettledrums,[240] Janáček clearly jumped at the chance of employing the drum rolls mentioned in the novel, using the side-drum rolls several times.[241] There is also a thunderous timpani solo at the end of Act 1; among unconventional instruments are the prisoners' chains, their tools, a rattle, and church bells.[242] A reduced orchestra, brilliantly evoking the band described by Dostoyevsky, is used in the show in Act 2.[243]

Janáček began revising almost immediately after finishing the first draft, and completed the opera in January 1928, less than eleven months since its inception; after a final revision, the score was copied out by 20 June 1928.[244] Janáček then checked through the first two acts, making further minor changes and additions in his own hand; he was unable to go through Act 3 before his unexpected death on 12 August.

For a while, contemporary directors steered clear of the work, and scholars who saw Janáček's autograph score, with its staves drawn freehand, were baffled.[245] In 1930, when Ota Zítek finally staged the opera in Brno, he added some text to the dialogue, and Janáček's pupils Osvald Chlubna and Břetislav Bakala, who felt that the full score – though in effect authorized – was incomplete, re-orchestrated it. In 1958, Chlubna maintained that they had made changes to Janáček's palette 'only in the most pressing cases', in order 'to fill in gaps in the sound which Janáček had overlooked'.[246] In fact, their changes and doublings substantially changed Janáček's original sound world; and by adding a celebratory male chorus they also distorted his ending.[247]

This version, published by Universal Edition, was used in subsequent productions, but in the early 1960s Universal Edition issued another edition, based on Janáček's autograph and prepared by the Czech conductor Rafael Kubelík.[248] This edition was used in the first English production in 1965, and was thought a revelation.[249] But only in 1980 was the opera recorded in a version based on Janáček's authorized full score, with all his additions to Act 1 and 2. The numerous instrumental adjustments in this version, the restoration of Janáček's original placing of the voice parts, some of the text and indeed of the music, show the true nature of the work.[250]

Yet even in the 1930s some discerning critics had understood Janáček's intentions and the value of this opera. Rosa Newmarch saw the Prague production in 1931; in the conclusion of her prophetic review,[251] she wrote the work's moving epitaph:

Is *The House of the Dead* only a mirror reflecting a sick and senile mind, or a flash-light turned upon such terrible verities as our eyes would prefer to evade: the Siberia of Dostoyevsky's time, the Bolshevik labour-camps of to-day? [. . .] 'In every creature there is a spark of God,' is written upon [Janáček's] score. This is the answer to the tragedy of life. Are we to believe he was thinking only of his own soul? Or even of the Russia he knew and loved in her continuous suffering and oppression? Those who knew Janáček will prefer to accept the widest possible application of the motto he inscribed upon his last creative effort.

Appendix

Janáček did not name a sole beneficiary in his will; he left his house in Hukvaldy and his land there to the village, and 100,000 crowns to the Faculty of Philosophy of the Masaryk University in Brno, with interest on this sum to be shared between Zdenka Janáčková and the University. Other capital was to be shared by other legally recognized beneficiaries. He also bequeathed Zdenka royalties of all operas except *Káťa Kabanová* and *From the House of the Dead*; after her death the royalties were to go to the University. However, on Sunday 5 August 1928 he assigned the interest on the 100,000 crowns to Kamila Stösslová, in a codicil to his will. He also bequeathed her the royalties of *Káťa Kabanová*, *The Diary of One who Disappeared*, *From the House of the Dead* and the Second String Quartet, *Intimate Letters*. This codicil was written in the album which Kamila kept for him to jot down his thoughts, in words as well as in music, during his visits to Písek; she brought it with her to Hukvaldy when she came at the end of July 1928.

In 1930 David Stössel contested the original will on behalf of his wife and the two sheets with the codicil and the beginning of a composition, 'Čekám Tě [I'm waiting for you]', were cut out of the album and used as evidence in court. The case dragged on for several years, but eventually the court decided in Kamila's favour. She was paid 70,000 crowns, a considerable sum at the time, and the University agreed to pay her royalties of *Káťa Kabanová* and *From the House of the Dead*. After another appeal she regained possession of the album. Although Zdenka was sufficiently provided for, she found the court case and any reminders of Kamila's relationship with Janáček degrading; for this reason she also tried to suppress the title of the Second String Quartet, *Intimate Letters*.

The history of the fate of Janáček's letters to Kamila is no less complicated. The editor of the Czech edition of the letters, which was published in 1990, described the story in full in the right hand column of her preface to the book; the following text draws on the comprehensive information given there.

Kamila had been saving Janáček's letters throughout their acquaintance, although she often cut out parts of them or inked out some passages. Two years after his death she made some of the letters available to Adolf Vašek, and allowed him to quote from them in his book, *Po stopách dra Leoše Janáčka* [In the tracks of Dr Leoš Janáček]. Soon after the publication of the book in 1930 an article appeared in the daily newspaper *Národní osvobození*, drawing the attention of the public to an enormous collection of about 1,000 letters in Kamila's possession. Fragments of Janáček's letters from London in 1926 and from Frankfurt in 1927 were quoted in the article. Zdenka was extremely upset by these developments, and through her

263

legal representative tried to suppress any further publication of Janáček's letters to Kamila.

However, the Czech musicologist and Janáček's first biographer Vladimír Helfert approached Kamila, hoping to acquire the collection for Janáček archive. Kamila refused to sell. After her death of cancer at the age of 43, in 1935, Helfert approached her husband. Again he was unsuccessful, owing to the court case over the Janáček estate; the Masaryk University also found David Stössel's price far too high.

In 1939, shortly before the Second World War, the situation changed. Rudolf Stössel, David and Kamila's eldest son, then 26, pawned the collection to Bedřich Hirsch for a loan of 20,000 crowns. In November 1939 Hirsch sold the collection for the sum of 22,000 crowns to the Faculty of Philosophy of the Masaryk University; this time, wishing to avoid any problems, Helfert asked the director of the Association of Authors' Rights Karel Balling to act for him. The collection included 713 letters and postcards, as well as some letters from Janáček to David Stössel, and seventeen letters from Janáček's sister Josefa to Kamila; there were also Kamila's album and two autograph scores (the *Chorus for the Laying of the Foundation Stone of the Masaryk University in Brno*, and the Second String Quartet, *Intimate Letters*). The pragmatic David Stössel emigrated to Switzerland, where he died in 1982, aged 93. His and Kamila's sons, married to gentiles, survived the war in Czechoslovakia, but the rest of Kamila's family perished.

Earlier in 1939, a mere eight days after the Masaryk University acquired the letters, Vladimír Helfert was arrested by the Gestapo and imprisoned. Even during his imprisonment he continued to take an interest in the correspondence and its fate, especially as he was under the impression that the collection was incomplete, and that many of Janáček's letters to Kamila from 1923 were not included. Tragically, Helfert died of the after-effects of his incarceration in the Terezín concentration camp, just before the liberation of Czechoslovakia in 1945.

After the Second World War all Janáček material in possession of the Faculty of Philosophy, including the correspondence, was transferred to the archive of the Music Division of the Moravian Museum. However, as Helfert's flat in Brno was ransacked at the end of the war, it was impossible to ascertain whether or not the collection was complete. Further letters were handed over by Helfert's widow in stages in the 1950s, another twenty-four letters were found in the estate of Janáček's niece Věra in 1967, and a few more letters and photographs were bought for the archive in 1970. Eventually, in 1988 (as the work began on the edition) the collection totalled 697 letters, postcards and correspondence cards addressed to Kamila, and thirty-two empty envelopes.

The letters between Janáček and Kamila chronicle the development of their relationship, and they also allow us a close look at the minutiae of Janáček's life and work. The collection – probably one of the largest of its kind – does help us to understand better the nature of Janáček's passion for Kamila. Yet there is still much that we shall never know, and perhaps this is for the best.

Notes

Introduction

1. See *Documenta Bartókiana* 1, Heft 3, Dennis Dille, ed., Akadémiai kiadó, Budapest and B. Schott's Söhne, Mainz, 1968, p. 122, fn. 1.
2. See his *feuilleton* 'Moravany! Morawaan!', *Lidové noviny*, 6 April 1918, in *Janáček's Uncollected Essays on Music*, selected, ed. and trans. Mirka Zemanová, Marion Boyars Publishers, London, 1989/1993, p. 40.
3. Cf. Ludvík Kundera, 'Janáčkova tvorba klavírní' [Janáček's piano works], *Musikologie*, iii, Prague, 1955, p. 309.
4. See 'What I admit', *Lidové noviny*, 13 February 1927, in Zemanová (ed.), *Janáček's Uncollected Essays*, p. 106.

Chapter 1: Beginnings

1. Letter to the National Theatre Association in Brno, 9 June 1916; first published by Leoš Firkušný in *Musikologie*, i, 1938; cf. also Bohumír Štědroň, ed., *Janáček ve vzpomínkách a dopisech* [Janáček in reminiscences and letters], Topič, Prague 1946, p. 189.
2. It has to be borne in mind, however, that – in Czech music at least – the concept of 'the Czech nation' in the modern sense of the word has existed only since Smetana.
3. Přemysl Otakar II of the native Přemyslids, known as the 'Iron and Gold King'; ruled 1253–78. The far-sighted Charles IV of Luxemburg (ruled 1346–76) founded Prague's New Town, the city's Charles University (1348), and built many monuments of great beauty. He became Roman King (1346), and Roman Emperor (in 1355, the first Czech king to do so); in 1356 he ratified the independence of the Czech kingdom.
4. In 1867 the new Austro-Hungarian Empire, based on the principle of dualism, was established; the monarchy was divided into two equal states (Austria and Hungary), with one ruler, and foreign policy, the army and army finance in common. This meant political equality for the Hungarians, but not for the Czechs, whose frustration manifested itself in many new ventures, from schools to patriotic choral societies.

Sušil, František (1804–68); priest, literary scholar and folk-song collector. His views on the character of Slavonic music and Moravian folk music, expressed in the preface to his collection, *Moravské národní písně* [Moravian folk-songs],

1835, had a direct influence on the growth of modern Czech music, particularly on Křížkovský.

Father Pavel Křížkovský (1820–85, christened Karel), composer, founder of choral style in Moravia. Active in Brno since 1843; music director of the Augustinian Queen's Monastery; choirmaster of the Brno Beseda Club (1860–3). He first harmonized and later reshaped and incorporated a number of texts and melodies from Sušil's collection in his unaccompanied male choruses. These 'ohlas' [echo] choruses were the first musical genre of the National Revival in Moravia, and some of them are still in the repertory of many Czech choirs. See also notes 16 and 17 below. Among other composers who used texts and melodies from Sušil's collection are Dvořák, Janáček, Vítězslav Novák and Bohuslav Martinů.

F.J. Klácel (1808–82), editor-in-chief of the daily newspaper *Moravské noviny*, founded in 1848.

5. From his introduction 'Několik slov o lidových písních moravských' [A few words about Moravian folk-songs]; František Bartoš, *Národní písně moravské nově nasbírané* [Moravian folk-songs newly collected], Brno, 1889, p. ii. Now usually referred to as Bartoš ii.

6. After the Hapsburg victory in 1620, Bohemia and Moravia underwent forcible re-Catholicization; 'heretical' books were destroyed and the Czech language was suppressed; Prague's Charles University was handed over to the Jesuits. A series of reforms was initiated in the eighteenth century but, while generally enlightened, these reforms also strengthened centralism and Germanization. The intellectual credibility of Czech as a language of the educated classes was only re-established during the Czech National Revival. Paradoxically, some of the first battles to revitalize the Czech language were fought in German.

Jan Ludevít Lukes (1824–1906) was a former fellow scholar at Queen's, founder and chorus master of Hlahol, the largest Czech choral society.

7. Bartoš ii, pp. lxxxi–xciv.

8. From Janáček's *feuilleton* 'Moje Lašsko' [My Lašsko], *Lidové noviny*, 22 May 1928 (also used in the preface to the 1928 edition of his *Dances from Lašsko*). See the complete edition of Janáček's *feuilletons*, *Fejetony z Lidových novin* [*Feuilletons* from *Lidové noviny*], ed. Jan Racek, Krajské nakladatelství, Brno, 1958, p. 15.

9. The family surname was first documented in the village of Smilovice near Těšín. Grandfather Jiří Janáček (1778–1848) was brought up by a country chaplain, Father Antonín Herman (1753–1801), for whom Jiří's widowed mother worked as a housekeeper. According to Vincenc Janáček, Jiří was born in 1780, and his father Jan died when Jiří was five; Jaroslav Vogel, however, gives Jan's dates as 1742–74, making it clear that Jiří was born four years after his father's death, and hence was illegitimate (though not Herman's son). Cf. Vladimir Helfert, *Leoš Janáček*, i, Oldřich Pazdírek, Brno, 1939, pp. 9, 17, 38ff; Vincenc Janáček, *Životopis Jiříka Janáčka (1778–1848)* [A biography of Jiřík Janáček (1778–1848)], ed. Jiří Sehnal, Opus Musicum, Brno, 1985, p. 11; Jaroslav Vogel, *Leoš Janáček*, Orbis Publishing, London, 1981. p. 34. Helfert gives 'around 1846' as the date of the family's arrival in Hukvaldy.

10. See Helfert, *Leoš Janáček*, p. 15ff.
11. Ibid.
12. Ibid.; see also Sehnal (ed.), *Životopis Jiříka Janáčka*, p. 31. As Sehnal notes, it is unlikely that Grandfather Jiří would be capable of improvising fugues; however, even if he were using only the basic technique of imitation, such a standard of playing would still be above-average for a country teacher.
13. Sehnal (ed.), *Životopis Jiříka Janáčka*, p. 56.
14. Josef (religious name Cölestin, ?–1887); Jan (1810–89); Jiří (1815–1866); Vincenc (1821–1901); Johanna (?–?) and Žofie (?–?).
15. Sigmund Freud's birthplace.
16. See Sehnal (ed.), *Životopis Jiříka Janáčka*, p. 59; Opava is a town in Silesia.
17. Neplachovice in 'small village Silesia', near the town of Opava. For Křížkovský, see note 4 above.
18. See Helfert, *Leoš Janáček*, p 35ff.
19. From Janáček's autobiographical reminiscences, *Leoš Janáček. Pohled do života a díla* [Leoš Janáček. A view of the life and work], ed. Adolf Veselý, Fr. Borový, Prague, 1924, p. 15. [Janáček/Veselý]
20. Ibid., p. 15.
21. See Helfert, *Leoš Janáček*, pp. 44–5.
22. Ibid., pp. 35ff.
23. Letter to Kamila Stösslová, 10 August 1918 (No. 79 in *Hádanka života. (Dopisy Leoše Janáčka Kamile Stösslové)* [The riddle of life. (Letters of Leoš Janáček to Kamila Stösslová)], ed. Svatava Přibáňová, Opus Musicum, Brno, 1990, p. 48.
24. See Janáček/Veselý, p. 15.
25. Ibid., p. 100. For Janáček's piano cycle *On the Overgrown Path*, see the present volume, pp. 105–6.
26. From Janáček's *feuilleton* 'Světla jitřní' [The lights of matins], *Lidové noviny*, 24 December 1909; cf. Racek (ed.), *Fejetony*, pp. 20–1.
27. 'An Interview in the journal *Literární svět*', 8 March 1928; see *Janáček's Uncollected Essays on Music*, selected, ed. and trans. Mirka Zemanová, Marion Boyars Publishers, London, 1989/1993, p. 121.
28. Secondary schools throughout the country sang Mass every morning and there was practical tuition on pupils' respective instruments in the afternoon. Keyboard players would usually be taught figured bass, and the best pupils organ playing. In 1772, Charles Burney observed during his journey through Bohemia that 'in all villages, where there is a reading and writing school, children of both sexes are taught music'; the Czech composer and organist Josef Seger (1716–82) told him that this was also the case 'in Moravia, Hungary, and part of Austria'. Cf. *The Present State of Music in Germany, the Netherlands and the United Provinces*, 2nd edn, corrected, 1773; new edn by Percy Scholes, OUP, London, 1959, ii, pp. 131–2 and 134–5.
29. See Věra Janáčkov, 'Můj strýc a smrt' [My uncle and death], *Lidové noviny*, 11 August 1940; quoted in Vogel, *Leoš Janáček*, p. 336: ' "A church," he told me, "is concentrated death. Tombs under the floor, bones on the altar, pictures full of torture and dying. Rituals, prayers, chants – death and nothing but death. I do not want to have anything to do with it." '
30. Both quotations are from Janáček's *feuilleton* 'Bez bubnů' [Without drums], *Lidové noviny*, 16 April 1911; cf. Racek (ed.), *Fejetony*, p. 17.

On the amount of instrumental music heard during the eighteenth and nineteenth centuries in Bohemian and Moravian parish churches, see John Tyrrell, *Czech Opera*, CUP, Cambridge, 1988, p. 214; even small churches often owned up to twenty instruments – virtually a small classical orchestra. Maria Theresa's 1754 ban on trumpets and drums was often ignored, especially in the country.

31. For example, the first movement of Janáček's *Sinfonietta* is written for brass instruments and timpani only; timpani also feature prominently in the closing Intrada of the *Glagolitic Mass* and the outer movements of Janáček's tone poem *Taras Bulba*.

32. For Křížkovský, see notes 4, 16 and 17 above. For Klácel, see note 4 above.

For Sušil, see note 4 above. He described the characteristic 'clear softness' – 'molezza dura' – of the tonality in Moravian and Slavonic folk-songs in the 1832 preface to his *Moravské národní písně* (Moravian folk-songs), published in 1835 (pp. v–vi). Janáček later tested Sušil's thesis, noted the vagueness and weaknesses of its conception, and challenged some of Sušil's statements.

The father of genetics, J.G. Mendel (1822–81), was the abbot of Queen's Monastery.

Moravian-born František Palacký (1798–1876) was one of the most important Czech Revivalists; between 1848 and 1876 he published *Dějiny národu českého* [The history of the Czech nation].

Josef Dobrovský (1753–1829) was a Czech historian, linguist and lexicographer, and a Catholic priest.

33. See note 16 above.

34. See Helfert, *Leoš Janáček*, p. 49ff; the spa was Škrochovice, near the town of Opava.

35. See Janáček/Veselý, p. 21.

36. Consequently, the city was German in character; a paradox but a historical fact. Several Czech suburbs merged with Brno in 1920, but even then a third of the city's population was German.

37. From Janáček's *feuilleton* 'Moje město' [My town], *Lidové noviny*, 24 December 1927; see Racek (ed.), *Fejetony*, p. 51.

38. See Zemanová (ed.), *Janáček's Uncollected Essays*, p. 121.

39. See Janáček/Veselý, pp. 22ff.; also Bohumír Štědroň, *Leoš Janáček. Vzpomínky, dokumenty, korespondence a studie* [Leoš Janáček. Reminiscences, papers, correspondence and studies], Editio Supraphon, Prague, 1986, p. 14.

40. Ibid.

41. See Helfert, *Leoš Janáček*, p. 54; Vogel, *Leoš Janáček*, p. 42, footnote **: Helfert believed that Janáček must have confused *Le prophète* with *L'africaine*, as the former was first performed in Brno before Janáček was born. However, there is no children's chorus in *L'africaine*. In his copy of the libretto of *Le prophète*, Janáček described the music of this opera as 'dramatic, full of effective passages in the orchestra and fascinating islands, which are like glowing light'. Cf. Vogel, *Leoš Janáček*, p. 20.

42. The city's Czechs and Germans held joint concerts until the 1860s. Before the opening of the Provisional Czech National Theatre in 1884 there were only occasional performances of operas in Czech in Brno; beween 1874 and

1884 some were given at the Beseda House, the centre of Czech community's social life. Cf. Tyrrell, *Czech Opera*, p. 57.

43. From a reminiscence included in Janáček's article 'Pavla Křížkovského význam v lidové hudbě moravské a v české hudbě vůbec' [The importance of Pavel Křížkovský in Moravian folk music and in Czech music in general], in the journal *Český lid* [The Czech nation], xi, 1902, pp. 257–63. Abridged reprint in Štědroň (ed.), *Leoš Janáček. Vzpomínky*, pp. 16–7.

44. This school was founded by the patriotic Matice school society of Brno, itself founded in 1878. The society also supported a private Czech primary school which had to be closed down in 1889 for lack of funds. See also note 4 above.

45. Latin remained the administrative language throughout the Empire until 1784.

46. From Janáček's *feuilleton* ' Pro pár jablek' [For a few apples], *Lidové noviny*, 4 September 1927; cf. Racek (ed.), *Fejetony*, p. 48.

47. Jiří Janáček (1815–66).

48. 'They took pride in him and believed that he would be famous one day,' recalled Janáček's maidservant Marie Stejskalová. See Marie Trkanová, *U Janáčků: podle vyprávění Marie Stejskalové* [At the Janáčeks: after the account of Marie Stejskalová], Panton, Prague, 1959, 2/1964, p. 30.

    Janáček's siblings were: Viktorie (1838–?), Eleonora (1840–1919), Josefa Adolfina (1842–1931); Karel (1844–1919), Bedřich (1846–1918), twins b. 1849 (one was stillborn; the other, František, died soon after), Rosalie (1850–?), Jiří (b. 1852, died in infancy), František (1856–1949), Josef (1858–1941), Adolf (b. 1861, died in infancy) and Marie (b. 1863, died in infancy).

49. Amalie Janáčková, nee Grulichouvá (1819–84); Eleonora Janáčková lived in Švábenice, in the district of Haná, central Moravia.

50. From Janáček's *feuilleton* 'Berlin', *Lidové noviny*, 15 May 1924: see Zemanová (ed.), *Janáček's Uncollected Essays*, pp. 220–1.

51. Janáček's uncle Jan (1810–89) was a priest in Blažice (later Znorovy); cf. Helfert, *Leoš Janáček*, p. 67.

52. Letter dated 26 May 1869; cf. *Leoš Janáček. Dopisy strýci. Dopisy matky* [Leoš Janáček. Letters to his uncle. Letters from his mother], ed. Svatava Přibáňová, Opus Musicum, Brno, 1985, pp. 80–1.

53. A reminiscence by Janáček's fellow chorister at the foundation, František Neumann, included in the Neumann family memoirs by his nephew, P.A.A. Neumann; under the title 'Fundatista ze Starého Brna' [The fundatista from the Old Brno], *Lidové noviny*, 12 March 1941. Abridged reprint in Štědroň (ed.), *Leoš Janáček. Vzpomínky*, p. 15.

    Sokol hat: a cap resembling the Scottish glengarry; part of the uniform worn by members of the Czech Sokol gymnastic organization (modelled on the German Turnverein founded earlier in the century).

54. See Janáček's letter of 14 August 1869, in Přibáňová (ed.), *Leoš Janáček*, p. 84.

55. Cf. P.A.A. Neumann, in Štědroň, *Leoš Janáček. Vzpomínky*, p. 15.

56. Ibid.

57. Studies there were also conducted in German, as the Institute did not come under Czech management until 1871.

58. W.M. Wundt (1832–1920), *Grundzüge der physiologischen Psychologie* (3 vols, 1874), and *Völkerpsychologie* (10 vols, 1900–20).
59. Mucha's first meeting with Janáček was described by his son, the Czech writer Jiří Mucha: 'Křížkovský, a dignified figure in a priest's habit . . . took the candidate [Alfons Mucha] to the piano and gave him a long test in intonation and harmony. He was clearly happy with the result, but when he wanted to offer the boy the only remaining place, an 18-year-old youth came in. "I have just taken on a new *fundatista*," he announced to Křížkovský who stopped in his tracks: "And I have just found such a good alto." He turned to the father and son who stood, disappointed, in the middle of the room: "This is my new deputy, the *regenschori* Leoš Janáček."' See Jiří Mucha, *Alfons Mucha*, Prague, 1982, pp. 18–19. Alfons Mucha left Brno in 1877, for Vienna and Paris; he and Janáček were not to meet again until after Mucha's return to Bohemia in 1910.
60. From a reminiscence included in Janáček's article cited in note 43 above.
61. See *Moravská orlice*, 11 December 1875; reprinted in Štědroň (ed.), *Leoš Janáček. Vzpomínky*, pp. 36–7. Janáček was elected choirmaster of Svatopluk on 13 February 1873, and conducted it until September 1874, when he left to study at the Prague Organ School.
62. *Dalibor*, 1 August 1873, p. 255; quoted in Štědroň (ed.), *Leoš Janáček. Vzpomínky*, p. 36.
63. Emilian Schulz (1836–1923), the director of the Brno Imperial and Royal Teachers' Training Institute and Janáček's future father-in-law.

Chapter 2: Prague and abroad

1. 'In the year 1874', see *Janáček's Uncollected Essays on Music*, selected, ed. and trans. Mirka Zemanová, Marion Boyars Publishers, London, 1989/1993, p. 103.
2. A man's long tunic.
3. See Stanley Buchholz Kimball, *Czech Nationalism: a Study of the National Theatre Movement, 1845–83*; Urbana, Illinois, 1966, p. 81.
4. The Rudolfinum, home of the Czech Philharmonic Orchestra, now houses two concert halls. Between 1919 and 1939 it was the seat of Czechoslovakia's interwar parliament.
5. František Skuherský (1830–92), Czech composer, theoretician and pedagogue; among his pupils were dozens of Czech composers, performers and teachers.
6. Robert von Zimmerman (1824–98). His *Allgemeine Aesthetik der Formwissenschaft* was published in 1865. Janáček also immersed himself in the study of *Allgemeine Aesthetik* (1875) by the Czech philosopher and theorist Josef Durdík (1837–1902).
7. Modal, from modes, also known as 'church modes', a system of scales which became established in the Middle Ages and was still accepted up to the 16th century. Derived from the modal system based on the Pythagorean scale, which was used by the ancient Greeks. Modes are easily identified by reference to the white notes on a piano keyboard; from the 17th century onwards,

two of the modes, Ionian and Aeolian, became known as the major and minor scales.

8. 12 April 1879; German original in Vladimír Helfert, *Leoš Janáček*, i, Oldřich Pazdírek, Brno, 1939, p. 110. Jan Ludevít Lukes (1824–1906), a popular Czech opera singer often engaged by Smetana; founder, director and chorus master of Hlahol, the largest Czech choral society (1861).
9. See *Leoš Janáček. Pohled do života a díla* [Leoš Janáček. A view of the life and works], ed. Adolf Veselý, Fr. Borový, Prague, 1924, p. 32. [Janáček/Veselý]
10. See 'In the year 1874' in Zemanová (ed.), *Janáček's Uncollected Essays*, p. 104. The concert probably took place on 4 April 1875; *Vltava* was premièred.
11. Ibid., p. 104.
12. Writing to his future wife Zdenka Schulz from Vienna, 14 April 1880; see *'Intime Briefe' 1879–80 aus Leipzig und Wien* ['Intimate Letters' 1879–80 from Leipzig and Vienna], ed. Jakob Knaus, Leoš Janáček-Gesellschaft, Zurich, 1985, p. 210.
13. The Neruda Quartet was active between 1859 and 1864. Only Amalie Wickenhauser, née Neruda (1834–90), settled in Brno; her brother and sisters lived largely abroad. Wilma Norman-Neruda (1839–1911) married first the Swedish composer L. Norman, then in 1888 the German pianist and conductor) Charles (later Lord) Hallé; she later gave regular concerts in London, and enjoyed an exceptional status in the turn-of-the-century English society. Marie Arlberg, née Neruda (1840–1922); František Neruda (1843–1915) was from 1864 active largely in Copenhagen.
14. See Vojtěch Kyas, 'Janáček se neměl o koho opřít?' [Janáček had no one to lean on?], *OM*, Brno, 1993, No. 2, p. 34; the Grieg sonata was performed on 13 January 1878.
15. Amalie Wickenhauser performed Rubinstein in Brno as early as 1855 (sonatas for violin and piano, op. 19, nos. 1 and 2), and the piano part of his Trio, op. 15, no. 1 in 1859; Janáček performed this part on 6 January 1878. At the Beseda, Amalie performed the first movement of Rubinstein's Piano Concerto no. 3 on 13 May 1876, and for the second time on 28 October 1877, when Rubinstein's Fantasia for Two Pianos was also on the programme. Cf. Kyas, 'Janáček', p. 35.
16. Mendelssohn on 28 October 1877 (Amalie Wickenhauser performed this concerto in Brno for the first time in 1851), and Saint-Saëns on 15 December 1878. It was highly unusual for a German conductor active in Brno, such as Ernst Wickenhauser, to perform at the city's Czech society. Cf. ibid., p. 37.
17. Ibid.
18. According to a review in *Dalibor*, 10 April 1879; quoted in Jaroslav Vogel, *Leoš Janáček*, Orbis Publishing, London, 1981, p. 60.
19. See a review of the concert on 13 January 1878, in *Moravská orlice*, 20 January 1989; cf. Kyas, 'Janáček', p. 39.
20. Kyas, 'Janáček', p. 34.
21. Cf. Vogel, *Leoš Janáček*, p. 78.
22. See Kyas, 'Janáček', p. 38.
23. For Janáček's adverse comments about Amalie Wickenhauser, see his letters to Zdenka dated 9, 14 and 31 October 1879; 1, 9 and 12 November 1879; 9 and 25 January 1880; 15 February 1880. See Knaus (ed.), *'Intime Briefe'*,

pp. 37, 43, 69, 70, 82, 85; 140 and 148; 180–1. Cf. also Kyas, 'Janáček', pp. 40–1. After her rift with Janáček Amalie Wickenhauser and some of her siblings performed only at the concerts of German music societies in Brno.

24. In 1880, Dvořák conducted his *Second Slavonic Rhapsody* and his Symphony in F major [no. 3] at the Beseda. His *Stabat Mater* and *Spectre's Bride* were performed there in 1882 and 1888 respectively, Symphony in D major [no. 1] in 1883, Symphony in D minor [no. 2] and *Hymnus* in 1886, all under Janáček's baton. See also Janáček's article 'Dr Antonín Dvořák and Brno', *Lidové noviny*, 27 April 1906, in Zemanová (ed.), *Janáček's Uncollected Essays*, pp. 180–2.

25. Cf. Vogel, *Leoš Janáček*, p. 62–3.

26. 15 December 1878; cf. ibid., p. 64.

27. See Janáček/Veselý, p. 41.

28. 'I was assigned to the first basses', recalled Janáček in 1927; see his reminiscence of Beethoven's *Missa Solemnis* in Zemanová (ed.), *Janáček's Uncollected Essays*, p. 193. Choral singing was taught in Leipzig by Professors Reinecke and Klesse; Janáček was happy with neither, and considered the level of choral singing in Brno much higher. Cf. his letters to Zdenka dated 9 and 16 October 1879 (Knaus (ed.), *'Intime Briefe'*, pp. 38 and 47).

29. See Janáček's *feuilleton* 'Moje děvče z Tater' [My girl from the Tatras], in *Fejetony z Lidových novin* [*Feuilletons* from *Lidové noviny*], ed. Jan Racek, Krajské nakladatelství, Brno, 1958, p. 46.

30. See Marie Trkanová, *Paměti: Zdenka Janáčková – můj život* [Memoirs: Zdenka Janáčková – my life], Šimon Ryšavý [Publishers], Brno, 1998, p. 22. [Trkanová/Janáčková]

31. Ibid., p. 18.

32. Ibid., p. 20.

33. Ibid., p. 22.

34. Ibid.

35. Ibid., p. 23.

36. Ibid.

37. Ibid.

38. Ibid., p. 34.

39. Letter dated 29 January 1880; see Knaus (ed.), *'Intime Briefe'*, p. 156.

40. Letters dated 7 and 15 November 1879 (ibid., pp. 80 and 89).

41. Letter dated 16 October 1879 (ibid., p. 47).

42. Letter dated 20 October 1879 (ibid., p. 52).

43. See Trkanová/Janáčková, p. 25.

44. Letter dated 31 October 1879, see Knaus (ed.), *'Intime Briefe'*, p. 69.

45. Letter dated 25 November 1879 (ibid., p. 103).

46. Lilli Lehmann (1848–1929); see letter dated 15 October 1879. Janáček's idol at the time, the composer and pianist Anton Rubinstein (1829–94), was present (ibid., p. 45).

47. Letter dated 29 October 1879 (ibid., p. 65).

48. Clara Schumann (1819–96); see letter 12 November 1879 (ibid., p. 85).

49. Arthur Nikisch (1855–1922); see Janáček's note in his diary and a letter dated 11 February 1880 (ibid., p. 174). See also footnote 352.

50. Letters dated 23 October, 20 and 22 November 1879 (ibid., pp. 96 and 99).

Further comments in letters dated 15, 19, 21 and 25 November (ibid., pp. 89, 95, 99 and 102).

51. Letters dated 25 October and 14 November 1879 (ibid., pp. 60 and 88).
52. Letter dated 29 November 1879 (ibid., p. 108).
53. Letter dated 16 October 1879 (ibid., p. 46).
54. Ibid.
55. Letter dated 30 January 1880 (ibid., p. 157).
56. Letter dated 29 January 1880 (ibid., p. 153).
57. Letter dated 1 April 1880 (ibid., p. 197).
58. Letter dated 6 April 1880 (ibid., p. 202).
59. Letter dated 3 April 1880, also 7 April 1880 (ibid., pp. 199 and 203; Knaus gives an erroneous date of 6 April).
60. Letter dated 5 April 1880 (ibid., p. 200).
61. Letters dated 4 April and 1 June 1880 (ibid., pp. 210 and 241).
62. Letter dated 31 May 1880 (ibid., p. 238).
63. Letter dated 6 October 1879, from Leipzig (ibid., p. 33).
64. Janáček rediscovered Moravian folk-song during trips to his native region in 1885 and 1888. See Chapter 4 of the present volume, pp. 60–2, 67, 69 and 70.

Chapter 3: Back in Brno

1. Letter dated 29 November 1879, see 'Intime Briefe' 1879–80 aus Leipzig und Wien ['Intimate Letters' 1879–80 from Leipzig and Vienna], ed. Jakob Knaus, Leoš Janáček-Gesellschaft, Zurich, 1985, p. 100.
2. It was a legal requirement for such schools to be run by corporations; the first general meeting of the Society for the Promotion of Church Music took place on 23 November 1881; Janáček was elected director of the new school at the first board meeting, 7 December 1881. Cf. Jaroslav Vogel, Leoš Janáček, Orbis Publishing, London, 1981. p. 77.
3. Letter dated 12 April 1880, Knaus (ed.), 'Intime Briefe', p. 207.
4. No. 36 Hlinky, where he lived until his marriage.
5. No. 46 Měšťanská (now Křížová) Street.
6. Vilém Heš (later Hesch, 1860–1908), Czech bass. Début Brno 1880; Prague, National Theatre 1882–94; Hamburg 1894; Vienna 1896–1908; leading bass during Mahler's régime (1897–1907). One of the greatest Czech singers, he was distinguished in Czech, Mozart and Wagner repertory.
7. This review was published in Moravská Orlice, 12 October 1880.
8. See Marie Trkanová, Paměti: Zdenka Janáčková – můj život [Memoirs: Zdenka Janáčková – my life], Šimon Ryšavý [Publishers], Brno, 1998, pp. 34–5. [Trkanová/ Janáčková]
9. Ibid., p. 35; cf. also Marie Trkanová, U Janáčků: podle vyprávění Marie Stejskalové [At the Janáčeks: after the account of Marie Stejskalová], Panton, Prague, 1959, p. 28. [Trkanová/Stejskalová]

Berthold Žalud (1856–86) was Janáček's friend, admirer and colleague at the Teachers' Training Institute; he was also choirmaster of the Beseda Society and a composer.

10. See Trkanová/Janáčková, p. 27.
11. Ibid., p. 29.
12. Even before his engagement to Zdenka, Janáček set his wedding date for 5 November 1881. Cf. Zdenka's grandmother's letter dated 30 September 1879 to the Schulz family.(Knaus (ed.), *'Intime Briefe'*, p. 247.)
13. See Trkanová/Janáčková, p. 28–9. When Zdenka's mother expressed the wish for the ceremony to be conducted in German, Janáček took umbrage. Although Zdenka was on his side, he stopped seeing her, and they only became reconciled when she begged the family to agree to his wishes.
14. In Obříství, in the wine region of Mělník; despite his German surname, Schulz, Zdenka's paternal grandfather was Czech.
15. 12 August 1881. The Janáčeks were shown round by the baritone Josef Lev (1832–98), one of the most famous and most popular Czech singers.
16. See Trkanová/Janáčková, p. 31.
17. Ibid.
18. Ibid., p. 32.
19. Ibid.
20. See Janáček's letter to Kamila Stösslová, 11 April 1928, in *Hádanka života. (Dopisy Leoše Janáčka Kamile Stösslové* [The riddle of life. (Letters of Leoš Janáček to Kamila Stösslová)], ed. Svatava Přibáňová, Opus Musicum, Brno, 1990, p. 340.
21. See Trkanová/Janáčková, p. 33.
22. 84 Austrian Gulden a month. Although from 1811 until the First World War there were approximately ten Gulden to one pound sterling, it is difficult to give a modern equivalent of Janáček's salary. In *Czech Opera*, CUP, Cambridge, 1988, p. xv, John Tyrrell offers some useful comparisons: in the 1890s, the Czech composer J.B. Foerster became the critic of a daily newspaper at 25 Austrian Gulden a month, rising to 50 Austrian Gulden after two years. Books and scores were expensive.
23. From an article by Josef Černík, 'Vzpomínání na Leoše Janáčka' [Remembering Leoš Janáček], *Lidové noviny*, 12 August 1933; abridged reprint in *Leoš Janáček. Vzpomínky, dokumenty, korespondence a studie* [Leoš Janáček. Reminiscences, papers, correspondence and studies], ed. Bohumír Štědroň, Editio Supraphon, Prague, 1986, p. 23.
24. From an article by Vladimír Sís, 'Pan profesor *Leoš Janáček*' [Professor Leoš Janáček], *Národní listy*, 15 August 1940; abridged reprint in Štědroň (ed.), *Leoš Janáček. Vzpomínky*, p. 25.
25. Alois Mrštík (1861–1925), Czech writer; with his brother Vilém (1863–1912) he wrote the play *Maryša*, which Janáček considered for an opera libretto in July 1908; in 1909 he approached the brothers for a libretto for *The Excursions of Mr Brouček* but they refused. Alois studied with Janáček at the Teachers' Training Institute, and sang under him at the Beseda. Cf. Alois Mrštík's reminiscence 'Chodníčkem života' [On the path of life], Sebrané spisy bratří Mrštíků [Collected writings of the brothers Mrštík], vol. 14, J. Otto, Prague, 1916, p. 260.
26. Janáček considered psychology to be of great importance for future composers.
27. During Janáček's directorship the school moved several times.

28. At the end of his directorship, in 1919, the school became the Brno Conservatoire of Music. Cf. pp. 157–9 of this volume.
29. The school's annual report, 1905; BmJA.
30. Jan Kunc, 'Leoš Janáček', *Hudební revue* [Musical review] iv, 1911, pp. 186–7; cf. Štědroň (ed.), *Leoš Janáček. Vzpomínky*, p. 49.
31. In Švábenice, central Moravia.
32. Letter No. 2 [December 1881], in *Leoš Janáček. Dopisy strýci. Dopisy matky* [Leoš Janáček. Letters to his uncle. Letters from his mother], ed. Svatava Přibáňová, Opus Musicum, Brno, 1985, p. 89.
33. Letter No. 3, March 1882 (ibid., p. 89). The reasons for her rift with Eleonora are unclear.
34. Zdenka's allowance amounted to 25 Austrian Gulden, and her parents also paid for the Janáčeks' fuel. Cf. Trkanová/Janáčková, p. 35.
35. Ibid.
36. Ibid., p. 36.
37. Ibid.
38. Ibid. Already in Leipzig, Janáček admitted to Zdenka (writing on 15 October 1879) that he 'lacked emotional delicacy'. Cf. Knaus, (ed.), *'Intime Briefe'*, p. 46.
39. Trkanová/Janáčková, p. 37.
40. No. 2, on the corner of Klášterní Street and Klášterní Square (now Mendlovo [Mendel] Square).
41. Trkanová/Janáčková, p. 38.
42. Ibid., p. 39.
43. Ibid.
44. Ibid.
45. The mediator was Father Anselm Rambousek, a Catholic priest and a friend of the Janáčeks; after hearing Zdenka's account of the marriage, he advised her to stay with her parents (ibid., p. 40).
46. Letter No. 8 [December 1882], cf. Přibáňová (ed.), *Leoš Janáček*, p. 91.
47. Schulz enclosed with his letter of 16 February 1883 an undated list of Janáček's misdeeds, written in Czech. See Bohumír Štědroň, 'Leoš Janáček na učitelském ústavě' [Leoš Janáček at the Teachers' Training Institute], *Rytmus*, xi, No. 9–10, p. 142.
48 In his letter of defence, dated 18 April 1883 (ibid., pp. 142–3), Janáček mentions that Schulz used to call him 'the rudest possible names'; on 2 March, Schulz 'tried to strangle me with such an awful passion that I was in [real] danger'. The police had to be present for the rest of Schulz's visit. In her account of this incident, Zdenka does not mention the police. See Trkanová/Janáčková, p. 40.
49. 22 June 1880; Arnošt Förchtgott-Tovačovský (1825–74) and Antonín Javůrek (1834–87) were active participants in the musical life of Brno.
50. Until his death from tuberculosis in 1886.
51. See this volume, p. 272, n. 24.
52. Cf. Bohumír Štědroň, 'Dvořák a Janáček'[Dvořák and Janáček], *Musikologie*, v, 1958. In fact, Janáček's promotion of Dvořák in Brno made possible the popularization of his music throughout Moravia. Janáček's articles, his analyses of Dvořák's compositions (especially of his four symphonic poems *The Water Goblin*, *The Noon Witch*, *The Golden Spinning-Wheel* and *The Wood*

Dove, published in 1897–8), and his arrangements of some of Dvořák's works further disseminated knowledge of Dvořák's music in the region.

53. As a young man, Janáček dreamt of one style of music common to all the Slavs, rather than specific Czech, Russian, Polish (etc.) music. He also suggested that a dictionary of Dvořák's motifs should be published. Cf. Vogel, *Leoš Janáček*, p. 21.

54. 'Dr Antonín Dvořák and Brno', in Zemanová (ed.), *Janáček's Uncollected Essays*, p. 181. Dvořák, a viola player by training, became a member of the orchestra of the National Theatre, Prague, at the age of 21.

55. From Dvořák's country house in Vysoká to Prachatice, Husinec (the birthplace of the Czech religious reformer Jan Hus), Strakonice, Orlík, Písek, Karlův Týn and the Říp Mountain (where the forefathers of the nation had decided, on their arrival, to announce that the Czech nation was to settle in the surrounding lands). They also stopped in Dvořák's birthplace, Nelahozeves.

   For their correspondence, see Artuš Rektorys, 'Dopisy A. Dvořáka L. Janáčkovi' [Antonín Dvořák's letters to Leoš Janáček], *České slovo*, 7 February 1933.

56. See 'Looking back at Antonín Dvořák' (*Hudební revue*, 1911, p. 432), in Zemanová (ed.), *Janáček's Uncollected Essays*, p. 186.

57. Vladimír Helfert reports that Janáček may have heard Smetana play one of Chopin's Nocturnes, op. 37 (G minor or G major, 1840) on 16 April 1873, at one of the concerts at the Beseda. See Vladimír Helfert, *Leoš Janáček*, i, Oldřich Pazdírek, Brno, 1939, p. 101, and Jan Racek, 'Leoš Janáček o skladebné struktuře klavírních děl Fryderyka Chopina' [Leoš Janáček about the structure of Frédéric Chopin's piano works], Sborník prací filosofické fakulty brněnské university, ix, Brno, 1960, p. 7.

58. According to Zdenka, Janáček was capable of practising for up to ten hours. Cf. Trkanová/Janáčková, pp. 33–4. But, as Helfert reports, Janáček's hands hampered his progress: 'Too small a span, chubby fist, thick fingers – all of that needn't have been an obstacle when playing an organ, but on a piano it was a real hindrance which, by practising, could only be subdued to a degree.' See Helfert, *Leoš Janáček*, p. 162.

59. Trkanová/Janáčková, p. 34.

60. He proposed the founding of the Beseda school in 1877, and resigned his directorship in 1890. This followed an incident in 1889 which profoundly hurt Janáček: having resigned his post of choirmaster at the Beseda, he was nevertheless willing to prepare and conduct a performance of Dvořák's oratorio *Sv. Ludmila*. Instead, the board decided to accept a later offer made by the then choirmaster, the operatic tenor Josef Kompit. See Vogel, *Leoš Janáček*, p. 79.

61. For an extra fee of 200 Austrian Gulden, see ibid.

62. Karel Hamák, 'Janáček, pán kůru' [Janáček, the lord of the musicians' gallery], *Lidové noviny* (afternoon edition), 12 August 1938; abridged reprint in Štědroň (ed.), *Leoš Janáček. Vzpomínky*, p. 35.

63. Karel Sázavský, 'Několik drobtů k životu a činnosti Janáčkově' [A few snippets regarding Janáček's life and activities], *Hudební rozhledy*, i, 1924/5, p. 36 (abridged reprint in Štědroň (ed.), *Leoš Janáček. Vzpomínky*, p. 38); also his *Dějiny Filharmonického spolku Beseda brněnská 1860–1900* [The history of the Brno, Beseda Philharmonic Society 1860–1900], Brno, 1900, p. 75ff.

64. František Mareš, 'K sedmdesátinám Leoše Janáčka' [For Leoš Janáček's 70th birthday], *Hudební rozhledy*, i, 1924–5, p.32ff.; abridged reprint in Štědroň (ed.), *Leoš Janáček. Vzpomínky*, p. 37–8.

65. Cf. Mareš, 'K sedmdesátinám', and Štědroň (ed.), *Leoš Janáček. Vzpomínky*, p. 38.

66. From a letter written in 1945 by Pavel Dědeček (1885–1954), then professor of conducting at the Prague Conservatoire, to Bohumír Štědroň. Dědeček taught under Janáček's directorship at the Organ School in Brno (1908–12), while also working as concert master, then conductor, at the Brno National Theatre (1912–14); see Štědroň (ed.), *Leoš Janáček. Vzpomínky*, pp. 40–1.

67. Ibid. Similarly, the conductor Karel Kovařovic had a high opinion of Janáček's abilities as a conductor; see his review of the concert Janáček gave on 10 January 1886 (*Hudební listy*, 15 January 1886; on the programme were, among other works, Dvořák's *Hymnus* and his Symphony no. 7, D minor). Reprinted in Štědroň (ed.), *Leoš Janáček. Vzpomínky*, p. 40. The singer Marie Calma, who sang under Janáček's baton in 1909 (in Gounod's oratorium *Mors et vita*, 1884), also thought highly of his abilities as a conductor. Cf. *Korespondence Leoše Janáčka s Marií Calmou a MUDr Františkem Veselým* [*Leoš Janáček's* correspondence with Marie Calma and MUDr František Veselý], Janáčkův archiv viii, ed. Jan Racek and Artuš Rektorys, Orbis Publishing, Prague, 1951 [JA viii], pp. 19–20. For a detailed account of Janáček's activities as a choirmaster and conductor, see Helfert, *Leoš Janáček*, pp. 176–258.

68. Janáček paid 25 Austrian Gulden for Olga's maintenance; see Trkanová/Janáčková, pp. 40–1.

69. Ibid, p. 42.

70. Ibid.

71. Ibid., p. 43. However, he did not attend any of the performances there, as he boycotted all German enterprise in Brno until 1918.

72. Ibid. Zdenka stated that, according to contemporary law, Janáček would have been entitled to take Olga away at the age of 7.

73. Ibid. However, it took a long time to convince Emilian Schulz that Zdenka should return to Janáček.

74. At Gleichenberg; paid for both of them by the Schulzes (ibid., p. 43).

75. Letter No. 16, probably at the beginning of October 1884; cf. Přibáňová (ed.), *Leoš Janáček*, p. 95. Amalie Janáčková died on 16 November 1884.

76. In fact, Janáček avoided funerals almost as a rule; according to his maidservant Marie Stejskalová, he was well enough to attend his mother's funeral. Cf. Trkanová/Stejskalová, p. 74.

77. See Trkanová/Janáčková, p. 44. The Schulzes continued to give Zdenka her monthly and dress allowance, and paid for the Janáčeks' fuel and Zdenka's insurance.

78. See *Hudební listy*, 3 January 1885; Leoš Firkušný, *Janáček kritikem brněnské opery* [Janáček as a critic of the Brno Opera], Oldřich Pazdírek, Brno, 1935, p. 50.

79. See 'National Theatre in Brno', *Hudební listy*, No. 9, 24 February 1886, in Zemanová (ed.), *Janáček's Uncollected Essays*, p. 137.

80. Ibid., p. 138.

81. The German Stadttheater in Brno, capacity 1,185, was the first theatre in Central Europe with electric light.

82. See 'National Theatre in Brno', in Zemanová (ed.), *Janáček's Uncollected Essays*, pp. 138–9.
83. Ibid., p. 140.
84. See 'Antonín Dvořák and Brno; *The Bartered Bride* and *Carmen*', *Hudební listy*, No. 4, 1 December 1886, in Zemanová (ed.), *Janáček's Uncollected Essays*, p. 143.
85. Ibid.
86. See 'The Academy of Music in Prague', *Hudební listy*, iii, No. 6, 1 January 1887, in Zemanová (ed.), *Janáček's Uncollected Essays*, p. 146.
87. See '*Carmen*', *Moravské listy*, 24 January 1891, in Zemanová (ed.), *Janáček's Uncollected Essays*, p. 159.
88. See his review of '*Dalibor*', *Hudební listy*, No. 4, 1 February 1888, in Zemanová (ed.), *Janáček's Uncollected Essays*, pp. 155 and 154.
89. In his speech melodies, Janáček notated the speech of people from all walks of life, during all sorts of activities. For a more detailed description of speech melodies, see the present volume, pp. 75–6. Janáček gave five different dates for the beginning of his speech melody studies (1879, 1881, 1888, 1897 and 1901). Some of his notations date from 1885, but the first evidence of his systematic notation of speech melodies dates from 1897, when the score of his third opera, *Jenůfa*, already existed in fair copy (as stated in the programme leaflet for the première in Brno, 21 January 1904).
90. See '*Carmen* and *The Bridegrooms*', *Hudební listy*, No. 7, 15 January 1887, in Zemanová (ed.), *Janáček's Uncollected Essays*, p. 149. See also note 67 above, regarding Kovařovic's very favourable review of Janáček's concert in 1886.
91. This review is often cited as the reason why *Jenůfa* was rejected by the National Theatre in Prague in 1903.
92. *Hudební listy* ceased publication in 1888. Between 1890 and 1892 Janáček wrote for *Moravské listy*, and between 1893 and 1928 most often for the popular Brno daily *Lidové noviny*.
93. The manuscripts of these two compositions were discovered by Dr Vladimír Telec. They are in the hand of Josef Kozlík (1862–1924), a teacher in the small town of Bílovice nad Svitavou in Moravia, who studied under Janáček at the Teachers' Training Institute around 1880. Cf. Vogel, *Leoš Janáček*, p. 82.
94. Jaroslav Tichý, real name František Rypáček (1853–1917); professor at the first Czech gymnasium in Brno. Author of various patriotic and other poems, librettist of Janáček's second opera, *The Beginning of a Romance*. Janáček also set Tichý's poem 'Your Beautiful Eyes' in 1885, and in 1897 his poem *Jarní píseň* [Spring song]; see the present volume, p. 80.

    The tune of a song about inconstant love used in *O Love* also appeared in Janáček's earlier choral work, *The Fickleness of Love*; another version later appeared as no. 1 in his *Moravian Folk Poetry in Songs*, 2nd edn (1908).
95. Letter dated 13 September 1886; see Rektorys, 'Dopisy A. Dvořáka', note 55 above; cf. also Helfert, *Leoš Janáček*, p. 361.
96. Janáček sent Urbánek the choruses on 20 June 1885; for Urbánek's reply (24 August 1886), and the reaction the work evoked in Prague, see Helfert, *Leoš Janáček*, p. 360, fn. 1.
97. At that time, standard Czech choral repertoire consisted of works by Křížkovský, Dvořák, Bendl and a few by Smetana (ibid., p. 360).
98. Ibid.

99. Trkanová/Janáčková, p. 44.
100. Ibid., p. 45.
101. Janáček heard the overture to Cherubini's opera *Les abencérages, ou L'étendard de Grenade* (based on the same story) in Leipzig. Cf. Helfert, *Leoš Janáček*, p. 362, and Vogel, *Leoš Janáček*, p. 86.
102. Julius Zeyer (1841–1901), Czech poet and writer. His father was of French Alsatian descent, his mother German Jewish. Although Zeyer's mother tongue was German, he eventually wrote masterly Czech. His extensive foreign travels aroused his enthusiasm for foreign literature, travel and the mythical. *Šárka*, in the last category, was written possibly at Dvořák's request but after some three years of dithering the composer rejected it.

   The earliest source of the myth of the Czech warrior women is provided by Cosmas (+1125), dean of the Prague chapter, in his *Chronica Boemorum*. Some scholars suggest that his picturesque description was his own invention, based on his knowledge of the Amazons of Scythia and other warrior women. Similarly, the maidens' fortress is often thought to be another variant of a medieval myth known throughout Europe (Magdeburg in Germany, for example, translates as 'maiden castle').
103. Karel Sázavský (1858–1930), music critic and art correspondent; also wrote for Janáček's *Hudební listy*. *Česká Thalie* was a fortnightly review; *Šárka* was published there in 1887. Janáček probably started working on the libretto in February.
104. Helfert, *Leoš Janáček*, p. 364.
105. Ibid., p. 366.
106. The first and second versions of the opera were written in 1887–8; the third in 1918.
107. See Helfert, *Leoš Janáček*, p. 368.
108. Cf. ibid.
109. Ibid.
110. Ibid.
111. Ibid., p. 369.
112. Ibid.
113. Ibid.
114. Ibid., p. 370.
115. Ibid.
116. Ibid.
117. Amalie Janáčková died on 16 November, 1884.
118. See Helfert, *Leoš Janáček*, p. 371.
119. In particular, *Jenůfa, Osud, Káťa Kabanová, The Cunning Little Vixen*, and *The Makropulos Affair*.
120. Cf. Helfert, *Leoš Janáček*, p. 371.
121. Ibid., pp. 371–2.
122. Ibid., p. 372.
123. Ibid.
124. Ibid., p. 373.
125. Ibid., p. 374.
126. Ibid.
127. *Rusalka* was completed in 1900; premièred in Prague in 1901.

128. Cf. Helfert, *Leoš Janáček*, p. 373.
129. Ibid., p. 374.
130. Ibid., p. 373.
131. Ibid., p. 375.
132. Ibid.
133. Ibid., p. 376.
134. Ibid.
135. Some time before 6 August 1887, from Cukmantl (now Zlaté hory in the Jeseníky Mountains, northern Moravia), where Janáček was taking a cure (ibid., 376).
136. On a card dated 6 August 1887, Dvořák states that looking through the opera will require 'much time'. His next card, inviting Janáček to Prague, bears the postmark 25 October 1887. (Cf. ibid.) However, Vogel, *Leoš Janáček*, p. 88, reports that Dvořák 'had personally given [Janáček] his opinion on 29 September'.
137. See Helfert, *Leoš Janáček*, p. 376, and Vogel, *Leoš Janáček*, p. 88.
138. Letters dated 10 November and 17 November 1887; first quoted in Max Brod, *Leoš Janáček: život a dílo* [Leoš Janáček: life and work], HMUB, Prague, 1924, pp. 69–70.
139. See Janáček's handwritten note on Zeyer's letter of 10 November 1887; cf. Helfert, *Leoš Janáček*, p. 377, fn. 1.
140. 11 November 1925, at the National Theatre in Brno.
141. Trkanová/Janáčková, p. 45.
142. Ibid., pp. 45–6.
143. Ibid., p. 46.
144. However, the Schulzes wanted Janáček at least to provide board for the wet nurse. As Janáček gave Zdenka no money for extra food, she used to give the wet nurse her own lunch, pretending at the table that she had no appetite, and eating scraps in the kitchen on the sly (ibid.).
145. Ibid.
146. See Helfert, *Leoš Janáček*, p. 376.

Chapter 4: Return to sources

1. See Janáček's *feuilletons* 'My Lašsko' and 'At the Harabiš Inn', in *Fejetony z Lidových novin* [Feuilletons from *Lidové noviny*], ed. Jan Racek, Krajské nakladatelství, Brno, 1958, pp. 15 and 30.
2. Published in *Hlídka*, iii, 1886, p. 314ff. and iv, 1887, p. 43ff; reprinted in *Leoš Janáček. O lidové písní a lidové hudbě* [Leoš Janáček. On folk-song and folk music], ed. Jiří Vysloužil, SNKLHU, Prague, 1955, pp. 121–31. The Czech folk-song collector, painter and writer Ludvík Kuba (1863–1956) published between 1884 and 1929 15 volumes of songs from various Slavonic countries (altogether 1,426 songs).
3. For Sušil, see this volume, p. 265, n. 4; his *Moravské národní písně s nápěvy to textu vřaděnými* [Moravian folk-songs with tunes included in the text (2,361 texts and 2,091 tunes)] came out as a serial publication over a period of seven years.

   František Bartoš (1837–1906), Czech folklorist and linguist.

4. Three editions of *Kytice z národních písní moravských* [A bouquet of Moravian folk-songs], 1890 (rev. 3/1901) and 1892–1901 (2/1908, as *Moravská lidová poesie v písních* [Moravian folk poetry in songs]).

5. See the present volume, p. 270, n. 7.

6. See Vladimír Úlehla, *Živá píseň*, Prague, 1949, pp. 55 and 220; quoted in Jaroslav Vogel, *Leoš Janáček*, Orbis, London, 1981, p. 120.

7. 'Moravian' scale: a melodic minor scale, identical up as well as down, starting and ending on the dominant (e.g. E–F sharp–G sharp–A–B–C–D–E); cf. Vogel, *Leoš Janáček*, p. 115.

   'Moravian modulation': to the key one whole tone lower (favourite in minor keys). Cf. ibid., p. 114.

8. Cf. ibid., p. 94.

9. 17 November 1891; reprinted in *Leoš Janáček. Vzpomínky, dokumenty, korespondence a studie* [Leoš Janáček. Reminiscences, papers, correspondence and studies], ed. Bohumír Štědroň, Editio Supraphon, Prague, 1986, p. 73.

10. No. 30, 1889; abridged reprint in ibid., p. 71.

11. Czech dancer and choreographer (1861–1945); he worked in Sweden, Paris, Toulouse and Milan, and between 1883 and 1924 largely as a soloist at the National Theatre, Prague (where he performed over 1,800 times); also in St Petersburg, London, and New York (the Metropolitan Opera, 1923–32). He was ballet master at the Dresden Hofoper (1900–10) and in Warsaw (1910–12); he worked also as a choreographer in Vienna, Berlin and Milan (La Scala). He had an enormous influence on Czech ballet.

12. Cf. Vogel, *Leoš Janáček*, p. 96.

13. See Marie Trkanová, *U Janáčků: podle vyprávění Marie Stejskalové* [At the Janáčeks: after the account of Marie Stejskalová], Panton, Prague, 1959, p. 41. [Trkanová/Stejskalová]

14. Painted by a folk painter Anežka Uprková, wife of the painter Joža Uprka. Among other works rediscovered there was the song-cycle *The Diary of One who Disappeared*.

15. See Marie Trkanová, *Paměti: Zdenka Janáčková – můj život* [Memoirs: Zdenka Janáčková – my life], Šimon Ryšavý [Publishers], Brno, 1998, p. 51. [Trkanová/Janáčková]

16. Jan Herben (1857–1936), a distinguished folklorist and writer, a long-standing acquaintance of Janáček.

17. See *Moravské listy*, iii, 29 July 1891; abridged reprint in Štědroň (ed.), *Leoš Janáček. Vzpomínky*, pp. 74–5.

18. Magazine *Prague*, ed. by Jan Herben and published during the summer of 1891 on the occasion of the Jubilee Exhibition. Reprinted in Štědroň (ed.) *Leoš Janáček. Vzpomínky*, p. 75.

19. See this volume, p. 280, nn. 139 and 140.

20. See Theodora Straková, 'Setkání Leose Janáčka s Gabrielou Preissovou' [Janáček's encounter with Gabriela Preissová], *ČMM*, xliii, 1958, p. 147.

21. Ibid., p. 149, letter dated 6 February 1888. Janáček's letter has not survived.

22. Ibid. Janáček and Preissová probably met in January 1891, when Preissová lectured in Brno about her two plays.

23. Ibid., p. 150, letter dated 2 April 1891.

24. For Jaroslav Tichý (1853–1917), see the present volume, p. 278, n. 94.

25. See Straková, 'Setkání, Leoše Janáčka', p. 153. Preissová's undated letter to Julie Kusá-Fantová was probably written at the end of July 1891.
26. Ibid. According to a brief report in *Moravská orlice* on 12 January 1892, Janáček had submitted the opera to the National Theatre in Brno, clearly expecting that Šubert's opinion of the work will be favourable. However, submitting the work in Prague was not necessarily a roundabout route to having the work accepted in Brno. Cf. John Tyrrell, *Janáček's Operas: A Documentary Account*, Faber, London, 1992, p. 28.
27. For Preissová's letter dated 16 December 1891 (in which she promised to intervene), and her letter dated 25 March 1892, see Straková, 'Setkání Leoše Janáčka', pp. 153 and 154–5.
28. Ibid., p. 157, Šubert's letter of 2 May 1892 to Janáček.
29. Ibid., p. 154, letter dated 13 March 1892.
30. Ibid., p. 156–7, letter dated 5 September 1891.
31. Between 1886 and his death in 1928 Janáček contributed to some fourteen different periodicals. Cf. Nigel Simeone, John Tyrrell and Alena Němcová, *Janáček's Works: A Catalogue of the Music and Writings of Leoš Janáček*, Clarendon Press, Oxford, 1997. Cf. also *Janáček's Uncollected Essays on Music*, selected, ed. and trans. Mirka Zemanová, Marion Boyars Publishers, London, 1989/1993.
32. *Feuilleton*: part of newspaper devoted to fiction, criticism, light literature etc.
33. See 'Hudba pravdy [Music of the truth], *Lidové noviny*, 16 December, 1893, in *Fejetony z Lidových novin* [*Feuilletons* from *Lidové noviny*], ed. Jan Racek, Krajské nakladatelství, Brno, 1958, pp. 67–8.
34. Dulcimer, or cymbalom, a shallow closed box over which are strung wires. The wires are struck by two wooden hammers held in the player's hands. The instrument, popular in the nineteenth century, is still played in Moravia, Hungary and Romania.
35. By the Hudební matice publishing house in Prague.
36. See Straková, 'Setkání Leoše Janáčka', p. 158. Janáček's letter to Preissová has not survived.
37. Ibid., letter dated 6 November 1893.
38. Ibid., p. 162.
39. Ibid., p. 161, an abridged reprint of an article by Josef Merhaut in *Moravská orlice*, 10 February 1893.
40. See his review in *Moravská orlice*, 13 February 1894; reprinted in Štědroň (ed.), *Leoš Janáček. Vzpomínky*, pp. 58–9.
41. It was revived for the Janáček festival in 1954.
42. See *Leoš Janáček. Pohled do života a díla* [*Leoš Janáček*. A view of the life and works], ed. Adolf Veselý, Fr. Borový, Prague 1924, p. 93–4. [Janáček/Veselý]
43. Cf. also Leoš Firkušný, 'Janáčkova opera, jež nebude provedena v cyklu' [Janáček's opera which will not be performed during the cycle of his operas], *Divadelní ročenka*, Brno, 1938, pp. 21–5, and Vogel, *Leoš Janáček*, pp. 99–101.
44. This was also the only time Janáček conducted his own opera.
45. Lucie Bakešová (1853–1935), a Czech folklorist.
46. See Janáček's article in *Lidové noviny*, 20 June 1894; an abridged reprint is in Štědroň (ed.), *Leoš Janáček. Vzpomínky*, pp. 75–6.
47. Janáček began orchestration on 16 February 1895. We saw from his letter to Otakar Nebuška (11 February 1917) that he wrote *Jenůfa* into full score.

However, from a single page of an autograph which has survived it seems that at least some of the music was first written in a rough two-stave version. Cf. John Tyrrell's preface to the full score of *Jenůfa*, UE 30 145, pp. 1–2.

48. See the present volume, pp. 73–4.

Chapter 5: Crystallization of style

1. Situated in the large Stromovka Park (Prague 7), formerly a large royal park founded in the thirteenth century.

2. As his maidservant Marie Stejskalová recalled in her memoirs; see Marie Trkanová, *U Janáčků: podle vyprávění Marie Stejskalové* [At the Janáčeks: after the account of Marie Stejskalová], Panton, Prague, 1959, p. 46. [Trkanová/Stejskalová]

3. Alois Jirásek (1851–1930), famous Czech novelist, author of several acclaimed historical novels; Hana Kvapilová (1860–1907), a prominent Czech actress, from 1888 one of the leading members of the National Theatre, Prague.

4. The brass octet included three trumpets, three trombones and two tubas. *Lord, Have Mercy* [in the original, *Hospodine pomiluj ny*] is a tenth-century Czech trope; Janáček did not use the oldest known version of the tune, but one used by Dvořák in his oratorio *Sv. Ludmila*. Cf. Jaroslav Vogel, *Leoš Janáček*, Orbis Publishing, London, 1981, pp. 124–5.

5. Janáček's review of *The Queen of Spades* was published in *Lidové noviny*, 21 January 1896. English translation in *Janáček's Uncollected Essays on Music*, selected, ed. and trans. Mirka Zemanová, Marion Boyars Publishers, London, 1989/1993, p. 179.

6. There were three 'partitions' of Poland: in 1771, the country was split betweeen Prussia, Austria and Russia; in 1793, between Russia and Prussia; and in 1795, between Prussia, Austria and Russia. The modern Polish state was founded in 1918.

7. On 12 July 1896 (according to the Gregorian calendar), i.e. 25 July.

8. See Janáček's article 'A few words from a holiday journey', ii, *Lidové noviny*, 15 August 1896, in Zemanová (ed.), *Janáček's Uncollected Essays*, p. 208.

9. 'A few words from a holiday journey', i–iii, 2 August, 15 August and 8 September 1896, in Zemanová (ed.), *Janáček's Uncollected Essays*, pp. 203–15.

10. See Janáček's letter dated 2 June, 1928 to the Moravan Choral Society (which gave the work's première on 2 December 1900). Reprinted in *Leoš Janáček. Vzpomínky, dokumenty, korespondence a studie* [Leoš Janáček. Reminiscences, papers, correspondence and studies], ed. Bohumír Štědroň, Editio Supraphon, Prague, 1986, p. 60.

11. 'How ideas came about', written in 1897 but not published in Janáček's lifetime; in Zemanová (ed.), *Janáček's Uncollected Essays*, pp. 69–70.

12. Ibid., pp. 70 and 71.

13. 8 June 1897; reprinted in Štědroň (ed.), *Leoš Janáček. Vzpomínky*, p. 60. Vrchlický also wrote that, with his help, Janáček was awarded a grant of 200 Gulden from the Czech Academy.

14. These four essays were published under the title *České proudy hudební* [Trends in Czech music] in the Brno magazine *Hlídka: The Water Goblin*, vol. ii [xiv], 1897, pp. 285–92; *The Noon Witch*, pp. 454–9; *The Golden Spinning-Wheel*,

pp. 594–604; *The Wood Dove*, vol. iii [xv], 1898, pp. 277–82. Reprinted, with explanatory notes, in Bohumír Štědroň's study 'Antonín Dvořák a Leoš Janáček' [Dvořák and Janáček], *Musikologie*, v, Prague, 1958, pp. 324–59.

K.J. Erben (1811–70), Czech poet and folklorist. In his enormously popular collection of twelve ballads, *Kytice z pověstí národních* [A garland of national tales], published in 1853, Erben created a new national style inspired by Czech folk poetry.

15. *The Water Goblin*, see Štědroň, 'Antonín Dvořák a Leoš Janáček', p. 331. As Štědroň points out in fn. 26, Janáček's comment shows him as a follower of formal aesthetics.

16. Ibid., p. 332, and fn. 29. As Štědroň states, Janáček's quotation from A.W. Ambros's *Geschichte der Musik*, 1862–78, is not altogether clear. In his review of *The Queen of Spades* (in Zemanová (ed.), *Janáček's Uncollected Essays*, p. 179), Janáček commented in a similar vein: 'Is Tchaikovsky here the true composer of these numbers, a *phone*tician and not just a sym*phonist?*'

17. *The Golden Spinning-Wheel*, see Štědroň, 'Antonín Dvořák a Leoš Janáček', p. 340.

18. See Janáček's *feuilleton* 'Smetana's daughter', in Zemanová (ed.), *Janáček's Uncollected Essays*, pp. 55–56.

19. See Janáček's article 'Last year and this year', *Hlídka, xxii*, 1905, p. 106; reprinted in Štědroň (ed.), *Leoš Janáček. Vzpomínky*, p. 84.

20. An interview in a Prague literary fortnightly, *Literární svět* [The literary world], 8 March 1928; in Zemanová (ed.), *Janáček's Uncollected Essays*, p. 121.

21. However, as his wife remarked, in his personal life Janáček was 'a poor psychologist and a poor diplomat'. See Marie Trkanová, *Paměti: Zdenka Janáčková – můj život* [Memoirs: Zdenka Janáčková – my life], Šimon Ryšavý [Publishers], Brno, 1998, p. 47. [Trkanová/Janáčková]

22. For example, on 16 September 1921 Janáček heard in the speech of the first Czech president, T.G. Masaryk, the key of 'pure A flat minor'. See Janáček's *feuilleton* 'Rytá slova', *Lidové noviny*, 22 September 1921; reprinted in *Triptychon*, ed. Jan Racek, Hudební matice, Prague, 1948, pp. 13–8.

23. From Janáček's article 'Alžběta', in *Lidová čítanka moravská* [Moravian Popular Reader], Prague, 1910; abridged reprint in Štědroň (ed.), *Leoš Janáček. Vzpomínky*, p. 85.

24. For Wundt (1832–1920), see the present volume, p. 270, n. 58. On phonetics, Janáček read works by the Norwegian Slavist Olaf Broch and the founder of experimental phonetics P.-J. Rousselot; among Czech authors he read Josef Chlumský, Antonín Frinta and the founder of modern Czech philology, Jan Gebauer. Cf. Vogel, *Leoš Janáček*, p. 160.

25. It seems that, apart from some preliminary sketches in 1894–5, Act 2 was written between late 1901 and the early summer of 1902.

26. The owner of the house, Julie Kusá-Fantová (1858–1908), was a well-known patriot and supporter of women's movement. See Trkanová/Stejskalová, p. 24 and p. 139., n. 5.

27. Ibid., p. 27.

28. For those interested in Janáček's culinary likes and dislikes, he loved meat, especially braised beef, game and frogs legs with parsley sauce, but disliked spinach! (Ibid., pp. 32 and 41.)

29. Ibid., p. 33.
30. Ibid., p. 27.
31. Letter to Josefa [Pepunka or Pepuška] Jungová, 3 December 1897 (ibid., p. 146, n. 17.)
32. Ibid., pp. 47–8.
33. Jaroslav Tichý, real name František Rypáček (1853–1917), see the present volume, p. 278, n. 94.
34. March 1898; the name of this college was Vesna (= spring).
35. Now usually referred to as Bartoš iii.
36. Brief, nervy interruptions and ostinatos, and the tension between the tune and the background – which are among the most distinctive traits of Janáček's mature style – are typical of decoration played against the tune by the *kontráš* (the second fiddler) of a small Moravian village band. At the most basic level, such a band (known as *hudecká muzika*) would consist of just two fiddlers and a bagpiper (the *gajdoš*); a better band would include another fiddle or two, a double bass, a cymbalom and bagpipes (later replaced by clarinets). The leading fiddler (the *hudec* or *primáš*), would richly embellish the tune of the folk-song; the second fiddle (the *kontráš*) would create a type of dialogue with the leading melody (not always strictly within the underlying harmony), using contrary, parallel and other motions in the accompaniment. This type of playing stresses linear thinking rather than the vertical. The musicians had their own expressions for the various instrumental techniques, such as 'okořenit' (to spice up), 'zahustit' (to thicken), 'zatvrdit' (to hold down, for the bass line).

   This type of decoration is represented, for example, in the accompaniment to 'Everyone is getting married' in the Conscripts scene in *Jenůfa* (Act 1). Cf. Jan Trojan, *Moravská Lidová píseň: melodika, harmonika* [Moravian folk-song: melodic and harmonic aspects], Prague, 1980, pp. 12–13. Cf. also John Tyrrell, *Czech Opera*, CUP, Cambridge, 1988, pp. 248–9.
37. Cf. Bartoš ii, pp. xiii–xiv.
38. In some communities a fallen girl would have her hair cut short in public by the other village women. In villages near Brno a cradle would be carried mockingly behind the wedding procession; in Maršovice, near the town of Znojmo, the girl would be chased through the village by the local shepherd with a whip (cf. ibid., p. xxviii).
39. Ibid., p. cxxxii.
40. Cf. Jiří Vysloužil, *Leoš Janáček*, Společnost Leoše Janáčka, Brno, 1978, p. 12. 'Chromatic major minor' was Janáček's own term. Chromatic intervals are such as introduce notes not forming a part of the prevailing key. Ionian, Lydian (with a raised fourth) and Mixolydian (with a flattened seventh) modes are major in character, while Aeolian and Dorian are minor in character. Cf. also the present volume, p. 270, n. 7.
41. See Vogel, *Leoš Janáček*, p. 137; cf. also John Tyrrell's preface to the full score of the Brno version (1908), Universal Edition, 1996, p. iii.
42. See Trkanová/Janáčková, p. 60.
43. From Janáček's letters to Olga, written between the end of May and July 1902; excerpts reprinted in Štědroň (ed.), *Leoš Janáček. Vzpomínky*, p. 92.
44. See Trkanová/Janáčková, p. 68.

45. See Trkanová/Stejskalová, p. 61. 'Dear heart': in the original Czech, 'duša moja' [my soul] – a term of endearment Janáček often used.
46. See Janáček's letter to Dvořák's biographer Otakar Šourek, 7 March 1920; first published in Štědroň (ed.), *Janáček ve vzpomínkách*, 1946 abridged reprint also in Štědroň (ed.), *Leoš Janáček. Vzpomínky*, pp. 127–8. However, Josef Němec, director of the Vesna College in Brno, wrote in his memoirs that Olga asked for the original of *Jenůfa's* prayer from Act 2 to be placed in her coffin, and that Janáček sometimes talked about this at the meetings of the Russian Circle in Brno. See Trkanová/Stejskalová, p. 151, n. 61.
47. See Trkanová/Janáčková, p. 75.

Chapter 6: Successes and obstacles

1. See Janáček's *feuilleton* 'My Luhačovice', *Hlídka*, xx, 1903, pp. 836–44; reprinted in Bohumír Štědroň, 'Leoš Janáček a Luhačovice' [Leoš Janáček and Luhačovice], *Výroční zpráva Městské spořitelny v Luhačovicích za rok 1938* (1939).
2. 28 April, 1903; see Alena Němcová, 'Brněnská premiéra Její pastorkyně' [The Brno première of *Jenůfa*], *ČMM*, lix, 1974, p. 135.
3. See the English translation of this review in *Janáček's Uncollected Essays on Music*, selected, ed. and trans. Mirka Zemanová, Marion Boyars Publishers, London, 1989/1993, p. 149.
4. See Marie Trkanová, *Paměti: Zdenka Janáčková – můj život* [Memoirs: Zdenka Janáčková – my life], Šimon Ryšavý [Publishers], Brno, 1998, p. 77. [Trkanová/Janáčková]
5. 21 May, 1903. *Louise* opened at the National Theatre on 13 February 1903 (Charpentier attended a performance on 29 March 1903), and stayed in the repertory until 1911; there were 48 performances in total. In 1922, Janáček was still interested in this opera and asked his publisher, Universal Edition, to order the full score for him from Paris. However, as it has never been published, it could not have been obtained. Cf. Jan Racek's study 'Leoš Janáček a Praha [Leoš Janáček and Prague], *Musikologie*, iii, Prague, 1955, p. 21, n. 34.
6. Prose was, in fact, first used in opera by the French composer and critic Alfred Bruneau (1857–1934) in *Messidor* (1897), to a libretto by Emile Zola. A reference to Bruneau was made in the programme leaflet for the Brno première of *Jenůfa* (21 January, 1904); Janáček may have been the author of this leaflet.
7. The first copy of Janáček's libretto, which he wrote himself, was called *Fragments of a Novel from Life*; like Charpentier, he called the first version a *roman musical*. In addition, the milieu of *Louise*, and some of Charpentier's ideas (such as employing a large chorus of many individual characters) may have suggested to Janáček some of the possibilities he explored in *Osud*. Cf. Theodora Straková, 'Janáčkova opera *Osud*' [Janáček's opera *Osud*], *ČMM*, xli, 1956, pp. 209–60; xlii, 1957, pp. 133–64.
8. See *Leoš Janáček. Pohled do života a díla* [Leoš Janáček. A view of the life and works], ed. Adolf Veselý, Fr. Borový, Prague, 1924, p. 94 [Janáček/Veselý]. Janáček also referred to the 'musicality' of Mrs Urválková's voice; see his undated letter to her, written probably in October 1903 (Janáček Archive of

the Music Division of the Moravian Provincial Museum [BmJA], shelfmark A 6164).

9. *Ukvalská lidová poesie v písních*, 13 songs, published in Brno in 1899.
10. Ludvík Vítězslav Čelanský (1870–1931), Czech conductor and composer. He often worked in Poland, where he founded the Lwow Opera and the Lwow Philharmonic Orchestra (1900 and 1902 respectively); he was also director of the Cracow and Lódz Operas, and director of the Warsaw Philharmonic (1905–6). In 1901 he helped create the Czech Philharmonic Orchestra from the members of the National Theatre who went on strike. He also worked in Kiev and Paris. In 1907 he founded and directed a new opera house at the Vinohrady Theatre, Prague and returned there in 1913. He was chief conductor of the Czech Philharmonic Orchestra (1918–9); chief conductor of the Šak Philharmonic Orchestra, Prague (1920–1). He was a gifted conductor and organizer, but his abilities were never fully exploited. Apart from one opera, he wrote orchestral, choral and sacred music, Lieder and seven melodramas (among others, to text by Turgenev and E.A. Poe).
11. Čelanský's opera, written to his own libretto, was performed nine times between 1897 and 1899.
12. See Trkanová/Janáčková, pp. 78–9.
13. Letter dated 2 October 1903 (BmJA, shelfmark E 1134); abridged version in Straková, 'Janáčkova opera *Osud*', p. 211.
14. Ibid.
15. Ibid.
16. See Janáček/Veselý, p. 98.
17. Letter dated 9 October 1903 (BmJA, shelfmark A 6161). Cf. Bohumír Štědroň, 'K Janáčkově opeře *Osud* [Janáček's opera *Osud*], *Živá hudba*, i, 1959, pp. 159–83.
18. Fedora Bartošová (1884–1941) had only a scant literary career; for her libretto and the fair copy sent to Janáček see Straková, 'Janáčkova opera *Osud*', p. 133ff. For her correspondence with Janáček and her reminiscences, see John Tyrrell, *Janáček's Operas: A Documentary Account*, Faber, London, 1992, p. 114–28.
19. Undated letter, written after Christmas 1903 (BmJA, shelfmark A 6169).
20. BmJA, shelfmark A 6174; cf. Bohumír Štědroň, *Dílo Leoše Janáčka: abecední seznam Janáčkových skladeb a uprav* [Janáček's works: an alphabetical catalogue of Janáček's compositions and arrangements], *HR*, Prague, 1959, pp. 180–1. Janáček's letter is undated but it was probably written on 19 January, and certainly before 21 January 1904 (the date of the première of *Jenůfa*). Cf. Tyrrell, *Janáček's Operas*, p. 54. The première was performed with an orchestra of twenty-nine and later performances with even smaller forces.
21. Jan Kunc, *Vzpomínky na premiéru Její pastorkyně* [Reminiscences of the première of *Jenůfa*], *Divadelní list*, ix, Brno 1933/4, pp. 78–80. Abridged reprint in Štědroň, *Leoš Janáček. Vzpomínky*, p. 95.
22. Cf. Bohumír Štědroň, 'Janáček and Kunc', *Rytmus*, viii, 1942/3, p. 90ff., and Štědroň, *Leoš Janáček. Vzpomínky*, pp. 96–7.
23. Letter dated 19 January 1903 (BmJA, shelfmark E 1135).
24. Letter dated 28 January 1904 (BmJA, shelfmark A 6175). Cf. Štědroň, *Dílo Leoše Janáčka*, p. 182.
25. Letter dated 9 February 1904; see *Korespondence Leoše Janáčka s Karlem*

Kovařovicem a ředitelstvím Národního divadla [Janáček's correspondence with Karel Kovařovic and the directorate of the National Theatre], Janáčkův archiv vii, ed. Artuš Rektorys, Hudební matice, Prague, 1950 [JA vii], pp. 17–18.

26. See Janáček's letter of 31 July 1908 to Dr Jaroslav Elgart, an executive of the Brno Theatre; quoted in Vogel, *Leoš Janáček*, pp. 148–9. There were no flutes on the first night of *Jenůfa*, and many orchestral colours were missing throughout the run of the opera. As Hynek Kašlík reported, the wind instruments were supplemented by members of a military band, and the strings by amateurs. Cf. also Hynek Kašlík, 'Retuše Karla Kovařovice v Janáčkově opeře Její pastorkyně' [Karel Kovařovic's 'retouchings' in Janáček's opera *Jenůfa*], *Hudební věstník*, xxxi, 1938, pp. 112–13, 130–1, 142–3, 159–60; reprinted separately (Unie čes. hudebníků z povolání), Prague, 1938.

27. Undated letter (written between 15 April and 9 May 1904); see František Pala, 'Janáček a Národní divadlo' [Janáček and the National Theatre (in Prague)], *Hudební rozhledy*, vi, 1953, p. 886. Cf. also Tyrrell, *Janáček's Operas*, p. 60.

28. See Mahler's letter of 9 December 1904, in Štědroň (ed.), *Leoš Janáček. Vzpomínky*, p. 98. Mahler was interested in Czech music throughout his life, and had lifelong friends among Czech singers and composers. The soprano Berta Lautererová (1869–1936), who was for several years a member of his ensemble in Hamburg and later, at his request, at the Vienna Hofoper, was the wife of the Czech composer and critic J.B. Foerster (1859–1951). Mahler was also acquainted with the renowned Czech bass Vilém Heš (1860–1908), the great Czech soprano Emmy Destinn (1878–1930) and others.

29. See Janáček's article 'Moje wspomnienia o Polsce' [My reminiscences of Poland], in the Polish magazine *Muzyka*, iii/5, May 1926, pp. 201–2. See also Vogel, *Leoš Janáček*, p. 150.

30. See Janáček's handwritten note on the commemorative programme brochure for Dvořák's 60th birthday (Umělecká Beseda, Prague, 1901). First quoted in Racek 'Leoš Janáček', p. 48.

31. See 'Looking back at Antonín Dvořák', *Hudební revue*, 1911, in Zemanová (ed.), *Janáček's Uncollected Essays*, p. 187.

32. Letter dated 25 January 1904 (BmJA, shelfmark E 1136).

33. František Mareš, 'K sedmdesátinám Leoše Janáčka' [For Leoš Janáček's seventieth birthday], *Hudební rozhledy*, i, 1924/5, p. 32ff. Reprinted in Štědroň (ed.), *Leoš Janáček. Vzpomínky*, p. 97.

34. In fact, František Pavlík was wounded on 2 October 1905, as the army cleared the building of the Beseda Society (the popular meeting place of the Czech community in Brno).

35. See Vogel, *Leoš Janáček*, p. 185.

36. Janáček probably visited this asylum (Mährische Landes-Irrenanstalt) in 1905–6. In an undated letter to an unknown doctor, which was found in Janáček's correspondence, the composer also requested to be permitted to listen to the female patients at the Prague mental asylum (BmJA, shelfmark A 3319); as is clear from a postcard to his wife, sent probably in December 1907, this visit did take place. Cf. Tyrrell, *Janáček's Operas*, p. 129.

37. Cf. Vogel, *Leoš Janáček*, p. 172: '. . . Janáček no doubt expressed [through Živný] many of his own thoughts: Živný's confessions about his work – in Act II to his wife, and especially in Act III to his pupils – are most moving.'

38. See John Tyrrell, *Czech Opera*, CUP, Cambridge, 1988, p. 124. Although a printed libretto was available, the score remained unpublished. Not only the names of protagonists (Míla and the conductor Lenský) refer to real-life characters. The painter Lhotský was thought to be a reference to Janáček's contemporary, the painter Jóža Uprka. Cf. Straková, 'Janáčkova opera *Osud*' (1957), pp. 136 and 144.

39. See the acclaimed 1990 recording of this opera by EMI, with the libretto translated by Rodney Blumer (1985).

40. Especially since the cause of the mother's madness is never made clear, although her pathological avarice and Janáček's portrayal of the conflict from the social point of view are contemplated in Straková, 'Janáčkova opera *Osud*' (1957), p. 135.

41. Janáček's comments written on Bartošová's letter; cf. Straková, 'Janáčkova opera *Osud*' (1956), p. 216. Cf. also Tyrrell, *Janáček's Operas*, p. 123.

42. Initially, he asked Bartošová (letter dated 12 November 1903) for the type of verse 'which Pushkin uses in *Onegin*'; her rhyme schemes were often quite complicated. Cf. BmJA, shelfmark A 5797, and Tyrrell, *Janáček's Operas*, p. 116.

43. Michael Ewans, *Janáček's Tragic Operas*, Faber, London, 1977, pp. 72–4. According to Jan Kunc, Janáček 'carried out successfully in music what [the Czech painter] Antonín Slavíček depicted in painting – the mood, at a health resort, of scorching sun beating down in a deluge of light'. See *Hudební revue*, iv, 1911, No. 3, p. 133, quoted in Vogel, *Leoš Janáček*, p. 173.

44. Act 1, Scene 9, 'Ty zlaté naše sluníčko' ['You golden little sun of ours'].

45. In Act 1, for example, the motif of the sun appears after the departure of the day-trippers, at the beginning of Živný's and Míla's monologues, and as her mother hears of her daughter's departure; it can also be heard in the glockenspiel as a student tries to steal a kiss from a young girl. In Act 2, this motif reappears, for example (though distorted) as the mother tries to deny her insanity.

46. Janáček picked up the speech melodies of the question and answer in Luhačovice in the summer of 1903, and quoted them in his *feuilleton* about the spa in November that year (see note 1 above). Before they found their way into *Osud*, he adapted them slightly (he disapproved of incorporating speech melodies intact). The fragment reappears in Act 3, as students quote a scene in Živný's opera.

47. The mother's entry is brief and unprepared; originally, Janáček wanted a longer scene here, and the mother was to sing a minor second below at the same time as Živný – an extremely bold proposal. See Ewans, *Janáček's Tragic Operas*, p. 87.

48. In an unmistakable 2/4 time, with a rhythmic figure on the word 'dost' [enough] typical both of Moravian folk music and Janáček's own music. According to the stage instructions, a bagpipe player is meant to strike up the tune.

49. For example, the harp and piccolo figurations in Živný's solo, Act 3, Scene 2. Cf. also the present volume, p. 285, n. 36.

50. Dr František Skácelík (1873–1944); the entire history of the text changes and negotiations with the Vinohrady Theatre is described in greater detail in Tyrrell, *Janáček's Operas*, pp. 135–58.

51. All conducted by Karel Kovařovic (though Janáček's programme for *Salome*, which he probably saw after 21 May 1906, has not been preserved). As he told the composer and chorus master Adolf Piskáček (1873–1919) that year, *Salome* 'had excited him'; he liked best the music for the Dance of the Seven Veils, and Jochanaan's death. In 1907 he also saw this opera at the Neues Deutsches Theater in Prague. Cf. Adolf Piskáček, 'Večer s Leošem Janáčkem' [An evening with Leoš Janáček], *Dalibor*, xxviii, 1905–6, p. 227, and Racek, 'Leoš Janáček a Praha', p. 23.

52. As he wrote in 1909; cf. Janáček/Veselý, p. 46.

53. See the interview mentioned in note 51 above; abridged reprint in Štědroň (ed.) *Leoš Janáček. Vzpomínky*, p. 72. Although it has often been stated that Janáček's notations of these 'nocturnes' from Rovné in Slovakia date from 1906, he had already notated numerous songs from Rovné in his diary in 1901–2, and probably visited the region several times. Cf. Jiří Vysloužil, 'Hudebně foikloristické dílo Leoše Janáčka' [Leoš Janáček's folklore work], in *Leoš Janáček. O lidové písni a lidové hudbě* [Leoš Janáček. On folk-song and folk music], ed. Jiří Vysloužil, SNKLHU, Prague, 1955, p. 47.

54. See note 53 above.

55. Subtitled 'Evening songs of the Slovak people from Rovné', they were first performed in Brno on 5 December 1907, and enthusiastically reviewed.

56. See his *feuilleton* 'Myšlenky cestou' [Thoughts on the road], *Dalibor*, xxix, 2 and 9 March 1907. Reprinted in Vysloužil (ed.), *Leoš Janáček. O lidové písni*. pp. 230–4.

57. *Hudební listy*, i/4 (3 Jan 1885), pp. 14–15; i/5 (12 Jan 1885), pp. 18–19; i/6 (19 Jan 1885), p. 22; i/8 (2 Feb 1885), pp. 29–30.

58. See Racek, 'Leoš Janáček', p. 22, fn. 37.

59. See Bohumír Štědroň, 'Janáček a Ruský kroužek v Brně' [Janáček and the Russian Circle in Brno], Hudobný archiv 2, Martin, 1977, p. 214; reprinted in Štědroň (ed.), *Leoš Janáček. Vzpomínky*, p. 122

60. 'Gero' was in fact a 10th-century German warlord who conquered Slavonic peoples settled between the rivers Elbe and Oder.

61. Cf. Karel Steinmetz, 'Metrorytmická stránka vztahu textu a hudby v Janáčkových sborech' [The metro-rhythmical aspect of the relationship between the text and music in Janáček's choruses]; Symposium *Hudba a literatura* [Music and literature] 1981, Frýdek-Místek, 1983, pp. 107–10.

62. 12 April 1907; cf. Bohumír Štědroň, *Leoš Janáček*, Panton, Prague, 1976, p. 106ff.

63. Not only in view of their social themes and Janáček's word-setting, but also the originality of his harmonic thinking.

64. See Firkušný's introduction to his recording of Janáček's piano music for RCA Victor, 1990 (RD60147), p. 7.

65. Janáček's letter dated 1 April 1912, reprinted in Štědroň, *Leoš Janáček. Vzpomínky*, p. 124. Ambros, a director of a school of music in the town of Prostějov, enquired about the meaning of the individual parts of the cycle. The Czech pianist Jaroslav Kvapil has pointed out that the rhythmic structure of the opening melody 'Come with us' (no. 3) clearly suggests the speech melody of the initial phrase of a Moravian folk-song 'Pojd'te s námi, vy mládenci' (Come with us, you lads).

66. Letter dated 6 June 1908; published by Artuš Rektorys in *Hudební rozhledy*, vii/14, 1954, p. 639.
67. See the present volume, pp. 179–81.
68. In this two-page extract, published on 1 February 1888, the author describes the cacophony into which his anti-hero walks on the moon, and his flight from the concert hall during a performance of a composition by a lunar composer. Čech's first Brouček novel was published in 1888, the sequel in 1889.
69. In 1889, Janáček asked Čech to arrange for him the text of a large folk-song cycle for choir and orchestra he planned, *Královničky* [The little queens], but the project came to nothing. Janáček's daughter Olga had a copy of the tenth edition of *Slave Songs* (1894), published in 1895.
70. *Excursions of Mr Brouček, One to the Moon, the Other to the Fifteenth Century*, *Lidové noviny*, 23 December 1917, in Zemanová (ed.), *Janáček's Uncollected Essays*, p. 95. For a more detailed story of the libretto, see the present volume, pp. 141–2.
71. Letter dated 26 September 1909; see *Korespondence Leoše Janáčka s Artuš em Rektorysem* [Janáček's correspondence with Artuš Rektorys], Janáčkův archiv iv, ed. Artuš Rektorys, with notes by V. Helfert, Hudební matice, 2nd enlarged edn, Prague, 1949 [JA iv], pp. 121.
72. Janáček/Veselý, p. 69.
73. Cf. Josef Sajner, 'Patografická studie o Leoši Janáčkovi' [A pathological study of Leoš Janáček'], *OM*, xiv, 1982, pp. 233–5.
74. Ibid.
75. 10 February 1910, in Brno; the 1923 version had a première the same year, at the Prague Mozarteum.
76. 2 July 1910.
77. Cf. Trkanová/Stejskalová, pp. 67 and 152, n. 11. The total cost was 20,000 crowns.
78. Ibid., p. 71.
79. See Trkanová/Janáčková, pp. 83–4.
80. See Trkanová/Stejskalová, p. 72.
81. See Trkanová/Janáčková, p. 84.
82. Janáček/Veselý, p. 71.
83. First published in the first volume of the magazine *Lumír*, 1873; in 1874 it appeared in Čech's collection *Poems*, and in 1899 in his *Collected Writings*, ii.
84. See 'The fiddler's child', *Hudební revue*, vi, 1913–14, in Zemanová (ed.), *Janáček's Uncollected Essays*, pp. 81–3.
85. 14 November 1917; the Czech Philharmonic Orchestra was conducted by Otakar Ostrčil. The first performance outside Czechoslovakia was given in London in 1923, under the baton of Sir Henry Wood.
86. See Ludvík Kundera, 'Janáčkova tvorba klavírní' [Janáček's works for the piano], *Musikologie*, iii, Prague, 1955, p. 307.
87. Ibid., p. 312.
88. See note 73 above.
89. See Trkanová/Stejskalová, p. 74.
90. This motif, according to Janáček, represents open arms longing to embrace the world; cf. Vogel, *Leoš Janáček*, p. 208.
91. Première 5 February 1917 in Prague; in 1924 Janáček revised the work.

Ladislav Vycpálek (1882–1969); his review appeared in *Hudební revue*, February 1927; cf. also Vogel, *Leoš Janáček*, p. 212.

92. Letter dated 2 July 1914; reprinted in Štědroň (ed.), *Leoš Janáček. Vzpomínky*, p. 99. The writer Alois Mrštík (1861–1925) was Janáček's former pupil at the Teachers' Training Institute, and sang under his baton at the Beseda. Janáček approached him and his brother Vilém (1863–1912) for a libretto for *The Excursions of Mr Brouček* but they refused. Cf. the present volume, p. 107.

93. Letter dated 6 July 1914; reprinted in Štědroň (ed.), *Leoš Janáček. Vzpomínky*, p. 100. Dr Janke (1865–1918) was an ear, nose and throat specialist, and worked both in Prague and the Luhačovice spa, where he and Janáček used to meet each summer. Janke also worked on the libretto of *The Excursions of Mr Brouček*. Cf. the present volume, p. 107.

Chapter 7: Recognition

1. See Marie Trkanová, *U Janáčků: podle vyprávění Marie Stejskalové* [At the Janáčeks: after the account of Marie Stejskalová], Panton, Prague, 1959, p. 75 [Trkanová/Stejskalová]. Cf. also Marie Trkanová, *Paměti: Zdenka Janáčková – můj život* [Memoirs: Zdenka Janáčková – my life], Šimon Ryšavý [Publishers], Brno, 1998, p. 86 [Trkanová/Janáčková].

2. See the present volume, pp. 72–3.

3. Ibid.

4. In addition, in May 1915 the leader of the 'Young Czechs' party, Karel Kramář, was arrested, tried and condemned to death (in 1917, he was granted an amnesty). Czech resistance movement therefore developed largely abroad, and in isolation; only a few Czech anti-Austrian politicians kept in contact with Masaryk, and attempted to act in the spirit of his politics.

5. See Jiří Horák, 'Zpráva o činnosti Ústavu pro lidovou píseň' [A report on the activities of the institute for folk-song], offprint, *Národopisný sborník českoslovanský*, xviii, No. 1, p. 13ff.; cf. Jiří Vysloužil, 'Hudebně folkloristické dílo Leoše Janáčka', in *Leoš Janáček. O lidové písni a lidové hudbě* [Leoš Janáček. On folk-song and folk music], SNKLHU, Prague, p. 61 (pp. 29–78 for Janáček and folk-song).

6. See Janáček's letter dated 21 January 1922, to Otakar Nebuška (1875–1952), administrator and writer on music. Quoted in Jaroslav Vogel, *Leoš Janáček*, Orbis Publishing, London, 1981, p. 213.

7. The main theme of the first movement is virtually identical with the closing motif of the penultimate scene of *Káťa*; the main theme of the third movement resembles the 'troika' motif in this opera, and its various variants.

8. According to the pianist Karel Šolc, who rehearsed the sonata for the first performance at the ISCM festival in Salzburg, August 1923 (although in the end he did not play the part). Cf. Vogel, *Leoš Janáček*, p. 213.

9. He wrote one in Leipzig (which he did not finish), and one in Vienna.

10. Ferdinand Vach (1860–1939); the Moravian Women Teachers' Choral Society, founded in 1917, gave many concerts throughout the war, to enthusiastic audiences.

11. Jaroslav Vrchlický (1853–1912); cf. also the present volume, pp. 73, 74, 114 and 156.

12. Cf. Vogel, *Leoš Janáček*, p. 219.

13. F.S. Procházka (1861–1939), poet and editor of the magazine *Zvon*. He worked on the final revision of *The Excursion of Mr Brouček to the Moon* and *Šárka*, and wrote the libretto for *The Excursion of Mr Brouček to the Fifteenth Century* (cf. also the present volume, pp. 107 and 141).

14. In fact, they used to house 24 of the Emperor's marksmen. Later, some of these houses had famous owners or lodgers: Franz Kafka rented No. 22 Golden Lane as a study, and wrote there most of the short stories published during his lifetime.

15. It was built by Tomáš Jaroš, bell-founder of the Hapsburg Emperor Ferdinand I, and stands in front of the summer palace, Belvedere (see next note).

16. Built in the middle of the 16th century by Ferdinand for his Queen, Anna Jagiełło.

17. By Klub přátel umění [Club of the Friends of Art], 18 March 1908. Dr Veselý (see next note) was chairman of the Club of the Friends of Art.

18. Dr František Veselý (1862–1923) created the spa at Luhačovice in Moravia, where Janáček got to know him.

19. See Hlava's letter dated 25 February 1911, *Korespondence Leoše Janáčka s Marií Calmou a MUDr Františkem Veselým* [Leoš Janáček's correspondence with Marie Calma and Dr František Veselý], Janáčkův archiv viii, ed. Jan Racek and Artuš Rektorys, Orbis Publishing, Prague, 1951 [JA viii], p. 27.

20. See the present volume, p. 288, note 28.

21. Cf. Jitka Ludvová, 'Německý hudební život v Praze 1880–1935' [German musical life in Prague, 1880–1935], *Uměnovědné studie*, iv, Prague, 1983, pp. 53–173. Cf. also John Tyrrell, *Czech Opera*, CUP, Cambridge, 1988, p. 48–9.

22. Letter dated 28 December 1913 (JA viii, pp. 35–6).

23. *The Dogheads* (1898) was Kovařovic's greatest success on the operatic stage, 1898.

24. Letter dated 29 September 1915 (JA viii, pp. 44–5).

25. Letter dated 3 October 1915 (ibid., pp. 45–7).

26. Letter dated 17 November 1915 (ibid., pp. 55–6).

27. Letter dated 9 December 1915 (ibid., p. 57).

28. Ibid., p. 59.

29. Letter dated 10 December 1915 (ibid., p. 60).

30. *Korespondence Leoše Janáčka s Karlem Kovařovicem a ředitelstvím Národního divadla* [Janáček's correspondence with Karel Kovařovic and the directorate of the National Theatre], Janáčkův archiv vii, ed. Artuš Rektorys, Hudební matice, Prague, 1950 [JA vii], pp. 27–8.

31. See Marie Calma-Veselá, 'Z boje pro Janáčkovu *Pastorkyni*' [From the battle for Janáček's *Jenůfa*], *Listy Hudební matice*, iv, 1924–5, p. 144.

32. Letter dated 25 February 1916 (JA viii, p. 66).

33. Letter dated 29 March 1916 (ibid., pp. 67–8).

34. František Mareš (1862–1941), director of the Vesna Society in Brno and the first chairman of the Club of the Friends of Art there; an ardent promoter of Czech music. He was a good friend and adviser of Zdenka Janáčková. He was unable to make a detour to Bohdaneč on his way to the première on 26 May 1916, and sent a telegram the previous day. Cf. JA viii, p. 68.

35. See letter dated 16 May, 1916, to Adéla Koudelová, president of the Vesna

Society. Reprinted in *Leoš Janáček. Vzpomínky, dokumenty, korespondence a studie* [Leoš Janáček. Reminiscences, papers, correspondence and studies], ed. Bohumír Štědroň, Editio Supraphon, Prague, 1986, p. 104.

36. Letter dated 4 June 1916; reprinted in ibid., p. 109.

37. See *Korespondence Leoše Janáčka s Gabrielou Horvátovou* [Janáček's correspondence with Gabriela Horvátová], Janáčkův archiv vi, ed. Artuš Rektorys, Hudební matice, Prague, 1950 [JA vi], p. 20, fn. 12.

38. Letter dated 28 May, 1916, see *Korespondence Leoše Janáčka s Otakarem Ostrčilem* [Janáček's correspondence with Otakar Ostrčil], Janáčkův archiv ii, ed. Artuš Rektorys, Hudební matice Umělecké besedy, Prague, 1948 [JA ii], pp. 18–19.

39. Letter dated 24 June 1916, reprinted in *Janáček ve vzpomínkách a dopisech* [Janáček in reminiscences and letters], ed. Bohumír Štědroň, Topič, Prague, 1946, p. 177.

40. See Nejedlý's review in *Smetana*, vi, Nos. 9–10, 4 August 1916; abridged reprint in Štědroň (ed.), *Leoš Janáček. Vzpomínky*, p. 106.

41. Among others, the composer Josef Suk and his family; personal problems played a part in this, as Dvořák's daughter Otilka rejected Nejedlý and married Suk. Cf. the present volume, pp. 187–8 and 193.

42. See *Vzpomínáme Karla Kovařovice* [We commemorate Karel Kovařovic], I.P. Kober, Prague, 1940, pp. 93–4. Dědeček was employed in the National Theatre orchestra between 1915 and 1917.

43. See Otakar Nebuška's letter to Janáček, dated 11 February 1917 (BmJA, shelf-mark D 143); an abridged version is in JA vii, p. 104.

44. See 'Janáčkova korespondence s Universal-Edition v letech 1916–1918 týkající se Její pastorkyně' [Janáček's correspondence with Universal Edition 1916–18, concerning *Jenůfa*], ed. Bohumír Štědroň, *Otázky divadla a filmu*, ii, 1971, pp. 259–60.

45. Beginning with Hynek Kašlík; see 'Retuše Karla Kovařovice v Janáčkově opeře Její pastorkyně' [Karel Kovařovic's 'retouchings' in Janáček's opera *Jenůfa*], *Hudební věstník*, xxxi, 1938, pp. 112–3, 130–1, 142–3, 159–60.

46. See Janáček's letter to Gustav Schmoranz, dated 27 October 1919 (JA vii, p. 81).

47. See letter dated 21 September 1923 (JA ii, pp. 75–61).

48. See Janáček's letter dated 30 October 1923, to his Brno lawyer Jaroslav Lecian (JA vii, pp. 90–1).

49. See Ostrčil's letter dated 3 January 1924 (JA vii, pp. 94–5). Janáček remained cool towards him for the rest of his life, although Ostrčil continued to conduct Janáček's operas, including the Prague premières of *The Cunning Little Vixen* and *The Makropulos Affair*, and a new production of *Jenůfa* in 1926.

50. See Janáček's letter dated 4 March, 1924 to Ostrčil (JA ii, pp. 79–80), and *Briefe an die Universal Edition*, ed. Ernst Hilmar; Hans Schneider, Tutzing, 1988, pp. 207–8. See also Janáček's letter dated 8 September 1926 to Dr Jan Löwenbach, in 'Jan Löwenbach a Leoš Janáček: vzájemná korespondence' [Jan Löwenbach and Leoš Janáček: mutual correspondence], ed. Ivo Stolařík, *Slezský sborník*, lvi, 1958, pp. 396–7.

51. A new edition was published in 1969 but apart from adding the Kostelnička's 'explanation' aria (which Janáček did not include in the 1908 vocal score),

his own version was ignored. Changes by various conductors were carefully explained in the footnotes.

52. Břetislav Bakala (1897–1958), Czech conductor, Janáček's pupil at the Organ School, he worked at the Brno National Theatre between 1920 and 1925. He was one of the few scholars who maintained that Janáček's own version was usable. Cf. *Rytmus*, viii, 1942–3, p. 85; reprinted in Štědroň (ed.), *Janáček ve vzpomínkách*, pp. 172–3.

53. See Jan Němeček, *Opera Národního divadla v období Karla Kovařovice 1900–1920* [The opera of the (Prague) National theatre in the time of Karel Kovařovic 1900–20], Divadelní ústav, Prague, 1968–9, ii, p. 86, fn. 136.

54. Cf. Sir Charles Mackerras's Decca recording of 1982. See also preface to Universal Edition score of *Jenůfa* (Brno version, 1908), UE 30 145, 1996, pp. x–xi.

55. Cf. JA viii, p. 69, n. 138: during his visit to Bohdaneč in June 1917, with Horvátová, Janáček 'wanted, or at least pretended that he wants' Marie Calma to sing the part. He invited the Veselýs to the performance on 17 August 1916.

56. Carmen, Brangäne, Brünnhilde and Elektra.

57. See Trkanová/Janáčková, p. 90.

58. Letter dated 20 May 1916, to his wife; see Jan Racek, 'Leoš Janáček a Praha' [Leoš Janáček and Prague], *Musikologie*, iii, 1955, p. 27.

59. See Trkanová/Janáčková, p. 90.

60. Ibid., pp. 90–1.

61. Ibid., pp. 91–2.

62. Janáček's inscription on the wreath he gave her after the première.

63. See Trkanová/Janáčková, p. 93.

64. BmJA, shelfmark Z 45, note dated '13.VI.1916'. Cf. also Trkanová/Janáčková, pp. 94 and 106. Later, during his relationship with Kamila Stösslová, Janáček also fantasized about Kamila being pregnant (letters of 16 February 1928, 19 and 26 April 1928), even though there was virtually no physical contact between them at the time.

65. Trkanová/Janáčková, p. 94; cf. also Trkanová/Stejskalová, p. 80.

66. Trkanová/Stejskalová, p. 80.

67. Trkanová/Janáčková, p. 95.

68. Ibid., p. 96.

69. Ibid.

70. Kateřina Hudečková, née Zemanová, from the village of Velká; much admired as a young woman at the 1895 exhibition in Prague. See the present volume, p. 761.

71. See JA viii, pp. 69–70, fn. 139.

72. Ibid., p. 70, n. 139.

73. Trkanová/Janáčková, p. 100.

74. Ibid., p. 101.

75. Ibid., pp. 101–2. According to Zdenka, Horvátová suggested that Zdenka had affairs of her own.

76. Ibid., p. 101.

77. Ibid., p. 104.

78. According to Zdenka, her brother claimed that both Horvátová and Janáček

could be imprisoned, and that Janáček would lose his social standing (ibid., p. 105).

79. Ibid., pp. 106, 108 and 109.

80. Ibid., p. 107.

81. Ibid., pp. 108–9. Cf. also *Intimate Letters: Leoš Janáček and Kamila Stösslová*, ed. and trans. John Tyrrell, Faber, London, 1994, Appendix 2, pp. 374–5. As is clear from Zdenka Janáčková's and Marie Stejskalová's memoirs, Janáček did not keep to the agreement.

82. 28 July 1916 (JA vii, p. 36).

83. See Jaroslav Vogel, *Leoš Janáček*, Orbis Publishing, London, 1981, p. 254.

84. See Trkanová/Janáčková, pp. 68 and 109.

85. JA viii, pp. 74–5, fn. 154.

86. Letter dated 3 May 1920 (ibid., p. 74).

87. The wife of his former pupil, the conductor Jožka Charvát; see Janáček's letter to Kovařovic, 18 March 1916 (JA vii, pp. 29–30).

88. Letter dated 31 January 1925 (JA viii, p. 77).

89. Some time in March 1925 Calma sang excerpts from the opera at the meeting of musicians and critics at the office of *La revue musicale*. Cf. her letter dated 2 March 1925 to Janáček (ibid., p. 78, and fn. 158).

90. See František Kožík, *Po zarostlém chodníčku* [On the overgrown path], Odeon, Prague, 1972, p. 120.

91. Charles Susskind, *Janáček and Brod*, Yale University Press, New Haven and London, 1985, p. 1.

92. Janáček met Strauss on 15 and 16 October 1916, and made a few notes about the meeting in his notebook. Strauss entered the box during the Kostelnička's aria 'Co chvíla' [One moment], Act 2, Scene 5. After this act he talked to Janáček and other guests, including Kovařovic and Gustav Schmoranz, and 'praised the originality' of the work. He left Prague the next day; Janáček met him that day at the railway station. Strauss kept coming back to the subject of *Jenůfa*: he liked Act 3 because of 'the brusque expression of the tragic in the music', and he loved the folk costumes. See Racek, 'Leoš Janáček a Praha', p. 28.

93. Max Brod, *Streitbares Leben*, Kindler Verlag, Munich, 1960, p. 425; also *Steitbares Leben, 1884–1968*, F.A. Herbig, Munich and Berlin, 1969, p. 271.

94. See Brod, *Streitbares Laben* (1960), p. 425; also 1969 edn, p. 271.

95. Jan Löwenbach (1880–1972), lawyer, writer on music' and librettist. He worked at the Hudební matice publishing house, and often gave Janáček legal advice, both in his dealings with foreign publishers and the National Theatre.

96. Alexander von Zemlinsky (1872–1942), Austrian conductor and composer; early supporter and later brother-in-law of Arnold Schoenberg. He worked in Vienna, Prague (Neues Deutsches Theater) and Berlin (collaborating there with Klemperer), and was the author of six operas, all performed during his lifetime.

97. Dr Emil Hertzka (1869–1932), publisher, managing director (1907–1932) of the Viennese publishing firm Universal Edition; Hugo Reichenberger (1873–1938), conductor at the Hofoper (1908–1935); Julius Bittner (1874–1939), Austrian critic and composer.

98. See Clemens Höslinger, 'Zur Vorgeschichte der Wiener *Jenůfa*-Première', *Mitteilungen des österreichischen Staatsarchivs*, Bd. 25, 1972.

99. Ibid.
100. Ibid.
101. See his letter to Horvátová, dated 25 January 1918 (JA vi, p. 64).
102. See Trkanová/Janáčková, p. 110, and Trkanová/Stejskalová, pp. 80 and 88–9.
103. In particular, *The Diary of One who Disappeared*, *Káťa Kabanová*, and the Second String Quartet.
104. Trkanová/Stejskalová, p. 107.
105. Trkanová/Janáčková, p. 111. By 8 July 1917, Janáček jotted down a fragment of Kamila's speech in his diary (reprinted in Tyrrell, *Intimate Letters*, p. 4); there are two more fragments in his letters (3 and 13 April 1928, both reprinted in Tyrrell, p. 243 and 250). In both of these letters, Janáček refers to Kamila's 'soft' words.

    Fragments of Kamila's speech also appear in Janáček's *feuilletons* 'Pro pár jablek?' [For a few apples], 1 April 1927, 'Schytali je' [They caught them], 3 July 1927, and 'Pepík a Jeník' [Pepík and Jeník], 2 April 1928. Reprinted in 'Fejetony z Lidových novin' [*Feuilletons* from *Lidové noviny*], ed. Jan Racek, Krajské nakladatelství, Brno, 1958. English translation of 'For a few apples' and 'They caught them' in *Leoš Janáček. Leaves from his Life*, ed. and trans. Vilem and Margaret Tausky, Kahn and Averill, London, 1982, pp. 110–12 and 108–9.
106. Letter dated 16 July, 1927; see *Hádanka života. (Dopisy Leoše Janáčka Kamile Stösslové)* [The riddle of life. (Letters of Leoš Janáček to Kamila Stösslová)], ed. Svatava Přibáňová, Opus Musicum, Brno, 1990, p. 13.
107. Letter dated 30 July 1917 (ibid., p. 13).
108. Ibid.
109. Trkanová/Janáčková, pp. 110 and 111.
110. Ibid., p. 111.
111. Ibid., pp. 111–2.
112. Ibid., p. 112.
113. Letter dated 10 August 1917, see Přibáňová (ed.), *Hádanka života*, p. 14.
114. Letter dated 22 August 1917 (ibid., p. 17).
115. Letter dated 6 December 1917 (JA vi, p. 39).
116. Letter dated 8 December 1917 (ibid., p. 40).
117. Letter dated 28 November 1917 (ibid., p. 32).
118. Letter dated 3 December 1917, see Přibáňová (ed.), *Hádanka života*, p. 26.
119. Undated letter to Artuš Rektorys, postmarked 29 March 1910 (JA iv, pp. 130–1).
120. The added characters are those of the Sacristan and his daughter Málinka. See also Tyrrell, *Janáček's Operas*, pp. 173–4.
121. The entire story is described in detail in Tyrrell, *Janáček's Operas*, pp. 161–247.
122. See note 13 above.
123. A school of writers associated with the literary magazine *Lumír*, founded in 1873 and known for its enthusiastic adoption and assimilation of foreign trends.
124. Domšík was introduced in the novel as 'Janek od Zvonu' [Janek from the bell], after a carved bell on his house. He was an historical character – his house with the carved stone bell still stands in the Old Town Square.
125. For example, the Mayor's daughter refers to an actual historical character, the popular preacher Jan of Rokycany (later to become the Hussite Archbishop of

Prague). Three of the Mayor's guests engage in a heated argument about religious doctrine. And the Hussite leader Jan Žižka, also an historical character, appears in a procession through Prague (although his is not a singing role).

126. Cf. Tyrrell, *Czech Opera*, p. 204.

127. See *The Excursions of Mr Brouček*, in *Janáček's Uncollected Essays on Music*, selected, ed. and trans. Mirka Zemanová, Marion Boyars Publishers, London, 1989/1993, p. 93.

128. In Part I, Act 1, for example, in Blankythý's and Etherea's arias. In Part II, Act 1, in Brouček's 'To je ňáká maškara' [It must be some masque], in Kunka's 'Aj, kázání' [Oh, the sermon] and elsewhere.

129. Notably in Part I, Act 1, in Brouček's 'Bez dluhů! Tvaroh!' [Without debts! Curd cheese!].

130. For example, in Part I, Act 1, in Brouček's 'Ztřeštěmy sem' [A crazy dream]; in Etherea's aria; in Brouček's 'Ďasa pláču! Jím!' [The deuce I'm crying! I'm eating!] and elsewhere in the other moondwellers' parts.

131. Diabolus in musica', 'the devil in music' (for example, C–F sharp).

132. Cf. Vogel, *Leoš Janáček* p. 237.

133. Letter to Gabriela Horvátová, dated 6 December 1917 (JA vi, p. 38).

134. Emmy Destinn (1878–1930) was given a score by Gabriela Horvátová and at first showed great interest, as the conductor Vincenc Maixner reported to Janáček on 16 December 1917. Destinn (known from 1918 under the Czech form of her name, Ema Destinnová), worked in Dresden, London (Covent Garden, 1904–14, 1919), New York (Metropolitan Opera, 1908–16 and 1919–21), and gave concerts throughout Europe and the USA. She was Senta in the first *Fliegende Holländer* in Bayreuth (1901); the first Berlin Salome (1906); at Covent Garden, the first Butterfly (1905), and the first Tatyana (1906). She created Minnie in the world première of Puccini's *La fanciulla del West* at the Metropolitan Opera (1911). Her voice was dark and heavy but her top notes were excellent; as she was also a fine actress, she invariably made a powerful impression. Puccini thought highly of her and Richard Strauss – who offered her the role of Ariadne – rated her as one of the greatest singers of the 20th century.

135. See letter dated 12 December 1917 (JA vi, p. 92).

136. See letter dated 14 December 1917 (ibid., p 93).

137. Ibid.

138. Letter dated 21 December 1917 (ibid., p. 94).

139. On 16 December 1918, in response to Janáček letter, Destinn wrote that she would be prepared to promote the role if she had an Italian translation; she also offered to sing the role in German to one of the conductors at Covent Garden, Percy Pitt (1870–1932). She also asked for 'some songs'. Sadly, this was the last communication between her and Janáček – Destinn could not be persuaded to study the role in Czech. (Cf. JA vi, pp. 96–7.)

140. Letter dated 29 December 1917 (JA vi, p. 49).

141. Letter dated 7 January 1918 (ibid., p. 54).

142. Letter dated 10 January 1918 (ibid., p. 55).

143. Letter dated 11 January 1918 (ibid., p. 56).

144. Cf. Susskind, *Janáček and Brod*, p. 47, and Tyrrell, *Janáček's Operas*, p. 97.

145. Cf. JA vi, p. 95, and Susskind, *Janáček and Brod*, pp. 49–50.

146. Cf. also note 153 below. For Janáček's praise of Horvátová, see his letter dated 7 February 1918 (JA vi, p. 67).

Maria Jeritza (Marie Jedličková, 1887–1982) was an Austrian soprano of Czech origin, a member of the Hofoper (later Staatsoper) in Vienna (1913–32). She also sang at Covent Garden, London and the Metropolitan Opera, New York, and was the first American Jenůfa and Turandot.

Lucie Weidt (1876–1940), also an Austrian soprano, was one of the most famous members of Mahler's ensemble in Vienna (1902-27); she created the Marschallin (*Der Rosenkavalier*) there.

147. See letter dated 9 February 1918 (JA vi, p. 69).
148. Letters dated 1 and 12 February 1918 (ibid., pp. 67 and 69).
149. See letter dated 18 February 1918 (ibid., pp. 72–3).
150. See Trkanová/Janáčková, p. 113.
151. Ibid., p. 114. Zdenka stayed with her parents, Janáček in the Hotel Post. He did not invite either her parents, or her brother for the première.
152. 16 February 1918 (JA vi, p. 72).
153. According to Zdenka, Horvátová was very disappointed that the Hofoper did not engage her for the role of the Kostelnička, and was cross with Janáček. See Trkanová/Janáčková, p. 115, and note 146 above.
154. See Max Brod, *Streitbares Leben*, 1960, pp. 429–30; also 1969 edn, p. 270.
155. See letter dated 12 February 1918 (JA vi, pp. 69–70).
156. See letter dated 18 February 1918 (ibid., p. 72).
157. Letter dated 20 February 1918 (ibid., p. 74).
158. František Mareš, 'Vzpomínky na Leoše Janáčka' [Reminiscences of Leoš Janáček], *Lidové noviny*, 17 February 1940; abridged reprint in Štědroň (ed.), *Leoš Janáček. Vzpomínky*, p. 112.
159. Max Kalbeck (1850–1921); Julius Korngold (1860–1945), Austrian critic and musicologist, father of the composer Erich Korngold; Richard Batka (1868–1822), Czech musicologist and critic, active in Prague as music editor of the monthly arts magazine *Kunstwart*.
160. 16 November 1918; Otto Klemperer (1885–1973), one of the greatest German conductors, then only 33. He was music director at Cologne 1917–24; he worked at the Neues Deutsches Theater in Prague (1907–10), a post he had been recommended for by Gustav Mahler.
161. See his letter to Horvátová, dated 25 March 1918 (JA vi, p. 83).
162. Including the October 1917 Revolution in Russia. On 12 March, 1920 he wrote to Kamila Stösslová: 'A terrible revolution, [and] now they purify it by rivers of blood'; on 16 December 1920, he wrote to her: 'And what about that Bolshevik spectacle?' See Přibáňová (ed.), *Hádanka života*, pp. 82 and 85. For Janáček's view of Communism, see the present volume, pp. 171–2 and 241.
163. See his letter to Horvátová, dated 25 March 1918 (JA vi, p. 83).
164. See Jarmil Burghauser, *Janáček. Souborné kritické vydání* [Complete critical edition], vol. 2, Supraphon-Bärenreiter, Kassel, 1980.
165. The Brno performance was conducted by Janáček's devoted advocate František Neumann; in the Prague performance, the Czech Philharmonic was conducted by Václav Talich (1883–1961), one of the greatest Czech conductors.
166. Letter dated 15 April 1918; see Přibáňová (ed.), *Hádanka života*, pp. 33–4.

167. Letter dated 23 April 1918 (JA vi, p. 88).
168. See Trkanová/Janáčková, p. 116.
169. See his letter dated 16 March 1928 (JA vi, p. 90).
170. See an interview with Horvátová, 'Za osobními vzpomínkami na L. Janáčka' [Personal reminiscences of Leoš Janáček], *Divadlo*, 30 November 1938; abridged reprint in JA vi, pp. 8–10.
171. See Kožík, *Po zarostlém chodníčku*, p. 127.
172. Letter dated 13 April 1918; see Přibáňová (ed.), *Hádanka života*, p. 35.
173. In addition, that year he applied for and was granted the Czech Academy prize of 5000 crowns (for 'lifetime work'). While this sum was far from adequate for a lifetime contribution to Czech music, it was sufficient to cover the Janáčeks' household expenses for almost a year (in a letter to Horvátová, dated 6 December 1917, cf. note 115 above, he claimed that household expenses cost him at that time 600 crowns a month). Janáček won further prizes from the Czech Academy in 1919 (first prize for *The Excursions of Mr Brouček*), in 1922 (for *The Diary of One who Disappeared*) and in 1925 (for the First String Quartet and the wind sextet *Mládí*), each prize 5000 crowns. (Cf. JA vi, p. 26, fn. 27; Janáček dates his prize for *The Excursions* 1921, see his letter to Brod, 18 December 1921, JA ix, p. 97.)
174. On 6 January 1918.
175. On 17 October 1918.
176. Trkanová/Stejskalová, p. 81. Janáček was well informed about the work of the Czech resistance abroad.

Chapter 8: The Indian summer begins

1. Letter dated 1 November, 1918. See *Hádanka života. (Dopisy Leoše Janáčka Kamile Stösslové* [The riddle of life. (Letters of Leoš Janáček to Kamila Stösslová)], ed. Svatava Přibáňová, Opus Musicum, Brno, 1990, p. 51.
2. Letter dated 27 July 1918 (ibid., p. 44).
3. Letter dated 28 July 1918 (ibid., p. 45).
4. Letter dated 2 September 1918 (ibid., p. 49).
5. Letter dated 9 September 1918 (ibid., p. 50).
6. Letter dated 3 December 1918 (ibid., p. 53).
7. Letter dated 13 February 1919 (ibid., p. 58).
8. Letter dated 11 March 1919 (ibid., p. 59).
9. Letter dated 10 August 1917 (ibid., p. 14).
10. Ozef [Josef] Kalda (1871–1921) was known chiefly for his novel *Ogaři* [The lads], and a book of stories *Jalovinky* [Idle talk], both set in his native region; his other works range from humour to children's stories. Karel Šípek thought Kalda 'a genius', and recommended *Jalovinky* to Janáček (cf. his letter dated 19 December 1915, JA v, p. 54). However, it is unlikely that Janáček would link Kalda with the anonymous author of *The Diary*.
11. Even a renowned Czech philologist František Trávníček tried to unravel the mystery. In his opinion, the author was the journalist Jan Misárek (1861–1932), author of several remarkable short stories set in Valašsko. He was acquainted with Jiří Mahen, the literary editor of *Lidové noviny* who published *The Diary* and who was known for similar pranks.

12. In a letter to Antonín Matula, 8 June 1916. Cf. Jiří Demel, 'Kdo je autorem Zápisníku zmizelého?' [Who is the author of *The Diary of One who Disappeared?*], and Jan Mikeska, 'Jak jsem přispěl k odhalení?' [How did I contribute to the revelation?], both in *OM*, xxix, 1997, No. 3, pp. 93–100.

13. Letter dated 24 July 1924; see Přibáňová (ed.), *Hádanka života*, p. 121.

14. Letter dated 25 June 1919 (ibid., p. 64).

15. Tessitura: a term which indicates the approximate average range of a piece of music in relation to the voice for which it had been written. Most of Janáček's music for the tenor has a high tessitura, i.e. lies high. This may have been the influence of Moravian folk music, cf. the present volume, p. 83.

16. Cf. Jaroslav Vogel, *Leoš Janáček*, Orbis Publishing, London, 1981, p. 257.

17. Letter dated 17 October 1921; see Přibáňová (ed.), *Hádanka života*, p. 91.

18. The first performances in London (27 October 1922) and in Paris (15 December 1922) were given by the Danish tenor Mischa Léon (real name Harry Haurowitz, 1889–?), second husband of the well-known Canadian soprano Pauline Donalda (1882–1970). He toured the United States, England and Europe and sang Don José at the National Theatre, Prague. He studied *The Diary* in Brno with Bakala, and sang it in the original Czech.

19. To increase the dramatic impact, several songs follow without a break, and short or longer breaks are indicated after other numbers.

20. This did not escape the notice of the publisher Oldřich Pazdírek in Brno who published it in 1943 as 'Intermezzo Erotico' for piano solo.

21. *Český deník*, February 1928.

22. Cf. Vogel, *Leoš Janáček*, p. 260.

23. From his collection *Selské balady* [Peasant ballads], 1885.

24. Cf. Vogel, *Leoš Janáček*, pp. 251–2.

25. The whole-tone scale, as its name suggests, consists of whole tones only. Although this scale appeared in the works of Liszt and Glinka, among others, the use of it is particularly associated with Debussy.

26. In the Brno première on 21 March 1920, Neumann added horns in the lower octave (Vogel, *Leoš Janáček*, p. 252).

27. Ibid., p. 250. The work is still played only rarely.

28. See letter to Jan Herben, dated 16 November 1918. First published by Gracian Černušák on 12 August 1938 in *Lidové noviny*; reprinted in Štědroň (ed.) *Leoš Janáček. Vzpomínky*, pp. 132–3.

29. Letter dated 11 March 1919; see Přibáňová (ed.), *Hádanka života*, p. 59.

30. See his *feuilleton* 'Úvodní slovo' [An introductory speech], *Lidové noviny*, 30 Setember 1919. Reprinted in *Fejetony z Lidových novin* [Feuilletons from *Lidové noviny*], ed. Jan Racek, Krajské nakladatelství, Brno, 1958, pp. 213–5.

31. Letter to Kamila dated 6 April 1919; see Přibáňová (ed.), *Hádanka života*, p. 61.

32. Letter to Kamila, dated 23 March 1920 (ibid., p. 82).

33. See Marie Trkanová, *U Janáčků: podle vyprávění Marie Stejskalové* [At the Janáčeks: after the account of Marie Stejskalová], Panton, Prague, 1959, p. 85. [Trkanová/Stejskalová]

34. See Rudolf Firkušný, 'My recollection of Janáček', introduction to the CD of Janáček's piano music, RCA Victor, RD60147, 1989, p. 5.

35. In May 1920; cf. Vogel, *Leoš Janáček*, p. 248.

36. Cf. Osvald Chlubna, 'Leoš Janáček a brněnské divadlo' [Leoš Janáček and the Brno theatre], *Divadelní list Zemského divadla v Brně*, viii, 1932/3, p. 9; abridged reprint in Štědroň (ed.), *Leoš Janáček. Vzpomínky*, p. 135. Both the theatre's orchestra and chorus were now over twice the size of those in the première of *Jenůfa* in 1904. Although the theatre always had fairly competent solo singers, now it was able to engage outstanding soloists. As a result, there were many important premières in Brno during the inter-war period: among others, four Janáček's operas (from *Káťa Kabanová* onwards), Ostrčil's later operas and the Czech première of Debussy's *Pelléas et Mélisande*. The City Theatre's ballet company gave the world première of Prokofiev's *Romeo and Juliet*, as well as some of the early ballets by Bohuslav Martinů. Cf. also John Tyrrell, *Czech Opera*, CUP, Cambridge, 1988, pp. 58–9.

37. For tessitura, see note 15 above. Janáček's suggestion of Otakar Mařák (1872–1939) was wholly unrealistic: Mařák, a fine lyric tenor (dubbed the Czech Caruso), was – apart from his many Czech roles – a favourite Don José and Cavaradossi in Prague. At Covent Garden, he was the first Bacchus (*Ariadne auf Naxos*, 1913); also sang Turiddu and Canio there. Among his Heldentenor roles were Parsifal (Chicago 1914), Dalibor (Prague 1927) and Tannhäuser (Prague 1932).

    Karel Hruška (1891–1966), a popular buffo tenor from Plzeň whom Janáček also mentioned in his letter to Kovařovic (19 October 1918, JA vii, pp. 67–8), joined the National Theatre in Prague in 1919, but took another part in *Brouček*. In the end the chief role went to the long-standing resident buffo tenor Miroslav Štork (1880–1953), whom Karel Šípek had suggested for the part in October 1915.

38. Cf. Kovařovic's letter to Janáček, dated 20 November 1919 (JA vii, pp. 83–4).

39. Cf. his letter to Kamila dated 26 November 1919, in Přibáňová (ed.), *Hádanka života*, p. 74.

40. See Kamila's letter dated 18 February 1920 (ibid., p. 81).

41. See Janáček's letter dated 23 March 1920 (ibid., p. 83).

42. See Janáček's letter dated 22 January 1918 (ibid., p. 28).

43. See Janáček's letter dated 23 March 1920 (ibid., p. 83).

44. See his letter to his wife dated 12 June 1916, in Jan Racek's study 'Leoš Janáček a Praha' [Leoš Janáček and Prague], *Musikologie*, iii, Prague, 1955, p. 47.

45. The Prague première was given on 23 April 1923. For his reminiscences, see Chlubna, *Leoš Janáček*, p. 125: reprinted in Štědroň (ed.), *Leoš Janáček. Vzpomínky*, p. 128.

46. See Janáček's letter dated 6 May 1920, in Přibáňová (ed.), *Hádanka života*, p. 83.

47. Ibid. As Kamila was spending some time in Semmering, she declined the invitation to accompany him to the première.

48. See, for example, Ostrčil's letters dated 30 January and 18 March 1920 (JA ii, pp. 29 and 32).

49. See Janáček's letter dated 29 January 1920 (ibid., p. 29).

50. See Ostrčil's letter dated 31 January 1920 (ibid.).

51. See Janáček's letters dated 25 and 27 April and 16 May 1920 (ibid., pp. 33–6 and 40–1).

52. See Ostrčil's letters dated 31 January and 28 April 1920 (ibid., pp. 29 and 39).

53. Kovařovic's choice of Václav Novák (1881–1928) for the role of Vürfl/Čaroskvoucí/Alderman was the only problem as far as the casting was concerned: Novák, an outstanding Heldentenor, was known for his fiery temperament. On 30 January 1920 he wrote a strongly-worded letter to Schmoranz, refusing the role; he claimed that Janáček knew nothing about voices and that the part was damaging his voice. This letter and Janáček's letter dated 2 February 1921 to Novák are quoted in František Pala, 'Janáček a Národní divadlo' [Janáček and the National Theatre], *Hudební rozhledy*, vi, 1953, p. 890.

54. 25 April 1920; abridged reprint in JA ii, p. 34.

55. 25 April 1920; abridged reprint in ibid., pp. 33–4.

56. 25 April 1920; abridged reprint in ibid., p. 40.

57. See letter dated 28 April 1920 (ibid., p. 39).

58. See his letter dated 25 April 1920 (ibid., p. 33).

59. '*The Excursions of Mr Brouček*', *Lidové noviny*, 23 December 1917, in *Janáček's Uncollected Essays on Music*, selected, ed. and trans. Mirka Zemanová, Marion Boyars Publishers, London, 1989/1993, pp. 92–6.

60. This may have been the reason for the doubt one can hear in another of Janáček's articles on the opera (in *Hudební revue*, xiii, 1919–20, pp. 177–9) and indeed the uncertainty in the reception of the piece.

61. See Šípek's undated letter [written probably between 19 and 31 December, 1915] to Marie Calma-Veselá' (JA v, p. 56).

62. See Max Brod, *Streitbares Leben*, Kindler Verlag, Munich, 1960, p. 246; also 1969 edn, F.A. Herbig, Munich and Berlin, p. 271. In his letter dated 7 June 1920 Brod listed two other reasons for wanting to suppress the second excursion (i.e. to the Hussite era) in the German version: its local patriotism, he believed, would not be understood by the German audiences, and this part of the opera – with its political debates and theological discussions – was not, in his view, sufficiently dramatic. Although Brod later modified his proposal, Janáček ignored all suggestions. As a result, Universal Edition did not issue *The Excursions* with a German translation, abridged and adapted, until 1959. A more authentic (though still adapted) version was issued in 1964. For Brod's correspondence, see *Korespondence Leoše Janáčka s Maxem Brodem* [Janáček's correspondence with Max Brod], Janáčkův archiv ix, ed. Jan Racek and Artuš Rektorys, SNKLHU, Prague, 1953 [JA ix], pp. 65–6.

63. See his letter dated 9 January 1920, in Přibáňová (ed.), *Hádanka života*, p. 77.

64. Cf. Vogel, *Leoš Janáček*, pp. 292 and 261.

65. The other two subjects were *Hájnikova žena* [The forester's wife] by P.O. Hviezdoslav (1849–1921), a Slovak poet, and *Hasanaginica* [= the wife of the Aga Hasan] by the Croatian writer Milan Ogrizović (1877–1923).

66. Cf. John Tyrrell, *Janáček's Operas: A Documentary Account*, Faber, London, 1992, p. 250–2.

67. Ibid., p. 248.

68. 16 February 1908, four years after its world première in Milan. Kovařovic was not fond of Italian opera. See also John Tyrrell, *Leoš Janáček: Káťa Kabanová*, CUP, Cambridge, 1982. Janáček's letter to Kamila is dated 5 December 1919. Cf Přibáňová (ed.), *Hádnka života*, p. 74. See also 'It's dusk', in Zemanová (ed.), *Janáček's Uncollected Essays*, p. 116.

69. See his inscription in Kamila's copy, dated 12 February 1928; reprinted in

'Janáček ve vzpomínkách a dopisech' [Janáček in reminiscences and letters], ed. Bohumír Štědroň, Topič, Prague, 1946, pp. 213–4.

70. See his letter dated 6 March 1921, in Přibáňová (ed.), *Hádanka života*, p. 86.

71. See his letter dated 31 March 1921 to Vincenc Červinka (1877–1942; translator from Russian, editor and critic) in Červinka's article 'Jak vznikla *Káťa Kabanová*' [How *Káťa Kabanová* came into being], *Národní politika*, 18 October 1938.

72. See his letter to Kamila dated 23 February 1920, in Přibáňová (ed.), *Hádanka života*, p. 80.

73. See his letter to Červinka: cf. note 71 above.

74. However, Janáček clearly did not want to reproduce actual Russian tunes. In Kudrjáš's song, he substituted a Ukrainian version (in Czech translation) of a well-known Russian folk-song, in order to fit the music he had originally written for Ostrovsky's original song (which does originate from the Volga region). Moreover, the music of this scale is based on a scale which does not occur in Russian folk-song. Cf. Lyudmila Polyakova, 'O "ruských" operách Leoše Janáčka' [About Janáček's 'Russian' operas], *Cesty rozvoje a vzájemné vztahy ruského a československého umění*, Prague, 1974, pp. 247–69; also Tyrrell, *Czech Opera*, p. 250.

75. Janáček seems to have used such oscillations with modal inflections when portraying a tragic death of a character he nevertheless saw as positive. Cf. Jiří Vysloužil, *Leoš Janáček*, Společnost Leoše Janáčka, Brno, 1978, p. 16. The diatonic scales are those of the major and minor keys; diatonic passages, intervals, chords and harmonies are therefore such as are made up of the notes of the key prevailing at the moment.

76. Cf. Marie Trkanová, *Paměti: Zdenka Janáčková – můj život* [Memoirs: Zdenka Janáčková – my life], Šimon Ryšavý [Publishers], Brno, 1998, pp. 120–3. A rift developed between Mr Schulz and his son Leo after Mrs Schulz's death.

77. See his letter dated 14 February 1921, in Přibáňová (ed.), *Hádanka života*, p. 85.

78. Cf. his letter of 23 October 1921 to Kamila (ibid., p. 92). Janáček's brother František, who died in 1908, invested his savings in Russian bonds which lost their value during the war. His widow went to live with her sister in Gliwice in Prussian Silesia (now in Poland). As she was unable to keep up the repayments on the cottage, Janáček bought it for 40,000 crowns, to keep the property in the family (his sister Josefka lived on the ground floor).

79. Cf. for example his letters dated 14 and 29 December 1921 (ibid., pp. 93–4).

80. Letter dated 28 December 1921 (ibid., p. 93).

81. Letter dated 9 January 1922 (ibid., p. 95).

82. See 'Nápěvky naší mluvy, vynikající pro svůj zvláštní dramatičností' [The speech melodies of our language which stand out for their particular dramatic effect], *ČMM*, iii, 1903, pp. 105–12, and his *feuilleton* 'Moje město' [My town], *Lidové noviny*, 24 December 1927; cf. also *Fejetony z Lidových novin* [*Feuilletons* from *Lidové noviny*], ed. Jan Racek, Krajské nakladatelství, Brno, 1958, p. 52.

83. In fact, Rudolf Těsnohlídek (1882–1928), the author of *The Cunning Little Vixen* serial in which Janáček became interested in 1922, also wrote a novel with a social theme, *Kolonia Kutejsík* [The Kutejsík colony], published in Brno that year. The novel won a state prize the same year. (*The Vixen* won a state

prize in 1923, the year it was published as a novel.) As in *The Cunning Little Vixen*, much of the text in *Kolonia Kutejsík* is in the local dialect, and Těsnohlídek was praised for fine portrayals of his characters and for the novel's humour. As the book's dedication is dated September 1917, he must have in fact completed the novel by the end of the First World War. It is not known whether Janáček knew of the novel, and unlikely that Těsnohlídek (who committed suicide in 1928) mentioned it to him during their encounter in 1922.

84. Although Janáček started writing for this newspaper in 1893, there were several gaps during which he did not contribute to it at all (especially in 1897–1906, 1913–17 and 1919–20). After 1919 he wrote for it more regularly, especially in 1921, 1922, 1924 and 1927.

85. Stanislav Lolek (1873–1836), at one time an apprentice forester; it was Bohumil Markalous, arts editor of *Lidové noviny*, who came across these drawings in Lolek's Prague studio. Janáček had known Lolek – in 1916 he asked him and the sculptor František Uprka to help with teaching the steps of the dances in the Prague production of *Jenůfa*.

86. Rudolf Těsnohlídek described in an article published in *Lidové noviny* on 1 November 1924 how the printers misread the vixen's original name Bystronožka [Fleetfoot].

87. This was written after his meeting with Janáček in 1922, but Janáček used only half of Těsnohlídek's text.

88. See Michael Ewans, *Janáček's Tragic Operas*, Faber, London, 1977, pp. 137–67.

89. Cf. also Charles Susskind, *Janáček and Brod*, Yale University Press, New Haven and London, 1985, pp. 76–7.

90. In Act 1, Scene 2 (with the captive Vixen living temporarily at the Forester's cottage); in Act 2, Scene 3, during her courtship. An amusing touch is the Crested Fowl's cry of 'Trrrp' (in the cottage yard); this word looks and sounds onomatopoeic, but 'trp' [with one 'r' only] is in fact Czech for the imperative of 'suffer'.

91. For example, in Act 1, Scene 1, the Blue Dragonfly, a non-singing character, comes looking in vain for the Vixen; at the end of Act 2, the squirrels giggle and a hedgehog sticks out its tongue.

92. From Líšeň, near Brno, on the edge of the Adamov forest. The village was famous for its poultry.

93. In this scene, both Těsnohlídek and Janáček seem to be poking fun at contemporary Czech politics: the country's Marxist Left was active throughout 1920, and the Communist Party of Czechoslovakia was founded in 1921.

94. BmJA, shelfmark S 60, quoted in Jarmila Procházková, 'Prezident a skladatel' [The President and the composer], *OM*, Brno, 1990, No. 6, pp. 179–80.

95. See his letter dated 16 June 1925, (JA ix, pp. 182–3).

96. See Veselý's interview in *Lidové noviny*, 15 May 1921.

97. See 'Stehlíček' [The little goldfinch], *Lidové noviny*, 1 June 1921; cf. also Racek (ed.), *Fejetony*, p. 113.

98. See his letter dated 14 December 1921, in Přibáňová (ed.), *Hádanka života*, p. 93.

99. Universal Edition, UE 30532, 1992.

100. See the undated letter (JA ix, p. 91), and letter dated 10 January 1922 (JA ix, pp. 99).

101. See his letter dated 10 February 1922, in Přibáňová (ed.), *Hádanka života*, p. 96.

102. Ibid.

103. See his letter dated 25 February 1922 (ibid., p. 97).

104. See her letter dated 13 February 1922 (ibid., p. 96).

105. See his letter dated 13 March 1922 (ibid., p. 97).

106. See her letter dated 16 March 1922 (ibid.).

107. See his letter dated 18 March 1922 (ibid.).

108. See her letter dated 25 August 1922 (ibid., p. 99).

109. See his letter dated 27 August 1922 (ibid.).

110. See his letter dated 2 September 1922 (ibid.).

111. Káťa was sung by the Prague Jenůfa, Kamila Ungrová, alternating with Marie Veselá, who created the part in Brno. Although Janáček's relationship with Gabriela Horvátová had by then been over for some three years, Janáček wrote to Ostrčil that she would have been more suitable for the role of Kabanicha than Marie Rejholcová. Cf. his letter dated 3 March 1922 (JA ii, p. 63).

112. See his letter to Kamila, dated 29 November, in Přibáňová (ed.), *Hádanka života*, p. 102.

113. Jaromír Borecký, *Národní politika*, 2 December 1922; cf. also JA ii, p. 70.

114. JA ii, p. 69–71.

115. *Lidové noviny*, 2 December 1922; cf. JA ii, p. 70.

116. See his letter dated 3 April 1923, in Přibáňová (ed.), *Hádanka života*, p. 105.

117. See his *feuilleton* 'Rabindranath Tagore', *Lidové noviny*, 22 June 1921; reprinted in Racek (ed.), *Fejetony*, pp. 94–7.

118. Cf. Karel Steinmetz, 'Metrorytmická stránka vztahu textu a hudby v Janáčkových sborech' (The metro-rhythmical aspect of the relationship between the text and music in Janáček's choruses); Symposium *Hudba a literatura* [Music and literature], 1981, Frýdek-Místek, 1983, pp. 107–10.

119. 'Ty lásky! [Those loves!], 'Milieu', 'Tři' [Three], 'Kohoutek' [The cockerel] and 'Sedm havranů' [Seven crows], all in Racek (ed.), *Fejetony*, pp. 113–32.

120. See J.V. Sládek, *Hukvaldské miniatury* [Hukvaldy miniatures], Profil, Ostrava, 1979, p. 42.

121. See Trkanová/Stejskalová, pp. 78–9.

122. Cf. also Tyrrell, *Janáček's Operas*, p. 297.

123. Scene 1, 'Bít, zabít, jen proto, že su liška!' [To kill, to club, only because I am a vixen].

124. Compare, for example, the Little Vixen's, 'Mami, mami' [Mummy, Mummy!] and the orchestral accompaniment in the opening scene of Act 1.

125. See also the present volume, pp. 61 and 281, no. 7.

126. 'Běží liška k Táboru' [The vixen runs to Tábor town]; Tábor, in southern Bohemia.

127. The Little Frog and the Foxcubs. Janáček also wanted the chickens to be sung by children, to differentiate their voices from those of the humans. See his letter dated 8 January 1925 to Ostrčil (JA ii, p. 87).

128. Ibid.

129. From Debussy's *Les fêtes galantes* (two series, each of three song settings of Verlaine, 1892 and 1904). Cf. Jiří Vysloužil, 'Leoš Janáček a naše doba' [Leoš Janáček and our time], *Hudební rozhledy*, xi, 1958, No. 18, pp. 731–44.

130. Ibid., p. 738.

131. He studied the score of *La mer* (which he bought in 1921), and also *Deux ara-besques* and *Children's Corner*, in the latter (which he bought probably in 1925) he made some notes on harmony. He also had a German libretto of *Pelléas et Mélisande*. Between 1919 and 1925 he heard Debussy's *Reflêts dans l'eau*, *Prélude à l'après-midi d'un faune*, *Pelléas et Mélisande* (in 1920 in Brno, in 1921 in Prague), the Violin Sonata, *Children's Corner*, some numbers from *Préludes*, and *Images*. (Ibid., p. 741.)

132. Janáček combined the harmony based on fourths with his favourite first inversion of a triad; in *The Cunning Little Vixen*, his strings, muted French horns and harp passages are also reminiscent of Debussy's style. (Ibid., p. 742.)

133. See Trkanová/Janáčková, p. 125.

134. 2 April 1909. The work was never published.

135. Dr Paul Wingfield has analysed a surviving page of sketches and the layout of the parts: the original trio parts are played in the quartet by the first violin and the cello, while the piano part is divided between the second violin and viola. Cf. 'Janáček's "Lost" Kreutzer Sonata', *Journal of the Royal Musical Association*, 112/2, 1987, pp. 229–56.

136. In a three-bar long *Adagio*.

137. *Con moto*, though the dance-like tempo is not sustained.

138. See letter dated 15 October 1923, in Přibáňová (ed.), *Hádanka života*, p. 129.

139. See František Kožík, *Po zarostlém chodníčku* [On the overgrown path], Odeon, Prague 1972, p. 217.

140. The director of the Berlin State Opera, Max von Schillings (1868–1933), conducted the Czech Philharmonic Orchestra in Prague on 22 February 1922. He heard *Jenůfa* at Brod's instigation; his future wife, the German soprano Barbara Kemp (1881–1959), was to sing *Jenůfa*. (Cf. JA ix, pp. 117–18.)

141. Cf. Janáček's letter to Kamila, dated 25 February 1922, in Přibáňová (ed.), *Hádanka života*, pp. 96–7.

142. Erich Kleiber (1890–1956), renowned Austrian (later Argentinian) conduc-tor. He studied in Prague; was the chief music director in Berlin State Opera (1923–34), and guest conductor at many leading opera houses. His director-ship of the Berlin State Opera was one of the greatest periods in the theatre's history, with the premières of Berg's *Wozzeck*, Milhaud's *Christophe Colomb*, and the introduction of *Jenůfa*.

143. 17 March 1924; see his *feuilleton* 'Berlin', *Lidové noviny*, 15 May 1926, in Zemanová (ed.), *Janáček's Uncollected Essays*, p. 220.

144. Letter dated 22 March 1924; cf. Vogel, *Leoš Janáček*, p. 296.

145. See his letter dated 30 June 1924, in Přibáňová (ed.), *Hádanka života*, p. 113.

146. Letter dated 1 July 1924 (ibid., pp. 113–4).

147. See Trkanová/Stejskalová, p. 110.

148. Ibid.

Chapter 9: The unbending spirit

1. Olin Downes (1886–1955), American music critic: *Boston Post*, 1906, then *New York Times*, 1924. He was the author of several popular books on music.

2. *New York Times*, 13 July 1924.
3. Ibid. For Janáček and Chopin, cf. the present volume, pp. 48, 184 and 276, n. 3; for Janáček and Dvořák, cf. the present volume, pp. 47–8 and 57.
4. *New York Times*, 13 July 1924.
5. Cf. Jarmil Burghauser's study 'Janáčkova tvorba komorní a symfonická' [Janáček's chamber works and orchestral music], *Musikologie*, iii, Prague, 1955, p. 238ff.
6. See the present volume, pp. 16–17.
7. See 'Berlin', *Lidové noviny*, 15 May 1924; in *Janáček's Uncollected Essays on Music*, selected, ed. and trans. Mirka Zemanová, Marion Boyars Publishers, London, 1989/1993, p. 220.
8. See his letter dated 24 July 1924, in *Hádanka života. Dopisy Leoše Janáčka Kamile Stösslové* [The riddle of life. (Letters of Leoš Janáček to Kamila Stösslová)], ed. Svatava Přibáňová, Opus Musicum, Brno, 1990, p. 121.
9. See 'Berlin', in Zemanová (ed.), *Janáček's Uncollected Essays*, pp. 218–20. Other structural devices, by now established in Janáček's music, are also apparent in *Mládí*, for example his typical intervallic structure.
10. See Jaroslav Vogel, *Leoš Janáček*, Orbis Publishing, London, 1981, p. 303; and Marie Trkanová, *Paměti: Zdenka Janáčková – můj život* [Memoirs: Zdenka Janáčková – my life], Šimon Ryšavý [Publishers], Brno, 1998, p. 135. [Trkanová/ Janáčková]
11. The Prague première took place on 23 November 1924 at the Vinohrady Theatre; the work was played by members of the Czech Philharmonic Orchestra.
12. The opera was performed there to great acclaim by the Brno City Theatre company on Janáček's birthday, 3 July (he left Brno that day for Hukvaldy, to avoid numerous well-wishers). The president planned to attend the performance on 9 July.
13. Cf. Jarmila Procházková, 'Prezident a skladatel' [The president and the composer], *OM*, No. 6, Brno, 1990, p. 174.
14. Ibid., pp. 174–5.
15. As explained in the present volume, Janáček respected Smetana for his patriotic stance, but much admired Dvořák for his wider Slavonic sympathies.
16. See the present volume, pp. 127–8 and 294, n. 41.
17. A matinée concert took place at the Vinohrady Theatre on 23 November 1924; on the programme were the piano cycle *On the Overgrown Path*, the song-cycle *The Songs of Hradčany*, the wind sextet *Mládí*, the Piano Sonata, and the song-cycle *The Diary of One who Disappeared*. On 27 November there was a concert of chamber music at the Prague Conservatoire. Cf. Procházková, 'Prezident', p. 182, n. 38.
18. See their letter dated 7 October 1924 (ibid., p. 175).
19. See his Christmas card to her dated 6 December 1924 (ibid.).
20. See the present volume, p. 75.
21. See his letter dated 3 April 1923, in Přibáňová (ed.), *Hádanka života*, p. 105.
22. See *Leoš Janáček. Pohled do života a díla* [Leoš Janáček. A view of the life and works], ed. Adolf Veselý, Fr. Borový, Prague, 1924, p. 99. [Janáček/ Veselý]
23. See his letter to Ostrčil dated 19 August 1926, in *Korespondence Leoše Janáčka s*

Otakarem Ostrčilem [Janáček's correspondence with Otakar Ostrčil], Janáčkův archiv ii, ed. Artuš Rektorys, HMUB, Prague, 1948 [JA ii], p. 96.

24. Chlubna's version was played on 2 May 1948 by the Brno Radio Orchestra, conducted by Břetislav Bakala. Dr Leoš Faltus (born 1937): Czech composer and musicologist; Dr Miloš Štědroň (born 1942): Czech composer and theoretician; both are based in Brno.

25. Alexander Insarov: pen name of Sonja Špálová (1898–1994), Czech poet and writer; 'Lola', which Janáček knew from *Lidové noviny*, comes from her collection of poems *Kamení* [The stones]. Pavla Křičková (1886–1972): Czech poet and teacher, sister of the composer Jaroslav Křička.

26. See Janáček/Veselý, p. 97.

27. Ibid., p. 98. For Janáček's fondness for viola d'amore, see also note 126 below.

28. Cf. Vogel, *Leoš Janáček*, p. 297.

29. On a card to his sister Josefka, see note 19 above.

30. See František Kožík, *Po zarostlém chodníčku* [On the overgrown path], Odeon, Prague, 1972, p. 243.

31. See Marie Trkanová, *U Janáčků: podle vyprávění Marie Stejskalové* [At the Janáčeks: after the account of Marie Stejskalová], Panton, Prague, 1959, p. 101. [Trkanová/Stejskalová]

32. See the present volume, p. 171, n. 92.

33. See his review in *Hudební rozhledy*, i, 15 November 1924; reprinted in *Leoš Janáček. Vzpomínky, dokumenty, korespondence a studie* [Leoš Janáček. Reminiscences, papers, correspondence and studies], ed. Bohumír Štědroň, Editio Supraphon, Prague, 1986, p. 144.

34. 6 December 1924; conducted by the Austrian conductor Artur Bodanzky (1877–1939), pupil of Alexander von Zemlinsky and Mahler's assistant (1902–4). The producer was Wilhelm von Wymetal, designer Hans Führinger.

35. *New York Times*, 13 July 1924.

36. Ernest Newman (1868–1959); music critic: *Manchester Guardian*, 1905; *Birmingham Post*, 1906; *Observer*, 1919; *Sunday Times*, 1920–58. Author of many acclaimed books, especially on Wagner.

37. Lawrence Gilman (1878–1939), distinguished critic, *New York Herald Tribune*, 1923–39, author of books on Strauss and Debussy.

38. It was not performed at the Met. until the 1974/5 season.

39. See his letter dated 21 December 1924, in Přibáňová (ed.), *Hádanka života*, p. 135.

40. Cf. Vogel, *Leoš Janáček*, p. 296.

41. Cf. Charles Susskind, *Janáček and Brod*, Yale University Press, New Haven and London, 1985, p. 88.

42. BmJA, shelfmark 50, p. 91; cf. also Procházková, 'Prezident', p. 169. On 16 and 17 September 1921 he notated the president's words in his *feuilleton* 'Rytá slova' [The engraved words], *Lidové noviny*, 22 November 1921. Reprinted in *Leoš Janáček, Triptychon*, ed. Jan Racek, HMUB, Prague, 1948, pp. 14–18. See also the present volume, p. 76.

43. Masaryk accepted the dedication on 5 May 1919. Cf. Procházková, 'Prezident', p. 169. Other dedicatees are Karel Kovařovic and Gabriela Horvátová.

44. 21 March 1920, at a matinée at the City Theatre. The performance was not a great success (ibid., p. 172).

45. Ibid., p. 173.
46. BmJA, shelfmark Z 60, pp. 123 and 125–7. See also Procházková, 'Prezident', pp. 175–6.
47. See his *feuilleton* 'Tvůrčí mysl' [The creative mind], *Lidové noviny*, 2 March 1924, in Zemanová (ed.), *Janáček's Uncollected Essays*, p. 190.
48. See Procházková, 'Prezident', p. 175.
49. See his letter dated 4 July 1924, in Přibáňová (ed.), *Hádanka života*, p. 114.
50. See her letter dated 9 July 1924 (ibid., p. 120).
51. See his letter dated 15 July 1924 (ibid., p. 116–20).
52. See her letter dated 25 July 1924 (ibid., p. 122).
53. See his letter dated 27 July 1924 (ibid.).
54. See his letter dated 20 August 1924 (ibid., p. 124).
55. See his letter dated 8 November 1924 (ibid., p. 131).
56. See his letter dated 22 November 1924 (ibid., p. 132).
57. See her letter dated 13 December 1924 (ibid., p. 135).
58. See Trkanová/Janáčková, p. 130.
59. Max Brod, *Leoš Janáček: život a dílo* [Leoš Janáček: life and works], HMUB, Prague, 1924. The German original was published in 1925 by the Wiener Philharmonischer Verlag, Vienna.
60. Janáček/Veselý.
61. Ibid., p. 100.
62. See his letter dated 5 February 1925, in Přibáňová (ed.), *Hádanka života*, p. 140.
63. See his letter dated 22 January 1925 (ibid., p. 139).
64. See his letter dated 26 March 1925 (ibid., p. 144).
65. See his letter dated 23 April 1925 (ibid., p. 145).
66. See his *feuilleton* 'Concertino', *Pult und Taktstock*, May–June 1927, in Zemanová (ed.), *Janáček's Uncollected Essays*, pp. 108–10.
67. Ibid., p. 108.
68. Ibid., p. 109.
69. Ibid.
70. The *Presto* starts off softly but soon picks up volume, though no instrument wins the 'quarrel'.
71. Cf. Vogel, *Leoš Janáček*, p. 306.
72. The Brno première took place on 16 February 1926, the Prague première on 20 February. Ilona Kurzová-Štěpánová (1899–1975) was a distinguished Czech pianist and teacher.
73. See his letter dated 7 February 1925, to the pianist Jan Heřman (1886–1946); quoted in Vogel, *Leoš Janáček*, p. 305.
74. See his letter dated 7 May 1925, in Přibáňová (ed.), *Hádanka života*, p. 147.
75. See his letter dated 6 May 1925 (ibid).
76. See his letter dated 15 May 1917, in *Korespondence Leoše Janáčka s Marií Calmou and MUDr Františkem Veselým* [Janáček's correspondence with Marie Calma and MUDr František Veselý], Janáčkův archiv viii, ed. Jan Racek and Artuš Rektorys, Orbis Publishing, Prague, 1951 [JA viii] pp. 70–1.
77. See Trkanová/Janáčková, p. 131–2.
78. See his letter dated 21 May 1925, in Přibáňová (ed.), *Hádanka života*, p. 150.
79. See his letter to Brod, *Korespondence Leoše Janáčka s Maxem Brodem* [Janáček's

correspondence with Max Brod], Janáčkův archiv ix, ed. Jan Racek and Artuš Rektorys, SNKLHU, Prague, 1953 [JA ix], pp. 181–3.

80. Cf. Trkanová/Janáčková, p. 132.
81. See his letter dated 3 June 1925, in Přibáňová (ed.), *Hádanka života*, p. 152.
82. See his letter dated 11 January 1918, in *Korespondence Leoše Janáčka s Gabrielou Horvátovou* [Janáček's correspondence with Gabriela Horvátová], Janáčkův archiv vi, ed. Artuš Rektorys, HM, Prague, 1950 [JA vi], p. 47.
83. See his letter dated 3 June 1925, in Přibáňová (ed.), *Hádanka života*, p. 153.
84. See his letter dated 30 May 1925 (ibid., p. 151).
85. See Trkanová/Stejskalová, p. 111.
86. See his letter dated 11 June 1925, in Přibáňová (ed.), *Hádanka života*, p. 154.
87. See his letter dated 16 June 1925 (ibid., p. 155).
88. See his letter dated 13 June 1925, in JA ix, pp. 179–81.
89. See his letter dated 11 July 1925 (ibid., pp. 188–9).
90. See his letter dated 26 June 1925 (ibid., pp. 185–6).
91. See Vogel, *Leoš Janáček*, p. 281.
92. See his letter dated 9 July 1925, in Přibáňová (ed.), *Hádanka života*, p. 156.
93. See his letter dated 30 July 1925 (ibid., p. 159).
94. See 'Basta!', *Lidové noviny*, 8 November 1925, in Zemanová (ed.), *Janáček's Uncollected Essays*, p. 225.
95. Ibid.
96. Ibid., p. 266.
97. See his card dated 7 September 1925, in Přibáňová (ed.), *Hádanka života*, p. 164.
98. See Trkanová/Stejskalová, p. 111.
99. See his letter dated 15 September 1925, in Přibáňová (ed.), *Hádanka života*, p. 165.
100. He made a final revision during the first few days of his summer break at Luhačovice; cf. John Tyrrell, *Janáček's Operas: A Documentary Account*, Faber, London, 1992, p. 12.
101. Cf. John Tyrrell, *Czech Opera*, CUP, Cambridge, 1988, pp. 292–7.
102. Ibid., p. 296.
103. The Brno première took place on 11 November 1925. See also his letters dated 6 and 23 November 1925, in Přibáňová (ed.), *Hádanka života*, pp. 167 and 168.
104. See Janáček's letter, dated 21 January 1926, and Ostrčil's reply of 31 January, in JA ii, pp. 91–4.
105. On 10 December 1922, at the Vinohrady Theatre. Čapek (1890–1938) was then 32.
106. *The Insect Play* was produced at the Regent Theatre by the actor-manager Nigel (from 1928 Sir Nigel) Playfair (1874–1934), who was also the joint translator. Playfair was the manager of the Lyric Theatre, Hammersmith (1918–34), where Čapek saw in 1924 Congreve's *The Way of the World*, and met Edith Evans, a celebrated Millamant. She expressed interest in *Makropulos*, which was finally produced in London (as *The Makropulos Secret*) in 1930.
107. Taking down the speech melody of a passer-by near the National Theatre, and probably also of Čapek himself; cf. Tyrell, *Janáček's Operas*, p. 304.

108. See his letter dated 28 December 1922, in Přibáňová (ed.), *Hádanka života*, p. 104.
109. Karel Čapek, *Věc Makropulos*, Aventinum, Prague, 1922.
110. See his undated letter (postmarked Prague, 27 February 1923), in JA ix, pp. 246–7.
111. See Helena Čapková, *Moji milí bratři* [My dear brothers], Československý spisovatel, Prague, 1962, p. 352.
112. See his letter dated 10 September 1923, in JA ix, pp. 247–8.
113. Among the scholars at the court were two famous astronomers, Johannes Kepler and Tycho de Brahe.
114. *České slovo*, 18 November 1926; cf. also Vogel, *Leoš Janáček*, p. 311.
115. 'Jsme věci a stíny!' [We are just objects and shadows!]; their scene totals a mere 25 words.
116. See 'An Interview from *Literární svět*', 8 March 1928, in Zemanová (ed.), *Janáček's Uncollected Essays*, p. 122.
117. For example, the protagonist is addressed either as, 'Marty', or 'Martyová', i.e., with a Czech suffix -ová.
118. For example, Marty's 'Ferdi byl přece Pepi syn!' [Ferdi was Joe's son after all!], Act 1, is not grammatically correct (though it has been said that, as Marty was Greek, her Czech was unlikely to be perfect!). In Act 3, Gregor's 'pečítko' [a seal] should have been 'pečetítko' – clearly too long a word here for Janáček.
119. Cf. Vogel, *Leoš Janáček*, p. 314.
120. In the part of Chambermaid and Machinist, at the beginning of Act 2.
121. This theme seems to be directly linked with the name Makropulos on several occasions. In Act 2, it is heard as Prus first mentions the name (to Marty's indignation), and later when Marty asks Albert Gregor whether he likes this name. In Act 3 it is heard soon after the arrival of the lawyer Kolenatý and the others, as well as after Marty at last utters her real name. It also appears before Hauk-Šendorf's entrance, and as Marty contemplates her life.
122. In Act 3, it is heard as Marty gives the name of her father, Hieronymus Makropulos, and his title, 'physician to the Emperor Rudolf II'; the theme recurs towards the end of the act, before Marty hands the secret document to Krista.
123. This is heard as Marty interrupts (twice) Kolenatý's narration in Act 1, and again twice during Gregor's scene; the instrument is used again on three occasions in Act 2, and recurs in Act 3, in the interlude before Marty's reappearance.
124. Act 2, 'Strada pískala' [Strada squealed]. 'Spanish' rhythms can be heard in Hauk-Šendorf's scene 'Dovolte, dovolte prosím' [Allow me, allow me, please], Act 2, as he recalls his stay in Spain with Marty (then known as Eugenia Montez).
125. Jiří Vysloužil, *Leoš Janáček*, Společnost Leoše Janáčka, Brno, 1978, p. 14.
126. In stage performances of *Makropulos* the viola d'amore is usually substituted by a viola or violin; only in modern recordings can the viola d'amore be heard clearly. Janáček had heard the viola d'amore in Brno and was familiar with its use in 19th- and 20th-century opera, but was probably attracted to this obsolete instrument both for its name and the sound – his scoring for it is not always practical. See also *Káťa Kabanová*, in the present volume, p. 166.

127. See his letter to Kamila dated 23 February 1925, in Přibáňová (ed.), *Hádanka života*, p. 142. As usual, he had to 'tidy up' the first version; he started on this in March 1925, and the end of Act 2 is dated 27 July 1925; cf. also his letter of that day to Kamila (ibid., p. 159).

128. See his letter dated 5 December 1925 (ibid., p. 169).

129. See his letter dated 29 March 1926 (ibid., p. 176).

130. In fact, Rosa Newmarch was the joint dedicatee, in recognition of her services. Janáček originally called the work *Military Symfonietta*; in 1928. he still referred to it under that name. Cf. also Vogel, *Leoš Janáček*, p. 322.

131. See his *feuilleton* 'Moje město' [My town], *Lidové noviny*, 24 December 1927, in *Fejetony z Lidových novin* [*Feuilletons* from *Lidové noviny*], ed. Jan Racek, Krajské nakladatelství, Brno, 1958, p. 52.

132. 'Ejhle, chase naša', according to Prof. Jiří Vysloužil.

133. Cf. Vogel, *Leoš Janáček*, p. 392.

134. See Miloš Štědroň, sleeve note of the CD recording of the *Sinfonietta* (Brno State Philharmonic Orchestra, conducted by František Jílek), Supraphon, Prague, 1988.

135. Cf. Trkanová/Stejskalová, pp., 112–3. Rosa Newmarch first visited Czechoslovakia in 1919, following an invitation by Karel Kovařovic. She saw *Jenůfa* on 1 July 1919, and wrote about the opera enthusiastically for *The Musical Times* ('A Slovak [sic!] Music-Drama', 1 December 1919). During her stay she also visited Moravia, with Kovařovic and his wife, but did not meet Janáček then, nor on her subsequent visits to Prague in 1920 and 1921.

136. Her two lectures took place in June 1922; *The Diary* was performed on 21 September 1922, at Bechstein Hall. In December that year Rosa Newmarch published an article on Janáček and the speech melodies, 'Janáček and Moravian Music Drama', in the *Slavonic Review*, London, i, No. 2, pp. 362–79.

137. *The Fiddler's Child* was conducted in October 1923 by Sir Henry Wood; it was the work's first performance outside Czechoslovakia. Sir Henry became an enthusiastic advocate of Janáček's music.

138. See her letter dated 11 February 1926, in *Janáček–Newmarch Correspondence*, ed. Zdenka E. Fischmann, Kabel Publishers, Rockville, Maryland, 1986, p. 91.

139. See his letter dated 24 February 1926 (ibid., p. 98).

140. Jan Mikota (1903–78), secretary of Janáček's Czech publisher, Hudební matice. Janáček got to know him during his trip to Venice in September 1925; Mikota also accompanied him to Frankfurt in 1927.

141. Adila Fachiri (1888–1962), a renowned British violinist, whose interpretation impressed Janáček. Leon Goossens (1897–1988), a famous British oboist. The reception at the School of Slavonic Studies took place on 4 May 1926. Two of Janáček's *Silesian Songs*, in Rosa Newmarch's translation, were sung by Herbert Hayner. The boys of L.C.C. Mansfield Road School, Gospel Oak (one of the best boys' choirs at the time in London) sang a number of English folk-songs.

142. See his undated letter (postmarked London, 6 May, 1926), in Přibáňová (ed.) *Hádanka života*, p. 179. The death of a driver he mentioned is sometimes thought to have been the inspiration for his Violin Concerto ('The Pilgrimage of a Soul'), which he began writing as soon as he returned to

Brno (and which, after a final revision, ended up as the overture to his last opera, *From the House of the Dead*). Cf. John Tyrrell, *Intimate Letters. Leoš Janáček to Kamila Stösslová*, Faber, London, 1994, p. 89.

143. Fanny Davies (1861–1934): 'an old hag – scarecrow', Janáček wrote to Kamila on 3 May 1926; in Přibáňová (ed.), *Hádanka života*, p. 178.

144. See his letter dated 8 September 1926, in Fischmann (ed.), *Janáček–Newmarch*, pp. 143–4.

145. See his letter from the Langham Hotel, BmJA, reprinted in Zemanová (ed.), *Janáček's Uncollected Essays*, p. 198.

146. See her letter dated 4 September 1926, in Fischmann (ed.), *Janáček–Newmarch*, pp. 140–2. Mrs Elizabeth Courtauld was on the board of the Royal Opera, Covent Garden. Between 1925 and 1927 she subleased the opera with her husband Samuel, and gave it a considerable subsidy.

147. Under the baton of the great Czech conductor Rafael Kubelík (1914–96).

148. See 'Moře, země' [The sea, the land], *Lidové noviny*, 13 June 1926, in Zemanová (ed.), *Janáček's Uncollected Essays*, pp. 230–1.

149. Fritz Zweig (1893–1984), German conductor, studied composition with Arnold Schoenberg. He worked at various opera houses throughout Europe: Berlin Volksoper, 1923; Berlin State Opera, 1927; Neues Deutsches Theater, Prague, 1934; Paris Opéra, 1938. From 1940 he worked in the USA.

150. See 'Moře, země' [The sea, the land], *Lidové noviny*, 13 June 1926, in Zemanová (ed.), *Janáček's Uncollected Essays*, p. 233.

151. For Kleiber, see the present volume, p. 307, n. 142; for Klemperer, see the present volume, p. 299, n. 160; for Zweig, note 149 above.

152. 'Glagolitic', on account of the Mass having originally been written in the Glagolitic script. 'Glagol' was the first alphabet of Old Slavonic, the language developed by Cyril (Constantine, *c.* 827–69), one of the Greek brothers invited in 863 by the Duke Rastislav of Great Moravia to disseminate Christianity throughout his empire. Cf. also the present volume, p. 7.

153. See 'An interview from *Literární svět*', 8 March 1928, in Zemanová (ed.), *Janáček's Uncollected Essays*, p. 122.

154. Ibid., p. 123.

155. See Trkanová/Janáčková, p. 152, and Trkanová/Stejskalová, p. 98.

156. See 'Glagolskaja missa' [The Glagolitic Mass], *Lidové noviny*, 27 November 1927, in Zemanová (ed.), *Janáček's Uncollected Essays*, p. 114.

157. Ludvík Kundera (1891–1971), Czech musicologist, father of the Czech writer Milan Kundera; his review appeared in *Tempo*, vii, p. 192. For Janáček's response, see his card dated 28 February 1928, BmJA, reprinted in Zemanová (ed.), *Janáček's Uncollected Essays*, p. 124.

158. Cf., for example, Vogel, *Leoš Janáček*, p. 336. Stejskalová reports that 'he had many good friends among priests', but that later in life he 'avoided anything that touched religion'. Cf. Trkanová/Stejskalová, p. 99; see also, for example, his letter to Kamila, dated 26 July 1926, in Přibáňová (ed.), *Hádanka života*, p. 178, about the new church bells in Hukvaldy: 'It would be nice, if they would not also toll to fool people.'

159. See Trkanová/Stejskalová, p. 99.

160. Milan Kundera, *Testaments Betrayed*, Faber, London and Boston, 1995, p. 183.

161. See his letter dated 29 October 1926, in Přibáňová (ed.), *Hádanka života*,

p. 191; the work was in fact completed by 30 October 1926. Otakar Hollmann (1894–1967); Bohuslav Martinů wrote the *Divertimento* for the left hand for him.

162. Cf. Vogel, *Leoš Janáček*, p. 344.

163. Ibid., p. 347.

164. On 27 December 1926, he wrote that he had just revised the work. Cf. Přibáňová (ed.), *Hádanka života*, p. 194.

165. Josef Lada (1887–1957), best known for his illustrations to Hašek's comic masterpiece, *The Good Soldier Švejk*; Ondřej Sekora (1899–1967), popular illustrator.

166. 26 October 1925, in Brno.

167. See the score of the original version, Editio Moravia, Brno, and Universal Edition, Vienna, UE 19994, 1993.

168. See Vogel, *Leoš Janáček*, p. 348.

169. See his letters dated 9 January, 12 and 24 February, 29 March, 15 and 30 June, 7, 15 and 24 August, 9 October, 23 November and 14 December, in Přibáňová (ed.), *Hádanka života*, pp. 171, 173, 174, 175, 183, 185–6, 188, 189, 190, 191, 192 and 193.

170. See, for example, his derisory comments about Otakar Ostrčil (who was devoted to Janáček) on 17 and 29 January 1926 (ibid., p. 172), and about Fanny Davies, on 3 May 1926 (ibid., p. 178).

171. See his letter dated 15 August 1926 (ibid., p. 189).

172. See his letter dated 29 October 1926 (ibid., p. 191).

173. See Trkanová/Janáčková, p. 139.

174. Ibid.

175. 18 December 1926, conducted by František Neumann, producer Ota Zítek, designer Josef Čapek. Alexandra Čvanová excelled in the title-role.

176. See his letter dated 14 December 1926, in Přibáňová (ed.), *Hádanka života*, p. 193.

177. See his letter dated 28 January 1927 (ibid., p. 195).

178. See Čapková, *Moji milí bratři*, p. 353.

179. See his letter dated 28 January 1927, in Přibáňová (ed.), *Hádanka života*, p. 193.

180. See Trkanová/Janáčková, p. 140.

181. See his letter dated 9 November 1926, in JA ix, p. 206; the changes proposed by Brod would naturally need to be reflected in the music, and he had no intention of writing any.

182. See his letter dated 11 November 1926 (ibid., p. 208).

183. See his letter dated 2 January 1927 (ibid., pp. 212–16).

184. See Janáček's letter dated 18 February 1927, to Universal Edition, in *Briefe an der Universal-Edition*, ed. Ernst Hilmar, Hans Schneider, Tutzing, 1988, pp. 301–2. Cf. also Susskind, *Janáček and Brod*, pp. 101–5, and Tyrrell, *Janáček's Operas*, pp. 313–4.

185. Among those who also attended that day were the great Czech painter Alfons Mucha, the writers Ignát Herrmann, Jiří Mahen and Gabriela Preissová, the renowned photographer František Drtikol, the actress Leopolda Dostalová, the soprano Kamila Ungrová and, apart from Janáček, two other composers, Josef Suk and J.B. Foerster. Cf. Procházková, 'Prezident', pp. 177–8.

186. See his letter dated 25 April 1927, in Přibáňová (ed.), *Hádanka života*, pp. 200–1.
187. In his next letter, dated 26 April 1927, he used the intimate form of address, 'Ty' (second person singular) rather than the formal 'Vy' (second person plural).
188. Janáček did so reluctantly, and also pleaded with her not to burn his letters.
189. As reported by him in his letter dated 30 April 1927, in Přibáňová (ed.), *Hádanka života*, pp. 202.
190. Ibid.
191. See his letter dated 2 May 1927 (ibid., p. 203).
192. See his letter dated 5 May 1927 (ibid., p. 205).
193. See his letter written probably on 6 May 1927 (ibid., p. 208).
194. See Trkanová/Janáčková, p. 140–1.
195. See his letter dated 21 May 1927, in Přibáňová (ed.), *Hádanka života*, p. 209.
196. See his letter dated 27–8 May 1927 (ibid., p. 209).

Chapter 10: The final masterpieces

1. See his letter dated 27 May 1927, in *Hádanka života*. (*Dopisy Leoše Janáčka Kamile Stösslové*) [The riddle of life. (Letters of Leoš Janáček to Kamila Stösslová)], ed. Svatava Přibáňová, Opus Musicum, Brno 1990, p. 210.
2. See his letter dated 19 February 1927 (ibid., p. 196).
3. See his undated letter, probably 16 October 1826 (ibid., p. 234).
4. See Kamila's letter dated 26 May 1927, and Janáček's letters dated 28 and 29 May 1927 (ibid., pp. 210–1).
5. See letter dated 29-30 May 1927 (ibid., p. 212).
6. Ibid.
7. Letter dated 30–31 May 1927 (ibid., p. 216).
8. See Marie Trkanová, *Paměti: Zdenka Janáčková – můj život* [Memoirs: Zdenka Janáčková – my life], Šimon Ryšavý [Publishers], Brno 1998, p. 141 [Trkanová/Janáčková]. Zdenka had to ask Janáček to give her written consent for the operation.
9. See his letter dated 8 June 1927, in Přibáňová (ed.), *Hádanka života*, p. 218.
10. See his letter dated 15 June 1927 (ibid.).
11. See his letter dated 13 June 1927 (ibid., pp. 218–19).
12. See Trkanová/Janáčková, p. 143.
13. Ibid., p. 144.
14. Ibid. This visit is not listed in John Tyrrell's list of Janáček's visits to Kamila's house in Písek (John Tyrrell, *Intimate Letters: Leoš Janáček to Kamila Stösslová*, Faber, London, 1994, p. 366). However, Janáček arrived in Prague on 26 June, and the wording of his letter dated 28 June 1927, from Prague ('. . . I will surely come back to you again!') seems to confirm that he had spent some time with Kamila in Písek. Cf. Přibáňová (ed.), *Hádanka života*, p. 219. Tyrrell dates Janáček's next letter, from Frankfurt, 28 June (p. 123); Přibáňová dates it 30 June (p. 220).
15. Cf. Trkanová/Janáčková, p. 145; cf. for example, Janáček's letter dated 11 July 1927, in Přibáňová (ed.), *Hádanka života*, p. 221.

16. 5–6 July 1927; cf. his letters dated 21 June, 1 and 11 July, in Přibáňová (ed.), *Hádanka života*, pp. 219–21.
17. See Trkanová/Janáčková, p. 144.
18. See Přibáňová (ed.), *Hádanka života*, p. 224.
19. See his letter dated 1 September 1927 (ibid., p. 227).
20. See his letter dated 4 September 1927 (ibid., p. 228). This visit is not mentioned in the list of meetings in Tyrrell, *Intimate Letters*.
21. See his letter dated 11 September (ibid., p. 229).
22. See Trkanová/Janáčková, p. 145.
23. See his letter dated 4 September, in Přibáňová (ed.), *Hádanka života*, p. 228.
24. He spent two days in Písek (1–3 October 1927).
25. See his letter dated 16 December 1927, in Přibáňová (ed.), *Hádanka života*, p. 234.
26. See his letter dated 16–17 October 1927 (ibid., p. 235).
27. See his letter dated 26 October 1927 (ibid., p. 240).
28. See his letter dated 30 October 1927 (ibid., p. 242).
29. See Trkanová/Janáčková, p. 147.
30. See his letter dated 9 November 1927, in Přibáňová (ed.), *Hádanka života*, p. 244.
31. See his letter dated 5 November 1927 (ibid., p. 242).
32. See his letter dated 11 November 1927 (ibid., p. 245).
33. See his letter dated 15 November 1927 (ibid., p. 249). *The Cunning Little Vixen* was in fact performed in Brno on 9 November 1927, the day before Mascagni conducted *Aida* there.
34. Ibid.
35. Cf. his letter dated 13–14 November 1927 (ibid., p. 247).
36. Cf. his letter dated 16 November 1927 (ibid., p. 250).
37. See his letter dated 22 November 1927 (ibid., p. 252).
38. Ibid.
39. Kamila burned some of his letters; in many of the surviving ones she tore off some pages, cut out certain parts with scissors, or blotted out words which she obviously thought too bold.
40. See his letter dated 24–5 November 1927, in Přibáňová (ed.), *Hádanka života*, p. 256.
41. See his letter dated 29 November 1927 (ibid., p. 259).
42. Ibid.
43. 25 April 1927; see the present volume, pp. 219–20, and 316, n. 186. For 'it seemed that the earth would split open', see Janáček's letter dated 7 May 1927, in Přibáňová (ed.), *Hádanka života*, p. 207.
44. See his letter dated 30 November 1927 (ibid., p. 259).
45. See his letter dated 1–2 December 1927 (ibid., p. 260).
46. Ibid., p. 261.
47. 13 December 1927, to mark the 20th anniversary of the Hudební matice society; on the programme were also works by Emil Axman, Boleslav Vomáčka and Jaroslav Křička.
48. See his undated letter, postmarked 12 December 1927, in Přibáňová (ed.), *Hádanka života*, p. 264.
49. See his letter dated 14 December 1927 (ibid., p. 265).

50. Ibid., and his letter dated 13 December 1927 (p. 264).
51. See undated letter, postmarked 16 December 1927 (ibid., p. 266).
52. See his letter dated 18 December 1927 (ibid., p. 268).
53. Ibid.
54. See his letter dated 19 December 1927 (ibid., p. 269).
55. See his letter dated 20 December 1927 (ibid., p. 270).
56. See his letter dated 21 December 1927 (ibid., p. 272).
57. See his letter dated 24 December 1927 (ibid.).
58. See his letter dated 25 December 1927 (ibid., pp. 273–4).
59. See his letter dated 31 December 1927 (ibid., p. 280). 'Heaven' or 'our Písek heaven' was Janáček's code for Kamila's home in Písek, but it seems that later he used it for a particular room at the back of the house, and towards the end of his life virtually for any room where Kamila was.
60. Ibid.
61. See Trkanová/Janáčková, p. 148.
62. Ibid.
63. Ibid.
64. Ibid., p. 149.
65. Ibid.
66. Ibid.
67. See his letter of 1–2 January 1928, in Přibáňová (ed.), *Hádanka života*, p. 281.
68. See his letter dated 2 January 1928 (ibid.).
69. See his letter dated 4 January 1928 (ibid., p. 283).
70. See his letter dated 10 January 1928 (ibid.).
71. Ibid.
72. See his letter dated 18 January 1928, in *Korespondence Leoše Janáčka s Maxem Brodem* [Janáček's correspondence with Max Brod], Janáčkův archiv ix, ed. Jan Racek and Artuš Rektorys, SNKLHU, Prague, 1953 [JA ix], p. 252.
73. See his letter dated 12 January 1928, in Přibáňová (ed.), *Hádanka života*, pp. 285–6.
74. Boleslav Vomáčka, *Lidové noviny*, 24 January 1928.
75. See his letter dated 23 January 1928, in Přibáňová (ed.), *Hádanka života*, p. 288.
76. See Trkanová/Janáčková, p. 150. Apparently, Janáček told David Stössel what Věra had heard. Stössel, accompanied by Janáček, then visited her, demanded to know the name of her source, and threatened to sue him for slander. However, when Věra agreed to name her source in court, Stössel left and took no further action. Janáček then severed relations with her.
77. Ibid., p. 151.
78. Ibid.
79. See his letter dated 29 January 1928, in Přibáňová (ed.), *Hádanka života*, p. 292. 'Love Letters' later became 'Intimate Letters'.
80. See his letter dated 1 February 1928 (ibid., p. 294).
81. See his letter dated 8 February 1928 (ibid., p. 299).
82. Ibid.
83. The performance took place on 12 February 1928; it was conducted by Jascha Horenstein. On 10 February, Sir Henry Wood conducted the work in London.

84. Přibáňová (ed.), *Hádanka života*, p. 300. Janáček visited Kamila in Písek (12–14 February).
85. See his letter dated 18 February 1928 (ibid., p. 304).
86. See his letter dated 19 February 1928 (ibid., p. 305).
87. See his letter dated 20 February 1928 (ibid., p. 306).
88. See his letter dated 26 February 1928 (ibid., p. 307).
89. See his letter dated 28 February 1928 (ibid., p. 308).
90. See his letter dated 28 February 1928, in the evening (ibid., p. 309).
91. See his letter dated 3 March 1928 (ibid., p. 311).
92. 'Bela [sic] Bartók, nebýt slovenských písní, z kterých sál, bylo by suché jeho dílo'. BmJA, shelfmark S 23, see Jiří Vysloužil, 'Janáček's Marginalia in *Moravian National Songs* of 1835', in *Colloquium Leoš Janáček et Musica Europaea*, ed. Rudolf Pečman, Brno, 1968, p. 260.

On meetings between Janáček and Bartók, see my Introduction, p. 4. Both Jan Racek ('Leoš Janáčeks und Béla Bartóks Bedeutung in der Weltmusik', *Sborník prací Filosofické fakulty brněnské university*, F6, Brno, 1962, pp. 5–16) and John Tyrrell (*Czech Opera*, CUP, Cambridge, 1988, p. 246) erroneously claim that Janáček and Bartók only met once. On the three meetings between the two composers and contacts in writing, see Denis Dille, *Documenta Bartókiana*, 1, Heft 3, Akadémiai Kiadó, Budapest – B. Schott's Söhne, Mainz, 1968, pp. 122; Vera Lampert, 'Zeitgenössische Musik in Bartóks Notensammlung', in the same series, Heft 5, pp. 142–68; James Porter, 'Bartók and Janáček: Contact, Context and Confluence', in *Ethnologische, historische und systematische Musikwissenschaft, Oskár Elschek zum 65. Geburtstag*, ed. Franz Födermayer und Ladislav Burlas, Institut für Musikwissenschaft, Bratislava, 1998, pp. 407–15. Cf. also James Porter, 'Bartók's *Concerto for Orchestra* (1943) and Janáček's *Sinfonietta* (1926): Conceptual and Structural Parallels', in *Bartók Perspectives, Man, Composer and Ethnomusicologist*, ed. Elliott Antokoletz, Benjamin Suchoff and Victoria Fischer OUP, Oxford, 2000, pp. 152–68.
93. See his letter dated 3 March 1928, in Přibáňová (ed.), *Hádanka života*, p. 311.
94. See his letter dated 13 March 1928 (ibid., p. 322).
95. See his letter dated 14 March 1928 (ibid.).
96. See his letter dated 3 March 1928 (ibid., p. 311).
97. See his letter dated 4 March 1928 (ibid., p. 312).
98. See his letter dated 6 March 1928 (ibid., p. 315).
99. See her letter dated 5 March 1928 (ibid.).
100. Cf. Trkanová/Janáčková, p. 151, and Janáček's letter dated 8 March 1928, in Přibáňová (ed.), *Hádanka života*, p. 317.
101. Ibid.
102. See Trkanová/Janáčková, p. 152.
103. See his letter dated 10–11 March 1928 in Přibáňová (ed.), *Hádanka života*, p. 319.
104. See his letter dated 14 March 1928 (ibid., p. 322).
105. See her letter dated 14 March 1928 (ibid., p. 325).
106. Cf. Germaine Greer, *The Female Eunuch*, Paladin, London, 1971, p. 206.
107. Ibid., p. 202.
108. For Janáček's fondness for the viola d'amore, see the present volume, pp. 167, 190, 208 and 312, n. 126.

109. The quartet was founded in 1923 as the Kudláček Quartet by the violinist and professor at the Brno Conservatoire, František Kudláček (1894–1972); it was renamed the Moravian Quartet in 1924. The ensemble gave concerts throughout Czechoslovakia until 1959, and in 1925 toured Austria, Germany and Italy. It successfully promoted quartets by Smetana and Dvořák, as well as by contemporary Czech composers.

110. At the Exhibition of Contemporary Culture on 7 September (a private performance for critics), and on 25 September 1928 for the public. Cf. Tyrrell, *Intimate Letters*, p. 362. Vogel gives the date of the first performance as 11 September 1928; cf. *Leoš Janáček*, p. 380.

111. See Přibáňová (ed.), *Hádanka života*, p. 330.

112. See his letter to Kamila dated 28 March 1928 (ibid.). He made a detour to Písek (23–5 March.).

113. Ibid., pp. 330–1.

114. Ibid., p. 331. See also the present volume, pp. 171–2, 211, 241, 299, n. 162, and 305, n. 93.

115. See his letter dated 5 April 1928, in Přibáňová (ed.), *Hádanka života*, p. 339.

116. See his letter dated 10 April 1928 (ibid.).

117. Ibid.

118. Dr Vlastimil Blažek (1878–1950), Czech musical archivist, founder of the Czechoslovak Mozart society. His father was an older colleague of Janáček's at the Teachers' Training Institute in Brno.

119. See his letter dated 11 April 1928, in Přibáňová (ed.), *Hádanka života*, p. 341.

120. Ibid.

121. See his letter dated 13 April 1928 (ibid., p. 342).

122. Cf. Trkanová/Janáčková, p. 152. The *Glagolitic Mass* was given at the Smetana Hall, Prague's Municipal House, on 8 April 1928. The composer and conductor Jaroslav Kvapil (1892–1958), then chorus master of the Brno Beseda Choral Society, conducted the Czech Philharmonic Orchestra, with soloists from Brno. In composition, Kvapil was a pupil of Janáček and Reger; after the Second World War he was professor of composition at the Janáček Academy in Brno (JAMU). He reintroduced works by Dvořák and Smetana at the Beseda, and introduced works by many contemporary Czech composers, including Janáček's cantatas and the *Glagolitic Mass* (first performance, broadcast live, on 5 December 1927).

123. See his letter dated 18 April 1928, in Přibáňová (ed.), *Hádanka života*, p. 349.

124. See his letter dated 25 April 1928 (ibid., p. 350).

125. Cf. Trkanová/Janáčková, pp. 153–4.

126. Ibid., p. 153.

127. See his letter dated 17 April 1928, in Přibáňová (ed.), *Hádanka života*, p. 347.

128. Cf. his letter dated 18 April 1928 (ibid., p. 348).

129. See her letter dated 29 April 1928 (ibid., p. 352).

130. The Exhibition of Contemporary Culture was staged to commemorate the tenth anniversary of the foundation of Czechoslovakia. It was held at a newly built permanent exhibition site in Pisárky, a Brno suburb (26 May – 30 September 1928). Cf. also his letter dated 30 April 1928 (ibid., p. 355).

131. See his letter dated 1 May 1928 (ibid., p. 357).

132. See his letter dated 5 May 1928 (ibid., p. 359).

133. See his letter dated 5-6 May 1928 (ibid., p. 360). Barbara Kemp (1881–1959) was a leading German soprano in Berlin (1913–31); she married Max von Schillings in 1923. Cf. also the present volume, p. 307, n. 140.

134. Bruno Walter conducted *Taras Bulba* at the Leipzig Gewandhaus on 25 October 1928; Sir Henry Wood conducted the work in London on 10 October 1928. Cf. also the present volume, p. 212.

135. See his letter dated 8 May 1928, in Přibáňová (ed.), *Hádanka života*, p. 362.

136. See his letter dated 11 May 1928 (ibid., p. 365).

137. See his letter dated 18–19 May 1928 (ibid., p. 373).

138. See his letter dated 25 May 1928 (ibid., p. 377).

139. See her letter dated 28 May 1928 (ibid.).

140. Cf. Trkanová/Janáčková, p. 153.

141. See his letter dated 29 May 1928, in Přibáňová (ed.), *Hádanka života*, p. 379.

142. See his undated letter, probably written 30 May 1928 (ibid.).

143. See her letter dated 2 June 1928 (ibid., p. 383).

144. See his letter dated 3 June 1928 (ibid., p. 384).

Gerhart Hauptmann, German writer and playwright (1862–1946), famous for his novels and especially for his play, *Die Weber* (1892), about the Saxon weavers during the Industrial Revolution. *Schluck und Jau* (1900) is a free adaptation of the Induction to *The Taming of the Shrew*; Christopher Sly is replaced by Jau, a tramp and a drunk; Schluck, another tramp, is dressed up as his 'princess'. The play was scheduled for an open-air production at Heidelberg Castle during the summer.

Gustav Hartung (1887–1946), German stage director at Frankfurt (1914–20), then Intendant at Darmstadt, Cologne and Berlin. He was noted for his public protest against the Nazi régime; in 1933 he left Germany for Switzerland. He became stage manager at Basle (1937–40); after the war, he was invited to work in Heidelberg.

145. See his letter dated 4 June 1928, in Přibáňová (ed.), *Hádanka života*, p. 385.

146. Ibid., p. 385–6.

147. See his letter dated 6 June 1928 (ibid., p. 387).

148. Ibid.

149. The concerts took place between 2 and 9 June. Vítězslav Novák (1870–1949) was sometimes considered a Czech representative of Impressionism. Other composers on the programme were Josef Klička, Rudolf Karel, Emil Axman, K.B. Jirák, Jaroslav Křička, Jan Kunc, Jaroslav Kvapil, Otakar Ostrčil, Jaroslav Řídký, Otakar Šín, Jaromír Weinberger and Bedřich Widermann.

150. See his letter dated 7–8 June 1928, in Přibánová (ed.), *Hádanka života*, p. 388.

151. See his letter dated 8 June 1928 (ibid., p. 389).

152. See his undated letter, probably written on 9–10 June 1928 (ibid., p. 390).

153. *Sbor při kladení základního kamene Masarykovy university v Brně* [Chorus for laying of foundation stone of Masaryk University in Brno], to words by Antonín Trýb. The work was sung by the male choir of the Beseda Society, conducted by Jaroslav Kvapil, its chorus master at the time.

154. See his undated letter, probably written on 9–10 June 1928, in Přibáňová (ed.), *Hádanka života*, p. 390.

155. Ibid.
156. See her letter dated 11 June 1928 (ibid., p. 393).
157. See his letter dated 14 June 1928 (ibid.).
158. See his letter dated 18 June 1928 (ibid., p. 395).
159. See her letter dated 27 June 1928, (ibid., p. 398).
160. See his letter dated 27 June 1928 (ibid., p. 399).
161. See his letter dated 29 June 1928 (ibid., p. 401). Karel Hoffman (1872–1936) was first violinist of the Bohemian Quartet which first performed the work, to great acclaim, at a festival of Czech music in Warsaw (October 1928).
162. See her letter dated 4 July 1928 (ibid., p. 404).
163. See his letter dated 4–5 July 1928 (ibid.).
164. See his letter dated 8–9 July 1928 (ibid., p. 408).
165. See his letter dated 16 July 1928 (ibid., p. 412).
166. See his letters dated 20–21 and 21–22 July 1928 (ibid., p. 415).
167. See Trkanová/Janáčková, p. 154.
168. See her letter dated 21 July 1928, in Přibánová (ed.), *Hádanka života*, p. 416.
169. See his letter dated 23–24 July 1928 (ibid., p. 418).
170. See Trkanová/Janáčková, p. 154.
171. See his letter dated 24 July 1928, in Přibánová (ed.), *Hádanka života*, p. 419.
172. Ibid.
173. See Trkanová/Janáčková, p. 154.
174. Ibid., p. 155.
175. See Marie Trkanová, *U Janáčků: podle vyprávění Marie Stejskalové* [At the Janáčeks: after the account of Marie Stejskalová], Panton, Prague, 1959, p. 118 [Trkanová/Stejskalová].
176. Ibid.
177. See Trkanová/Janáčková, p. 155.
178. See Trkanová/Stejskalová, p. 118.
179. See Jaroslav Procházka, *Lašské kořeny života i díla Leoše Janáčka* [The Lašsko roots of the life and work of *Leoš Janáček*], Okresní a místní rada osvětová, Frýdek-Místek, 1948, pp. 170–1.
180. See Hrstka's article in *Lidové noviny*, 16 August 1928; quoted in Vogel, *Leoš Janáček*, p. 377. Adolf Hrstka (1864–1931) was a medical doctor in the small town of Štramberk.
181. William Marie Ritter (1876–1955), Swiss critic, novelist and writer on music, he visited Prague in 1903, and lived there in 1904–5, writing for *Le mercure de France*, Author of the first French book on Smetana (1907), he offered Janáček two librettos and visited him in Moravia in 1927–8; he planned to write a book about Janáček and had several long conversations with him. Cf. also note 187 below.
182. See Trkanová/Stejskalová, p. 119, and Trkanová/Janáčková, p. 155.
183. See Trkanová/Janáčková, p. 155.
184. Private communication, cf. also Tyrrell, *Intimate Letters*, p. 344.
185. Cf. Tyrrell, *Intimate Letters*. The sum in question was 100,000 crowns.
186. Adolf Vašek, 'Po stopách dra Leoše Janáčka' [In the tracks of Dr Leoš Janáček], Brno, 1930; Věra Janáčková, 'Poslední dny Leoše Janáčka' [Leoš Janáček's last days], *Národní politika*, 13 August 1940; reprinted in *Leoš Janáček. Vzpomínky, dokumenty, korespondence a studie* [Leoš Janáček. Reminiscences, papers,

correspondence and studies], ed. Bohumír Štědroň, Editio Supraphon, Prague, 1986, p. 168.

187. Cf. Charles Susskind, *Janáček and Brod*, Yale University Press, New Haven and London, 1985, p. 129. This seems to tally with Zdenka's report that Otto stayed in a local hotel; see note 188 below.

188. Cf Trkanová/Janáčková, p. 165.

189. Cf. Tyrrell, *Intimate Letters*, p. 344.

190. Now known as Ostrava; the car had been standing by. (Cf. Vogel, *Leoš Janáček*, p. 377.)

191. Ibid., p. 378, and Trkanová/Janáčková, p. 158.

192. Vogel, *Leoš Janáček*, p. 378. Kamila had been taken for a relative, and given an adjacent room at the sanatorium.

193. See Susskind, *Janáček and Brod*, p. 129.

194. See Vogel, *Leoš Janáček*, p. 378.

195. Ibid. Apparently, Kamila was at his bedside (Tyrrell, *Intimate Letters*, p. 343); cf. also Stanislav Tauber (*Můj hudební svět* [My musical world], Brno, 1949, pp. 102–3). However, Zdenka and Janáček's niece Věra do not mention this. Cf. Trkanová/Janáčková, p. 158.

196. Trkanová/Janáčková, p. 156.

197. Stanislav Tauber (1878–1959), a notable Czech tenor, was a long-standing member of the Moravian Teachers' Choral Society, with whom he toured extensively. He had known Janáček for a long time and performed in many of his works, including the cantata *Amarus* and the *Glagolitic Mass*. Cf. also note 195 above.

198. See Tauber, *Můj hudební svět*, p. 102.

199. See Trkanová/Janáčková, p. 157.

200. Ibid.

201. See Tauber, *Můj hudební svět*, p. 103.

202. Ibid.

203. See Trkanová/Janáčková, p. 158.

204. See Tauber, *Můj hudební svět*, p. 103, and Trkanová/Janáčková, p. 158.

205. See Tauber *Můj hudební svět*, p. 103

206. See Trkanová/Janáčková, p. 159.

207. Ibid.

208. See Tauber, *Můj hudební svět*, p. 103.

209. See Trkanová/Janáčková, p. 159.

210. See Tauber, *Můj hudební svět*, p. 103.

211. Ibid., p. 104.

212. See Trkanová/Janáčková, p. 159.

213. Ibid., p. 155.

214. Ibid., p. 164.

215. Ibid., p. 160.

216. Ibid.

217. See his remark about Zdenka's 'low intelligence' and the belittling comments she had reportedly made about Janáček's music; Tauber, *Můj hudební svět*, p. 99.

218. Zdenka had already signed a contract with Charitas, a funeral parlour in Brno, but the City of Brno – who had a funeral parlour of its own – wanted

the honour of arranging the funeral. In the end, Charitas was paid off and the City took over.

219. See Trkanová/Janáčková, p. 160–1.

220. See Trkanová/Stejskalová, p. 153.

221. See Trkanová/Janáčková, p. 162.

222. See Vogel, *Leoš Janáček*, p. 379.

223. Ibid.

224. Ibid., p. 380.

225. See his letter written probably on 29 November 1927, in Přiváňová (ed.), *Hádanka života*, p. 259; cf. also the present volume, pp. 228–9.

226. See his letter dated 6 March 1921; the comment refers to the fact that many of his operas have a female protagonist rather than a male one: *Šárka, Jenůfa, The Cunning Little Vixen, Káťa Kabanová* and *The Makropulos Affair*. Cf. also the present volume, p. 164.

227. See her review of *From the House of the Dead*, 'New Works in Czechoslovakia', *The Chesterian*, xii, 1931, and the reprint in Fischmann (ed.), *Janáček–Newmarch*, p. 167.

228. 'What I admit', *Lidové noviny*, 13 February 1927, in Zemanová (ed.), *Janáček's Uncollected Essays*, pp. 105–7. He also referred to the opera briefly in three letters to Kamila Stösslová (28 May, 2–4 and 8 June 1927), and in a *feuilleton* he wrote for *Lidové noviny*, ' Schytali je' [They caught them], 28 June 1927. On 29 July 1927 this newspaper carried an interview about his 'new opera'.

229. For a more detailed account of Janáček's work on the libretto, see Tyrrell, *Janáček's Operas*, pp. 328–30.

230. Janáček even continued to use a Cyrillic rather than a Latin character for 'P' in the name of Petrovič.

231. He added this date on the title-page of the final autograph score; his first scenario was probably written between 23 and 28 February 1927. Cf. also Tyrrell, *Janáček's Operas*, pp. 330–1.

232. See his letters dated 28 May and 8 June 1927, in Přibáňová (ed.), *Hádanka života*, pp. 210 and 218.

233. Moreover, no major Russian composer at the time turned to luminaries of Russian prose and drama. Boris Asafyev's *The Storm* (based on Ostrovsky's play) was not written until 1940, and although there are two Russian settings of Dostoyevsky, Prokofiev's *The Gambler* (1929), and Tsvetayev's *White Nights* (1933), only Janáček chose *From the House of the Dead* as an operatic subject. However, another Czech composer, Otakar Jeremiáš (1892–1962), chose Dostoyevsky's *The Brothers Karamazov* for his opera of the same name (1928). Among Tolstoy's works, only *War and Peace* was set to music by a major Russian composer, Prokofiev (1946). However, Czech operas on Tolstoy's works include Otakar Ostrčil's *Honzovo království* [Honza's kingdom] (1924), based on *The Tale of Ivan the Jester*, J.B. Foerster's *Bloud* [The simpleton] (1936), based on *The Two Old Men*, and a radio opera by Bohuslav Martinů, *Čím člověk žije* [What men live by] (1953).

234. For example, the characters mentioned in his open letter to Brod are included in the draft scenario (and one of them, Baklušin, had a small part in the earliest musical draft of Act 1), but they do not appear in the opera. Janáček gave Baklušin's love story to Skuratov; in the entry of Petrovič [Petrovich] he

incorporated the character of a Pole, a political prisoner. In Dostoevsky, the Commandant's apology at the end of the opera is also addressed to the Pole, who does not appear in Janáček's setting.

235. His conversation with Petrovič now takes place in Act 2, his stay at the hospital and his parting from Petrovič in Act 3.

236. Cf. Derek Katz, 'Don Juan in Prague and Brno: Janáček and 20th-century Czech Don Juans', International Conference *A Tale of Three Cities, Janáček's Brno between Vienna and Prague*, University of London, 22–24 October 1999. The story of the beautiful miller's wife is a Russian folk-tale; Gogol's account of this tale, *Christmas Eve*, was set to music by various Russian composers, including Tchaikovsky (*Vakula the Smith*, 1874, revised as *Cherevichki* [The slippers], 1885).

237. 'An Interview from *Literární svět*', in Zemanová (ed.), *Janáček's Uncollected Essays*, p. 123.

238. 'There are two drafts of the concerto; it is unclear whether the work's various subtitles ('The pilgrimage of a soul', 'Soul' and 'Little soul') are related to *From the House of the Dead* or to another opera which Janáček might have contemplated (William Ritter's *L'âme et la chair*). Also, 'soul' or 'little soul' is a familiar term of endearment in Moravia, which Janáček often used when addressing Kamila.

239. For example, as in the various versions which alternate with the prisoners' 'departure' chorus in Act 1.

240. See the present volume, pp. 14, 260 and 268, n. 31.

241. In the prison camp described by Dostoyevsky drum rolls signalled the beginning and end of work. Janáček used side-drum rolls for the various entries of the prison guards. This is particularly effective at the end of Act 2: the drum roll starts as the guards rush on to the stage after the Small Prisoner attacks Aljeja, and it fades out as the curtain falls.

242. The prisoners' chains are heard not only in the overture but also at other points in the opera; Janáček specified the 'chains' (read: prison chains) among the percussion even in the draft of the Violin Concerto. Various work tools such as a saw and an anvil are used at the beginning of Act 2, and a rattle in the Don Juan play. Bells accompany the arrival of the priest in Act 2 – a clear reminiscence of the recently completed *Glagolitic Mass*.

243. Janáček underlined in his copy of the novel the instruments enumerated by Dostoyevsky: two violins, three balalaikas, two guitars, a tambourine and two accordions.

244. On 19 June 1928 Janáček wrote to Kamila that the copyists 'will be finished here tomorrow, on Wednesday'; see Přibáňová (ed.), *Hádanka života*, p. 396. Cf. also Tyrrell, *Janáček's Operas*, p. 335.

245. Cf. Osvald Chlubna, 'K úpravě opery "Z mrtvého domu"' [On the revision of the opera *From the House of the Dead*], in Václav Nosek, *Opery Leoše Janáčka na brněnské scéně* [Janáček's operas on the Brno stage], Státní divadlo, Brno, 1958 [unpaginated]. Janáček had used his method of drawing his own staves in many of his other works, but this was the first time – apart from some sketches for *The Excursions of Mr Brouček* – that he used it in an opera. Perhaps he did so, as John Tyrrell argues in his introduction to the 1980 CD recording, in order to achieve a chamber-like texture.

246. See Chlubna, 'K uprave opery "Z mrtvého domu"'; the article includes a verbal description of the changes.
247. They 'thickened' the orchestration with extra wind instruments and a harp; the prisoners' words, 'svoboda, svobodička' [freedom, dear freedom] were set against Janáček's 'motto' theme (the sharply dissonant chords which, for example, open the opera).
248. The first score was published by Universal Edition in 1930. In Kubelík's later version many, though not all, of the additions by Bakala and Chlubna were pasted over; in 1961 Kubelík conducted his version in a concert performance in Munich.
246. This production, at Sadler's Wells, was conducted by Charles (later Sir Charles) Mackerras. However, even then some doubling was needed – as Sir Charles explained in the programme note, the scoring seemed at times too transparent for the theatre.
250. Decca CD recording, 430 375–2.
251. See her review mentioned in note 227 above and Fischmann (ed.), *Janáček–Newmarch*, p. 169. 'In every creature [there is] a spark of God': in his scenario for the final scene, Janáček described Aljeja as 'a symbol of *the spark of God in man*', and the above-mentioned version of this comment found its way on to the title-page of his final autograph score.

Bibliography

Items are arranged alphabetically by author, then chronologically under that author. Editions and translations of Janáček's autobiographical reminiscences, correspondence and writings are listed briefly under his name, with a cross-reference for the editor/translator under whose name detailed information about the edition is then given.

Czech diacritics are ignored in alphabetization.

All translations in the book are mine unless otherwise stated. As I do not quote from Dr John Tyrrell's edition of Janáček's correspondence with Kamila Stösslová, I have only given the dates of Janáček's and Stösslová's letters; I do not refer to the numbering used by Dr Tyrrell.

Abbreviations

BmJA	Janáček Archive of the Music Division, Moravian Provincial Museum, Brno [Hudební oddělení Moravského zemského muzea]
ČMM	*Časopis Moravského musea/muzea v Brně* [periodical]
DL	*Divadelní list Zemského divadla v Brně* [periodical]
HM	Hudební matice [publisher]
HMUB	Hudební matice Umělecké Besedy [publisher]
HR	*Hudební rozhledy* [periodical]
JA	Janáčkův archiv [Janáček's archive], first series, general ed. Vladimír Helfert (i) and Jan Racek (ii–ix)

i *Korespondence Leoše Janáčka s Artušem Rektorysem* [Leoš Janáček's correspondence with Artuš Rektorys], ed. Artuš Rektorys, HMUB, Prague, 1934
[2nd enlarged edn, Prague, 1949 = iv]

ii *Korespondence Leoše Janáčka s Otakarem Ostrčilem* [Leoš Janáček's correspondence with Otakar Ostrčil], ed. Artuš Rektorys, HMUB, Prague, 1948

iii *Korespondence Leoše Janáčka s F.S. Procházkou* [Leoš Janáček's correspondence with F.S. Procházka], ed. Artuš Rektorys, HMUB, Prague, 1949

iv   *Korespondence Leoše Janáčka s Artušem Rektorysem* [Leoš Janáček's
      correspondence with Artuš Rektorys], ed. Artuš Rektorys, 2nd
      enlarged edn, HMUB, Prague, 1949

v   *Korespondence Leoše Janáčka s libretisty Výletů Broučkových* [Leoš
      Janáček's correspondence with the librettists of *The Excursions of
      Mr Brouček*], ed. Artuš Rektorys, HM, Prague, 1950

vi   *Korespondence Leoše Janáčka s Gabrielou Horvátovou* [Janáček's cor-
      respondence with Gabriela Horvátová], ed. Artuš Rektorys,
      HM, Prague, 1950

vii   *Korespondence Leoše Janáčka s Karlem Kovařovicem a ředitelstvím
      Národního divadla* [Janáček's correspondence with Karel Kova-
      řovic and the directorate of the National Theatre], ed. Artuš
      Rektorys, HM, Prague, 1950

viii *Korespondence Leoše Janáčka s Marií Calmou a MUDr Františkem
      Veselým* [Leoš Janáček's correspondence with Marie Calma and
      MUDr František Veselý], ed. Jan Racek and Artuš Rektorys,
      Orbis, Prague, 1951

ix   *Korespondence Leoše Janáčka s Maxem Brodem* [Janáček's corre-
      spondence with Max Brod], ed. Jan Racek and Artuš Rektorys,
      SNKLHU, Prague, 1953

LN   *Lidové noviny* [newspaper]
OM   *Opus Musicum* [periodical]
SNKLHU   Státní nakladatelství krásné literatury, hudby a umění [State publishing
           company of *belles lettres*, music and art]

Bakala, Břetislav, 'Její pastorkyňa' [Jenůfa], *Rytmus*, viii, 1942–3, p. 85; reprinted in
    Štědroň, ed., 1946, pp. 172–3
Bartoš, František, *Národní písně moravské v nově nasbírané* [Moravian folk-songs newly
    collected], Brno, 1889 (with an introduction about the importance of the
    songs and a short essay by Janáček) [now usually referred to as Bartoš ii]
Beckerman, Michael, *Janáček as Theorist*, Pendragon Press, Stuyvesant, New York,
    1994
Brod, Max, *Sternenhimmel: Musik- und Theatererlebnisse*, Orbis, Prague, and Kurt
    Wolf, Munich, 1923; 2nd edn as *Prager Sternenhimmel*, Paul Zsolnay, Vienna
    and Hamburg, 1966
——*Leoš Janáček: život a dílo* [Leoš Janáček: life and works], HMUB, Prague, 1924;
    German original, Wiener Philharmonischer Verlag, Vienna, 1925; 2nd
    enlarged edn, Universal Edition, Vienna, 1956
——*Streitbares Leben*, Kindler Verlag, Munich, 1960; also as *Streitbares Leben,
    1884–1968*, F.A. Herbig, Munich and Berlin, 1969
Burghauser, Jarmil, 'Janáčkova tvorba komorní a symfonická' [Janáček's chamber
    and orchestral music], *Musikologie*, iii, Prague, 1955, pp. 211–305
Burney, Charles, *The Present State of Music in Germany, the Netherlands and the United
    Provinces*, 2nd edn, corrected, 1773; new edn by Percy Scholes, OUP,
    London, 1959

Calma-Veselá, Marie, 'Z boje pro Janáčkovu *Pastorkyni*' [From the battle for Janáček's *Jenůfa*], *Listy Hudební matice*, iv, 1924–5, pp. 137–47.

——'Ze vzpomínek na Leoše Janáčka' [From my recollections of Leoš Janáček], *Hudební výchova*, xix, 1938, pp. 99–100

Čapková, Helena, *Moji milí bratři* [My dear brothers], Československý spisovatel, Prague, 1962; 3rd edn, 1986

Černohorská, Milena, 'K problematice vzniku Janáčkovy theorie nápěvků' [On the origin of Janáček's theory of speech melodies], *ČMM*, xlii, 1957, pp. 165–78

——'Nápěvková theorie Leoše Janáčka' [On Janáček's theory of speech melodies], *ČMM*, xliii, 1958, pp. 129–44.

Červinka, Vincenc, 'Jak vznikla *Káťa Kabanová*' [How *Káťa Kabanová* came into being], *Národní politika*, 18 October 1938

Československý hudební slovník osob a institucí [The Czechoslovak music dictionary of people and institutions], ed. Gracian Černušák, Bohumír Štědroň and Zdenko Nováček, Státní hudební vydavatelství, Prague, 1963–5

Chlubna, Osvald, 'Dr Leoš Janáček: Z mrtvého domu' [Dr Leoš Janáček: *From the House of the Dead*], *DL*, v, 1929–30, pp. 177 and 189–94

——'Vzpomínky na Leoše Janáčka' [Reminiscences of Leoš Janáček], *DL*, vii, 1931–2, pp. 101–4, 125–7, 169, 172, 289–90

——'Leoš Janáček a brněnské divadlo' [Leoš Janáček and the Brno theatre], *DL*, viii, 1932–33, p. 9; abridged reprint in Štědroň, ed., 1986, p. 135

——'K úpravě opery "Z mrtvého domu"' [On the revision of the opera *From the House of the Dead*]; in Václav Nosek, ed., *Opery Leoše Janáčka na brněnské scéně* [Janáček's operas on the Brno stage], Státní divadlo, Brno, 1958 (unpaginated)

Dědeček, Pavel, 'Karel Kovařovic a "Její pastorkyňa"' [Karel Kovařovic and *Jenůfa*]; in Jan Petr, ed., *Vzpomínáme Karla Kovařovice* [We commemorate Karel Kovařovic], I.P. Kober, Prague, 1940

Demel, Jiří, 'Kdo je autorem Zápisníku zmizelého?' [Who is the author of *The Diary of One who Disappeared?*], *OM*, xxix, 1997, No. 3, pp. 93–100

Dille, Denis, *Documenta Bartókiana*, 1, Heft 3, Akadémiai Kiadó, Budapest and B. Schott's Söhne, Mainz, 1968, p. 122

Downes, Olin, 'The Music of Janacek [sic], Composer of "Jenufa" [sic] to Be Heard at [the] Metropolitan', *New York Times*, 13 July 1924

Michael Ewans, *Janáček's Tragic Operas*, Faber, London, 1977

Fiala, Otakar, 'Libreto k Janáčkově opeře Počátek románu' [The libretto to Janáček's opera *The Beginning of a Romance*], *ČMM*, xlix, 1964, pp. 199–222

Firkušný, Leoš, ed., *Janáček kritikem brněnské opery* [Janáček as a critic of the Brno Opera], Oldřich Pazdírek, Brno, 1935; reprinted in *Otázky divadla a filmu*, i, 1970, pp. 207–48

——'Poslední Janáčkova opera Z mrtvého domu' [Janáček's last opera *From the House of the Dead*], *DL*, xii, 1936–7, pp. 358–68 and 386–400; also printed separately, Pazdírek, Brno, 1937; reprinted in Firkušný, *Odkaz Leoše Janáčka české opeře* [Janáček's legacy to Czech opera], Dědictví Havlíčkovo, Brno, 1939, pp. 54–70

——'Janáčkova opera, jež nebude provedena v cyklu' [Janáček's opera which will not be performed during the cycle of his operas], *Divadelní ročenka spolku členů Národního divadla*, Brno, 1938, pp. 21–5

──ed., 'Dopisy Leoše Janáčka z archivu Družstvá Národního divadla v Brně' [Janáček's letters from the archive of the Consortium of the National Theatre in Brno], *Musikologie*, i, 1938, pp. 130–9

Firkušný, Rudolf, 'My recollection of Janáček', introduction to the CD of Janáček's piano music, RCA Victor, RD60147, 1989

Fischmann, Zdenka E., ed., *Janáček–Newmarch Correspondence*, Kabel Publishers, Rockville, Maryland, 1986

Greer, Germaine, *The Female Eunuch*, Paladin, Grafton Books, London, 1971

Hamák, 'Janáček, pán kůru' [Janáček, the lord of the musicians' gallery], *LN*, 12 August 1938; abridged reprint in Štědroň, ed., 1986, p. 35

Helfert, Vladimír, *Leoš Janáček*, i, Oldřich Pazdírek, Brno, 1939

──*O Janáčkovi* [About Janáček], ed. Bohumír Štědroň, HMUB, Prague, 1949

Heyworth, Peter, *Otto Klemperer: His Life and Times*, i, 1885–1933 CUP, Cambridge, 1983

Hilmar, Ernst, ed., *Briefe an die Universal Edition*, Hans Schneider, Tutzing, 1988

Horvátová, Gabriela, 'Za osobními vzpomínkami na L. Janáčka' [Personal reminiscences of L. Janáček], *Divadlo*, 30 November 1938; abridged reprint in JA vi, pp. 8–10

Höslinger, Clemens, 'Zur Vorgeschichte der Wiener *Jenůfa*-Première', *Mitteilungen des österreichischen Staatsarchivs*, Bd. 25, 1972

Janáček's autobiographical reminiscences: see Veselý, Adolf, ed. [Janáček/Veselý]

Janáček's correspondence with Jan Löwenbach: see Stolařík, Ivo, ed.

Janáček's correspondence with Rosa Newmarch: see Fischmann, Zdenka E., ed.

Janáček's correspondence with Kamila Stösslová: see Přibáňová, Svatava, ed., 1990

'Janáčková korespondence s Universal-Edition v letech 1916–1918 týkající se Její pastorkyně' [Janáček's correspondence with Universal Edition 1916–18, concerning *Jenůfa*]: see Štědroň, Bohumír, ed., 1971

For Janáček's complete correspondence with Universal Edition, see also Hilmar, Ernst, ed., 1988

Janáček's correspondence with his future wife Zdenka: see Knaus, Jakob, ed., 1985

Janáček's letters to his uncle and his mother's letters: see Přibáňová, Svatava, ed., 1985

Janáček's articles and *feuilletons*: for collections, see Racek 1948 and Racek 1958; Tausky 1982; Zemanová 1989/1993; also *Leoš Janáček. O lidové písni a lidové hudbě* [Leoš Janáček. On folk-song and folk music], Vysloužil, ed., 1955

Other articles and *feuilletons* by Janáček quoted in the book:

'Ženichové' [The bridegrooms], *Hudební listy*, iii, 15 January 1887, p. 54; reprinted in Štědroň, ed., 1946, pp. 111–2; trans. in Zemanová, ed., 1989 1993, pp. 148–9

'Moje Luhačovice' [My Luhačovice], *Hlídka*, xx, 1903, pp. 836–44; reprinted in Bohumír Štědroň, 'Leoš Janáček a Luhačovice' [Leoš Janáček and Luhačovice], *Výroční zpráva Městské spořitelny v Luhačovicích za rok 1938* [1939]

'Nápěvky naší mluvy, vynikající pro svůj zvláštní smysl dramatičností' [The speech melodies of our language which stand out for their particular dramatic effect], *ČMM*, iii, 1903, pp. 105–12; *Hlídka*, xx, 1903, pp. 636–7

'Loni a letos' [Last year and this year], in *Hlídka*, xxii, 1905, p. 106; abridged reprint in Štědroň, ed., 1986, p. 84

'Myšlenky cestou' [Thoughts on the road], *Dalibor*, xxix, 2 and 9 March 1907; reprinted in Vysloužil, ed., 1955

'Výlety páně Broučkovy' [The Excursions of Mr Brouček], *Hudební revue*, xiii, 1919–20, pp. 177–9

'Rytá slova' [The engraved words], *LN*, 22 September 1921; reprinted in Racek, ed., 1948

For reviews and analyses by Janáček see also:

České proudy hudební [Trends in Czech music], *Hlídka: The Water Goblin*, vol. ii [xiv], 1897, pp. 285–92; *The Noon Witch*, pp. 454–9; *The Golden Spinning-Wheel*, pp. 594–604; *The Wood Dove*, vol. iii [xv], 1898, pp. 277–82. Reprinted, with explanatory notes, in Bohumír Štědroň, 'Antonín Dvořák a Leoš Janáček', *Musikologie*, v, 1958, pp. 105–23; appendix, pp. 324–59

Janáček kritikem brněnské opery [Janáček as a critic of the Brno Opera], see Firkušný, Leoš, ed., 1935

'Leoš Janáček kritikem brněnské opery v letech 1890–1892' [Leoš Janáček as critic of the Brno Opera 1890–2], see Štědroň, ed., 1970

Janáček ve vzpomínkách a dopisech [Janáček in reminiscences and letters], see Štědroň, ed., 1946

Leoš Janáček: Letters and Reminiscences, see Štědroň, ed., 1955 [rev. version, in English, of Štědroň, ed., 1946]

Leoš Janáček. Vzpomínky, dokumenty, korespondence a studie [Leoš Janáček. Reminiscences, papers, correspondence and studies]; see Štědroň, ed., 1986

Janáček's works: A Catalogue of the Music and Writings, see Simeone, Nigel, Tyrrell and Němcová, 1997

Janáček, Vincenc, *Životopis Jiříka Janáčka (1778–1848)* [A biography of Jiřík Janáček (1778–1848)], ed. Jiří Sehnal, Opus Musicim, Brno, 1985

Janáčková, Věra, 'Poslední dny Leoše Janáčka' [Leoš Janáček's last days], *Národní politika*, 13 August 1940; reprinted in Procházka, 1966, p. 219; abridged reprint in Štědroň, ed., 1986, p. 168

Janáčková, Zdenka, memoirs: see Trkanová, Marie

Jiříkovský, Václav, 'Vzpomínky na Leoše Janáčka' [Reminiscences of Leoš Janáček], *DL*, vii, 1931–2, pp. 248–50

Kašlík, Hynek, 'Retuše Karla Kovařovice v Janáčkově opeře Její pastorkyně' [Karel Kovařovic's 'retouchings' in Janáček's opera *Jenůfa*], *Hudební věstník*, xxxi, 1938, pp. 112–13, 130–1, 142–3, 159–60; reprinted separately (Unie čes. hudebníků z povolání), Prague, 1938

Kimball, Stanley Buchholz, *Czech Nationalism: A Study of the National Theatre Movement, 1845–83*; Urbana, Illinois, 1966

Knaus, Jakob, ed., '*Intime Briefe' 1879–80 aus Leipzig und Wien* ['Intimate Letters' 1879–80 from Leipzig and Vienna], Leoš Janáček-Gesellschaft, Zurich, 1985

Konečná, Haná, ed., *Soupis repertoáru Národního divadla v Praze 1881–1983* [List of repertoire of the National Theatre in Prague, 1881–1983), Národní divadlo, Prague, 1983

Kožík, František, *Po zarostlém chodníčku* [On the overgrown path], Odeon, Prague, 1972

Kunc, Jan, 'Leoš Janáček', *Hudební revue*, iv, 1911, pp. 121–34 and 185–9

——*Vzpomínky na premiéru Její pastorkyně* [Reminiscences of the première of *Jenůfa*], *DL*, ix, Brno 1933–4, pp. 74–81; abridged reprint in Štědroň, ed., 1986, p. 95

Kundera, Ludvík, 'Janáčkova tvorba klavírní' [Janáček's works for the piano], *Musikologie*, iii, Prague,1955, pp. 306–29

——'Glagolskaja missa' [*Glagolitic Mass*], *Tempo*, vii, 1927–8, p. 186–93

Kundera, Milan, *Testaments Betrayed*, Faber, London, 1995

Kyas, Vojtěch, *Janáček se neměl o koho opřít?* [Janáček had no one to lean on?], *OM*, v, 1993, No. 2, pp. 33–42

Lampert, Vera, 'Zeitgenössische Musik in Bartóks Notensammlung', *Documenta Bartókiana*, 1, Heft 5, Akadémiai Kiadó, Budapest and B. Schott's Söhne, Mainz, 1968, pp. 142–68

Ludvová, Jitka, 'Německý hudební život v Praze 1880–1935' [German musical life in Prague, 1880–1935], *Uměnovědné studie*, iv, Prague 1983, pp. 53–173

Mareš, František, 'K sedmdesátinám Leoše Janáčka' [For Leoš Janáček's 70th birthday], *HR*, i, 1924–5, pp. 33–5; abridged reprint in Štědroň, ed., 1986, pp. 37–8

——'Vzpomínky na Leoše Janáčka' [Reminiscences of Leoš Janáček], *LN*, 17 February 1940; abridged reprint in Štědroň, ed., 1986, p. 112

Mikeska, Jan, 'Jak jsem přispěl k odhalení?' [How did I contribute to the revelation?], *OM*, xxix, 1997, No. 3, pp. 93–100

Mucha, Jiří, *Alfons Mucha*, Mladá Fronta, Prague, 1982

Němcová, Alena, 'Brněnská première Její pastorkyně' [The Brno première of *Jenůfa*], *ČMM*, lix, 1974, pp. 136–46

——'Otazníky nad Její pastorkyní' [Questions about *Jenůfa*], *OM*, xvi, 1984, pp. 24–7

Němeček, Jan, *Opera Národního divadla v období Karla Kovařovice 1900–1920* [The opera of the (Prague) National theatre in the time of Karel Kovařovic 1900–20], Divadelní ústav, Prague, 1968–9

Newmarch, Rosa, 'A Slovak Music-Drama', *The Musical Times*, 1 December 1919

——'Janáček and Moravian Music Drama', *The Slavonic Review*, i, No. 2 December, 1922, pp. 362–79

——'New Works in Czechoslovakia' [review of *From the House of the Dead*], *The Chesterian*, xii, 1931, pp. 213–19; reprinted in Fischmann, ed., 1986, pp. 165–9

——Janáček–Newmarch Correspondence, see Fischmann, ed., 1986

Nosek, Václav, ed., *Opery Leoše Janáčka na brněnské scéně* [Leoš Janáček's operas on the Brno stage], Státní divadlo, Brno, 1958 (unpaginated)

Pala, František, 'Janáček a Národní divadlo' [Janáček and the National Theatre (in Prague)], *HR*, vi, 1953, pp. 882–91

——'Jevištní dílo Leoše Janáčka' [The stage works of Leoš Janáček], *Musikologie*, iii, 1955, pp. 61–210

Piskáček, Adolf, 'Večer s Leošem Janáčkem' [An evening with Leoš Janáček], *Dalibor*, xxviii, 25 May 1906, p. 227; abridged reprint in Štědroň, ed., 1986, p. 72

Polyakova, Lyudmila, 'O "ruských" operách Leoše Janáčka' [About Janáček's 'Russian' operas], *Cesty rozvoje a vzájemné vztahy ruského a československého umění*, Prague, 1974, pp. 247–69

Porter, James, 'Bartók and Janáček: Contact, Context and Confluence', in *Ethnologische, historische und systematische Musikwissenschaft, Oskár Elschek zum 65. Geburtstag*, ed. Franz Födermayer and Ladislav Burlas, Institut für Musikwissenschaft, Bratislava, 1998, pp. 407–15

——'Bartók's *Concerto for Orchestra* (1943) and Janáček's *Sinfonietta* (1926): Conceptual and Motivic Parallels', in *Bartók Perspectives, Man, Composer, and Ethnomusicologist*, ed. Elliott Antokoletz, Benjamin Suchoff and Victoria Fischer, OUP, Oxford, 2000, pp. 152–68

Přibáňová, Svatava, 'Operní dílo Janáčkova vrcholného údobí' [The operas of Janáček's culminative period], *ČMM*, lxv, 1980, pp. 165-71 [includes a list of musical sources in BmJA for *The Excursions of Mr Brouček, Káťa Kabanová, The Cunning Little Vixen, The Makropulos Affair* and *From the House of the Dead*]

——ed., *Leoš Janáček. Dopisy strýci. Dopisy matky* [Leoš Janáček. Letters to his uncle. Letters from his mother], Opus Musicum, Brno, 1985

——ed., *Hádanka života. (Dopisy Leoše Janáčka Kamile Stösslové)* [The riddle of life. (Letters of Leoš Janáček to Kamila Stösslová)], Opus Musicum, Brno, 1990

Procházka, Jaroslav, *Lašské kořeny života i díla Leoše Janáčka* [The Lašsko roots of the life and work of Leoš Janáček], Okresní a místní rada osvětová, Frýdek-Místek, 1948

——'Leoš Janáček, Václav Talich a Česká filharmonie' [Leoš Janáček, Václav Talich and the Czech Philharmonic], *OM*, x, 1978, pp. 184–7; No. v–vi, pp. xix–xxix

Procházková, Jarmila, 'Prezident a skladatel' [The President and the composer], *OM*, 1990, No. 6, pp. 168–82

Racek, Jan, ed., Leoš Janáček's *feuilleton* 'Rytá slova' [The engraved words], *LN*, 22 September 1921; reprinted in *Triptychon*, HM, Prague, 1948, pp. 13–8

——'Leoš Janáček a Praha [Leoš Janáček and Prague], *Musikologie*, iii, 1955, pp. 11–50

——*Fejetony z Lidových novin* [Feuilletons from *Lidové noviny*], Krajské nakladatelství, Brno, 1958

——'Leoš Janáček o skladebné struktuře klavírních děl Fryderyka Chopina' [Leoš Janáček about the structure of Frédéric Chopin's piano works], Sborník prací Filosofické fakulty brněnské university, F4, Brno, 1960, pp. 5–8

——'Leoš Janáčeks und Béla Bartóks Bedeutung in der Weltmusik', *Sborník prací Filosofické fakulty brněnské university*, F6, Brno, 1962, pp. 5–16

Rektorys, Artuš, 'Dopisy A. Dvořáka L. Janáčkovi' [Antonín Dvořák's letters to Leoš Janáček], *České slovo*, 7 February 1933

Sajner, Josef, 'Patografická studie o Leoši Janáčkovi' [A pathological study of Leoš Janáček'], *OM*, xiv, 1982, pp. 233–5

Sázavský, Karel, *Dějiny Filharmonického spolku Beseda brněnská 1860–1900* [The history of the Brno Beseda Philharmonic Society 1860–1900], Brno, 1900

——'Několik drobtů k životu a činnosti Janáčkově' [A few snippets regarding Janáček's life and activities], *HR*, i, 1924–5, p. 36; abridged reprint in Štědroň, ed., 1986, p. 38

Simeone, Nigel, Tyrrell, John and Němcová, Alena, *Janáček's Works: A Catalogue of the Music and Writings of Leoš Janáček*, Clarendon Press, Oxford, 1997

Sládek, Jan Václav, *Hukvaldské miniatury* [Hukvaldy miniatures], Profil, Ostrava, 1979

Šourek, Otakar, ed., *Antonín Dvořák přátelům doma* [Antonín Dvořák to his friends at home], Melantrich, Prague and Pazdírek, Brno, 1941

Štědroň, Bohumír, 'Janáček a Kunc', *Rytmus*, viii, 1942–3, p. 90ff., and Štědroň, ed., 1986, pp. 96–7

——ed., *Janáček ve vzpomínkách a dopisech* [Janáček in reminiscences and letters], Topič, Prague, 1946; partial English translation in Štědroň, ed., 1955

——'Leoš Janáček na učitelském ústavě' [Leoš Janáček at the Teachers' Training Institute], *Rytmus*, xi, 1947, No. 9–10, pp. 140–5

——ed., *Leoš Janáček: Letters and Reminiscences*, Artia, Prague, 1955 [revised version, in English, of Štědroň, ed., 1946]

——'Antonín Dvořák a Leoš Janáček' [Dvořák and Janáček], *Musikologie*, v, 1958, pp. 105–53; appendix, pp. 324–59

——*Dílo Leoše Janáčka: abecední seznam Janáčkových skladeb a úprav* [Janáček's works: an alphabetical catalogue of Janáček's compositions and arrangements], *HR*, 1959; English trans., ibid.

——'K Janáčkově opeře *Osud* [Janáček's opera *Osud*], *Živá hudba*, i, 1959, pp. 159–83

——ed., 'Leoš Janáček kritikem brněnské opery v letech 1890–1891' [Leoš Janáček as critic of the Brno Opera 1890–1891], *Otázky divadla a filmu*, i, 1970, pp. 207–48

——ed., 'Janáčkova korespondence s Universal-Edition v letech 1916–1918 týkající se Její pastorkyně' [Janáček's correspondence with Universal Edition 1916–18, concerning *Jenůfa*], *Otázky divadla a filmu*, ii, 1971, pp. 259–60

——*Leoš Janáček*, Panton, Prague, 1976

——'Janáček a Ruský kroužek v Brně' [Janáček and the Russian Circle in Brno], Hudobný archiv 2, Martin, 1977, p. 214

——ed., *Leoš Janáček. Vzpomínky, dokumenty, korespondence a studie* [Leoš Janáček. Reminiscences, papers, correspondence and studies], Editio Supraphon, Prague, 1986

Štědroň, Miloš and Faltus, Leoš, 'Znovu Janáčkova symfonie Dunaj' [Once again Janáček's *Danube* symphony], *OM*, vii, 1985, pp. 193–6

——'Janáčkův Houslový concert – torzo nebo vrcholné dílo posledního údobí skladatele?' [Janáček's Violin Concerto – torso or culminative work of the composer's final period?], *OM*, xx, 1988, pp. 89–96

Steinmetz, Karel, 'Metrorytmická stránka vztahu textu a hudby v Janáčkových sborech' [The metro-rhythmical aspect of the relationship between the text and music in Janáček's choruses'; Symposium *Hudba a literatura* [Music and literature] 1981, Frýdek-Místek, 1983, pp. 107–10

Stejskalová, Marie, memoirs, see Trkanová, Marie

Stolařík, Ivo, ed., 'Jan Löwenbach a Leoš Janáček: vzájemná korespondence' [Jan Löwenbach and Leoš Janáček, mutual correspondence], *Slezský sborník*, lvi, 1958, pp. 360–411

Straková, Theodora, 'Janáčkovy operní náměty a torsa' [Janáček's operatic subjects and fragments], *Musikologie*, iii, 1955, pp. 417–49

——'Janáčkova opera *Osud*' [Janáček's opera *Osud*], *ČMM*, xli, 1956, pp. 209–60; xlii, 1957, pp. 133–64

——'Setkání Leoše Janáčka s Gabrielou Preissovou' [Leoš Janáček's encounter with Gabriela Preissová], *ČMM*, xliii, 1958, pp. 145–63

Sušil, František, *Moravské národní písně* [Moravian folk-songs], 1835

Susskind, Charles, *Janáček and Brod*, Yale University Press, New Haven and London, 1985

Tauber, Stanislav, *Můj hudební svět* [My musical world], Brno, 1949

Tausky, Vilem and Margaret, ed. and trans., *Janáček: Leaves from his Life*, Kahn and Averill, London, 1982

Trkanová, Marie, *Paměti: Zdenka Janáčková – můj život* [Memoirs: Zdenka Janáčková – my life], Šimon Ryšavý [Publishers], Brno, 1998 [Trkanová/Janáčková]

——*U Janáčků: podle vyprávění Marie Stejskalové* [At the Janáčeks: after the account of Marie Stejskalová], Panton, Prague, 1959 [Trkanová/Stejskalová]

Trojan, Jan, *Moravská lidová píseň: melodika, harmonika* [Moravian folk-song: melodic and harmonic aspects], Prague, 1980

Tučapský, Antonín, *Mužské sbory Leoše Janáčka a jejich interpretační tradice* [Janáček's male-voice choruses and their performance tradition], Státní pedagogické nakladatelství, Prague, 1971

Tyrrell, John, *Leoš Janáček: Káťa Kabanová*, CUP, Cambridge, 1982

——*Czech Opera*, CUP, Cambridge, 1988

——*Janáček's Operas: A Documentary Account*, Faber, London, 1992

——ed. and trans., *Intimate Letters: Leoš Janáček and Kamila Stösslová*, Faber, London, 1994

Úlehla, Vladimír, *Živá píseň*, Prague, 1949

Vašek, Adolf, 'Po stopách dra Leoše Janáčka' [In the tracks of Dr Leoš Janáček], Brno, 1930

Veselý, Adolf, ed., *Leoš Janáček. Pohled do života a díla* [Leoš Janáček. A view of the life and work], Fr. Borový, Prague, 1924 [Janáček/Veselý]

Vogel, Jaroslav, *Leoš Janáček: A Biography*, revised 2nd English edn, Orbis Publishing, London, 1981

Vysloužil, Jiří, 'Hudebně folkloristické dílo Leoše Janáčka', in *Leoš Janáček. O lidové písni a lidové hudbě*, SNKLHU, Prague, 1955, pp. 29–78

——ed., *Leoš Janáček. O lidové písni a lidové hudbě* [Leoš Janáček. On folk-song and folk music], SNKLHU, Prague, 1955

——'Leoš Janáček a naše doba' [Leoš Janáček and our time], *HR*, xi, 1958, No. 18, pp. 731–44

——'Janáček's Marginalia in *Moravian National Songs* of 1835', in *Colloquium Leoš Janáček et Musica Europaea*, ed. Rudolf Pečman, Brno, 1968, pp. 251–60

——*Leoš Janáček*, Společnost Leoše Janáčka, Brno, 1978

Wingfield, Paul, 'Janáček's "Lost" Kreutzer Sonata', *Journal of the Royal Musical Association*, 112/2, 1987, pp. 229–56

——*Janáček: Glagolitic Mass*, CUP, Cambridge, 1992

——ed., *Janáček Studies*, CUP, Cambridge, 1999

Zemanová, Mirka, selected, ed. and trans., *Janáček's Uncollected Essays on Music*, Marion Boyars Publishers, London, 1989; 1993 (PB)

Index

Within entries, LJ = Leoš Janáček, Z = Zdenka Janáčková.
The alphabetical order ignores diacritical marks, and articles at the start of titles.

3/2/09